JOHN WESLEY'S LONDON
A GUIDEBOOK

Courtesy of the Central Illinois Conference,
United Methodist Church

JOHN WESLEY'S LONDON
A GUIDEBOOK

Samuel J. Rogal

Texts and Studies in Religion
Volume 34

The Edwin Mellen Press
Lewiston/Queenston

Library of Congress Cataloging-in-Publication Data

Rogal, Samuel J.
    John Wesley's London, A Guidebook

    (Texts and studies in religion ; v. 34)
    Biblilography: p.
    Includes index.
    1. London (England)--History--18th century.
2. London (England)--Church history. 3. London
(England)--Description--1981- --Guide-books.
4. Wesley, John, 1703-1791--Homes and haunts--
England--London--Guide-books. 5. Methodist Church--
England--Clergy--Biography. I. Title. II. Series.
DA682.R64 1988   941   87-22038
ISBN 0-88946-823-0 (alk. paper)

This is volume 34 in the continuing series
Texts and Studies in Religion
Volume 34 ISBN 0-88946-823-0
TSR Series ISBN 0-88946-976-8

The Edwin Mellen Press
Box 450
Lewiston, New York
USA 14092

The Edwin Mellen Press
Box 67
Queenston, Ontario
L0S 1L0 CANADA

Printed in the United States of America

TO THE FAMILY

"Rejoice we are allied
To That which doth provide . . ."

SAMUEL J. ROGAL is Chair
Division of Humanities and Fine Arts
Illinois Valley Community College
Oglesby, Illinois

TABLE OF CONTENTS

Preface   ix

CHAPTER ONE
  A General View of John Wesley's London   1

CHAPTER TWO
  Northern Section   19

CHAPTER THREE
  North-Central Section   33

CHAPTER FOUR
  South-Central Section   231

CHAPTER FIVE
  Southern Section   357

APPENDICES
  A. A Chronology of Important Events   385
  B. Eighteenth-Century Archbishops of Canterbury   399
  C. Eighteenth-Century Bishops of London   401
  D. Sir Christopher Wren's London Churches   405

LIST OF WORKS CITED AND CONSULTED   409

INDEX OF BIBLICAL REFERENCES   415

INDEX OF NAMES, PLACES AND EVENTS   433

Preface

My purpose in preparing a guide to and survey of John Wesley's London has been to introduce the student and general reader to England's capital during the greater part of the eighteenth century--to present it as John Wesley observed it and as he reacted to it. In that context and for that purpose, credit for the largest portion of this project must go to John Wesley himself, for I have relied heavily upon his words (and even his own thoughts) as he journeyed throughout the city streets and lanes in the performance of what he believed to have been his principal duty while on earth: the salvation of his fellow human beings. For the most part, he noted little in terms of outward appearances of public buildings, streets, and courts, and even the churches. Instead, he focused upon the people--their spiritual conditions and their necessities. London served as Wesley's organizational headquarters, so to speak--the place to which he would write, record, summarize and generally administer the organization known as British Methodism. Therefore, to fill obvious gaps relative to description and general background, I have consulted the reactions of others whose eyes focused more sharply upon such items as the sizes and shapes of exterior settings and structures.

In organizing this book, I have borrowed from the traditional format of the travel guide in an effort to identify easily key locales and sites, a considerable number of which no longer exist. Thus, the main body of my text contains four sections: Northern, North-Central, South-Central, and Southern. Within each section, the order of streets, buildings and districts follows

generally, a west to east direction. As far as possible,
I have attempted to provide complete information on
Wesley's activities in a specific locality, to include the
dates and times of day. There are times and places
and dates where I have been unable to provide information
beyond the reference to a Biblical text from which Wesley
developed a particular sermon. An entry for a specific
place that reads, simply, "Hebrews 3:12," means that
Wesley preached from and developed that text; I have not
thought it necessary to write, "He preached on Hebrews
3:12." However, I have thought it necessary to transcribe
as completely as possible the passage from Scripture
upon which he based a particular sermon text, so that
the reader can grasp at least some idea of the thesis
of a specific sermon address. Such a practice proves
especially helpful in light of Wesley's sermons having
been, for the most part, delivered extempore. He
wrote only a small proportion of his pulpit orations, and
those he later published in larger collections.

The major source for John Wesley's activities in
London between February 1738 (the return from the Georgia
mission) and March 1791 (his death) continues to be
The Journal of the Rev. John Wesley, A.M. Enlarged from
Original Mss., and Illustrations. 8 vols. London: Charles
H. Kelly, 1909-1916--edited chiefly by the Rev. Nehemiah
Curnock, and others after his death. Curnock's
standard edition (at some time to be supplanted by the
completed Bicentennial Edition of the Works of John Wesley,
under the editorial direction of Dr. Frank Baker)
contains not only the complete journal, but a large portion
from the diaries (written originally in a shorthand code)
and Wesley's complete Sermon Register, the latter
dating from 14 January 1747 to 25 December 1761. Since
by far the highest percentage of quoted material in my
text comes from the Curnock edition of the Journal, I
have elected not to clutter the page with documentation.
Rather, the reader need only to compare my account for
a given date with that of the same date in Wesley's
Journal (since, of course, the latter work proceeds
chronologically) to observe the complete context of the

quotation, paraphrase, and entire day's event. Thus, for example, when my own text indicates that "on Saturday, 19 December 1761, he (Wesley) 'visited many near Oxford Market,'" the reader will find the direct quotation in the Curnock edition of the Journal under 19 December 1761 (4:481).

Following the Appendices, I have placed the complete list of sources that I have consulted for the preparation of this project. As a collection, those volumes have provided me with an overall image of life in eighteenth-century London--its people, its buildings, its streets, and its districts. Again, to avoid unnecessary documentation and to follow current practice, I have, simply, placed as parantheticals, short titles and page references directly following particular quotations and paraphrases. To obtain the full bibliographical references for sources, the reader need only check the short titles or names of authors/editors against the complete entries in the list.

In Appendix A, particularly, the "Chronology of Important Events" attempts to place John Wesley's London activities and thoughts within the larger context of eighteenth-century British history, both cultural and intellectual. Certainly, one of the most respected of John Wesley's qualities focuses upon his sensitivity to the actions and reactions of his own world. Indeed, he stands now before the present century as a man of and for the times during which he lived and worked.

Oglesby, Illinois   S.J.R.
August 1987

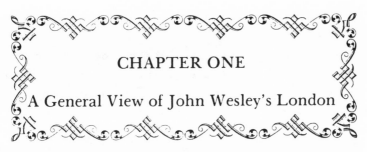

CHAPTER ONE

A General View of John Wesley's London

The verity of true Religion's known
By no description better than its own
Of Truth and Wisdom it informs the Mind,
And nobly strives to Civilize Mankind;
With potent Vice maintains Eternal Strife,
Corrects the Manners, and reforms the Life.
(Defoe,Reformation of Manners, 1702)

On 1 February 1738, John Wesley returned to England
after an absence of more than twenty-five months. Since
5 February 1736, he had been in General James Oglethorpe's
colony of Georgia, striving vainly to gain access to the
Indians of that region who had not the least yearning
for his instruction or moral guidance. During the last
months of that mission, he had spent considerable time
denying the charges and the grievances of the colonial
magistrates that he did "deviate from the principles and
regulations of the Established Church in many particulars
inconsistent with the happiness and prosperity of this
colony. . . ." (Tyerman, Life 1:155) Yet, upon his return
from America, Wesley wasted little time in reflecting
upon what could be termed, at least, an unfruitful
experience. "But what have I learned myself in the
meantime?" he lamented upon landing at Deal. "Why, what
I the least of all suspected, that I, who went to
America to convert others, was never myself converted to
God" (Journal 1:422).

Nonetheless, Wesley spent the following eight months preaching throughout Great Britain, finding additional time for travel to Germany and visits there with Count Nicholas von Zinzendorf and his Moravian Brethren. And, above all, 1738 witnessed the religious conversion of John Wesley, indeed the beginning of what would become British Methodism and, perhaps, one of the brightest of moments in the social and general religious history of Great Britain. On 24 May 1738, one of the most powerful of hearts and certainly the most active of souls throughout the island-kingdom began a socio-religious quest that would culminate in the founding of a religious denomination known throughout the Western world for its organization and its influence.

Epithets employed to describe John Wesley's activities during his long and productive life have, by now, almost become clichés: "Wrestling Jacob," "Man of Fire," "Missionary on Horseback," "Horseman with a Torch," "Knight of the Burning Heart," "The Lord's Horseman," "Friend of the People," and "The World His Parish." Such attempts at epic association, mainly in the form of book and essay subtitles, tend to convey the image of Wesley as a transient evangelist, roaming the countryside at random, paying little attention to the necessity for organization or to the details of an itinerary. Such subtitles and general epithets outline a romantic but hardly accurate historical personage. Actually, Methodism's founder and leader was also its singular administrator--its finance officer, travel agent, public relations spokesman, and moderator. Rarely, in the history of movements, institutions, or societies, do we observe such rigid control--control bordering upon pure autocracy. Rarely, do we discover an individual so amazingly aware of when, where, and how often he must visit

a particular locality within the relatively vast realm
of his geographic and religious responsibilities.

Naturally, Wesley quickly and early selected a base
for all of his activities, a city that demanded perhaps
as much of his seemingly limitless time and labor as did
all the rest of the nation combined. London became the
heart of John Wesley's large but loose network of Methodist
societies, a place where he might gather all that
proved necessary and important to him, a place where he
might pause on occasion to take stock of what he had
done and what he needed to do. ". . .all that life can
afford," wrote Samuel Johnson of his nation's capital.
Within that context of John Wesley's own definition and
understanding of life, the statement accurately synthe-
sizes and summarizes his activities there between the
return from Savannah in early 1738 and his death fifty-
three years later.

The London of the middle and later eighteenth century presented little in the way of comparison with the
present metropolis--the City of London and the twelve
inner boroughs comprising some 2,700,000 people. Prior
to 1750, London Bridge stood unchallenged as the principal means of walking or riding across the River Thames.
Covered with antique houses from one side to the other,
it formed a picturesque extension of Gracechurch Street
from Middlesex to the Surrey shore. Further, it existed
as a narrow, dark, and dangerous thoroughfare. At
each end, the citizen of London could observe an arched
gateway, generally bristling with spikes and--at regular
intervals--adorned with the heads of traitors. True,
that in 1722 a second bridge at Westminster had been
suggested, but five distinct groups presented a firm and
united stand against the project: the Company of Watermen, who found the Thames their principal (and sometimes

only) source of revenue; the west-county bargemen; the
Borough of Southwark; the City of London Corporation;
the inhabitants of London Bridge. Twelve years later
(1734), a small band of gentlemen joined with the Archbishop of Canterbury, William Wake, in funding prelimi-
nary plans and surveys for a new bridge. In 1736, Parliament passed an act for the building of a structure
across the river, to be financed through lotteries and
grants. And thus, from 1739 to 1750, the Swiss architect Charles Labeyle erected Westminster Bridge--1223
feet long (and thus 300 feet longer than London Bridge),
fifteen arches, and alcoves similar in style with those
on the London Bridge.

Between the proposal for Westminster Bridge in
1722 and its completion in 1750, a second structure,
Putney Bridge, had been erected in 1729 at a cost to the
City of £23,975. That bridge extended 789 feet in its
length and 24 feet in width, with openings through which
vessels might pass. The largest of those openings bore
the name "Walpole Lock," since Robert Walpole (1676-
1745) had helped to procure the original act of Parliament that brought about the project. Shortly after
the opening, foot passengers found themselves confronted with a halfpenny toll, which doubles to a single
penny on Sundays. Officials divided that revenue
between the widows and children of poor watermen living
in Stepney and Fulham; apparently, after the completion
of Putney Bridge, those men were not permitted to ply
on Sundays. Finally, citizens of London could observe
the construction of Blackfriars Bridge from 1760 to 1779,
as well as that of the picturesque wooden Battersea
Bridge between 1771 and 1773. Upon the opening of the
former structure, foot passengers again found themselves
forced to pay a halfpenny toll on weekdays and twice

that amount on Sundays. Opposition to the toll led to
frequent riots, culminating in the burning of the toll
house in 1780; the government then purchased the bridge
and eliminated the charges.

Upon his return from Germany in 1739, Wesley may
well have noticed the construction of the Mansion House,
the official residence of the lord mayors of London, on
the site previously occupied by the Stocks Market--or
Woolchurch Market. There, fruit, roots, and herbs had
been sold in an area adorned on one side by a row of
shady trees and on the other by a conduit surmounted by
an equestrian statue of Charles II. All of that adorn-
ment disappeared by 1752, and in its place rose a stately
building, the creation of George Dance the elder. In
the following year, 1753, the Lord Mayor Sir Crisp
Gascoigne assumed occupancy of the new residence, an edifice that appeared as "sedate, severe, churchy, and dig-
nified, a kind of Hallelujah Chorus in stone" (Kent,
Encyclopaedia 470).

However, the scene associated with London during
the middle and late eighteenth century cannot be described
only in terms of replacing trees and open markets
with stately government houses, or by noting the construction of new bridges across the River Thames. To the
contrary, a pastoral atmosphere dominated the area,
especially in districts immediately without the old city
walls. Islington, Hoxton, Hackney, and Bethnal Green
existed as little more than country villages. On the
Surrey side of the Thames, fields and open country rolled
beyond the King's Bench Prison. Newington, Walworth,
Camberwell, Brixton, Peckham, and Clapham lay out of ear-
shot of the noises and general commotion generated by
activity within the City. Lambeth appeared as one great
garden, extending from Kensington Common to Westminster

Bridge. To the east, Blackwell, Poplar, Bow, and
Stepney could be identified merely by clusters of houses
surrounded by fields and gardens. To the west, Chelsea,
Knightsbridge, Marylebone, and Tottenham obscured themselves beneath layers of neatness, cleanliness, affluence, and--above all--isolation. Belgravia seemed an
immense farm of arable pasture land in contrast to Tothill
Fields--a dreary place of stunted, dusty, and trodden
grass, a pleasure palace for all varieties of disreputable characters.

The major problem confronted by eighteenth-century
London focused, of course, upon its growth: from (and
these are approximate figures based upon a number and
variety of sources) half a million in 1700, to 750,000
in 1750, to 900,000 by the end of the century. Those
few statistics can best be understood when viewed
beside the populations of other "cities" in the island-
kingdom: Bristol and Norwich each housed about 30,000
inhabitants in 1700; Manchester and Liverpool could
claim around 80,000 persons each by 1800. The growth
of London during the first half of the eighteenth century appears to have been, primarily, in the direction
of Deptford, Hackney, and Bloomsbury. The City spread
also on the southern bank of the Thames after the construction of Westminster Bridge. Supposedly, Richard
Boyle, Lord Burlington, built his greathouse in Picadilly
(1665-1668) because he determined to have not a
single building behind him. However, by 1750, Burlington
House found itself surrounded by so many new avenues
that it actually stood in the very heart of London's
west end. During the reign of Anne (1702-1714),
Bloomsbury Square, Lincoln's Inn Fields, Soho Square, and
Queen's Square (Westminster) represented the ultimate in
fashionable quarters. In the reign of George II (1727-

1760), the wealthy of London could lay claim to Leicester
Fields, Golden Square, and Charing Cross.   From
Greenwich to the West End, the newly fashionable Portland
stone interrupted the sea of red, yellow, and grey
brick and created monuments out of churches, public office
buildings, and even private residences.

By 1776, sixteen years into the reign of George III,
slow but definite progress could be observed in the
ambitious projects for widening of the City's streets.
Laborers removed cobbles and kennels and installed paving-
stones and gutters.   Eight of the ancient city gates had
already been taken down simply because they could no longer
function as city gates! Only Temple Bar and Newgate
remained.   Within the poor sections of the City, workmen
busied themselves with the demolition of old buildings--
or stood by while those structures crumbled to the ground,
independent of human labor or their equipment, into their
own dust.   Simply, a significant number of old dwellings
in the poorer districts had been constructed with bricks
mixed with "the slop of the streets, ashes, scavengers'
dirt, and everything that will make the brick earth and
clay go as far as possible" (London Chronicle, 2 June
1764; George, London Life 74, 345).   In addition to the
paradoxical combination of destruction and construction,
a project came forth from that dust to make London the
most brilliantly lighted city in Europe--if not in the
entire eighteenth-century world.   Johann W. von Archenholz
observed that in "Oxford Street alone, there are
more lamps [fueled by cheap fish-oil] than in all of Paris"
(Picture of England 1:135).   Whether the light proved
just compensation for the thick smoke and the especially
strong stench of the fuel can only be left to speculation
and imagination.

If London, during the middle and late eighteenth

century, could boast of its wealth and growth and improvement, it could also display to the world the pitiful
state of its poor. Obviously, when one-eighth of a nation's
population endures in a single city, poverty, with
its natural complements of crime and general ill-health,
will not only survive, but it will also thrive. The
plight of the poor souls packed into eighteenth-century
London streets and dwellings comes down to us today almost
as one large collection of stereotypes represented
by a set of William Hogarth's drawings: <u>Industry and
Idleness</u> (1747), <u>Gin Lane</u>, <u>Beer Street</u>, <u>The Four Stages
of Cruelty</u> (all 1751). Nonetheless, the conditions captured by the mind and the pen of Hogarth proved extremely
accurate, obviously real and even painful to anyone
who walked the streets and the lanes of Hanoverian London
.". . .such scenes, who could see unmoved?" wrote
John Wesley in his journal for 8 February 1753. "There
are none such to be found in a pagan country. If any of
the Indians in Georgia were sick (which, indeed, exceedingly rarely happened till they learned gluttony and
drunkenness from the Christians), those that were near
gave him whatever he wanted. Oh who will convert the
English into honest heathens?" On Friday and Saturday,
9-10 February of that same year, he again walked among
the poor and the sick. "I found some in their cells under
ground, others in their garrets, half starved both
with cold and hunger, added to weakness and pain. But
I found not one of them unemployed who was able to crawl
about the room. So wickedly, devilishly false is that
common objection, 'They are poor only because they are
idle.' If you saw these things with your own eyes,could
you lay out money in ornaments or superfluities?"

    Wesley's closing question seems never to have been
answered; ignoring such problems and issues remained the
order of the day during the eighteenth century. Extra-

vagance functioned as the common denominator for the upper
classes. Splendid residences arose almost everywhere,
contending in richness with palaces and estates reserved,
traditionally, for kings and princes. The number of
carriages had increased practically threefold from the
beginning to the middle of the century. Ridottos (public dances and masquerades), formal balls, masquerades,
and midnight banquets seemed never to cease, while under
the new lamps that illuminated public gardens, the maca-
ronis (those fops and dandies of fiction come to life)
lounged about in gilded alcoves, wasting time and dulling
their own senses. The more conservative among the ladies
of high fashion and means contented themselves with coif-
fures merely one or two feet high, adorned with scarves,
ostrich feathers, or strands of pearls; others surpassed
that elevation and went so far as to adorn their heads
with heaps of flowers, herbs, and fruit. Gamblers,
actors, and prostitutes donned masks and mingled with
persons of wealth and title. Even clerks and apprentices,
servant girls and cooks, adorned themselves in gaudy
attire in tasteless attempts to emulate their masters and
mistresses. As early as 1744, the grand jury of the county of Middlesex declared that "the advertisements in the
newspapers were seducing the people to places for the
encouragement of luxury, extravagance, and idleness; and
that, by this means, families were ruined, and the kingdom dishonoured; and that, unless some superior authority
put a stop to such riotous living, they feared it would
lead to the destruction of the nation" (Tyerman, Life of
Wesley 1:216). The nation and its capital did survive,
of course, although both of them did endure moments of
moral discomfort.

Religion seemed the obvious answer to national salvation, or at least a balm to ease the moral discomforts.

However the Anglican Church did not escape the effects
of wealthy eighteenth-century Londoners' appetites for
unexampled wealth and display. Out of the cinder piles
of the Great Fire (2-6 September 1666), Christopher Wren
(1632-1723), Nicholas Hawksmoor (1661-1736), James Gibbs
(1682-1754), George Dance the elder (1695-1768) and George
Dance the younger (1741-1825) constructed new temples for
the adherents to the nation's Established Church. In fact,
in 1711, the newly elected High Church Tory government
celebrated its victory by passing the Fifty New Churches
Act, financed by a tax on coal.

Not surprisingly, the upper classes absented themselves from Sabbath and weekday worship services frequently
and consistently. "People of fashion," stated Archbishop
Thomas Secker--half in complaint, half in defense--
"especially of that sex which ascribes to itself most knowledge, have nearly thrown off all observation of the Lord's
day. . .and if to avoid scandal they sometimes vouchsafe
their attendance on Divine worship in the country, they
seldom or never do it in town" (Lecky, History of England
2:533). By the reign of George II (1727-1760), the day
traditionally and legally set aside for public worship
began to lose its distinctively religious character for
those holding membership in the upper classes. Cabinet
councils and Cabinet dinners were consistently held on
the Lord's Day, while Sunday card parties became increas-
ingly fashionable entertainments. Even Sunday concerts
had gained considerable popularity by the time (1760)
George III reached the throne of England.

Despite the tendency for persons of wealth, title,
and fashion to disregard Sunday and weekday public worship
in favor of more pleasurable activities, the Anglican
Church itself could not be held blameless. Those
persons who did attend service regularly and who professed

to some degrees of piety complained of dull sermons
preached in a dull manner by dull clerics. Certainly,
in the pulpit rhetoric of Joseph Butler, George Berkeley,
Thomas Secker, Laurence Sterne, George Whitefield,
and John Wesley, the eighteenth-century sermon address
became a major literary form; however, for every Anglican
priest resembling the former list, at least twice
the number of less imaginative clerics came to resemble
the type described by the poet George Crabbe in 1807:

> Good master ADDLE was the Parish-Guide;
> His Clerk and Sexton, I beheld with Fear
> His stride majestic, and his Frown severe;
> A noble Pillar of the Church he stood,
> Adorn'd with College-Gown and Parish-Hood;
> Then,as he pac'd the hallow'd aisles about,
> He fill'd the sevenfold Surplice fairly out!
> But in his Pulpit, wearied down with Prayer,
> He sat, and seem'd as in his Study's Chair;
> For while the Anthem swell'd, and when it
>   ceas'd,
> Th' expecting People view'd their slumbering
>   Priest;--
> Who, dozing, died.

The Parish Register 3:820-831

The larger churches of London, with interiors
designed almost as replicas of theatres or indoor stadia,
gave to worshippers a sense of distance from the entire
service; they had the feeling of university students com-
pelled to sit for a specified period in a large lecture
hall. The liturgy of the Anglican service not only cen-
sured any attempts at enthusiasm, but also did well to
suppress most forms of outward and spontaneous religious
expression on the part of the congregation. The function
of the Anglican clergy focused, most assuredly, upon the

creation of good and happy men, although incumbents
appreciated only the most rational of methods. And, in
general, the rank and file clerics were terribly under-
provided and not especially well-read or enlightened.
Essentially, the leaders of the eighteenth-century Church
of England possessed and expressed perfect confidence of
their faith having nothing to fear from the fullest and
most searching investigations.

Little wonder, then, that after 1742, the Methodism
of John and Charles Wesley began to exercise considerable
influence over all classes of people, both in London and
throughout Great Britain. Simply, Wesleyan Methodism
filled a number of religious and social voids among those
Anglicans who found little or no spiritual gratification
from the traditional doctrines and practices within their
own parish churches. Seldom heard from a Church of England
pulpit were such subjects as the utter depravity of
human nature, the lost conditions of human beings in
general, the vicarious atonement of Christ, the necessity
for believing in the sustaining action of the Divine Spirit
upon the believer's soul. John Wesley's form of evan-
gelicalism, tempered with his desire to remain within the
legal and traditional boundaries of the Established Church,
awoke in the minds of his followers the strong (but certainly not radical) emotions of hope, fear and love. The
Methodism of Wesley sought to transfer the character,
while arresting and reclaiming the thoroughly depraved
individual.

At the close of the year 1738, John Wesley--ordained
deacon and priest of the Church of England, Fellow
of Lincoln College, Oxford--suddenly but not unexpectedly
found himself almost entirely excluded from the pulpits
of Establishment churches. During the whole of 1739,
the thirty-six year-old Wesley could express his philo-

sophy of reform to the congregations of only four London
Anglican churches: Basingshaw, Islington, St. Giles,
and St. Katherine's. In addition, the churches at Clif-
ton, Durnmer, Runwich, and St. Mary's Exeter were closed
to him. That expulsion lasted for over forty years, after
which time London bishops and incumbents--sensing the
rising popularity of British Methodism--began to issue
invitations to their pulpits on a fairly regular basis.
Most important, one must never forget that John Wesley
lived and died a member of the Church of England; one
must keep in mind that he never once considered himself
anything but a priest of that Church.

In the early months of 1739, Wesley found himself
forced to restrict his oratory to the living rooms of
three or four private homes. In essence, he lived the
part of an exiled minister; denied access to Established
churches, he followed the example of his former Oxford
pupil, George Whitefield, and took his message to the
open fields, to the residences of devoted friends and of
loyal adherents, to the upper rooms of reclaimed buildings and barns, and eventually to his own chapels. Again,
in the face of such hardships and distractions, not to
mention pure physical inconvenience, Wesley spent his
entire working life trying to function as a clergyman
within the established institutions of church and state.
Long a fervent believer in Apostolical succession--
although he gradually modified his commitments to other
Anglican doctrines--he continued to profess his warm
adherence to the creed and the worship of the state religion. He even exhorted his followers to attend Anglican
worship service (prior to or following his own), to
abstain from attacking Anglican clergy, to avoid embracing
any of the Dissenting sects. In an essay dated 11 December 1789, and published in his own Arminian Magazine for
1790, the eighty-six year-old Wesley declared "once more

that I live and die a member of the Church of England;
and that none, who regarding my judgment or advice, will
ever separate from it" (Tyerman, Life of Wesley 3:634-
635). And, as we know, that separation did not occur
until five years after the death of Methodism's founder
and leader.

The preceding discussion--including Wesley's purpose, his problems, and his influences--brief and general as it may (and necessarily must) be, proves sufficient, at least, to establish the key point about and
purpose for this entire volume: John Wesley's perspec-
tive of London in no way resembled the views of the city
as presented by other London noteworthies of the same and
even earlier periods. Throughout the diaries of Samuel
Pepys, covering the period 1 January 1660 through 1668,
the writer observed a city undergoing dramatic and trau-
traumatic change, enduring dramatic and traumatic events:
the Restoration of Charles II, the Great Fire, the equally
great plague, threatened invasion. Nonetheless, in
the midst of such tense activities, Pepys managed to discover and to practice the good life: to travel in high,
merry, and important company; to observe and record the
boisterous amusements and splendid fashions; to stride
with kings, ministers, and their ladies; to accumulate
wealth and to maintain health.
For James Boswell, at age twenty-two, the London
of 1762-1763 proved the perfect place for casting off,
if only for a brief and temporary moment, the oppressive
grip of his father's Calvinistic Presbyterianism and discipline. In coffee-houses, theatres, brothels, ladies'
bed-chambers, taverns, streets and alleys, and even in
the pews of churches of several denominations, young
Boswell attempted to see and to do, within a single year,
all that had hitherto been denied him. "London is

undoubtedly a place where men and manners may be seen to
the greatest advantage. The liberty and whim that reigns
there occasions a variety of perfect and curious characters. Then the immense crowd and hurry and bustle of
business and diversion, the great number of public
places of entertainment, the noble churches and the su-
perb buildings of different kinds, agitate, amuse, and
elevate the mind. Besides, the satisfaction of pursuing
whatever plan is most agreeable, without being known or
looked at, is very great. Here a young man of curiosity
and observation may have a sufficient fund of present entertainment, and may lay up ideas to employ his mind in
old age" (London Journal 68-69). Certainly, Boswell's
mentor and intellectual father image, Samuel Johnson,
shared a similar liking for his young companion's pleasure palaces, although the great sage was, no doubt, re-
stricted in a number of areas because of advanced age.
However, Johnson's concept of London exists principally
on an intellectual level that becomes extremely difficult to describe or even to synthesize. Perhaps that
concept of the capital can best be understood in terms of
his oft-quoted description of his attitude toward the
city: ". . .when a man is tired of London, he is tired
of life; for there is in London, all that life can afford" (Boswell, Life of Johnson 859).

No one will deny for a moment that the same scenes
(the same men, women, manners, institutions, and buildings) that existed for James Boswell and Samuel Johnson
also existed for John Wesley. The significant difference,
of course, lies in the realization that while Boswell and
Johnson rode the waves of London's energy and intellectual stimulation, the patriarch of British Methodism
plodded through the muck and the waste of what can only
be described as the worst that life within that city had

to afford. Almost from the outset of his return to Lon-
London from Georgia, Wesley set out to strengthen and then
elevate the souls of the poor within the city, to provide them with some forms of relief, physical and spiritual, from the daily miseries that characterized their
lives. Thus, he plunged into the filthy garrets and under-
ground cellars of St. Giles parish, Cripplegate, visited
the wretched inmates of Newgate Prison, and even
rode along side the condemned as they made their way to
the gallows at Tyburn. Denied the rights granted to him
upon ordination as an Established Church deacon and
priest, he took to the open fields of Kennington Common,
Whitechapel, and Moorfields. When the weather turned
wet and cold, he transferred his activities indoors--
not to St. Paul's Cathedral, Christ Church, or Holy Trinity,
but to a drafty, second-story meeting-house in Fetter
Lane, a reclaimed government armory in Upper Moorfields,
or a refurbished Dissenters' chapel in the West
End. Palaces, inns, or impressive temples of public
worship had little or no meaning for John Wesley, as evi-
denced by a comment in his journal for Saturday, 1 October 1763: "I returned to London, and found our house in
ruins, great part of it being taken down, in order for a
thorough repair. But as much remained as I wanted: six
foot square suffices me by day or night." In his heart
and mind, the only splendor lay with God and with His impoverished human creatures on earth.

The smattering of details presented in this intro-
ductory discussion--these and others which have been set
forth with considerably more specificity in the main section of the text--provide the reason for looking most
carefully at the London of John Wesley. Simply, his London
don emerges from history as the city that students of the
eighteenth century, of its literature and its culture, do

not always see, nor do they always want to see it.
Wesley's London is not a pleasant sight, nor does it offer
to students and general readers much in the way of ideal
and sometimes romantic notions they may possess about the
"good life" in eighteenth-century England. Instead, John
Wesley's London presents to the late twentieth century a
panorama of serious experiences and equally serious activities. Sermons, **meetings**, chapel and church worship services, outdoor meetings, charity work, writing, reading,
meditation, rejection, disappointment, physical abuse:
all of those and more stand clear but harsh against a
taut background of life, creating a scene in which hope
and despair vie continually with each other to control
the physical and spiritual existence of eighteenth-
century Londoners. On Thursday, 1 March 1791, on the day
before his death, John Wesley lay in his bed and recited
these lines:

> Happy the man whose hopes rely
> On Israel's God; He made the sky,
>> And earth, and seas with all their
>>> train;
> His truth for ever stands secure,
> He saves th' oppressed, He feeds the
>> poor,
>> And none shall find His promise
>>> vain.

(<u>Journal</u> 8:138)

Those words proved, practically, the last utterance of
John Wesley--his final sustained comment upon his long
life. The passage from that hymn accurately describes
Wesley's purpose in life as he practiced it throughout
the island-kingdom of Great Britain and, particularly,
in the crowded capital of England.

CHAPTER TWO

Northern Section

Though you through cleanlier alleys wind by day,
　　To shun the hurries of the public way,
Yet ne'er to those dark paths by night retire;
　　Mind only safety, and contemn the mire.
Then no impervious courts thy haste detain,
　　Nor sneering alewives bid thee turn again.
(Gay, Trivia; Or, The Art of Walking the Streets of London,
　　1716)

Kentish Town. Kentish Town exists as the oldest
village wholly within the borough of St. Pancras. A
chapel dedicated to St. John the Baptist was created
there during the reign of Henry III (1216-1272) or
Edward I (1272-1307) and torn down late in the eighteenth
century. In 1783, James Wyatt (1746-1813) erected a new
chapel near the foot of Highgate Road. Generally during
the eighteenth century, visitors from London came to
Kentish Town to frequent the several hospitable inns of the
area and to escape the smoke of the City.

John Wesley notes, in his diary for Wednesday, 18
February 1789, that at 2:00 in the afternoon he arrived
in "K[enti]sh town." Almost two years later, on Wednesday,
19 January 1791, the aged patriarch records another
visit to the village--at 1:00 in the afternoon, "at Mr.
Clulow's within. . . ." As Wesley's solicitor, William
Clulow witnessed the Deed of Declaration (formally known
as the Declaration and Appointment of the Conference of
the People Called Methodists) on 28 February 1784; he also
witnessed Wesley's will, dated 25 February 1789.

Islington. The borough of Islington serves well to
exemplify the overall growth and development of London
during the eighteenth century. In 1708, only 325 houses
stood in a section known for handsome and elaborately
adorned mansions and accompanying gardens and orchards.
By 1793, two years after John Wesley's death, that figure
had reached 1200. The population of Islington for 1800
was estimated at 10,212. Notable residents of the area
included the poet William Collins (1721-1759); John
Nichols (1745-1826), editor of The Gentleman's Magazine;
the actor-manager-laureate Colley Cibber (1671-1757) and
his daughter, Virginia Clarke. The parish church dedicated
to St. Mary the Virgin, remained the only church in
Islington until the nineteenth century. The original
structure of that building was demolished in 1751; three
years later, Launcelot Dowbiggin erected a new church,
opened by James Colebrook, lord of the manor.

George Stonehouse (1714-1793) became vicar of
Islington in 1738. Wesley visited him often and
frequently discharged the curate's duties there--although
he never received a formal appointment to that post. In
both his journal and diary, Wesley noted thirty-three
occasions between Wednesday, 10 May 1738, and Monday, 6
October 1740, upon which he preached at Islington or conversed with Rev. Stonehouse. For example, he noted in
his journal for 10 May 1738 that "Mr. Stonehouse was convinced of the 'truth as it is in Jesus.'" After 1740,
Welsey seemed to have lost his interest (or need) in
Islington, either religious or social. However, on Good
Friday, 16 April 1747, he recorded an occasion upon
which "I was desired to call on one that was ill at
Islington. I found there several of my old acquaintance
who loved me once as the apple of their eye. By staying with them but a little I was clearly convinced that,

was I to stay but one week among them. . .I would be
as <u>still</u> as poor Mr. St[onehouse]." Clearly, anti-
Methodist sentiment had come to that part of greater London,
indicating the extent to which Wesley had been cut off
from the establishment that he once had served and into
whose arms he had been more than welcome.

Finally, there exists one passing reference to
Islington, a short notation of a walk there at 6:00 p.m.,
Friday, 27 February 1789.

<u>Highbury Place, Islington</u>. At No. 25, **Highbury** Place
lived John Horton--by vocation a drysalter, but also one
who served on the London Common Council and as one of
John Wesley's executors. Thus, Wesley proved a frequent
visitor to Highbury Place, and Horton's house served him
as one of several places to which he retired for rest and
literary work. One must note, however, that those visits
occurred rather late in Wesley's life, after the strong
anti-Methodist sentiment in Islington had generally sub-
sided.

Thus, on Wednesday, 20 December 1786, Wesley noted in
his journal that "I retired to Highbury Place; but how
changed! Where are those three amiable sisters? One is
returned to her father, one deprived of her reason, and
one in Abraham's bosom!" The Methodist patriarch refers
here to the daughters of a local Methodist, Henry Durbin:
Alice became deranged; another (d. 1834) lived with
Mr. Durbin; a third, Mary, married John Horton and died
on 16 May 1786. Three years earlier, Wesley had visited
25 Highbury Place, where on Sunday, 9 November 1783, at
1:00 p.m., he christened the Hortons' infant daughter.

From the journals, we know that Wesley "retired" to
Highbury Place on Monday, 13 November 1786; Monday, 21

July 1788; Tuesday, 6 January 1789; and Tuesday, 12 January 1790.   There also exist diary references to visits
there on the following occasions: Sunday, 29 December
1782 (for communion at 9:30 a.m.); Monday, 6 January
1783 (at 9:30 a.m.); Thursday, 5 June 1783 (8:30 p.m.);
Thursday, 10 July 1783 (at 6:30 p.m., for supper and
prayer); Thursday, 20 November 1783 (at 1:30 p.m., when
he "writ society")' Friday, 19 November 1784 (5:45 a.m.);
Wednesday, 3 August 1785 (at noon); and Tuesday, 22 February 1791, at 1:00 p.m.--less that two weeks before his
death.

Marshall Claxton's painting of The Death-bed of John
Wesley identifies John Horton as the figure with the hand-
kerchief to his face (see Journal, ed. Curnock, 8:140-
141).   The son of a Methodist preacher, Claxton (1811-
1881) was native to Bolton.   A pupil of John Jackson, he
entered the Royal Academy School in 1831; he received the
gold medal of the Society of Arts four years later.

Stoke Newington.   Nearly all of the physical associations
of Stoke Newington with the eighteenth century have been
destroyed.   For example, on the south side of Church
Street, Daniel Defoe wrote Robinson Crusoe (published in
1719) on or near the site later occupied by a house on
the northeast corner of Defoe Road.   That dwelling,
bound on the west by Cut-throat Lane, was demolished in
1875.   It supposedly had an unusual number of doors, with
strong locks and bolts, serving to protect the writer
from real or imagined intruders (or creditors!).

Stoke Newington became the home of the Independent
minister and hymnodist, Rev. Isaac Watts (1674-1748), who
served, initially as a tutor to the family of Sir John
Hartopp from 1696 to 1702.   Watts then spent the final
thirty years of his life at Abney Park, the residence of
Sir Thomas Abney.   That dwelling came down in 1840 to

make way for Abney Park Cemetery. Because Stoke Newington
became a refuge for Dissenters prohibited from living
in the City of London proper, a number of Nonconformist
chapels and meeting-houses arose there during the eighteenth century.

For John Wesley, Stoke Newington provided still
another place of periodic retirement, where he could rest
from his travels, perform his administrative functions,
and prepare his various prose tracts and poetic revisions.
On Monday, 25 November 1745, he went there to finish
A Further Appeal to Men of Reason and Religion (London:
William Strahan, 1745). Other works written and/or
completed there include A Letter to a Friend Concerning
Tea (London: William Strahan, 1748), dated "Newington,
Dec. 10, 1748"; the third volume of his Sermons on Var-
ious Occasions (London: William Strahan, 1750), comple-
ted between Monday, 11 December 1749, and Saturday, 16
December 1749; A Short Account of the Rev. John Fletcher
(London: John Paramore, 1786), a portion of which he
wrote at Newington on Wednesday, 27 September 1786. Dur-
ing the period that William Strahan (1715-1785) served
as Wesley's printer, his printing office stood in Wine-
Office Court, off Fleet Street; he then moved to New
Street.

At the end of his journal in the entry for Friday, 9
October 1747, Wesley indicated that he had spent several
weeks at Newington and at Lewisham working on literary
labors; again, on Monday, 21 December 1747, he stated
that he had retired to Newington to write--and to read
of the deaths of some of the Order de la Trappe. Finally,
he devoted the evening of Wednesday, 3 December 1777,
to visiting with John Fletcher at the home of Mr. Charles
Greenwood (d. 1783); Fletcher was then ill with consumption. A biographical word about the latter, an

important figure in the history of eighteenth-century
British Methodism, is in order at this point.

John William Fletcher (originally de la Flechere),
a native of Nyon, Switzerland, came to England in 1752
from the Swiss military, then in service to the King of
Portugal. He obtained a tutorship in the family of
Thomas Hill, M.P., at Tern Hill, Shropshire. At the time
of the parliamentary session, he accompanied the Hill
family to London, came in contact with the Wesleyan
Methodists, and promptly joined the society at West
Street(see under Chapter Three, "North-Central Section").
Wesley encouraged Fletcher to take Orders; thus, in 1757,
he received ordination at Whitehall, after which he rushed
off to assist the leader of the Methodists, with whom
he remained in close association until his own death in
1785. In 1760, he received appointment as vicar of
Madely, some ten miles from Tern Hall; ten years later,
Selina Shirley, Countess of Huntingdon and the patroness of
George Whitefield and the Calvinist Methodists, appointed
Fletcher head of her seminary in Trevecca, Wales. He
served there for only one year, his departure necessi-
tated by the Countess's purge of Wesleyan Methodists from
her institution. From Wales, Fletcher returned to London,
then to Switzerland, back to Madeley, then (because
of continued ill-health) to the hot wells outside
Bristol. In November 1781, he wed Mary Bosanquet, one of
John Wesley's most devoted female workers, and the couple
settled in Madeley. Throughout adulthood, Fletcher
suffered terribly from consumption; his death in middle
August 1785 proved a severe blow to the aged Wesley, who
preached his friend's funeral sermon on 6 November. By
early August 1786, the Methodist patriarch was at work
on Fletcher's biography. The preface, written at Amsterdam,
bears the date 12 September 1786, and the work

appeared in December under the title <u>A Short Account</u>
<u>of the Life and Death of the Reverend John Fletcher</u>.

Others of John Wesley's visits to Stoke Newington oc-
cured on Thursday, 8 December 1785; Wednesday, 18 January
1786; Tuesday, 13 January 1789; and Wednesday, 5 January
1791. From Wesley's Sermon Register--a summary of his
pulpit activity from 14 January 1747 through 25 December
1761, and arranged in three columns (date, place, and Biblical text reference)--we may note the following entries
for Stoke Newington; Scripture quotations <u>were not</u> included in the Register, but are supplied here--and elsewhere
throughout this volume, for information and for the the-
matic sense of the sermon:

Wednesday, 18 December 1747

> <u>2 Corinthians</u> 4:6--For it is the God who said,
> "Let light shine out of darkness," who has
> shone in our hearts to give the light of
> the knowledge of the glory of God in the
> face of Christ.

> <u>Luke</u> 16:26--And besides all this, between us and
> you a great chasm has been fixed, in order
> that those who would pass from here to you
> may not be able, and none may cross from
> there to us.

> <u>2 Corinthians</u> 3:18--And we all with unveiled
> face, beholding the glory of the Lord, are
> being changed into his likeness from one de-
> gree of glory to another; for this comes from
> the Lord who is the Spirit.

(?) November 1748

> <u>Ephesians</u> 2:2--. . .in which you once walked,
> following the course of this world, following
> the prince of the the power of the air,
> the spirit that is now at work in the sons

of disobedience.

John 6:45--It is written in the prophets,"And
they shall be taught by God." Every one
who has heard and learned from the Father
comes to me.

John 4:13--Jesus said to her, "Every one who
drinks of this water will thirst again. . ."

1 Peter 4:7--The end of all things is at hand;
therefore, keep sane and sober for your
prayers.

Monday, 5 December 1748

Micah 6:7--Will the Lord be pleased with thousands of rams, with ten thousands of rivers
of oil? Shall I give my first born for my
transgression, the fruit of my body for the
sin of my soul?

Psalms 147--Praise the Lord, for it is good to
sing praises to our God. . . .

2 Corinthians 4:6--See above for Wednesday, 18
December 1747.

Matthew 24:4--And Jesus answered them, Take
heed that no one leads you astray.

Luke 7:36--One of the Pharisees asked him, and
he went into the Pharisee's house, and sat
at table.

Luke 15:11--And he said, "There was a man who
had two sons. . . ."

Mark 1:15--The time is fulfilled, and the kingdom of God is at hand; repent, and believe
in the gospel.

Revelation 22:17--The Spirit and the Bride say,
"Come." And let him who hears say, "Come."
And let him who is thirsty come, let him who
desires take the water of life without price.

Monday, 2 January 1749

2 Corinthians 8:9--For you know the grace of
our Lord Jesus Christ, that though he was
rich, yet for your sake he became poor, so
that by his poverty you might become rich.

Isaiah 55:7--Let the wicked forsake his way,
and the unrighteous man his thoughts; let
him return to the Lord, that he may have mercy on him, and to our God, for he will abundantly pardon.

Jeremiah 18:22--May a cry be heard from their
houses, when thou bringest the marauder suddenly upon them! For they have dug a pit to
take me, and laid snares for my feet.

1 John 5:7--And the Spirit is the witness, because the Spirit is the truth.

Matthew 11:28--Come to me, all who labor and
are heavy laden, and I will give you rest.

Revelation 20--Then I saw an angel coming down
from heaven. . . .

(?) November 1749

Acts 11:26--And when he had found him, he
brought him to Antioch. For a whole year
they met with the church, and taught a large
company of people; and in Antioch the disciples were for the first time called Christians.

Psalms 90:12--So teach us to number our days
that we may get a heart of wisdom.

Matthew 16:26--For what will it profit a man,
if he gains the whole world and forfeits
his life? Or what shall a man give in return for his life?

Tuesday, 1 January 1751

Dueteronomy 12:10--But when you go over the
Jordan and live in the land which the Lord
your God gives you to inherit, and when he
gives you rest from all your enemies round
about, so that you live in safety. . . .

1 Corinthians 13:13--So faith, love, hope,
abide, these three; but the greatest of
these is love.

John 17:3--And this is eternal life, that they
know thee the only true God, and Jesus Christ
whom thou hast sent.

(?) October 1751

1 John 5:11--And this is the testimony, that
God gave us eternal life, and this life is
in his Son.

1 John 5:12--He who has the Son has life; he
who has not the Son of God has not life.

John 4:24--God is spirit, and those who worship him must worship in spirit and truth.

Thursday, 21 November 1751

Jeremiah 8:22--Is there no balm in Gilead? Is
there no physician there? Why then has the
health of the daughter of my people not been
restored?

Philippians 2:16-17--. . .holding fast to the
word of life, so that in the day of Christ
I may be proud that I did not run in vain
or labor in vain. Even if I am to be poured
as a libation upon the sacrificial offering
of your faith, I am glad and rejoice with
you all.

1 John 5:3--For this is the love of God, that
we keep his commandments. And his commandments are not burdensome.

Tuesday, 7 January 1752

   Romans 3:22--The righteousness of God through
      faith in Jesus Christ for all who believe.
      For there is no distinction. . . .

   Psalms 147:3--He heals the brokenhearted, and
      binds up their wounds.

   Galatians 3:22--But the scripture consigned all
      things to sin, that what was promised to
      faith in Jesus Christ might be given to
      those who believe.

   Galatians 6:14--But far be it for me to glory
      except in the cross of our Lord Jesus Christ,
      by which the world has been crucified to me,
      and I to the world.

Newington Green, Stoke Newington.   Although the
Green was enclosed in 1742, at least four houses therein
dated from 1658, and thus the area contained some of the
oldest houses in greater London.   Further, a Unitarian
congregation built a chapel there in 1708.

     Isaac Watts (1674-1748) spent the years 1690 to 1694
as a student at Newington Green Academy, the successor
to an earlier institution where Daniel Defoe had studied
sixteen years previously.   The school held a reputation
for its realistic and liberal (at least for the times)
attitude toward education.   The Rev. Thomas Rowe, the son
of one of Cromwell's chaplains and the minister of an
Independent congregation meeting at Girdlers' Hall (Basinghall Street), served as the principal of Newington Green
Academy during Watts' tenure there.   For a full discussion of Rowe, Watts, and Newington Green Academy, see
Escott 18-19.

     On Monday, 13 October 1740, at 3:00 p.m., Wesley
visited Newington Green--"at Mrs. Clark's, conversed, tea."

Adylena Clark, described as a remarkably holy woman, was
the wife of George Clark, a prominent London Methodist.

   Hackney. According to Daniel Defoe (Tour 337), who
last observed the borough of Hackney in 1724, the town
"is of great extent, containing no less than 12 hamlets
or separate villages." He labeled the area as being
"remarkable for the retreat of wealthy citizens," observing
"that there is at this time near a hundred coaches kept
in it; though I will not join with a certain satirical
author, who said of Hackney, that there were more coaches
than Christians in it." Defoe's "certain satirical
author" could possibly have been Tom Brown (1663-1764),
a miscellaneous writer of unusual longevity best known
for his Amusements Serious and Comical (1700).
   John Wesley seemed to have visited Hackney on two
occasions during the middle of 1741. Initially, on Friday, 29 May, he paused at the home of a Mr. Clare; then,
on Monday, 27 July, he preached there on Ephesians 2:8--
"For by grace you have been saved through faith; and
this is not your own doing, it is the gift of God. . . ."
He informs us of an additional visit, that on Tuesday,
3 January 1786, when, between 4:00 and 5:00 p.m., he conversed and prayed.

   Shacklewell, Hackney. Shacklewell, which adjoins
Hackney to the south, at one time achieved recognition
as a separate district. At present, however, it belongs
to the borough of Hackney. One prominent residence,
Shacklewell House, belonged to the Heron (or Hern) family;
afterward, it passed into the possession of the Rowe
family. Henry Rowe, who was still living in 1715, sold
the dwelling to Francis Tyssen--who occupied the building

as late as 1720.

Wesley spent the hours between 1:00 and 2:00 p.m., Thursday, 15 December 1785, at Shacklewell, working on The Arminian Magazine--the Methodist miscellany of prose and verse that he edited until the final month before his death.

CHAPTER THREE
North-Central Section

Wherever God erects a House of Prayer
The Devil always builds a Chappel there:
And 'twill be found upon Examination,
The latter has the largest Congregation:
For ever since he first debauch'd the Mind,
He made a perfect Conquest of Mankind.
With Uniformity of Service, he
Reigns with a general Aristocracy.
No Nonconforming Sects disturb his Reign,
For of his Yoak there's very few complain.

  Defoe, The True-Born Englishman (1701)

Paddington. Paddington--in the eighteenth century
a small, pleasant village, but not a part of London proper
--served as one of the many places of retirement for
the busy and oft-traveled Wesley. He was certainly not
alone in that regard, for a number of "artists sought
rustic themes at Paddington, in whose churchyard several
painters, engravers, and sculptors of the late eighteenth
century lie buried" (Rude 62). Wesley went there on a
Thursday morning, 4 May 1754, spending "some weeks in
writing; only going to town on Saturday evenings, and
leaving it [London] again on Monday morning."

Marylebone Fields. During Wesley's day, Marylebone
proved sparsely populated--consisting mostly of garden
walks and broad, green fields. In 1793, the Treasury
offered a prize of £1000 for the best plan for developing

Marylebone Fields. Later, George, Prince of Wales
(who also functioned as Regent), determined to create a
new park and to name it (indirectly) for himself. Thus,
Regent's Park came into being. Charles Wesley moved to
Marylebone in 1771; thirty years prior to that event,
his brother had discovered Marylebone Fields a convenient area in which to hold outdoor worship services. In
that context, we can compile a summary of John Wesley's
services and sermons in Marylebone Fields between the
middle of June 1740 and early May 1741:

> 6:00 p.m., Wednesday, 18 June 1740
>> Acts 5:30--The God of our fathers raised Jesus
>> whom you killed by hanging him on a tree.
>
> 6:00 p.m., Wednesday, 2 July 1740
>> Romans 14:17--For the kingdom of God does not
>> mean food and drink, but righteousness and
>> peace and joy in the Holy Spirit. . . .
>
> 6:00 p.m., Wednesday, 16 July 1740
>> Hosea 14:4--I will heal their faithlessness; I
>> will love them freely, for my anger has
>> turned from them.
>
> 6:00 p.m., Wednesday, 30 July 1740
>> 1 Timothy 2:4--No soldier on service gets en-
>> tangled in civilian pursuits, since his aim
>> is to satisfy the one who enlisted him.
>
> 6:00 p.m., Wednesday, 13 August 1740
>> Acts 28:22--But we desire to hear from you what
>> your views are; for with regard to this sect
>> we know that everywhere it is spoken against.
>
> 5:30 p.m., Sunday, 26 April 1741
>> Isaiah 1:18--Come now, let us reason together,
>> says the Lord; though your sins are like
>> scarlet, they shall be as white as snow;
>> though they are red like crimson, they shall

become like wool.

6:15 p.m., Saturday, 2 May 1741

2 Corinthians 5:7--. . .for we walk by faith,
not by sight.

5:30 p.m., Sunday, 3 May 1741

Micah 6:7--Will the Lord be pleased with
thousands of rams, with ten thousands of
rivers of oil? Shall I give my first-born
for my transgression, the fruit of my body
for the sin of my soul?

Tottenham Court Road Chapel.   In 1756, George Whitefield (1714-1770) built--with funds supplied by his patroness, Selina Shirley, Countess of Huntingdon, as well as
a contribution of £500 from actor-manager David Garrick--
his chapel at Tottenham Court Road. He laid the founda-
tion-stone at the beginning of June 1756; on 7 November,
Whitefield opened the chapel for divine worship, basing
his initial sermon text there upon 1 Corinthians 3:11--
Other foundation can no man lay than that is laid, which
is Jesus Christ.

Surrounding the chapel--known generally and sarcas-
tically as "Whitefield's Sout Trap"--were fields and
gardens. In fact, one could find only two houses on the
north side of the area. When first erected, the chapel
spread seventy feet square within the walls; in 1758,
Whitefield ordered the addition of twelve alm-houses and
a minister's house. Eighteen months later, he determined
the chapel to be too small for his needs; thus, he
enlarged the building to 127 feet by 70 feet, with a
dome 114 feet high. Beneath, Whitefield provided burial vaults, in which he intended that he and the Wesleys
be interred. "I have prepared a vault in this chapel,
where I intend to be buried, and Messers. John and Charles

Wesley shall also be buried here. We will all lie
together. You [the members of the Tottenham Court Road
Chapel] will not let them [the Wesleys] enter your chapel
while they are alive. They can do you no harm when
they are dead" (Tyerman, Life of Wesley 3:76-77).

On Saturday, 10 November 1770, Wesley returned to
London from Norwich. He then received news of Whitefield's death (on 30 September, at Newburyport, near
Boston) and also learned of the request from the latter's
executors that he preach the funeral sermon. "The
time appointed for my beginning at the Tabernacle,"
noted Wesley in his journal for that day, "was half-hour
after five [Sunday, 18 November 1770], but it was quite
filled at three; so I began at four. At first the noise
was exceeding great; but it ceased when I began to speak;
and my voice was again so strengthened that all who were
within could hear, unless an accidental noise hindered
here or there for a few moments. Oh that all may hear
the voice of Him with whom are the issues of life and
death; and who so loudly, by this unexpected stroke,
calls all His children to love one another."

Whitefield's chapel, known also as the Tabernacle,
stood until 1880, in which year it was pulled down.

Oxford Market, Oxford Street. On the north side
of Oxford Street, near John Street, stood Oxford Market,
built in 1731 for Robert Harley, Earl of Oxford (1661-
1724), and designed by James Gibbs (1682-1754). Sometimes known as Portland Market, it house stalls for the
sale of meat, fish, and vegetables--lasting until 1880,
when the building came down.

Originally, Oxford Market stood in open fields, ad-
joining the farmland from which most of its commodities
originated. There, servants of the wealthy Soho residents

came to buy their provisions. The area--but not
the building--appears on a plan of Marylebone drawn in
1719 by John Prince; its initial reference in the rate
books dates 1724, at which time the market contained
but six stalls. In 1727, the stall-holders increased to
eighteen; about the middle of the century, the structure
underwent further expansion with the addition of out-
buildings.

Wesley stated, merely, that on Saturday, 19 December 1761, he "visited many near Oxford Market. . . ."

Chesterfield Street, Marylebone. When Charles Wesley
moved to No. 1 Chesterfield Street in 1771, Marylebone
appeared a pleasant rural village. In fact, little
else but green fields stretched from Whitefield's Chapel
in Tottenham Court Road (see pp. 35-36) to the younger
Wesley's new home. Because of the distance (approximately three miles) from the Foundry in Moorfields, John
Wesley objected to his brother's new residence. Simply,
the two could not consult easily or frequently with each
other on matter related to the London Methodist societies.

In 1779, Charles Wesley's two sons, Charles (1757-
1834) and Samuel (1766-1837), embarked upon a series of
private subscription concerts, twelve each year, at the
house on Chesterfield Street, which itself contained two
organs and a harpsichord. They performed works by Handel,
Corelli, and contemporary composers, as well as their own
improvisations of those pieces. The series lasted until
1785; by that time, Samuel Wesley had become a rather
prolific composer, and Charles Wesley (despite objec-
tions from brother John) determined to permit both of
the young musical geniuses to enter the profession of
music.

The boys' uncle noted, in his journal for Thursday,

25 July 1781, that he "spent an agreeable hour at a concert of my nephews.   But I was a little rune out of my
elements among lords and ladies.   I love plain music and
plain company best."

Charles Wesley died on Saturday, 29 March 1788, and
his body was laid to rest in the graveyard of Marylebone
parish church (built in 1740 to replace the original
structure).   The churchyard itself has become a small
paved garden with seats, but Wesley's monument remains
in full view. After Charles Wesley's death, his widow,
Sarah (nee Gwynne), continued to occupy the house on
Chesterfield Street, and we know of at least two occasions upon which her brother-in-law visited her there.
On Saturday, 19 July 1788, "I spent an hour in Chesterfield Street with my widowed sister and her children."
Only a year before, young Samuel had suffered a serious head injury from a fall into a builder's excavation,
and his father's death served only to increase the boy's
despondency and irritability. At any rate, more than two
years after his brother's death, on Monday, 17 January
1791, the aged John Wesley came again to Chesterfield
Street, this time for dinner, conversation, and prayer.

St. Pancras ("Pancridge").   Two diary notations in-
form us of Wesley's activities in that (then) small section of the city known as St. Pancras. As late as 1776,
the area contained a population of less that six hundred.   On Friday, 14 September 1739, Wesley "walked to
Pancridge"; more than two weeks later (Sunday, 30 September), the diary entry reads, "Pancras, 12,000, Acts
xx. 28 [". . .I bought this citizenship for a large sum."
Paul said, "But I was born a citizen."]. . . ." The figure of 12,000 proves most confusing. Certainly, that
number could refer to the attendance at one of the open
air worship services, but that appears highly unlikely,

considering the date. Simply, neither Wesley nor his
evangelical organization had become popular (or even
known)by late 1739. If the reference is to the number
of persons in attendance, it would not have been the only
instance upon which Wesley inflated the numbers of
people who came to hear him preach (perhaps overestima-
ted would be a more kind term).

     Bloomsbury. Wesley states that between 12:15 and
1:30 p.m., Friday, 22 December 1738, he "conversed, [had]
communion, conversed" at Bloomsbury. For more specific
and detailed references to this section of the city, see
individual places set forth in the entries immediately
below.

     The British Museum (Montague House). The Museum
originated as an institution in 1753, with the purchase
of the library and collection of Sir Hans Sloan (1660-
1752)--Physician to Christ's Hospital, London; President
of the College of Physicians; President of the Royal Society, 1727-1740; and Physician-General to the army. He
bequeathed to the British nation his collection of over
50,000 books and 3516 manuscripts on the condition that
£20,000 should be paid to his heirs. The government accepted those terms and raised the amount through public
lottery. Increased by addition of the Cottonian collection and the Harleian manuscripts--the former having
been private property for a considerable period--the Museum, arranged in Montague House, opened its doors to
the public in 1759. The present building was erected
between 1823 and 1847 from the designs of Robert Smirke
(1781-1867); his brother, Sydney (1799-1877), completed
the west wing of the building and the reading room in

1854.

Wesley spent part of the afternoon of Wednesday, 12
December 1759, in the British Museum. There, he noticed
"a large library, a great number of curious manuscripts,
many uncommon monuments of antiquity, and the whole collection of shells, butterflies, beetles, grasshoppers,
&c., which the indefatigable Sir Hans Sloane, with such
vast expense and labour, procured in a life of fourscore
years." The leader of the Methodists returned to the Museum
on Friday, 22 December 1780, accompanied by friends.
"What an immense field is here for curiosity to range in!
What room is filled from top to bottom with things brought
from Otaheite; two or three more with things dug out
of the ruins of Herculaneum! Seven huge apartments are
filled with the curious books, five with manuscripts, two
with fossils of all sorts, and the rest with various animals. But what account will a man give to the judge of
quick and dead for a life spent in collecting all these?"

Church of St. George, Hart Street, Bloomsbury.
Built by Nicholas Hawksmoor (1661-1736) in 1731, St.
George's possessed a handsome portico and an extraordi-
nary steeple, planned from the description of Pliny of
the tomb of King Mausolus in Caria. For the eighteenth-
century version, Hawksmoor surmounted the steeple with a
statue of King George I in Roman toga, a gift of one Mr.
Huck, a brewer to the Royal household. The cost of construction, including the minister's house, amounted to
£31,000--more than three times the original estimate of
£9,790 17s 4d. The Whig government objected to the cost;
later in the century, Horace Walpole termed St. George's
Bloomsbury "a masterpiece of absurdity."

As for the steeple, a popular epigram reflected the
people's political sentiments:

> When Harry the Eighth left the Pope in the lurch,
> The Protestants made him head of the Church;
> But George's good subjects, the Bloomsbury people,
> Instead of the church, made him head of the
>   steeple.

Supposedly, the steps of the steeple were left there to
demonstrate how the King ascended to the top, while the
artist William Hogarth (1697-1764) gave that part of the
church a prominent spot in the background for his Gin
Lane (1751).

John Wesley preached at St. George's on Sunday morning, 28 May 1738, on the theme, "This is the victory
that overcometh the world, even our faith." He returned
on Sunday, 22 October 1738, at 10:00 a.m., when he once
more delivered the sermon.

St. Giles-in-the-Fields, High Street. Until the beginning of the seventeenth century, St. Giles existed as
a pleasant village, consisting of broad fields, a handful of cottages grouped around a stone cross, and some
shops. Soon, however, the fields disappeared, and St.
Giles began to spread toward--and eventually to connect
with--London.

The Church of St. Giles-in-the-Fields, in High
Street near the northern end of Shaftesbury Avenue, was
built originally (c. 1118) as the chapel of a leper hospital by Matilda, queen of Henry I. The year 1734 saw
the completion of the third construction of the church.
Until the development of New Oxford Street, the main
highway to the west went round by the present Broad
Street, and malefactors on their way to Tyburn received
a final bowl of ale as they stood on the Steps of St.
Giles' Church.

Thus, within the context of those malefactors, we
notice an entry from Wesley's diary for Wednesday, 8 November 1738: "10 at St. Giles', tea. . . ." On that day,
at 6:30 a.m., John and Charles Wesley had gone first to
Newgate Prison "to do the last good office to the condemned malefactors." At 9:00 a.m., they boarded a coach
for Tyburn, and the procession from Newgate must have
reached St. Giles' Church an hour later. While the condemned drank their ale, the brothers sat in their coach
and drank tea--provided, perhaps, by members of one of
the religious societies who lived in the neighborhood.
They arrived at Tyburn about 10:30.

On Sunday, 4 February 1739, at 3:00 p.m., John Wesley
preached at St. Giles' Church on the subject, "'Whosoever believeth in Me, out of his belly shall flow rivers
of living water.' How was the poor of God present
with us! I am content to preach here no more." Nevertheless, he did return to St. Giles' on two further
occasions. On Friday, 7 August 1747, at 6:00 p.m., he
accompanied the body of Jane Muncy(one of the first women
to join the society meeting in Fetter Lane) from Short's
Gardens, Drury Lane (see the entry immediately below),
to St. Giles' churchyard, "where I performed the last
office in the presence of such an innumerable multitude
of people as I ever saw gathered together before. Oh
what a sight it will be when God saith to the grave,
'Give back,' and all the dead, small and great, shall
stand before Him!" More than forty years later, Wesley
again preached at St. Giles', the date being Sunday, 29
October 1786. "My subject [Luke 15:7] was the joy in
heaven over one sinner that repenteth; and truly God
confirmed His word. Many seemed to be partakers of that
joy, and a solemn awe sat on the whole congregation."

Short's Gardens, Drury Lane.   Short's Gardens lay
between King's Street in St. Giles, southwest, and Drury
Lane, northeast (a distance of 220 yards in length), and
from Charing Cross, northwesterly (a distance of 850
yards).   Wesley states, in his journal for Monday, 20
October 1740, that he "began declaring that 'gospel of
Christ' which 'is the power of God unto salvation'
[Romans 1], in the midst of the publicans and sinners, at
Short's Gardens, Drury Lane."   From the journal and diary
entries, we may note that John Wesley met with people
and preached in the area on at least thirty-three
occasions between Wednesday, 22 October 1740, and Friday,
7 August 1741. He based his sermon texts almost exclu-
sively upon Romans, with the exception of 10 July 1741
(Acts 3:12), and 7 August 1741 (Revelation 14). Most
important, however, one should note the order and the
consistency of those entries; they represent Wesley's
methodist approach to and within his overall evangelical
scheme.   Thus--

    5:00 p.m., Wednesday, 22 October 1740

        Romans 1--Paul. . .set apart for the gospel of
           God which he promised beforehand through his
           prophets in the holy scriptures. . . .

    6:15 p.m., Monday, 27 October 1740

        Romans 2--Therefore, you have no excuse, O man,
           whoever you are, when you judge another. . .

    5:00 p.m., Wednesday, 29 October 1740

        Romans 2--Continued

    5:15 p.m., Friday, 31 October 1740

        Romans 3--Then what advantage has the Jew? Or
           what is the value of circumcision?

    5:15 p.m., Monday, 3 November 1740

        Romans 3--Continued

    5:30 p.m., Friday, 7 November 1740

        Romans 3--Continued

6:00 p.m., Monday, 24 November 1740
   Romans 3--Continued
5:00 p.m., Wednesday, 26 November 1740
   Romans 3--Continued
5:15 p.m., Friday, 28 November 1740
   Romans 3--Continued
5:30 p.m., Monday, 1 December 1740
   Romans 4:5--And to one who does not work but
      trusts him who justifies the ungodly, his
      faith is reckoned as righteousness.
5:00 p.m., Wednesday, 3 December 1740
   No text indicated
4:00 p.m., Wednesday, 10 December 1740
   Romans 5--Therefore, since we are justified by
      faith, we have peace with God through our
      Lord Jesus Christ.
6:00 p.m., Friday, 23 January 1741
   Romans 5:14--Yet death reigned from Adam to
      Moses, even over those whose sins were not
      like the transgression of Adam, who was a
      type of the one who was to come.
5:45 p.m., Monday, 26 January 1741
   Romans 6--What shall we say then? Are we to
      continue to sin that grace may abound?
6:00 p.m., Friday, 30 January 1741
   Romans 6--Continued
5:15 p.m., Friday, 6 February 1741
   Romans 6--Continued
5:30 p.m., Friday, 13 February 1741
   Romans 7--Do you not know, brethren--for I am
      speaking to those who know the law--that the
      law is binding only on a person during his
      life?
6:00 p.m., Friday, 3 April 1741

Romans 7--Continued

6:00 p.m., Friday, 10 April 1741

    Romans 8:1--There is therefore now no condem-
       nation for those who are in Christ Jesus.

1:15 p.m., Saturday, 11 April 1741

    No text indicated

5:30 p.m., Friday, 17 April 1741

    Romans 8:29-30--For those who he foreknew he
       also predestined to be conformed by the im-
       age of his Son, in order that he might be
       the first-born among many brethren. And
       those whom he predestined he also called;
       and those whom he called he also justified;
       and those whom he justified he also glori-
       fied.

7:00 p.m., Wednesday, 22 April 1741

    Romans 8:15--For you did not receive the spi-
       rit of slavery to fall back into fear, but
       you have received the spirit of sonship.

6:15 p.m., Friday, 24 April 1741

    Romans 8:2--For the law in the Spirit of life
       in Christ Jesus has set me free from the
       law of sin and death.

7:00 p.m., Sunday, 26 April 1741

    No text indicated

6:15 p.m., Friday, 1 May 1741

    Romans 8:4--. . .in order that the just require-
       ment of the law might be fulfilled in us,
       who walk not according to the flesh, but ac-
       cording to the Spirit.

7:00 p.m., Sunday, 3 May 1741

    No text indicated

6:00 p.m., Friday, 8 May 1741

    Romans 8:7-15--For the mind that is set on the

flesh is hostile to God; it does not sub-
mit to God's law, indeed, it cannot. . . .
. . .For you did not receive the spirit of
slavery to fall back into fear, but you have
received the spirit of sonship.

6:15 p.m., Friday, 29 May 1741

Roman 8:16--. . .it is the Spirit himself bearing witness with our spirit that we are children of God. . . .

6:15 p.m., Friday, 5 June 1741

Romans 8--There is therefore now no condemna-
tion for those that are in Christ Jesus.

5:45 p.m., Friday, 10 July 1741

Acts 3:12--And when Peter saw it he addressed
the people, "Men of Israel, why do you wonder at this, or why do you stare at us, as
though by our own power or piety we had made
him walk?

6:00 p.m., Friday, 31 July 1741

Romans 8--See above for Friday, 5 June 1741.

4:30 p.m., Friday, 7 August 1741

Revelation 14--Then I looked, and lo, on Mount
Zion stood the Lamb, and with him a hundred
and forty-four thousand who had his name
and his Father's name written on their foreheads.

One cannot help but note that amazing "regularity" of Wesley's visits to Short's Gardens: he came there mostly on
Wednesdays and Fridays, occasionally on Mondays, rarely
on Saturdays and Sundays, never on Tuesdays or Thursdays.
With the exception of Saturday, 11 April 1741, he arrived
no earlier than 4:00 p.m., and no later than 7:00 p.m.

Two additional references to Wesley's association
with Short's Gardens exist. On Friday, 22 January 1742,
he met the Methodist society there for the first time.

Eleven years later, on Sunday, 24 July 1753, he heard a
sermon there delivered by the celebrated Irish Methodist,
Thomas Walsh--one of Wesley's most gifted preachers, who
had joined the Methodists on 29 September 1749: "Abundance of his countrymen flocked to hear," remarked
Wesley, "and some were cut to the heart. How many means
does God use to bring poor wanderers back to himself!"

   West Street Chapel, Seven Dials.   In the 1680's,
Nicholas Barbon planned the original West Street on the
estate owned by the Earl of Newport. Until 1725, residents knew and referred to the street as "Hog Lane"--a
continuation of an ancient thoroughfare that eventually
became a part of Charing Cross Road. A.M. Grossley, a
French visitor to the area in 1765, observed it as "crowded
with people waiting to hear a poor wretch stand in
the pillory, whose punishment was deferred to another
day. The mob, provoked at this disappointment, vented
their rage upon all that passed their way, whether afoot
or in coaches, and threw at them dirt, rotten eggs, dead
dogs, ordure, which they had provided to pelt the unhappy
wretch, according to their custom" (Phillips 219).
   French Protestants erected a building in West
Street about 1683 and named it La Tremblade ("The Tre-
mor"), perhaps a reminiscence of a scene of persecution
in France. One Mrs. Elizabeth Palmer bequeathed £500
to be invested for the benefit of the poor widows of St.
Clement Danes, in the Strand. With that sum, trustees
purchased, in 1728, the West Street freehold and premises
and then rented the property for £16 per year (raised
to £30 in 1760). Wesley leased the chapel in 1743
for what he termed a period of "several years." He preached
his first sermon there on Trinity Sunday, 29 May
1743, and continued to preach there until the end of

February 1790. Thus, from the diary and the journals, we
note the other important instances upon which the founder
and leader of British Methodism occupied the pulpit
at West Street, as well as the Scriptural texts from which
he preached:

Wednesday, 18 December 1745. A national fast day;
the Pretender, Prince Charles Edward, and his army of
Highlanders had reached Derby, and there he proclaimed
his father King of England. No text indicated.

Sunday, 7 January 1750

>   Luke 2:21--And at the end of eight days, when
>   he was circumcised, he was called Jesus, the
>   name given by the angel before he was con-
>   ceived in the womb.
>
>   Deuteronomy 10:12--And now, Israel, what does
>   the Lord your God require of you, but to
>   fear the Lord your God, to walk in all his
>   ways, to love him, to serve the Lord your
>   God with all your heart and with all your
>   soul. . . .
>
>   Hebrews 2:15--. . .and deliver all those who
>   through fear of death were subject to life-
>   long bondage.

Friday, 19 January 1750. Wesley read prayers and
George Whitefield "preached a plain, affectionate dis-
course." That marked the first of several cooperative
efforts from the same pulpit between Wesley and Whitefield, brought about from pressures exerted by Selina
Shirley, Countess of Huntingdon, who wished unity and
harmony between the Calvinist Whitefield and the Armi-
Arminian Wesley.

Wednesday, 24 January 1750

>   Hebrews 4:9--So then, there remains a sabbath
>   rest for the people of God. . . .

Isaiah 55:7--. . .let the wicked forsake his
way, and the unrighteous man his thoughts;
let him return to the Lord, that he may
have mercy on him, and to our God, for he
will abundantly pardon.

1 Corinthians 2:14--But thanks be to God, who
in Christ always leads us in triumph, and
through us spreads the fragrance of the
knowledge of him everywhere.

Isaiah 58:12-13--And your ancient ruins shall
be rebuilt; you shall raise up the foundations of many generations; you shall be
called the repairer of the breach, the restorer of streets to dwell in. If you turn
back your foot from the sabbath, from doing
your pleasure on my holy day, and call the
sabbath a delight and the holy day of the
Lord honorable; if you honor it, not going
your own ways, or seeking your own pleasure,
or talking idly. . . .

1 John 3:1--See what love the Father has given
us, that we should be called children of
God; and so we are. The reason why the
world does not know us is that it did not
know him.

Hebrews 6:10-11--For God is not so unjust as
to overlook your work and the love which
you showed for his sake in serving the
saints, as you still do. And we desire
each one of you to show the same earnestness in realizing the full assurance of
hope until the end. . . .

2 Corinthians 13:8--For we cannot do anything
against the truth, but only for the truth.

Numbers 13--The Lord said to Moses, "Send men
to spy out the land of Canaan. . . ."

Numbers 23:10--Who can count the dust of Jacob,
or number the fourth part of Israel?
Let me die the death of the righteous, and
let my end be like his!

Saturday, 3 February 1750

Luke 12:19--And I will say to my soul, Soul,
you have ample goods laid up for many
years; take your ease, eat, drink, be
merry.

Matthew 11:25--At that time Jesus declared,"I
thank thee, Father, Lord of heaven and earth,
that thou hast hidden these things from the
wise and understanding and revealed them to
babes. . . ."

1 Corinthians 13:1-3--If I speak in the tongues
of men and of angels, but have not love, I
am a noisy gong or a clanging cymbal. And
if I have prophetic powers, and understand
all mysteries and knowledge, and if I have
all faith, so as to remove mountains, but
have not love, I am nothing. If I give away
all I have, and if I deliver my body to be
burned, but I have not love, I have gained
nothing.

Sunday, 9 September 1750

Psalms 46:10--Be still and know that I am God.
I am exalted among the nations; I am exalted in the earth!

Acts 26:8--Why is it thought incredible by any
of you that God raises the dead?

2 Corinthians 2:2--For if I cause you pain,
who is there to make me glad but the one

whom I have pained?

Romans 13:11--Besides this you know what hour
it is, how it is full time now for you to
wake from sleep. For salvation is nearer to
us now than when we first believed. . . .

1 Corinthians 13:13--So faith, love, hope abide,
these three; but the greatest of these is
love.

Philippians 3:10--. . .that I may know him and
the power of his resurrection, and may share
his sufferings, becoming like him in death
. . . .

Galatians 5-18--But if you are led by the
Spirit you are not under the law.

Hebrews 10:38--. . .but my righteous one shall
live by faith, and if he shrinks back, my
soul has no pleasure in him.

Sunday, 23 September 1750. The worship service at
West Street Chapel continued from 9:00 a.m. until 10:00
p.m.

Thursday, 1 November 1750

Revelation 7:9--After this I looked, and behold, a great multitude which no man could
number, from every nation, from all tribes
and peoples and tongues, standing before the
throne and before the Lamb, clothed in white
robes, with palm branches in their hands. . .

Romans 8:22--We know that the whole creation
has been groaning in travail together until now. . . .

Revelation 17:15--And he said to me, "The
waters that you saw, where the harlot is
seated, are peoples and multitudes and nations
and tongues.

Hebrews 12:2--. . .looking to Jesus the pioneer
and perfecter of faith, who for the joy that
was set before him endured the cross, despising the shame, and is seated at the right
hand of the throne of God.

Luke 16:9--And I tell you, make friends for
yourselves by means of unrighteous mammon,
so that when it fails they may receive you
into the eternal habitations.

Hebrews 10:35--Therefore, do not throw away
your confidence, which has a great reward.

Hebrews 12:5-6--And have you forgotten the exhortation which addresses you as sons?--My
son, do not regard lightly the discipline of
the Lord, nor lose courage when you are
punished by Him. For the Lord disciplines
him whom He loves, and chastises every son
whom He receives.

1 Peter 2:2--Like newborn babes, long for the
pure spiritual milk, that by it you may
grow up to salvation. . . .

Exodus 32:10--. . .now therefore let me alone,
that my wrath may burn hot against them and
I may consume them; but of you, I will make
a great nation.

John 17:3--And this is eternal life, and they
know thee the only true God, and Jesus Christ
whom thou hast sent.

Philippians 1:23--I am hard pressed between
the two. My desire is to depart and be
with Christ, for that is far better.

Romans 15:5-6--May the God of steadfastness
and encouragement grant you to live in such
harmony with one another, in accord with

Christ Jesus, that together you may with one voice glorify the God and Father of our Lord Jesus Christ.

Hebrews 13:9--Do not be led away by diverse and strange teachings; for it is well that the heart be strengthened by grace, not by foods, which have not benefited their adherents.

Hebrews 13:1--Let brotherly love continue.

Isaiah 30:18--Therefore, the Lord waits to be gracious to you; therefore, he exalts himself to show mercy to you. For the Lord is a God of justice; blessed are all those who wait for him.

Sunday, 25 November 1750

Titus 3:5--. . .he saved us, not because of deeds done by us in righteousness, but in virtue of his own mercy, by the washing of regeneration and renewal in the Holy Spirit. . . .

1 John 5:19--We know we are of God, and the whole world is in the power of the evil one.

Psalms 139--O Lord, thou hast searched me and known me!

Proverbs 28:14--Blessed is the man who fears the Lord always; but he who hardens his heart will fall into calamity.

Revelation 14:4-5--It is these who have not defiled themselves with women, for they are chaste; it is these who follow the Lamb wherever he goes; these have been redeemed from mankind as first fruits for God and the Lamb, and in their mouth no lie was found, for they are spotless.

Galatians 4:3--So with us; when we were children,

we were slaves to the elemental spirits
of the universe.

Sunday, 10 February 1751. Earlier that morning,
Wesley had fallen on ice while crossing London Bridge and
had sprained his ankle. "It was with much difficulty
that I got up into the pulpit. . . ."

Mark 10--And he left there and went to the
region of Judea and beyond the Jordan, and
crowds gathered to him again; and again, as
his custom was, he taught them.

Psalms 118:28--Thou art my God, and I will give
thanks to thee; thou art my God, I will ex-
tol thee.

Deuteronomy 10:12--See above (p. 48) for Sunday, 7 January 1750.

Sunday, 3 March 1751

1 Thessalonians 4:7--For God has not called us
for uncleanliness, but in holiness.

Romans 2:23--You who boast in the law, do you
dishonor God by breaking the law?

Hebrews 9:13--For if the sprinkling of defiled
persons with the blood of goats and bulls
and with the ashes of a heifer sanctifies
for the purification of the flesh. . . .

Monday, 25 March 1751

Luke 1:26--In the sixth month the angel Gabriel
was sent from God to a city of Galilee
named Nazareth. . . . .

John 14:16--And I will pray the Father, and
he will give you another Counselor, to be
with you for ever. . . .

John 14:21--He who has my commandments and
keeps them, he it is who loves me; and he
who loves me will be loved by my Father, and

I will love him and manifest myself to him.

Galatians 5:22--But the fruit of the Spirit is
love, joy, peace, patience, kindness, goodness, faithfulness. . . .

Thursday, 30 May 1751

John 16:22--So you have sorrow now, but I will
see you again and your hearts will rejoice,
and no one will take your joy from you.

Ephesians 1:13--In him you also, who have heard
the word of truth, the gospel of your salvation, and have believed in him, were sealed
with the promised Holy Spirit. . . .

John 3:7--Do not marvel that I said to you,
"You must be born anew."

1 Corinthians 2:5--. . .that your faith might
not rest in the wisdom of men, but in the
power of God.

1 John 4:19--We love, because he first loved us.

Matthew 22:21--They said, "Caesar's." Then he
said to them, "Render therefore to Caesar
the things that are Caesar's, and to God
the things that are God's."

John 18:36--Jesus answered, "My kingship is not
of this world; if my kingship were of this
world, my servants would fight, that I might
not be handed over to the Jews; but my
kingship is not from the world."

Thursday, 13 June 1751

John 3:14--And as Moses lifted up the serpent
in the wilderness, so must the Son of man be
lifted up. . . .

2 Corinthians 13:5--Examine yourselves, to see
whether you are holding to your faith. Test
yourselves. Do you not realize that Jesus

Christ, any incentive of love, any parti-
cipation in the Spirit, any affection and
sympathy, complete my joy by being of the
same mind, having the same love, being in
full accord and of one mind.

Luke 13:23--And some one said to him, "Lord,
will those who are saved be few?"

1 Kings 18:21--And Elijah came near to all the
people, and said, "How long will you go limping with two different opinions? If the
Lord is God, follow him; but if Baal, then
follow him." And the people did not answer
him a word.

John 5:12--They asked him, "Who is the man who
said to you, 'Take up your pallet and walk'?"

Philippians 1:27--Only let your manner of life
be worthy of the gospel of Christ, so that
whether I come and see you or am absent, I
may hear of you that you stand firm in one
spirit, with one mind striving side by side
for the faith of the gospel. . . .

Philippians 1:30--. . .engaged in the same
conflict which you saw and now hear to be
mine.

Psalms 50:22--Mark this, then, you who forget
God, lest I rend, and there be none to
deliver!

John 16:8--And when he comes, he will convince
the world of sin and of righteousness and
of judgment. . . .

Romans 15:5--See above for Thursday, 1 November
1750 (p. 52).

Philippians 3:8--Indeed, I count everything as
loss because of the surpassing worth of

knowing Christ Jesus my Lord. For his sake
I have suffered the loss of all things, and
count them as refuse, in order that I may
gain Christ. . . .

Wednesday, 30 October 1751. No text indicated.

Monday, 16 December 1751

Philippians 3:3--For we are the true circumcision, who worship God in spirit,and glory
in Christ Jesus, who put no confidence
in the flesh.

James 2:22--You see that faith was active
along with his works, and faith was completed by works. . .

Galatians 4:4--But when the time had fully
come, God sent forth his Son, born of
woman, born under the law. . . .

1 John 5:12--He who has the Son has life; he
who has not the Son has not life.

Romans 12:2--Do not be conformed to this
world, but be transformed by the renewal
of your mind, that you may prove what is
the will of God, what is good and acceptable and perfect.

Acts 28:22--But we desire to hear from you
what your views are; for with regard to
this sect, we know that everywhere it is
spoken against.

Wednesday, 1 January 1752

Romans 2:28--For he is not a real Jew who is
one outwardly, nor is true circumcision
something external and physical.

Deuteronomy 10:12--See above for Sunday, 10
February 1751 (p. 54), and for Sunday, 27
January 1750 (p. 48). Thus, we note the

third instance upon which Wesley preached
from this text.

Philippians 3:20--But our commonwealth is in
heaven, and from it we wait a Savior, the
Lord Jesus Christ.

Philippians 3:9-11--. . .and be found in him,
not having a righteousness of my own,based
on law, but that which is through faith in
Christ, the righteousness from God that de-
pends on faith; that I may know him and the
power of his resurrection, and may share his
sufferings, becoming like him in his death,
that if possible I may attain the resurrection from the dead.

Philippians 3:14--. . .I press on toward the
goal for the prize of the upward call of
God in Christ Jesus.

Philippians 4:7--And the peace of God which
passes all understanding, will keep your
hearts and minds in Christ Jesus.

Philippians 1:13--. . .so that it has become
known throughout the whole praetorian guard
and to all the rest that my imprisonment is
for Christ. . . .

1 Corinthians 6:9--Do you know now that the
unrighteous will not inherit the kingdom
of God?   Do not be deceived; neither the
immoral, nor idolators, nor adulterers,
nor homosexuals. . . .

1 Timothy 6:17--As for the rich in this world,
charge them not to be haughty, nor to set
their hopes on uncertain riches, but on
God, who richly furnishes us with everything to enjoy.

Psalms 10:14--Thou dost see; yea, thou dost
note trouble and vexation, that thou mayst
take it into thy hands; the hapless commits
himself to thee; thou hast been the helper
of the fatherless.

Malachi 3:2--But who can endure the day of his
coming, and who can stand when he appears?

Matthew 18:15--If your brother sins against
you, go and tell him his fault, between you
and him alone. If he listens to you, you
have gained your brother.

Colossians 1:19--For in him all the fulness of
God was pleased to dwell. . . .

Wednesday, 29 January 1752

Colossians 2:9--For in him the whole fulness
of deity dwells bodily. . . .

Hebrews 9:13--See above under Sunday, 3 March
1751 (p. 54).

Colossians 3:4--When Christ, who is our life,
appears, then you also will appear with him
in glory.

Psalms 10:14--See above for Wednesday, 1 January 1752 (p. 59).

Sunday, 15 March 1752. Wesley preached in the midst
of "one of the most violent storms I ever remember." A
part of the house opposite the Chapel collapsed from the
high winds.

Sunday, 5 November 1752

Colossians 3:11--Here there cannot be Greek or
Jew, circumcised and uncircumcised, barbarian,
Scythian, slave, free man, but Christ is
all and in all.

Colossians 3:16--Let the word of Christ dwell
in you richly, as you teach and admonish

>   one another in all wisdom, and as you sing
>   psalms and hymns and spiritual songs with
>   thankfulness in your hearts to God.
>
> Colossians 3:18--Wives, be subjects to your
>   husbands, as fitting in the Lord.
>
> Romans 13:11--See above for Sunday, 9 Septem-
>   ber 1750 (p. 51).

Monday, 25 December 1752

> Acts 17:23--For as I passed along, and obser-
>   ved the objects of your worship, I found
>   also an altar with this inscription, "To
>   an unknown god." What therefore you wor-
>   ship is unknown, this I proclaim to you.
>
> 1 John 3:8--He who commits sin is of the devil;
>   for the devil has sinned from the beginning.
>   The reason the Son of God appeared
>   was to destroy the works of the devil.
>
> John 21:22--Jesus said to him, "If it is my
>   will that he remain until I come, what is
>   that to you? Follow me!"
>
> Galatians 4:5--. . .to redeem those who were
>   under the law, so that we might receive
>   adoption as sons.
>
> Acts 24:14--But this I admit to you, that
>   according to the Way,which they call a sect,
>   I worship the God of our fathers, believing
>   everything laid down by the law or written
>   in the prophets. . . .
>
> Ecclesiastes 6:12--For who knows what is good
>   for man, while he lives the few days of his
>   vain life, which passes like a shadow? For
>   who can tell a man what will be after him
>   under the sun?
>
> Acts 26:24--And as he thus made his defense,
>   Festus said with a loud voice, "Paul, you
>   are mad; your great learning is turning you

mad."
Monday, 8 January 1753
> Matthew 1:21--. . .she will bear a son, and
> you shall call his name Jesus, for he will
> save his people from their sins.
> Matthew 3:8--Bear fruit that befits repentance
> . . . .
> Romans 14:17--For the kingdom of God does not
> mean food and drink, but righteousness and
> peace and joy in the Holy Spirit. . . .
> Matthew 12:43--When the unclean spirit has gone
> out of a man, he passes through waterless
> places seeking rest, but he finds none.
> 1 Corinthians 1:17--For Christ did not send me
> to baptize, but to preach the gospel, and
> not with eloquent wisdom, lest the cross of
> Christ be emptied of its power.
> Matthew 19:29--And any one who has left hou-
> ses or brothers or sister or father or
> mother or children or lands, for my name's
> sake, will receive a hundredfold, and in-
> herit eternal life.
> 1 Corinthians 7:29--I mean, brethren, the ap-
> pointed time has grown very short; from now
> on let those who have wives live as though
> they had none. . . .
> Matthew 25:1--Then the kingdom of heaven shall
> be compared to ten maidens who took their
> lamps and went to meet the bridegroom.
> 1 Corinthians 14:20--Brethren, do not be chil-
> dren in your thinking; be babes in evil,
> but in thinking be mature.
Tuesday, 30 January 1753
> Jeremiah 5:29--Shall I not punish them for

these things? says the Lord, and shall I
not avenge myself on a nation such as this?
Hebrews 12:1--Therefore, since we are surrounded
by so great a cloud of witnesses, let
us also lay aside every weight, and sin
which clings so closely, and let us run
with perseverance the race that is set
before us. . . .
Ephesians 6:13-14--Therefore, take the whole
armor of God, that you may be able to with-
stand in the evil day, and having done all,
to stand. Stand, therefore, having girded
your loins with truth, and having put on
the breastplate of righteousness. . . .
Saturday, 3 February 1753
Mark 4:1--Again, he began to teach beside the
sea. And a very large crowd gathered about
him, so that he got into a boat and sat on
it on the sea; and the whole crowd was beside the sea on the land.
1 Thessalonians 5:12--But we beseech you, brethren, to respect those who labor among you
and are over you in the Lord and admonish
you. . . .
Hebrews 5:12--For though by this time you ought
to be teachers, you need someone to teach
you again the first principles of God's
word. You need milk, not solid food. . . .
1 Thessalonians 5:19--Do not quench the Spirit
. . . .
Luke 8:18--Take heed then how you hear; for to
him who has will more be given, and from
him who has not, even what he thinks he has
will be taken away.

2 Corinthians 9:10--He who supplies seed to
the sower and bread for food will supply
and multiply your resources and increase
the harvest of your righteousness.

Sunday, 7 April 1754

2 Corinthians 5:8--We are of good courage, and
we would rather be away from the body and
at home with the Lord.

Philippians 3:10--See above for Wednesday, 1
January 1752 (p. 58).

1 Peter 2:24--He, himself, bore our sins in
his body on the tree, that we might die to
sin and live to righteousness. By his
wounds you have been healed.

Sunday, 5 May 1754

John 16:22--See above for Thursday, 30 May
1751 (p. 55).

1 Peter 1:6--In this you rejoice, though now
for a little while you may have to suffer
various trials. . . .

John 15:22--If I had not come and spoken to
them, they would not have sin; but now they
have no excuse for their sin.

Isaiah 42:19--Who is blind but my servant, or
deaf as my messenger whom I send? Who is
blind as my dedicated one, or blind as the
servant of the Lord?

Sunday, 16 June 1754

Luke 16:31--He said to him, "If they do not
hear Moses and the prophets, neither will
they be convinced if some one should rise
from the dead."

Luke 12:20--But God said to him, "Fool! This
night your soul is required of you;and the

things you have prepared, whose will they
be?"

Romans 6:23--For the wages of sin is death, but
the free gift of God is eternal life in
Christ Jesus our Lord.

Ephesians 4:1--I, therefore, a prisoner for
the Lord, beg you to lead a life worthy of
the calling to which you have been called
. . . .

Sunday, 11 August 1754

Job 22:21--Agree with God, and be at peace;
thereby good will come to you.

Ephesians 4:28--Let the thief no longer steal,
but rather let him labor,doing honest work
with his hands, so that he may be able to
give to those in need.

Philippians 1:21--For me to live is Christ,and
to die is gain.

Sunday, 3 November 1754

Matthew 16:23--But he turned and said to Peter,
"Get behind me, Satan! You are a hindrance
to me; for you are not on the side of God,
but of men."

Philippians 1:9--And it is my prayer that your
love may abound more and more, with knowledge and all discernment. . . .

Sunday, 8 December 1754

Romans 15:4--For whatever was written in former days was written for our instruction,
that by steadfastness and by the encouragement of scriptures we might have hope.

Proverbs 19:7--All a poor man's brother hate
him; how much more do his friends go far
from him! He pursues them with words,but

does not have them.

Acts 26:18--. . .open their eyes that they may
turn from darkness to light, and from the
power of Satan to God, that they may receive
forgiveness of sins and a place among those
who are sanctified by faith in me.

1 John 1:3--. . .that which we have seen and
heard we proclaim also to you, so that you
may have fellowship with us; and our fellowship is with the Father and with his Son
Jesus Christ.

Sunday, 5 January 1755

Romans 4:7--Blessed are those whose iniquities
are forgiven and whose sins are
covered. . . .

Psalms 10:4--In the pride of his countenance
the wicked does not see him; all his
thoughts are, "There is no God."

Matthew 10:16--Behold, I send you out as sheep
in the midst of wolves; so be wise as ser-
pents and innocent as doves.

Sunday, 9 February 1755

Mark 9:24--Immediately the father of the child
cried out and said, "I believe; help my un-
belief!"

Joel 2:16--. . .gather the people. Sanctify
the congregation; assemble the elders; gather the children, even nursing infants.
Let the bridegroom leave his room, and the
bride her chamber.

Ecclesiastes 11:1--Cast your bread upon the
waters, for you will find it after many
days.

Friday, 28 February 1755

2 <u>Peter</u> 3:7--But by the same word the heavens
and earth that now exist have been stored
up for fire, being kept until the day of
judgment and destruction of ungodly men.

<u>Luke</u> 13:24--Strive to enter by the narrow door;
for many, I tell you, will seek to enter
and not be able.

1 <u>John</u> 3:7--Little children, let no one deceive
you. He who does right is righteous, as he
is righteous.

Sunday, 16 March 1755

<u>John</u> 3:7--See above for Thursday, 30 May 1751
(p. 55).

<u>Matthew</u> 16:20--Then he strictly charged the
disciples to tell no one that he was the
Christ.

<u>John</u> 8:32--. . .and you will know the truth,
and the truth will make you free.

<u>Ephesians</u> 2:19--So when you are no longer
strangers and sojourners, but you are fellow citizens with the saints and members
of the household of God. . . .

Thursday, 19 June 1755

<u>Psalms</u> 147:20--He has not dealt thus with any
other nation; they do not know his ordinan-
ces. Praise the Lord!

1 <u>Corinthians</u> 10:22--Shall we provoke the Lord
to jealousy? Are we stronger than he?

<u>Galatians</u> 6:14--But far be it from me to glory
except in the cross of our Lord Jesus Christ,
by which the world has been crucified to me,
and I to the world.

Sunday, 22 June 1755

<u>Romans</u> 8:18--I consider that the suffering of

this present time are not worth comparing
with the glory that is to be revealed to
us.

John 1:47--Jesus saw Nathanael coming to him,
and he said of him, "Behold, an Israelite
indeed, in whom is not guile!"

1 Kings 19--Ahab told Jezebel all that Elijah
had done, and how he had slain all the
prophets with the sword.

Saturday, 28 June 1755

Ephesians 5:16--Let no one deceive you with
empty words, for it is because of these
things that the wrath of God comes upon
the sons of disobedience.

Psalms 66:18--If I had cherished iniquity to
my heart, the Lord would not have listened.

John 15--I am the true vine, and my Father is
the vinedresser.

Jeremiah 6:13--For from the least to the
greatest of them, every one is greedy for
unjust gain;and from prophet to priest,
every one deals falsely.

John 8:29--And he who sent me is with me; he
has not left me alone, for I always do what
is pleasing to him.

Jeremiah 18:5--Then the word of the Lord came
to me.

John 15:7--This I command you, to love one
another.

Hebrews 12:28--Therefore, let us be grateful
for receiving a kingdom that cannot be shaken,
and thus let us offer to God acceptable
worship, with reverence and awe. . . .

Sunday, 29 June 1755

Acts 3:26--God, having raised up his servant,
sent him to you first, to bless you in
turning every one of you from wickedness.

Acts 1:4--And while staying with them he charged
them not to depart from Jerusalem, but
to wait for the promise of the Father, which
he said, "you heard from me. . . ."

Galatians 2:17--But if in our endeavor to be
justified in Christ, we ourselves were found
to be sinners, is Christ then an agent of
sin? Certainly not!

Luke 18:42--And Jesus said to him, "Receive
your sight; your faith has made you well."

Monday, 21 July 1755

Psalms 37:1--Fret not yourself because of the
wicked; be not envious of wrongdoers!

2 Timothy 3:4--. . .treacherous, reckless,
swollen with conceit, lovers of pleasure
rather than lovers of God. . . .

1 Timothy 4:5-6--. . .for then it is consecrated
by the words of God and prayer. If you
put these instructions before the brethren,
you will be a good minister of Christ Jesus,
nourished on the words of the faith and of
the good doctrine which you have followed.

Titus 2:11--For the grace of God has appeared
for the salvation of all men. . . .

Hebrews 3:7--Therefore, as the Holy Spirit
says, "Today, when you hear His voice. . ."

1 Corinthians 1:27--If any speak in a tongue,
let there be only two, or at most three,
and each in turn; and let one interpret.

Luke 19:41--And when he drew near and saw the
city, he wept over it. . . .

Jeremiah 50:4-5--In those days and in that
time, says the Lord, the people of Israel
and the people of Judah shall come together,
weeping as they come; and they shall seek
the Lord their God. They shall ask the way
to Zion, with faces turned toward it, saying, "Come, let us join ourselves to the
Lord in an everlasting covenant which will
never be forgotten."

Saturday, 2 August 1755

Hebrews 5:14--But solid food is for the mature, for those who have their faculties
trained by practice to distinguish good
from evil.

Acts 8:13--Even Simon himself believed, and
after being baptized he continued with
Philip. And seeing signs and great miracles
being performed, he was amazed.

1 Peter 1:6--See above for Sunday, 5 May 1754
(p. 63).

Acts 15:18--. . .says the Lord, who has made
these things known from old.

Romans 1:3--. . .the gospel concerning his Son,
who was descended from David according to
the flesh. . . .

Monday, 4 August 1755

Psalms 37:1--See above for Monday, 21 July
1755 (p. 68)

Psalms 76:11--Make your vows to the Lord your
God, and perform them; let all around him
bring gifts to him who is to be feared. . . .

Acts 8:13--See above for Saturday, 2 August
1755 (p. 69).

Luke 21:34--But take heed to yourselves lest
your hearts be weighed down with dissipa-
tion and drunkenness and cares of this life,

and that day come upon you suddenly like a
snare. . . .

Galatians 2:17--See above for Sunday, 29 June
1755 (p. 68).

Hebrews 3:15--. . .while it is said, "Today,
when you hear his voice, do not harden your
hearts as in the rebellion."

Luke 22:37--For I tell you that this scripture
must be fulfilled in me, "And he was reckoned
with transgressors"; for what is written
about me has its fulfillment.

John 8:36--So if the Son makes you free, you
will be free indeed.

Sunday, 26 October 1755

Luke 12:7--Why even the hairs of your head are
all numbered. Fear not; you are of more
value than many sparrows.

Revelation 19:8--. . .it was granted to her
to be clothed with fine linen, bright and
pure--for the fine linen is the righteous
deeds of the saints.

1 Timothy 4:8--. . .for while bodily training
is of some value, godliness is of value in
every way, as it holds promise for the
present life and also for the life to come.

Isaiah 40:1--Comfort, comfort my people, says
your God.

Psalms 101:1-2--I will sing of loyalty and of
justice; to thee, O Lord, I will sing. I
will give heed to the way that is blameless.
O when wilt thou come to me?

Luke 12:7--See above, first entry under this
date (p. 70).

Matthew 9:22--Jesus turned, and seeing her he

said, "Take heart, daughter; your faith has
made you well." And instantly the woman was
made well.

Mark 2:11--I say to you, rise, take up your
pallet and go home.

Acts 1:8--But you shall receive power   when
the Holy Spirit has come upon you; and you
shall be my witness in Jerusalem and in all
Judea, Samaria, and to the end of the earth.

John 15:2--Every branch of mine that bears no
fruit, he takes away, and every branch that
does bear fruit he prunes, that it may bear
more fruit.

Luke 12:20--See above for Sunday, 16 June 1754
(pp. 63-64).

Luke 19:17--And he said to him, "Well   done,
good servant! Because you have been faithful
in a very little, you shall have authority
over ten cities."

Daniel 9:7--To thee, O Lord, belongs righteousness, but to us confusion of face,   as at
this day,   to the men of Judah, to the
inhabitants of Jerusalem,and to all Israel,
those that are near and those that are far
away, in all the lands to which thou hast
driven them, because of the treachery which
they have committed against thee.

Jeremiah 23:6--In his days Judah will be saved,
and Israel will dwell securely. And this is
the name by which he will be called: "The Lord
is our righteousness."

Monday, 10 November 1755

Mark 2:11--See above for Sunday, 26 October
1755 (p. 71).

Acts 1:8--See above for Sunday,   26 October

1755 (p. 71).

Luke 21:34--See above for Monday, 4 August
1755 (pp. 69-70).

Sunday, 26 November 1755. No text indicated.

Sunday, 7 December 1755

Luke 21:36--But watch at all times, praying
that you may have strength to escape all
these things that will take place, and to
stand before the Son of man.

Isaiah 26:21--For behold, the Lord is coming
forth out of this place to punish the inhabitants of the earth for their iniquity,
and the earth will disclose the blood shed
upon her, and will no more cover her slain.

Matthew 23:23--Woe to you, scribes and Pharisees, hypocrites! for you tithe mint and
dill and cummin, and have neglected the
weightier matters of the law, justice and
mercy and faith; these you ought to have
done, without neglecting the others.

Hebrews 2:4--. . .while God also bore witness
by signs and wonders and various miracles
and by gifts of the Holy Spirit distributed according to his own will.

Friday, 19 December 1755

Amos 4:12--Therefore, thus will I do to you, O
Israel; because I will do this to you, prepare to meet your God, O Israel!

Psalms 101:1-2--See above for Sunday, 26 October 1755 (p. 70).

Matthew 23:37--O Jerusalem, Jerusalem, killing
the prophets and stoning those who are sent
to you! How often would I have gathered
your children together as a hen gathers her

brood under her wings, and you would not!

Revelation 14:1--Then I looked, and lo, on
Mount Zion stood the Lamb, and with him a
hundred and and forty-four thousand who had
his name and his Father's name written on
their foreheads.

Acts 26:23--. . .that the Christ must suffer,
and that, by being the first to rise from
the dead, he would proclaim light both to
the people and to the Gentiles.

Thursday, 25 December 1755

Haggai 2:7--. . .and I shall shake all nations
so that the treasures of all nations shall
come in, and I will fill this house with
splendor, says the Lord of Hosts.

Thursday, 1 January 1756

2 Corinthians 5:17--Therefore, if any one is
in Christ, he is a new creation; the old
has passed away; behold, the new has come.

Matthew 3:8--See above for Monday, 8 January
1753 (p. 61).

Isaiah 44:22--I have swept away your transgressions like a cloud, and your sins like a
mist; return to me, for I have redeemed you.

Sunday, 12 September 1756

Matthew 13:27--And the servants of the householder came and said to him, "Sir, did you
not sow good seeds in your field? How,
then, has it weeds?"

Galatians 6:14--See above for Thursday, 19
June 1755 (p. 66).

Psalms 91:11--For he will give his angels
charge of you to guard you in all your
ways.

(?) September 1756

    Matthew 13:27--See above for Sunday, 12 Sep-
       tember 1756 (p. 73).

    2 Corinthians 4:2--We have renounced disgrace-
       ful, underhanded ways; we refuse to practice
       cunning or to tamper with God's word, but
       by the open statement of the truth we would
       commend ourselves to every man's conscience
       in the sight of God.

    Galatians 6:14--See above for Thursday, 19 June
       1755 (p. 66), and Sunday, 12 September 1756
       (p. 73).

    Matthew 6:24--No one can serve two masters;
       for either will he hate the one and love
       the other, or he will be devoted to the one
       and despise the other. You cannot serve
       God and mammon.

    Psalms 91:11--See above for Sunday, 12 Septem-
       ber 1756 (p. 73).

    Psalms 34:8--O taste and see that the Lord is
       good! Happy is the man who takes refuge in
       him!

    2 Timothy 4:5--As for you, always be steady,
       endure suffering, do the work of an evan-
       gelist, fulfil your ministry.

    Ephesians 4:3. . .eager to maintain the unity
       of the Spirit in the bond of peace.

    Ephesians 4:29--Let no evil talk come out of
       your mouths, but only such as good for edi-
       fying, as fits the occasion, that it may
       impart grace to those who hear.

    John 15:16--You did not choose me, but I chose
       you and appointed you that you should go
       and bear fruit and that your fruit should

abide; so that whatever you ask the Father
in my name, he may give it to you.
Colossians 1:14--. . .in whom we have redemption, the forgiveness of sins.
Revelation 7:9-10--After this I looked, and
behold, a great multitude which no man
could number, from every nation, from all
tribes and peoples and tongues, standing
before the throne and before the Lamb,
clothed in white robes, with palm branches
in their hands, and crying out with a loud
voice, "Salvation belongs to our God who
sits upon the throne, and to the Lamb!"
(?) November 1756
Revelation 19:9--And the angel said to me,
"Write this: Blessed are those who are invited to the marriage supper of the Lamb."
And he said to me, "These are the true words
of God."
2 Timothy 2:20--In a great house there are
not only vessels of gold and silver, but
also of wood and earthenware, and some for
noble use, and some for ignoble. . . .
Habakkuk 2:5--Moreover,wine is treacherous;
the arrogant man shall not abide. His
greed is as wide as Sheol; like death, he
has never enough. He gathers for himself
all nations, and collects as his own all
peoples.
John 13:27--Then after the morsel, Satan entered into him. Jesus said to him, "What
you are going to do, do quickly."
Proverbs 12:27--A slothful man will not catch
his prey, but the diligent man will get

precious wealth.

2 Thessalonians 2:7--for the mystery of law-
lessness is already at work; only he who
now restrains it will do so until he is out
of the way.

Psalms 93:1--The Lord reigns; he is robed in
majesty; the Lord is robed; he is girded
with strength. Yea, the world is established;
it shall never be moved. . . .

Luke 16:9--See above for Thursday, 1 November
1750 (p. 52).

Proverbs 23:23--Buy truth and do not sell it;
buy wisdom, instruction, and understanding.

1 John 3:9--No one born of God commits sin; for
God's nature abides in him, and he cannot
sin because he is born of God.

1 John 1:7--. . .but if we walk in the light,
as he is in the light, we can have fellowship with one another, and the blood of
Jesus his Son cleanses us from all sin.

Acts 2:42--And they devoted themselves to the
apostles' teaching and fellowship, to the
breaking of bread and the prayers.

John 20:27--Then he said to Thomas, "Put your
finger here, and see my hands; and put out
your hand, and place it on my side; do not
be faithless, but believing."

(?) January 1757

Ephesians 4:22--Put off your old nature, which
belongs to your former manner of life and
is corrupt through deceitful lusts. . . .

Romans 4:13--The promise of Abraham and his
descendants, that they should inherit the
world, did not come through the law, but

through the righteousness of faith.

Ephesians 3:14--For this reason I bow my knees
before the Father. . . .

Isaiah 51:11--And the ransomed of the Lord
shall return, and come to Zion with singing; everlasting joy shall be upon their
heads; they shall obtain joy and gladness,
and sorrow and sighing shall flee away.

Isaiah 51:22--Thus says your Lord, the Lord
your God who pleads the cause of his people: "Behold, I have taken from your hand
the cup of staggering; the bowl of my wrath
you shall drink no more. . . .

Isaiah 53:5-6--But he was wounded for our
transgressions, he was bruised for our iniquities; upon him was the chastisement
that made us whole, and with his stripes
we are healed. All we, like sheep, have
gone astray; we have turned, every one, to
his own way; and the Lord has laid on him
the iniquity of us all.

Matthew 18:3--. . .and he said, "Truly I say
to you, unless you turn and become like
children, you will never enter the kingdom
of heaven.

Ephesians 6:14--See above for Tuesday, 30 January 1753 (p. 62).

Matthew 9:24--. . .he said, "Depart; for the
girl is not dead, but sleeping." And they
laughed at him.

Matthew 11:25--See above for Saturday, 3 February 1750 (p. 50).

1 Corinthians 13:10--. . .but when the perfect
comes, the imperfect will pass away.

Ephesians 5:8--. . .for once you were darkness, but now you are light in the Lord;
walk as children of light. . . .

1 Thessalonians 4:13--But we would not have
you ignorant, brethren, concerning those
who are asleep, that you may not grieve
as others do who have no hope.

Hebrews 9:11--But when Christ appeared as a
high priest of the good things that have
come, then through the greater and more
perfect tent (not made with hands, that is,
not of this creation). . . .

1 Corinthians 15:20--But in fact Christ has
been raised from the dead, the first fruits
of those who have fallen asleep.

Sunday, 30 January 1757. The service at West Street
Chapel lasted "between four and five hours."

Sunday, 7 August 1757

1 Kings 18:21--See above for Thursday, 13
June 1751 (p. 56).

Matthew 10:21--Brother will deliver up brother
to death, and the father his child,
and children will rise against parents
and have them put to death. . . .

Philippians 3:20--See above for Wednesday, 1
January 1752 (p. 58).

Hebrews 10:36--For you have need of endurance,
so that you may do the will of God and
receive what is promised.

Romans 13:12--. . .the night is far gone, the
day is at hand. Let us then cast off the
works of darkness and put on the armor of
light. . . .

Romans 10--Brethren, my heart's desire and

prayer to God for them is that they may be
saved.

2 Kings 5:12--Are not Abana and Pharpar, the
rivers of Damascus, better than all the
waters of Israel? Could not I wash in them,
and be clean? So he turned and went away
in a rage.

1 John 1:7--See above for November 1756 (p.
76).

1 Peter 1:9--As the outcome of your faith you
obtain the salvation of your souls.

Revelation 1:8--"I am the Alpha and the Omega,"
says the Lord God, who is one and who was
and who is to come, the Almighty.

Wednesday, 9 November 1757

Psalms 49:6--. . .men who trust in their
wealth and boast of the abundance of their
riches?

Hebrews 3:14--For we share in Christ, only if
we hold our first confidence firm to the
end. . . .

1 Peter 1:9--See above for Sunday, 7 August
1757 (p. 79).

Wednesday, 7 December 1757

Hebrews 13:8--Jesus Christ is the same yesterday
and today and forever.

Hebrews 13:20--Now may the God of peace who
brought again from the dead our Lord Jesus
Christ, the great shepherd of the sheep, by
the blood of the eternal covenant. . . .

Philippians 4:7--See above for Wednesday, 1
January 1752 (p. 58).

1 Corinthians 9:24--Do you not know that in a
race all the runners compete, but only one
receives the prize? So run that you may

obtain it.

Sunday, 25 December 1757

1 John 3:8--See above for Monday, 25 December
1752 (p. 60).

Matthew 26:12--In pouring this ointment on my
body, she has done it to prepare me for
burial.

1 Peter 2:13--Be subject for the Lord's sake
to every human institution, whether it be
to the emperor as supreme. . . .

Wednesday, 1 February 1758

Romans 12:21--Do not be overcome by evil, but
overcome evil with good.

Mark 2:17--And when Jesus heard it, he said to
them, "Those who are well have no need of a
physician, but those who are sick; I came
not to call the righteous, but sinners."

Leviticus 26:34--Then the land shall enjoy its
sabbaths as long as it lies desolate, while
you are in your enemies' land; then the
land shall rest, and enjoy its sabbaths.

Genesis 6:5--The Lord saw that the wickedness
of man was great in the earth, and that
every imagination of the thoughts of his
heart was only evil continually.

2 Corinthians 11:2--I feel a divine jealousy
for you, for I betrothed you to Christ to
present you as a pure bride to her one husband.

1 Peter 2:17--Honor all men. Love the brother-
hood. Fear God. Honor the emperor.

Psalms 25:13--He, himself, shall abide in
prosperity, and his children shall possess
the land.

1 <u>Thessalonians</u> 4:8--Therefore, whoever disregards this, disregards not man, but God,
who gives his Holy Spirit to you.

<u>Matthew</u> 11:28--Come to me, all who labor and
are heavy laden, and I will give you rest.

<u>Acts</u> 11:21--And the hand of the Lord was with
them, and a great number that believed turned
to the Lord.

Friday, 17 February 1758. A public fast day.   No
text indicated.

Sunday, 22 October 1758

<u>Proverbs</u> 2:1-6--My son, if you receive my words
and treasure up my commandments with you. . .
from his mouth came knowledge and understanding. . . .

<u>John</u> 4:24--God is spirit, and those who wor-
ship him must worship in spirit and truth.

<u>Psalms</u> 101:2--See above for Sunday, 26 Octo-
ber 1755 (p. 70).

<u>Daniel</u> 9:24--Seventy weeks of years are de-
creed concerning your people and your holy
city, to finish the transgression, to put
and end to sin, and to atone for iniquity,
to bring in everlasting righteousness, to
seal both vision and prophet,and to anoint
a most holy place.

2 <u>Timothy</u> 2:6--It is the hard-working farmer
who ought to have the first share of the
crops.

<u>Jeremiah</u> 23:6--See above for Sunday, 26 Octo-
ber 1755 (p. 71).

<u>James</u> 1:27--Religion that is pure and undefiled
before God and the Father is this: to visit
orphans and widows in their affliction,

and to keep oneself unstained from
the world.

Saturday, 9 December 1758

Isaiah 38:18--For Sheol cannot thank thee,
death cannot praise thee; those who go down
to the pit cannot hope for thy faithfulness.

Isaiah 40:1--See above for Sunday, 26 October
1755 (p. 70).

Genesis 49:5--Simeon and Levi are brothers;
weapons and violence are their swords.

Isaiah 5:25--Therefore, the anger of the Lord
was kindled against his people, and he
stretched out his hand against them and
smote them, and the mountains quaked; and
their corpses were as refuse in the midst
of the streets. For all his anger is not
turned away and his hand is stretched out
still.

Sunday, 14 January 1759

Romans 12:11--Never flag in zeal, be aglow
with the Spirit, serve the Lord.

Hebrews 11:1--Now faith is the assurance of
things hoped for, the conviction of things
not seen.

1 Peter 4:11--. . .whoever speaks, as one who
utters oracles of God; whoever renders service, as one who renders it by the strength
which God supplies; in order that in everything God may be glorified through Jesus
Christ. To him belong glory and dominion
for ever and ever.

1 Corinthians 6:19--Do you not know that your
body is a temple of the Holy Spirit within

you, which you have from God? You are not
your own. . . .

1 Peter 4:19--Therefore, let those who suffer
according to God's will do right and en-
trust their souls to a faithful Creator.

Galatians 6:10--So then, as we have opportunity, let us do good to all men, and especially to those who are of the household
of faith.

Galatians 4:18--For a good purpose it is
always good to be made much of, and not
only when I am present with you.

1 Corinthians 10:20--No, I imply that what
pagans sacrifice they offer to demons and
not to God. I do not want to be partners
with demons.

Luke 8:10--To you it has been given to know
the secrets of the kingdom of God; but for
others, they are in parables, so that seeing they may not see, and hearing they may
not understand.

1 Corinthians 15:19--If for this life only we
have hoped in Christ, we are of all men
most to be pitied.

1 Peter 5:5--Likewise, you that are younger,
be subject to the elders. Clothe yourselves, all of you, with humility toward
one another, for "God opposes the proud,
but gives grace to the humble."

2 Corinthians 3:8--. . .will not the dispensa-
tion of the Spirit be attended with greater
splendor?

Mark 11:24--Therefore, I tell you, whatever
you ask in prayer, believe that you receive

it, and you will.

Matthew 20:15--Am I not allowed to do what I
choose with what belongs to me? Or do you
begrudge my generosity?

Joel 2:12--"Yet even now," says the Lord,
"return with me all your heart, with fasting,
with weeping, and with mourning. . . ."

Ephesians 5:16--But I say, walk by the Spirit,
and do not gratify the desires of the
flesh.

Saturday, 25 August 1759

Acts 24:16--So I always take pains to have a
clear conscience toward God and toward men.

Philippians 4:4--Rejoice in the Lord, always;
again I will say, "Rejoice."

Psalms 103:2--Bless the Lord, O my soul, and
forget not all His benefits. . . .

Saturday, 15 September 1759. On the preceding day,
Wesley had returned to London from Sundon. In his absence,
he had left orders for the immediate repairing of
West Street Chapel. "The main timbers were so rotten,"
he noted, "that in many places one might thrust his
fingers into them. So that probably, had we delayed till
spring, the whole building must have fallen to   the
ground."

Thursday, 8 November 1759

1 Peter 4:17--For the time has come for judgment to begin with the household of God;
and if it begins with us, that will be the
end of those who do no obey the gospel of
God?

Acts 9:31--So the church throughout all Judea
and Galilee and Samaria had peace and was
built up; and walking in the fear of the

Lord and in the comfort of the Holy Spirit
it was multiplied.

Psalms 62:1--For God alone my soul waits in
silence; from him comes my salvation.

Thursday, 29 November 1759. On this day, Londoners
celebrated a general thanksgiving. In August, the Battle
of Minden had saved Hanover for the British Crown; in
September, General James Wolfe had captured Quebec, thus
winning Canada for England.

Sunday, 9 December 1759

James 2:12--So speak and so act as those who
are to be judged under the law of liberty.

2 Peter 3:8--But do not ignore this one fact,
beloved, that with the Lord, one day is as
a thousand years, and a thousand years as
one day.

2 Peter 3:10--But the day of the Lord will
come, like a thief, and then the heavens
will pass away with a loud noise, and the
elements will be dissolved with fire, and
the earth and the works that are upon it
will be burned up.

2 Peter 3:18--But grow in the grace and knowledge of our Lord and Savior Jesus Christ.
To him be the glory, both now and to the
day of eternity.

Sunday, 13 January 1760. By now, West Street Chapel
had been thoroughly repaired and enlarged. "When I
took this, eighteen years ago," noted Wesley, "I little
thought the world would have borne us until now."

Thursday, 17 January 1760

Romans 14:23--But he who has doubts is condemned; if he eats, because he does not
act from faith; for whatever does not pro-

proceed from faith is sin.

1 Corinthians 5:11--But rather I wrote to you
not to associate with any one who bears the
name of brother if he is guilty of immorality or greed, or is an idolator, reviler,
drunkard, or robber--not even to eat with
such a one.

James 3:2--For we all make many mistakes, and
if any one makes no mistakes in what he
says, he is a perfect man, able to bridle
the whole body, also.

Matthew 18:3--See above for January 1757 (p.
77).

Sunday, 27 January 1760

Nehemiah 13:16--Men of Tyre, also, who lived
in the city, brought in fish and all kinds
of wares and sold them on the sabbath to
the people of Judah, and in Jerusalem.

Revelation 7:13--Then one of the elders
addressed me, saying, "Who are these, clothed
in white robes, and whence have they come?"

1 Corinthians 4:12--. . .and we labor, working with our own hands. When reviled, we
bless; when persecuted, we endure. . . .

Saturday, 9 February 1760

1 Corinthians 7:29--See above for Monday, 8
January 1753 (p. 61).

Psalms 51:8-9--Fill me with joy and gladness;
let the bones which thou hast broken rejoice.
Hide thy face from my sins, and blot out
all my iniquities.

2 Corinthians 11:3--But I am afraid that as
the serpent deceived Eve by his cunning,
your thoughts will be led astray from a

sincere and pure devotion to Christ.

2 Corinthians 11:14--And no wonder, for even
Satan disguises himself as an angel of
light.

Wednesday, 20 February 1760

Joel 2:13--. . .and rend your hearts and not
your garments. Return to the Lord your
God, for he is gracious and merciful, slow
to anger, and abounding in steadast love,
and repents of evil.

Galatians 5:22--See above for Monday, 25 March
1751 (p. 55).

Matthew 20:15--See above for Sunday, 14 January 1759 (p. 84).

Matthew 11:28--See above for Wednesday, 1 February 1758 (p. 81).

Sunday, 24 February 1760

Acts 1:25--. . .to take the place in this
ministry and apostleship from which Judas
turned aside to go to his own place.

Galatians 2:20--I have been crucified with
Christ; it is no longer I who live, but
Christ who lives in me; and the life I now
live in the flesh I live by faith in the
Son of God, who loved me and gave himself
for me.

Psalms 35:27--Let those who desire my vindi-
cation shout for joy and be glad, and say
evermore, "Great is the Lord, who delights
in the welfare of his servant!"

Hebrews 2:1--Therefore, we must pay the closer
attention to what we have heard, lest we
drift away from it.

Sunday, 9 November 1760

Matthew 21:21--And Jesus answered them, "Truly,
I say unto you, if you have faith and
never doubt, you will not only do what has
been done to the fig tree, but even if you
say tho this mountain, 'Be taken up and be
cast into the sea,' it will be done.

Galatians 3:3--Are you so foolish? Having begun with the Spirit, are you now ending with
the flesh?

James 5:20--. . .let him know that whoever
brings back a sinner from the error of his
way will save his soul from death and will
cover a multitude of sins.

Exodus 14:15--The Lord said to Moses, "Why do
you cry to me? Tell the people of Israel
to go forward.

Sunday, 21 December 1760. Wesley preached a charity
sermon at both morning and afternoon services; he
based his texts upon the following:

Ephesians 2:19--See above for Sunday, 16 March
1755 (p. 66).

John 20:22--And when he had said this, he
breathed on them, and said to them, Receive
the Holy Spirit.

Acts 21:14--And when he could not be persuaded, we ceased and said, "The will of the
Lord be done."

John 21:19--After this he said to him, "Follow
me."

Thursday, 25 December 1760

Hebrews 1:1-4--In many and various ways God
spoke of old to our fathers by the prophets;
but in these last days he has spoken to us
by a Son, whom he appointed the heir of all

things, through whom also he created the
world. He reflects the glory of God and
bears the very stamp of his nature, uphold-
ing the universe by his word of power. When
he had made purification for sins, he sat
down at the right hand of the Majesty on
high, having become as much superior to angels as the name he has obtained is more
excellent than theirs.

Galatians 3:12--. . .but the law does not rest
on faith, for "He who does them shall live
by them."

Matthew 23:37--See above for Friday, 19
December 1755 (pp. 72-73).

Philippians 3:1--Finally, my brethren, rejoice
in the Lord. To write the same things to
you is not irksome to me, and is safe for
you.

Thursday, 1 January 1761

2 Corinthians 5:19--. . .that is, God was in
Christ reconciling the world to himself,
not counting their trespasses against
them, and entrusting to us the message of
reconciliation.

2 Corinthians 10:5--We destroy arguments and
every profound obstacle to the knowledge of
God, and make every thought captive to obey
Christ. . . .

Psalms 141:3--Set a guard over my mouth, O
Lord, keep watch over the door of my lips!

Matthew 3:12--His winnowing fork is in his
hand, and he will clear his threshing floor
and gather his wheat into the granery, but
the chaff he will burn with unquenchable

fire.

Romans 3:22--. . .the righteousness of God
through faith in Jesus Christ for all who
believe.

Ephesians 3:3--. . .how the mystery was made
know to me by revelation, as I have written
briefly.

Luke 13:2--And he answered them, "Do you think
that these Galileans were worse sinners
than all the other Galileans, because they
suffered thus?

Friday, 13 February 1761. A general fast-day; Wesley
preached on--

Revelation 3:6--He who has an ear, let him
hear what the Spirit says to the churches.

Joel 2:14--Who knows whether he will not turn
and repent, and leave a blessing behind
him, a cereal offering and a drink offering for the Lord, your God?

1 Thessalonians 4:7--See above for Sunday, 3
March 1751 (p. 54).

Sunday, 15 February 1761

Matthew 15:28--Then Jesus answered her, "O
woman, great is your faith! Be it done for
you as you desire." And her daughter was
healed instantly.

Galatians 4:18--See above for Sunday, 14
January 1759 (p. 83).

Galatians 5:5--For through the Spirit, by
faith, we wait for the hope of righteousness.

Ephesians 4:30--And do not grieve the Holy
Spirit of God, in whom you were sealed for
the day of redemption.

Sunday, 22 February 1761

Romans 6:23--See above for Sunday, 16   June
1754 (p. 64).

Hebrews 7:19--. . .in the other hand,a better
hope is introduced through which we draw
near to God.

Romans 12:5--. . .so we, though many, are one
body in Christ, and individually members
of one another.

Romans 14:7--None of us lives to himself, and
none of us dies to himself.

Sunday, 1 March 1761

Galatians 4:30--But what does the scripture
say? "Cast out the slave and her son; for
the son of the slave shall not inherit with
the son of the free woman."

Galatians 5:6--For in Christ Jesus neither
circumcision nor uncircumcision is of any
avail, but faith working through love.

Luke 12:20--See above for Sunday, 16   June
1754 (pp. 63-64), and for Sunday, 26
October 1755 (p. 71).

Philippians 3:8--See above for Sunday,13 June
1751 (pp. 56-57).

Sunday, 23 August 1761

Hebrews 9:13--See above for Sunday, 3 March
1751 (p. 54), and for Wednesday, 29 January 1752 (p. 59).

Galatians 5:22--See above for Monday, 25 March
1751 (p. 55), and for Wednesday, 20 February 1760 (p. 87).

Luke 15:22--But the father said to his servants,
"Bring quickly the best robe, and put it
on him; and put a ring on his hand,

and shoes on his feet. . . ."

Jude 22--And convince some, who doubt. . . .

1 Corinthians 2:12--Now we have received not
the spirit of the world, but the Spirit
which is from God, that we might understand
the gifts bestowed on us by God.

Matthew 7:20--Thus, you will know them by their
fruits.

Romans 7:24--Wretched man that I am! Who will
deliver me from this body of death?

Ephesians 4:30--See above for Sunday, 15 February 1761 (p. 90).

1 Timothy 4:5--See above for Monday, 21 July
1755 (p. 68).

Galatians 6:3--For if anyone thinks he is something, when he is nothing, he deceives himself.

Matthew 22:37--And he said to him, "You shall
love the Lord your God with all your heart,
and with all your soul, and with all your
mind.

1 John 5:19--See above for Sunday, 25 November 1750 (p. 53).

Sunday, 1 November 1761

Revelation 7:8--. . .twelve thousand of the
tribe of Zebulun, twelve thousand of the
tribe of Joseph, twelve thousand sealed
out of the tribe of Benjamin.

Hebrews 12:5--See above for Thursday, 1 November 1750 (p. 52).

1 Samuel 17--Now the Philistines gathered
their armies for battle. . . .

1 Peter 1:9--See above for Sunday, 7 August
1757 (p. 79), and for Wednesday, 9 November 1757 (p. 79).

Friday, 6 November 1761

> Luke 10:42--. . .one thing is needful. Mary
> has chosen the good portion, which shall
> not be taken away from her.

> 2 Peter 3:11--Since all these things are thus
> to be dissolved, what sort of persons ought
> you to be in lives of holiness and godli-
> ness. . . .

> 1 John 2:1--My little children, I am writing
> this to you so that you may not sin; but if
> any one does sin, we have an advocate with
> the Father, Jesus Christ the righteous. . .

> 1 John 2:20--But you have been anointed by
> the Holy One, and you all know.

> Hebrews 6:1--Therefore, let us leave the ele-
> mentary doctrines of Christ and go on to
> maturity, not laying again the foundation
> of repentence from dead works and of faith
> toward God. . . .

Sunday, 29 November 1761

> Isaiah 1:3--The ox knows its owner, and the
> ass its master's crib; but Israel does not
> know, my people does not understand.

> Isaiah 2:22--Turn away from man in whose nos-
> trils is breath, for of what account is he?

> Acts 22:16--And now, why do you wait? Rise
> and be baptised, and wash away your sins,
> calling on his name.

Friday, 4 December 1761

> Isaiah 26:12--O Lord, thou wilt ordain peace
> for us, thou has wrought for us all our
> works.

Friday, 20 August 1762. Wesley conducted a meeting
of the London society at West Street Chapel.

Sunday, 7 October 1764. No text indicated.

Sunday, 22 January 1766. On Wednesday, the 18th,
Wesley had a serious accident: his horse collapsed under
him, he was tossed from her, and he suffered serious
bruises to his right arm, chest, knee, and leg. His
ankle "swelled exceedingly." On the 22nd, he could not
complete the service at West Street Chapel and required
assistance.

Sunday, 26 October 1766. He preached in the morning to a "crowded audience."

Saturday, 1 November 1766. All Saints Day; no text
indicated.

Saturday, 26 September 1767. No text indicated.

Sunday, 5 March 1769. No text indicated.

Tuesday, 25 December 1770. No text indicated.

Sunday, 14 January 1776. "As I was going to West
Street Chapel, one of the chaise-springs suddenly snapped
asunder; but, the horses instantly stopping, I stepped
out without the least inconvenience."

Whit Sunday, 18 May 1777. No text indicated.

Sunday, 14 December 1777. No text indicated.

Friday, 25 December 1778. Christmas Day: "I read
prayers. . .and preached and administered the sacrament
to several thousand people."

Sunday, 8 August 1779. No text indicated.

Friday, 31 December 1779. "We concluded the year
. . .with a solemn watch-night." Wesley had instituted
the monthly post-midnight watch-night service in 1742;
later, the practice became, for Methodists and other
Protestant denominations,a New Year's eve service that
extended beyond midnight.

Sunday, 24 December 1780. No text indicated.

Wednesday, 21 February 1781. A national fast-day;
no text indicated.

Tuesday, 1 January 1782. No text indicated.

Monday, 29 July 1782. No text indicated.

Sunday, 8 December 1782

> Romans 15:4-5--See above for Sunday, 8 Decem-
> ber 1754 (p. 64); for Thursday, 13 June
> 1751 (p. 55); for Thursday, 1 November 1750
> (pp. 52-53).

Sunday, 12 October 1783

> Ephesians 4:3--See above for September 1756
> (p. 74).

Saturday, 25 December 1784. Christmas Day

> Luke 2:14--"Glory to God in the highest, and
> on earth, peace among men with whom he is
> pleased!"

Sunday, 23 January 1785

> Matthew 20:15--See above for Sunday, 14 Janu-
> ary 1759 (p. 84); and for Wednesday, 20
> February 1760 (p. 87).

Sunday, 24 July 1785. ". . .both the largeness and
earnestness of the congregation gave me a comfortable
hope of blessing at the ensuing Conference." The forty-
second Methodist Conference began on Tuesday, 26 July
1785, ending on Wednesday, 3 August 1785. All of the
sessions held forth at West Street Chapel.

Sunday, 7 August 1785

> Luke 18:10--Two men went up to the temple to
> pray, one a Pharisee and the other a tax
> collector.

Sunday, 25 December 1785. Christmas Day

> Luke 2:14--See above for Saturday, 25 Decem-
> ber 1784 (p. 95).

Sunday, 26 February 1786

> Ephesians 2:8--For by grace you have been saved
> through faith; and this is not your own doing;
> it is the gift of God.

Monday, 17 July 1786
    1 Timothy 1:5--. . .whereas the aim of our
    charge is love that issues from a pure
    heart and a good conscience and sincere
    faith.
Sunday, 22 October 1786
    Ephesians 4:30--See above for Sunday, 15 Feb-
    ruary 1761 (p.90), and for Sunday, 23
    August 1761 (p.92).
Sunday, 26 November 1786
    Colossians 1:10--. . .to lead a life worthy
    of the Lord, fully pleasing to him, bearing
    fruit in every good work and increasing in
    the knowledge of God.
Monday, 1 January 1787
    2 Corinthians 5:17--See above for Thursday, 1
    January 1756 (p.73).
Sunday, 25 February 1787
    2 Corinthians 6:1--Working together with him,
    then, we entreat you not to accept the
    grace of God in vain.
Sunday, 14 October 1787
    Daniel 3--King Nebuchadnezzar made an image
    of gold, whose height was sixty cubits and
    its breadth six cubits. He set it up on
    the plain of Dura, in the province of
    Babylon.
Sunday, 25 November 1787. On this day, Wesley preached
two "charity sermons" on behalf of the poor children.
    Psalms 14:1--The fool says in his heart, "There
    is no God." They are corrupt, they do abomi-
    nable deeds, there is none that does good.
Monday, 25 February 1788. No text indicated. Wesley "took a solemn leave of the congregation at West

Street, by applying once more what I had enforced fifty
years before, 'By grace ye are saved, through faith.'
At the following meeting, the presence of God, in a mar-
vellous manner, filled the place."

Friday, 6 February 1789. The "Quarterly day for
meeting the local preachers took place at West Street
Chapel.

Sunday, 14 February 1790. Wesley preached a sermon to the children; his text--

> Psalms 34:11--Come, O sons, listen to me, I
> will teach you the fear of the Lord.

Monday, 22 February 1790. A meeting of the leaders of the London society convened.

Sunday, 28 February 1790. "The chapel would not
near contain the congregation. All that could squeeze
in seemed much affected, and it was with difficulty I
broke through and took chaise for Brentford. . . ." He
preached on

> Ephesians 5:1-2--Therefore, be imitators of
> God, as beloved children.And walk in love,
> as Christ loved us and gave himself up for
> us, a fragrant offering and sacrifice to
> God.

In all, Wesley's journal, diary, and Sermon Register
indicate that he preached at West Street Chapel on at
least 135 separate occasions (or days) during the period from Wednesday, 18 September 1745, through Sunday,
28 February 1790.

Bear Yard, Sheffield Street. Bear Yard, as its name
suggests, comprised an open tract on the west side of
Sheffield Street, by Clare Market--and not far from West
Street and Great Queen Street. Clare Market came into

existence in 1657, and functioned on Tuesdays, Thursdays,
and Saturdays for the sale of meat and fish.

On Tuesday evening, 19 September 1738, Wesley attended a meeting of of a Church of England religious society at Bear Yard, where he "preached repentance and re-
mission of sins." He returned there for meetings on the
evenings of Tuesday, 3 October 1738; Tuesday, 31 October
1738; and Tuesday, 7 November 1738.

Furnival's Inn, Holborn. Wesley visited this Inn
of Chancery on one occasion only: Wednesday, 21 February 1739, at 8:00 a.m., for "communion, singing." The
Inn itself--named after Sir William de Furnival, fourth
Lord Furnival, who leased the property to law students
in 1383--was attached to Lincoln's Inn. Its buildings,
with a front designed by Inigo Jones (1573-1652), were
for the most part pulled down during the reign of
Charles I (1625-1649). In 1818, new owners completely rebuilt the Inn and leased it to Henry Peto, the prominent London builder, on a building lease of one hundred
years.

Gray's Inn Walks (Gardens), Holborn. From the Restoration until at least the end of the eighteenth century, Gray's Inn Walks served as a fashionable public
promenade. Samuel Pepys went there on a Lord's Day
(Sunday) in 1661 and observed the fine ladies on parade.
A year later, he returned with his wife, on that occasion to examine the latest in ladies fashions.

At 3:00 p.m., Thursday, 3 September 1741, Wesley
met at Gray's Inn Walks with Count Nicholaus Ludwig von
Zinzendorf (1700-1760), the leader of the German Moravian

Brethren. The dialogue from that meeting (which
Wesley transcribed in his journal in the original Latin)
marked the beginning of the end of Wesley's relationship
with the Moravians. Simply, there could no longer exist
the possibility of a healing of their divergent views concerning Christian perfection and the means by which to
attain grace.

   The Gardens (or "Walks") resulted from the land-
scaping efforts of Sir Francis Bacon in 1606.   Throughout the seventeenth century, the area served not only to
accommodate the fashionable strollers, but to provide a
convenient place for duelling.

   St. Dunstan's Church, Fleet Street. The original
St. Dunstan's dates from about 1530; the structure nar-
rowly escaped destruction from the Great Fire of 2-4
September 1666. Eventually, the building gave way, between 1831 and 1833, to the Church of St. Dunstan in the
West. In 1671, Thomas Harrys of Water Lane supplied a
new clock for the church at a cost of £35. Affixed to
that instrument, the figures of two giants struck the
hour. The poet William Cowper (1731-1800) commemorated
the old church in his Table Talk (1782):
         When Labour and when Dulness, club in hand,
         Like the two figures of St. Dunstan's stand,
         Beating alternately, in measured time,
         The clock-work tintinabulum of rhyme.
In 1701, the church benefited from extensive repairs:
the old arched roof came off, to be replaced by a square
roof at a higher elevation. Later, in 1730, fire once
again threatened the structure, but the blaze somehow
stopped just short of its walls.   John Wesley's uncle,
Dr. Matthew Wesley, the surgeon, was buried in St.

Dunstan's churchyard in 1737.

Within the same month after his return to England
from Herrnhut and Zinzendorf's Moravian brethren (16
September 1738), Wesley--on Friday, 29 September--arose
at 6:30 a.m. (fairly late for him!) and dressed for
prayers and communion at St. Dunstan's. He repeated
that activity on the mornings of Thursday, 21 December
1738; Saturday, 30 December 1738; Saturday, 6 January
1739; and Saturday, 16 June 1739.

Colebrook Row, Islington. Opposite the point where
City Road joins Goswell Road, the eighteenth-century
Londoner came upon Colebrook Row, a long street upon
which stood houses dominated by their terraces. Some
four months before Wesley's death, this entry appears
in his diary (for Wednesday, 15 December 1790): ". . .
12.30 chaise, Colebrook Row, conversed. . . ." There
exists no evidence to identify the individual(s) with
whom he conducted this early afternoon conversation,
nor does the aged Methodist leader identify the content
of the discussion.

The Baptist's Head, St. John's Lane, Clerkenwell.
The old public house of Baptist's Head (named for Sir
Baptist Hicks, Viscount Campden of Campden) had originally been the house of Sir Thomas Forster, a judge who
died in 1612. The judge's coat of arms appeared over a
fireplace in the taproom. Such literary noteworthies as
Samuel Johnson, Richard Savage, Oliver Goldsmith, and
David Garrick met there on several occasions. Wesley
went to the Baptist's Head only once, on Thursday evening, 7 October 1740; all he noted in his journal was

that at 8:00 "the gentlemen met. . . ."

   The Charterhouse, Charterhouse Square (near Smithfield). Built in 1371 as one of the houses of the Car-
tusian Order, Charterhouse was taken from the monks during the dissolution of the monasteries in the reign of
Henry VIII. After passing through the hands of various
nobles (including Sir Edward North and the Duke of Norfolk), the property came(1611)into possession of Thomas
Sutton, the Queen's Master of Ordnance, who purchased
it for £13,000 and endowed it as a school for forty
poor boys and as a hospital for eighty poor men. Among
the notable pupils who attended Charterhouse School, in
addition to young John Wesley (from 28 January 1714 to
June 1720), were Richard Lovelace, Richard Steele, Joseph
Addison, William Blackstone. In 1872, the old school was
transferred to Godalming (Surrey), and the Merchant
Taylors took its place until 1933.
   John Wesley entered Charterhouse on 28 January
1714, at age ten, and remained there until he entered
Christ Church, Oxford, on 24 June 1720. Nonetheless,
he would return there upon a number of occasions, for
he looked upon the school as a place where he might seek
periodic respite from his travels and his evangelical
labors. Thus, at 3:30 p.m., Monday, 25 September 1738,
he conversed there with Mr. Jonathan Agutter (d. 1762)--
a pensioner at the Charterhouse who, on more than one
isntance, provided Wesley with a quiet room wherein
he could draft his sermons, correct proofs, write letters,
or simply sit and think.   The Methodist leader returned
to the school at least five times during January 1739:
Saturday, the 13th; Thursday, the 18th; Saturday the 20th;
Tuesday, the 23rd; and Monday, the 29th.

Of interest is Wesley's reaction to the students
while walking through the Charterhouse on Monday, 8
August 1757:"I wondered that all the squares and buildings, and especially the school-boys, looked so little.
But this is easily accounted for. I was little myself
when I was at school, and measured all about me by myself. Accordingly, the upper boys, being bigger than
myself, seemed to me very big and tall; quite contrary
to what they appear now, when I am taller and bigger
than them. I question if this is not the real ground
of the common imagination that our forefathers, and in
general men of past ages, were much larger than now--
an imagination current in the world eighteen hundred
years ago." Wesley, himself, stood only slightly above
five feet and weighed approximately one hundred and
twenty-two pounds.

Pardon Church, Charterhouse. On Friday, 17 November 1769, Wesley wrote in his journal that he
"preached at a chapel near John Street, built on the very
spot of ground whereon, many hundred years ago, Pardon
Church stood." When a pestilence devastated London in
1348, Bishop Ralph Stratford consecrated three acres of
waste ground between the lands of the Abbey of Westminster and those of St. John Clerkenwell. There he erected a chapel where masses were said for the repose of
the dead, and he named the ediface Pardon Churchyard.
In 1361, Michael de Northburgh died, having bequeathed
£2000 for building a Carthusian prior at Pardon Churchyard (Charterhouse).

The New Prison, Clerkenwell. In 1615, the City of

London erected, in the fields north of Newcastle House,
a prison to ease the rising population of Bridewell Prison
(built originally between 1515 and 1520). Then, the
Corporation authorized a second "new: structure, "New
Prison"--also known as the House of Detention--to relieve
the overcrowdedness of Newgate. The "new" Bridewell of
1615 was demolished in 1804; the so-called "New Prison"
(the second structure) underwent complete rebuilding during 1845-1846.

On two occasions, John Wesley attempted to enter
New Prison, located near Clerkenwell Green. Reverend
Mr. Wilson, the parish curate, refused to allow him (on
Tuesday, 19 August 1740) "to go and pray with one who
had sent for me several times before, lying in the New
Prison, under sentence of death, which was to be execu-
ted in a few days." Again, on Wednesday, 1 April 1741,
Wesley went there to see another prisoner awaiting exe-
cution. "But the keeper told me Mr. Wilson. . .had given
charge I should not speak with him. I am clear from
the blood of this man. Let Mr. Wilson answer for it to
God."

New Wells, Lower Rosomon Street, Clerkenwell. From
Wesley's journal we learn that on Monday, 29 April 1756,
he "preached at Sadler's Wells , in what was formerly a
play-house." That does not refer, in any way, to the
more noted Sadler's Wells, but to another place of entertainment not far from there. The following notice
appeared in The Gentleman's Magazine for May 1752. "The
theatrical edifice now called the New Wells, near the
London Spaw, was preached in [17 May] for the first time
by a clergyman methodist, it being taken by the Rev.
John Wesley for a tabernacle." Actually, as we know from

Wesley's journal, he had preached there at least once
prior to 17 May; the latter date may well be the beginning of his lease arrangement for the building. At
any rate, New Wells had been closed as a theatre since
1750, while Sadler's Wells remained a place of entertainment until the original building was shut down in 1906.

Wesley preached again at New Wells on Monday, 10
November 1755.   A year later, the building came to the
ground to make way for the expansion of Rosomon Street.

Finsbury Dispensary, Rosomon Street, Clerkenwell.
The Finsbury Dispensary, founded by a Quaker, George
Friend (!), opened on 12 August 1780. Selina Shirley,
Countess of Huntingdon (and patroness of George Whitefield and the Calvinist Methodists), became a subscriber
and ordered sermons preached at Spa Fields on behalf of the institution.   Rowland Hill (1744-1833),the
founder of the Surrey Chapel (London), preached several
times at St. Luke's Church for the cause of the Finsbury
Dispensary. In the list of contributions for the
Dispensary for 1787, the following entry appears: "To
sermons at St. John's, Clerkenwell, by the Rev. John
Wesley and the Rev. Rowland Hill,£20.0s.4d." The institution moved to Number 16, Woodbridge Street,
Clerkenwell, and then to Brewer Street, Goswell Road.

Although Wesley remarked, in his journal for Sunday, 16 December 1787, that "I would gladly countenance
every institution of this kind," there exists no hard
evidence of the Methodist patriarch ever having actually visited Finsbury Dispensary.

St. John's Church, St. John Square, Clerkenwell.

In the early eighteenth century, St. John's stood as a
Presbyterian meeting house, only to be ransacked during
the Sacheverell riots of 1710 and its contents burned at
the door. By 1716, this once famous abbey of Clerkenwell
stood for sale. Five years later (1721), Mr. Simon
Michel bought the structure, but then sold it in 1723 to
the Commissioners of Queen Anne's Bounty for £500. At
that point, the Commissioners reconstructed the building
as the parish church of St. John's, Clerkenwell, and it
remained as such until 1931--when the parish united with
St. James's, Clerkenwell, and the church passed over to
the Order of St. John of Jerusalem.

John Wesley preached twice at St. John's on Sunday,
24 September 1738. Almost fifty years later, on Sunday,
16 December 1787, he preached the charity sermon there
for the benefit of the Finsbury Dispensary (see. pp. 104-
105).

Middlesex House, Bartholomew Close, Smithfield.
Middlesex Court, part of a large building known as Mid-
Middlesex House, functioned as an old Presbyterian place of
worship. It adjoined the Church of St. Bartholomew. John
Wesley, who preached there on Monday, 26 December 1764,
termed it "a large, commodius place."

St. Bartholomew's Hospital, Smithfield. The oldest
hospital in London (dating from 1123), the buildings of
St. Bartholomew surrounded a large square with a handsome fountain. One approached the place from Smithfield
by a gateway (built in 1702), adorned with a statue of
Henry VIII and the symbolic figures of Sickness and Lame-
ness. The quadrangle, begun by James Gibbs (1682-1754)
in 1730, marks, supposedly, the first instance of con-

struction with Bath stone. Gibbs's work was gratuitous,
and public subscription defrayed the cost of rebuilding.
William Hogarth, himself born near the Hospital (in
1697), in 1736 presented two pictures--The Pool of
Bethesda and The Good Samaritan--to the institution. He
based his figures upon actual patients, leaving instructions that the two pieces should never be varnished.
However, after the artist's death in 1764, his wish was
violated. In 1935, workers removed the coats of varnish
and restored the paintings to their original conditions.

   Wesley's only recorded visit to St. Bartholomew's
Hospital came about on Friday, 15 December 1738, at 9:15
a.m. He conversed, led prayers, and stayed there no
longer than forty-five minutes.

   Fetter Lane Chapel, Fetter Lane.   On Monday, 1
May 1738, John Wesley informs us that: our little society began, which afterward met in Fetter Lane."   That
group, founded principally by John and Charles Wesley
and James Hutton, on advice from Peter Bohler (and thus
its obvious ties with the Moravians), met first at
Hutton's residence and bookseller's shop--The Bible and
Sun, Little Wild Street, west of Temple Bar and not far
from Drury Lane. In 1740, Hutton leased Fetter Lane
Chapel from a Mr. Ketterage; the building had been vacant
since 1732.

   A word about Hutton (1715-1795) may be in order
here. Educated at Westminster School, he secured, in
1725, an apprenticeship to Mr. William Innys, the bookseller. At the expiration of that service, he opened a
bookseller's shop at the Bible and Sun; having been
converted by the Wesleys a short time prior to that, he
began to hold religious services in his shop. Soon,

however, he joined the Moravians and began to publish
works by Count Nicholaus von Zinzendorf. Later, he became a bookseller to George Whitefield, and eventually
published the calvinist Methodist's journal. Eventually,
he gave up his business to become secretary to the
Moravian Society and to preach and perform charitable work.
Hutton died at Oxted Cottage, Surrey, on 3 May 1795 (see
Plomer, Dictionary 1726-1775, 134-135).

   The disruption of the Fetter Lane religious society began in November 1739; in fact, the Wesleys and
their few followers occupied the Foundery on 11 November 1739 (see p. 162). Not until Sunday evening, 20
July 1740, however, did John Wesley and "eighteen or
nineteen" others actually withdraw from Fetter Lane.
The former set forth the reasons for the group's actions:
"About nine months ago certain of you began to speak
contrary to the doctrine we had till then received.
The sum of what you heard was this:
   1.   That there is no such thing as a weak
        faith: That there is no justifying faith
        where there is ever any doubt or fear,
        or where there is not, in the full
        sense, a new, clean heart.
   2.   That a man ought not to use those or-
        dinances of God which our Church [the
        Church of England] terms 'a means of
        grace,' before he has such a faith as
        excludes all doubt and fear, and im-
        plies a new, clean heart."
   Wesley's departure allowed the pro-Moravian element
of the society at Fetter Lane to form its own group of
Moravian Brethren. On 30 October 1742, that organization of seventy-two persons achieved status as a church
(or congregation) of the Brethren's Unity; the members

chose William Holland as their elder, while James Hutton
received appointment as warden. Essentially, the Fetter
Lane religious society, during its brief existence, proved neither Moravian nor Methodist, but functioned as a
pure religious society attached (unofficially) to the
Church of England. Its members followed the Book of Com-
Common Prayer and took the sacrament of Holy Communion in
parish churches.

Fetter Lane itself, named from the beggars called
Faitours or Fewters, deserves notice also as the street
on which John Dryden and Thomas Otway lived--opposite
each other, in fact. In Newton Hall, none other than
Sir Isaac Newton convened his first meeting of the Royal
Society of London.

Newgate Prison, Holborn Viaduct. The principal
west gate of the ancient city of London was termed "New
Gate," probably because it existed as a reconstruction
of an earlier gate dating from Roman times--at the point
where Watling Street reached London, or, roughly, along
the line of Oxford Street and Holborn. From the twelfth
century, its gatehouse functioned as a prison; funds
left by Sir Richard Whittington (d. 1423) allowed for
the enlargement, reconstruction, and general improvement of that structure. John Howard (1726-1790), the
noted prison reformer, drew attention to the unsanitary
conditions within the institution--particularly after
two Lord Mayors died of jail fever caught at the sessions. In 1780, the Gordon anti-popery rioters burned
Newgate to the ground; it was rebuilt shortly thereafter,
but finally demolished during 1902-1903, when the Central Criminal Court was built on that very site.

For a contemporary view of Newgate Prison, we may

wish to consider the reaction of a relatively young
James Boswell, who visited there on Tuesday, 3 May 1763:

> I. . .thought we should see prisoners of
> one kind or other, so went to Newgate. I
> stepped into a sort of court before the
> cells. They are surely most dismal places.
> There are three rows of 'em, four in a row,
> all above each other. They have double win-
> dows, and within these, strong iron rails;
> and in these dark mansions are the unhappy
> criminals confined. I did not go in, but
> stood in the court, where were a number
> of strange black-guard beings with sad
> countenances, most of them being friends
> and acquaintances of those under sentence
> of death.
>
>   (Boswell's London Journal 250-251)

John Wesley preached to and prayed with the Newgate
inmates on a fairly regular schedule between the autumn
of 1738 and the winter of 1739-1740: Tuesday, 19 September 1738; Saturday, 23 September 1738; Tuesday, 7 November 1738; Thursday, 14 December 1738; Tuesday, 13 February 1739; Thursday, 15 February 1739; Friday, 2 March
1739; Saturday, 29 September 1739; Wednesday, 6 February
1740. From that time, his visits become less frequent,
most probably because of his commitments in other parts
of London and throughout the British Isles. Thus, we
observe him at Newgate on Monday, 11 January 1742; Saturday, 4 September 1742; Friday, 10 August 1744; Friday,
20 Nove.nber 1767; Thursday, 18 November 1784; Sunday,
26 December 1784; Saturday, 23 December 1786.

Perhaps Wesley's most striking reaction to Newgate
Prison will be observed from his journal entry for 26
November 1784. "I preached the condemned criminals'

sermon in Newgate. Forty-seven were under sentence of
death. While they were coming in there was something
very awful in the clink of their chains. But no sound
was heard, either from them or the crowded audience, after
the text was named: 'There is joy in heaven over one
sinner that repenteth, more than over ninety and nine
just persons that need not repentence' [Luke 15:7]. The
power of the Lord was eminently present, and most of the
prisoners were in tears. A few days after twenty of
them died at once, five of whom died in peace."

St. Sepulchre's Church, Snow Hill, Holborn. Founded about 1100, St. Sepulchre's Church suffered severely
from the Great Fire of 1666. Renatus Harris the elder
(1640-1715) built the great organ there in 1677, seven
years after Sir Christopher Wren had superintended
the rebuilding of the church (1670). Known formally as
the Church of the Holy Sepulchre without Newgate, St.
Sepulchre's underwent further alteration in 1790 and
again in 1879. Its bell traditionally tolled upon the
occasion of an execution at Newgate Prison. Also, by a
custom that ended in 1744, every condemned prisoner on
his way from Newgate to the gallows at Tyburn stopped
at St. Sepulchre's to receive a nosegay. Until 1882,
the church clock regulated the hours for executions,
and the church bellman would proceed under the walls of
Newgate Prison the night before an execution, ring his
bell, and recite these lines:

> All you that in the condemned hold do lie,
> Prepare you, for to-morrow you shall die;
> Watch all and pray, the hour is drawing near
> That you before the Almighty must appear;
> Examine well, yourselves, in time repent,

That you may not to eternal flames be sent;
And when St. Sepulchre's bell to-morrow tolls,
The Lord above have mercy on your souls.
        Past twelve-o'clock!
During the period 1767, Thomas Weales, D.D., served as
the incumbent there.

Wesley preached at St. Sepulchre's on the evening
of Friday, 25 December 1778. He described the structure
as "one of the largest parish churches in London. It
was warm enough, being sufficiently filled; yet I felt
no weakness or weariness, but was stronger after I had
preached my fourth sermon than I was after the first."
Thus, we may observe a typical day for John Wesley, then
in his eighty-first year. He had begun with a service
at 4:00 a.m. ("as usual") in City Road Chapel (see below,
pp. 138-147), another later in the morning at West
Street Chapel (see above, p. 94), returned to City Road
in the afternoon, and finished at St. Sepulchre's in the
evening.

Snow Hill, Holborn. Snow Hill extends, currently,
from the Central Markets to Holborn Viaduct. The viaduct itself did not see completion until the middle of
the nineteenth century; prior to that, especially during
Wesley's day, roving gangs of aristocratic ruffians
known as Mohocks (a variation on the spelling of the
North American Indian tribe, Mohawks) enjoyed waylaying
elderly women, stuffing them into barrels, and rolling
them down Snow Hill.

Shortly after 4:00 a.m., Sunday, 14 August 1743,
Wesley experienced another of his frequent accidents.
After prayers, he rode to Snow Hill, at which point "the
saddle slipping quite upon my mare's neck, I fell over

her head, and she ran back into Smithfield." However,
on that occasion, at least, he suffered no serious injury.

    St. Andrew's Church, Holborn. St. Andrew's esca-
ped serious damage during the Great Fire of 1666. Nonetheless, Wren rebuilt the structure during 1684-1690,
at a cost of £9000. It thus stood as one of the great
architect's largest parish churches, measuring 105 feet
by 63 feet. Wren left the original tower (built about
1446), which proved to be in better condition than the
main body of the church; however, he did resurface the
tower with Portland stone in 1704. During 1714-1724,
Dr. Henry Sacheverell (1674-1724) served as the rector,
his appointment being a reward of sorts for the trial
that he had undergone. That appointment resulted principally through the influence of Jonathan Swift, who
interested Lord Bolingbroke on Sacheverell's behalf.
Continuing as the rector until his death in 1724,
Sacheverell was buried in the chancel. Also buried there
were the poets John Hughes (1677-1720) and the young
Thomas Chatterton (1752-1770). James Boswell, who attended services at St. Andrew's on Sunday, 22 May 1763,
labeled it "a very fine building. At one end of it is
a window of very elegant painted glass" (Boswell's London Journal 265). In that church, on 26 February 1689,
Samuel Wesley the elder--the father of Samuel, John,
and Charles Wesley--had been ordained priest by Bishop
Henry Compton (1632-1713).

    John Wesley preached at St. Andrew's on Sunday, 22
February 1738, from 1 Corinthians 13:3--"'Though I give
all my goods to feed the poor, and though I give my body
to be burned, and have not charity, it profiteth me

nothing.'Oh, hard sayings! Who can hear them? Here, too,
it seems, I am to preach no more." Interestingly enough,
that was the same sermon that he had preached at Savannah,
Georgia, on 20 February 1736, as he entered upon his unfortunate ministry in and mission to America.

The Church of St. Bartholomew the Great, Smithfield.
One of the oldest of the London churches, St. Bartholomew's dates from around 1123, although only a small portion of the nave and choir remained from the original
Augustinian priory church. Additions and rebuildings
occurred in 1336, 1405-1406, 1515, and 1628; restora-
tions went forward during 1863-1885, 1893, and 1932.

Wesley preached at St. Bartholomew's on Sunday morning, 17 December 1738, and again at 10:00 a.m. on the
following Sunday, 24 December. At the invitation of the
rector, Richard Thomas Bateman, he preached a charity
sermon there on Sunday afternoon, 31 May 1747. Bateman,
one of Wesley's friends at Christ Church, Oxford, had
been converted to the Methodist cause in Wales by Rev.
Howell Davies. His name appears in a very interesting
note sent by Wesley to Dr. Thomas Sherlock (1678-1761),
Bishop of London, which identifies Wesley's status within the Established Church:

> My Lord,--Several years ago the church-
> wardens of St. Bartholomew's informed Dr.
> [Edmund] Gibson [1669-1748], then [1723-
> 1748] Lord Bishop of London, "My Lord, Mr.
> Bateman, our rector, invites Mr. Wesley
> very frequently to preach in his church."
> The Bishop replied, "And what would you
> have me do? I have no right to hinder him.
> Mr. Wesley is a clergyman regularly

ordained and under no ecclesiastical
censure."--I am, my Lord,
             Your Lordship's obedient servant.
       [London, 23 June 1755; Telford, _Letters_ 3:132]
       Returning to the afternoon of 31 May 1747, we will
note that Wesley based his sermon text on 1 _Peter_ 4:7--
The end of all things is at hand; therefore, keep sane
and sober for your prayers. Wesley commented, in his
journal for that Sunday, that "it was with much difficulty that I got in--not only the church itself, but all
the entrances to it, being so thronged with people ready
to tread upon one another. The great noise made me afraid
at first that my labour would be in vain; but. . .
all was still as soon as the service began." Two weeks
later, Wesley returned (Sunday, 14 June 1747), at which
time he paused to admire "the behaviour of the people;
none betrays either lightness or inattention." He was
back there again on yet the following Sunday (21 June)
and preached on the story of Dives and Lazarus.
       Wesley waited an entire year before Bateman issued
him another (and one of the last) invitation to preach
at St. Bartholomew's. At 11:00 a.m., Sunday, 12 June
1748, he noticed that "Deep attention set on every face
while I explained. . .those words, 'Thou art not from
the kingdom of God.'" Three days later (Wednesday, 15
June), he preached there on _Philippians_ 1:21--For to
me to live is Christ, and to die is gain. "How strangely
is the scene changed!" reads the journal entry for
that day. "What laughter and tumult was there, among
the best of the parish, when we preached in a London
church ten years ago! And now all are calm and quietly
attentive, from the least even to the greatest."

St. Bride's Church, Fleet Street. St. Bride's

suffered total destruction from the Great Fire of 1666.
Between 1671 and 1680, Sir Christopher Wren engaged himself in the rebuilding of one of his largest and most
expensive churches, the cost reaching £ 11,430 5s. 11d.
Wren added the spire in 1703, that part of the building
rising some 234 feet and consisting of four octagonal
arcades of diminishing size, topped by an obelisk and
finished by a ball and chain. The bells were installed
in 1710; James Boswell heard their "merry chimes" on 12
January 1763, after a successful love encounter with his
actress friend, Mrs. "Louisa" Lewis (Boswell's London
Journal 137-138). Richard Lovelace was buried in this
church in 1658; the tombstone of novelist Samuel Richardson (1689-1761) lies in the central aisle; Samuel
Pepys (1633-1703) received baptism there; and John
Milton (1608-1674) lived in a house that once overlooked
the churchyard of St. Bride's. Thus, because of its
memorials to men of letters, the church has been termed
"the Cathedral of Fleet Street."
     Wesley came to St. Bride's Church late in the after-
noon (5:30) of Sunday, 29 October 1738, for "prayers,
singing, Bible, singing, prayer."

     Bolt Court, Fleet Street. First mentioned on a map
in 1677, Bolt Court derives its name from the Bolt-in-
Tun on the opposite side of Fleet Street. Samuel Johnson
(1709-1784) moved there from Johnson's Court on Friday,
15 March 1776, where he remained until his death in 1784.
He resided at Number 8, which belonged to Edmund Allen,
a printer, whose house and shop were located in
Bolt Court from 1726 to 1780. Allen died on 28 July
1780. James Boswell found his friend's new house
"much better" than the one in Johnson's Court: "good

rooms and a pretty little spot of background (Boswell:
The Ominous Years 255). Sir John Hawkins (1719-1789),
the other Johnsonian Biographer, informs us (Life of
Johnson 236) that "Behind it [the house] was a garden,
of which he [Johnson] took delight in watering; a room
on the ground floor was assigned to Mrs. [Anna] Williams
[1706-1783, a friend of Johnson], and the whole of
the two pair of stairs floor was made a repository for
his books; one of the rooms thereon being his study."
The house burned to the ground in 1819.

On Thursday, 18 December 1783, at 2:00 p.m., the
eighty year-old John Wesley visited the seventy-
four year-old Samuel Johnson at Number 8 Bolt Court.
He remained there until 4:00 p.m., during which time
(according to Wesley's diary) the two dined and conversed.
Wesley's only comment focused upon his observation
that Johnson "is sinking into the grave by gentle
decay." Unfortunately, Boswell, in his grand biography,
makes no mention of the visit; he spent that winter
back in his native Scotland. However, one cannot
help but reflect opon the latter's introduction, in
that same biography, to the "final chapter," so to
speak, in his subject's life.

> 1784: AETAT. 75]--And now I am arrived
> at the last year of the life of Samuel
> Johnson, a year in which, although passed in
> severe indisposition, he nevertheless gave
> many evidences of the continuance of those
> wondrous powers of mind, which raised him
> so high in the intellectual world. His con-
> versation and his letters of this year were
> in no respect inferiour to those of former
> years.   (Life of Johnson 1263)

Notwithstanding, one year following Wesley's visit, on

13 December 1784, Johnson died in the house in Bolt
Court.

    <u>Gutter Lane, Cheapside</u>. Gutter Lane, a corruption
of "Guthrum's Lane" (from an early association with
King Alfred's godson), lies between Cheapside on the
south and Maiden Lane on the north.   The stalls of German
merchants, or <u>Easterlings</u>, were located there; their
so-called "good money" gave rise to the British monetary
term <u>sterling</u>.
    Wesley addressed a religious society in Gutter Lane
on Thursday, 21 September 1738, but he "could not declare the mighty works of God there. . . ." He returned,
presumably for the same purpose, at 6:00 p.m.,
Thursday, 2 November 1738.

    <u>St. Luke's Church, Old Street</u>. Built in 1732 from
designs by John James and Nicholas Hawksmoor (1661-1736),
St. Luke's Church received consecration on 16 October
1733. The tower, diminishing in the upper stages,was surmounted by a tall fluted obelisk instead of the traditional spire. William Nicholls, its first rector, also
served as vicar of St. Giles Church, Cripplegate.Wesley
remarked, on Sunday, 3 August 1740, that "our parish
church was such a sight as, I believe, was never seen
there before: several hundred communicants, from whose
very faces one might judge that they indeed sought Him
that was crucified." The diary records his attendance at
St. Luke's on Sunday, 5 October 1740; Sunday, 2 November
1740; Wednesday, 4 February 1741; Ash Wednesday, 11 February 1741; Friday, 27 March 1741; and Sunday, 29 March
1741.

Wesley preached a charity sermon at St. Luke's on
Sunday, 29 December 1778. "I doubt," he noted, "whether it was ever so crowded before; and the fear of God
seemed to possess the whole audience." Several years later (Sunday, 27 November 1785), he preached there to
another large audience on Romans 13:11--Besides this
you know what hour it is, how it is full time now for
you to wake from sleep. For salvation is nearer to us
now than when we first believed. . . . Finally, he delivered a sermon at St. Luke's on Sunday, 27 December
1789, to "a very numerous congregation on 'The Spirit and
the Bride say, Come.'" (Revelation 22:17) Of more
than passing interest is his comment on that day: "So
are the tables turned, that I have now more invitations
to preach [in London] churches than I can accept of."

Beech Lane, Whitecross Street. At Beech Lane--be-
tween Redcross Street by Barbican, and Whitecross
Street--a large religious society met, beginning sometime in 1738. When in London, Wesley frequently preached
in this area, usually on Saturdays. Thus, we find
him there on 13 January 1739, 17 February 1739, and 11
December 1762--all of those dates falling on a Saturday.
He described the meeting of 11 December 1762 in a letter
to his brother Charles: "Like a bear garden; full of
noise, brawling, cursing, swearing, blasphemy, and confusion. Those who prayed were partly the occasion of
this, by their horrid screaming and unscriptural, en-
thusiastic expressions. Being determined either 'to
mend them or to end them, I removed the meeting to the
Foundery" (Telford, Letters 4:196). The meeting took
place in the house of John Guildord (d. 1777), one of
John Wesley's aged and faithful preachers and itinerant
travelers. He, himself, had been converted at the

Foundery. "Surely," wrote Wesley in his journal for Whit
Sunday, 18 May 1777, "never before did a man of so weak
talents do so much good! He died, as he lived, in the
full triumph of faith, vehemently rejoicing and praising
God."

Quaker Meeting-House, Bull-and-Mouth Street. Bull-
and-Mouth Street, a cross-route leading from St. Martin's-
le-Grand to Butcher Hall Lane, commemorates, in
its corruption of Boulogne Moth, the capture of Boulogne
Harbor by Henry VIII in 1544. On that street, the Bull
and Mouth Inn stood as one of the principal centers from
which coaches commenced their journeys to the provinces.
There, George Fox (1624-1691), the founder of the Society
of Friends (Quakers), preached during the period of
the Commonwealth (1649-1660). After the restoration of
Charles II in 1660, the inn quickly transformed into a
place for the persecution of Quakers.

      On the Bull-and-Mouth Street stood a meeting-house
built originally for the Quakers, who occupied it in
1665, five years after Charles II returned to the
English throne. The sect relinquished the building in
1760, when Sandemanians moved there. Wesley first preached
in the meeting-house on Friday, 10 September 1756;
he returned the following Sunday (19 September) and
again on Friday, 17 February 1758--a public fast-day.
His final appearance at the Quaker Meeting-House came
on Wednesday, 21 December 1763: "I took my leave of the
Bull-and-Mouth, a barren, uncomfortable place, where
much pains has been taken for several years--I fear to
little purpose." From Wesley's Sermon Register we may
observe other occasions on which he preached at the old
Quaker meeting-house, as well as the texts upon which he

based his sermons:

(?) October 1756

> 1 Peter 2:1--So put away all malice and all
> guile and insincerity and envy and all slan-
> der.
>
> Revelation 20:8--. . .and will come out to de-
> ceive the nations which are at the four cor-
> ners of the earth, that is Gog and Magog,
> to gather them for battle; their number is
> like the sand of the sea.

(?) November 1756

> John 17:3--And this is eternal life, that they
> know thee the only true God, and Jesus
> Christ whom thou hast sent.
>
> Romans 3:22--. . .the righteousness of God
> through faith in Jesus Christ for all who
> believe. For there is no distinction. . . .
>
> Hebrews 12:28: Therefore, let us be grateful
> for receiving a kingdom that cannot be sha-
> ken, and thus let us offer to God accepta-
> ble worship, with reverence and awe. . . .
>
> Romans 8:33--Who shall bring any charge against
> God's elect? It is God who justifies. . . .
>
> Galatians 3:22--But the scripture consigned
> all things to sin, that what was promised
> to faith in Jesus Christ might be given to
> those who believe.

(?) February 1757

> Mark 12:34--And when Jesus saw that he ans-
> wered wisely, he said to him, "You are not
> far from the kingdom of God." And after
> that no one dared to ask him any question.
>
> Psalms 147:3--He heals the brokenhearted, and
> binds up their wounds.

Luke 15:7--Just so, I tell you, there will be
more joy in heaven over one sinner who repents than over ninety-nine righteous persons who need no repentence.

Job 7:18--. . .dost visit him every morning,
and test him every moment?

Hebrews 8:11--And they shall not teach every
one his fellow or or every one his brother,
saying, "Know the Lord," for all shall know
me, from the least of them to the greatest.

John 11:48--If we let him go on thus, every
one will believe in him, and the Romans
will come and destroy both our holy places
and our nation.

Isaiah 1:3--The ox knows its owner, and the
ass its master's crib; but Israel does not
know, my people does not understand.

1 Corinthians 1:24--. . .but to those who are
called both Jews and Greeks, Christ the
power of God and wisdom of God.

Luke 12:42--And the Lord said, "Who then is
the faithful and wise steward, whom his
master will set over his household, to give
them their portion of food at the proper
time?

Wednesday, 30 March 1757

John 7:37--On the last day of the feast, the
great day, Jesus stood up and proclaimed,
"If any one thirst, let him come to me and
drink.

2 Corinthians 5:15--And he died for all, that
those who might live no longer for themselves, but for him who for their sake died
and was raised.

Luke 24:8--And they remembered his words. . .
Friday, 11 November 1757
    2 Corinthians 5:18--We are of good courage,
       and we would rather be away from the body
       and at home with the Lord.
    1 Peter 1:24--. . .for "All flesh is like
       grass and all its glory like the flower of
       grass. The grass withers, and the flower
       falls. . . ."
    Romans 12:21--Do not be overcome by evil, but
       overcome evil with good.
(?) November 1757
    John 11:49--But one of them, Caiaphas, who was
       high priest that year, said to them, "You
       know nothing at all. . . ."
    Titus 2:15--Declare these things; exhort and
       reprove with all authority. Let no one
       disregard you.
    Galatians 5:18--But if you are led by the
       Spirit, you are not under the law.
    2 Corinthians 5:18--All this is from God, who
       through Christ reconciled us to himself and
       gave us the ministry of reconciliation. . .
    Ecclesiastes 11:1--Cast your bread upon the
       waters, that you will find it after many
       days.
    Mark 12:34--See above for February 1757 (p.
       120).
    Mark 4:26--And he said, "The kingdom of God
       is as if a man should scatter seed upon the
       ground. . . ."
(?) December 1757
    Deuteronomy 10:12--"And now, Israel, what
       does the Lord your God require of you,

but to fear the Lord your God, to walk in
all his ways, to love him, to serve the
Lord your God with all your heart and with
all your soul. . . ."

James 2:22--You see that faith was active,
along with his works, and faith was completed by works. . . .

John 3:8--The wind blows where it wills, and
you hear the sound of it, but you do not
know whence it comes or whither it goes;
so it is with every one who is born of the
Spirit.

Friday, 3 February 1758

Ezekiel 37:1--The hand of the Lord was upon me,
and he brought me out by the Spirit of the
Lord, and set me down in the midst of the
valley; it was full of bones.

Galatians 5:25--If we live by the Spirit,
let us also walk by the Spirit.

Friday, 10 February 1758

Colossians 3:9--Do not lie to one another,
seeing that you have put off the old nature with its practices. . . .

Colossians 4:5--Conduct yourselves wisely toward outsiders, making the most of the
time.

Isaiah 58:5-6--Is such the fast that I choose,
a day for a man to humble himself? Is it
to bow down his head like a rush, and to
spread sackcloth and ashes under him? Will
you call this a fast, and a day acceptable
to the Lord? Is not this the fast that I
choose: to loose the bonds of wickedness,
to undo the thongs of the yoke, to let the

oppressed go free, and to break every yoke?

Matthew 22:4--Again, he sent other servants,
saying, "Tell those who are invited, 'Behold, I have made ready my dinner, my oxen
and my fat calves are killed, and everything is ready; come to the marriage feast.'

Friday, 3 March 1758

1 Corinthians 13:13--So faith, hope, love
abide, these three; but the greatest of
these is love.

Lamentations 3:39--Why should a living man complain, a man, about the punishment of his
sins?

Psalms 101:2--I will give heed to the way that
is blameless. O when wilt thou come to me?
I will walk with integrity of heart within
my house. . . .

Saturday, 25 November 1758

2 Timothy 2:6--It is the hard-working farmer
who ought to have the first share of the
crops.

Colossians 3:22--Slaves, obey in everything
those who are your earthly masters, not
with eyeservice , as men-pleasers, but in
singleness of heart, fearing the Lord.

1 John 3:1--See what love the Father has given
us, that we should be called children
of God; and so we are. The reason why the
world does not know us is that it does not
know him.

1 Peter 3:8--Finally, all of you, have unity
of spirit, sympathy, love of the brethren,
a tender heart and a humble mind.

Tuesday, 5 December 1758

Matthew 18:15--If your brother sins against
you, go and tell him his fault, between

you and him alone. If he listens to you,
you have gained a brother.

Sunday, 31 December 1758

Genesis 49:4--Unstable as water, you shall
not have pre-eminence because you went up
to your father's bed; then you defiled it;
you went up to my couch!

Isaiah 1:3--See above for February 1757 (p.
121).

Acts 18:19--And then they came to Ephesus, and
he left them there; but he himself went into the synagogue and argued with the Jews.

Friday, 30 November 1759

Psalms 50:13--Do I eat the flesh of bulls, or
drink the blood of goats?

2 Peter 3:8--But do not ignore this one fact,
beloved, that with the Lord one day is as a
thousand years, and a thousand years as one
day.

Acts 10:35--. . .but in every nation any one
who fears him and does what is right is acceptable to him.

2 Peter 3:17-18--You therefore, beloved, knowing this beforehand, beware lest you be carried away with the error of lawless men and
lose your own stability. But grow in the
grace and knowledge of our Lord and Savior,
Jesus Christ. To him be the glory both now
and to the day of eternity.

Friday, 11 January 1760

Hebrews 7:19--. . .on the other hand, a better
hope is introduced, through which we draw
near to God.

Romans 12:2--Do not be conformed to this world,
but be transformed by the renewal of your

mind, that you may prove what is the will
of God, what is good and acceptable and
perfect.

Hebrews 9:13--For if the sprinkling of defiled
persons with the blood of goats and bulls
and with the ashes of a heifer sanctifies
for the purification of the flesh. . . .

Romans 14:23--But now, since I no longer have
any room for work in these regions, and
since I have longed for many years to come
to you. . . .

James 3:2--For we all make many mistakes, and
if any one makes no mistakes in what he
says, he is a perfect man, able to bridle
the whole body, also.

1 Corinthians 7-35--I say this for your own
benefit, not to lay any restraint upon you,
but to promote good order and to secure
your undivided devotion to the Lord.

Romans 14:7--None of us lives to himself, and
none of us dies to himself.

1 Corinthians 7:37--But whoever is firmly
established in his heart, being under no
necessity but having his desire under
control, and has determined this in his heart,
to keep her as his betrothed, he will do
well.

Wednesday, 6 February 1760

1 Corinthians 7:29--I mean, brethren, the appointed time has grown very short; from now
on, let those who have wives live as though
they had none. . . .

Joel 2:13--". . .and rend your hearts and not
your garments." Return to the Lord your
God, for he is gracious and merciful, slow

to anger, and abounding in steadfast love,
and repents of evil.

Psalms 35:27--Let those who desire my vindi-
cation shout for joy and be glad, and say
evermore, "Great is the Lord, who delights
in the welfare of his servant!"

Galatians 3:20--Now an intermediary implies
more than one; but God is one.

Thursday, 7 February 1760

1 John 3:22--. . .and we receive from him
whatever we ask, because we keep his commandments and do what pleases him.

Mark 9:23--And Jesus said to him, "If you can!
All things are possible to him who believes."

Galatians 6:12--It is those who want to make a
good showing in the flesh that would compel
you to be circumcised, and only in order
that they may not be persecuted for the
cross of Christ.

Luke 10:42--. . .one thing is needful. Mary
has chosen the good portion, which shall
not be taken away from her.

1 Peter 1:9--As the outcome of your faith you
obtain the salvation of your souls.

Wednesday, 19 November 1760

Proverbs 3:17--Her ways are ways of pleasant-
ness, and all her paths are peace.

Hebrews 2:1--Therefore, we must pay the closer
attention to what we have heard, lest we
drift away from it.

Ecclesiastes 3:18--I said in my heart with regard to the sons of men that God is testing
them to show them that they are but beasts.

Galatians 3:22--See above for November 1756, p.

120).

Wednesday, 11 November 1761

Galatians 4:4--But when the time had fully
come, God sent forth his Son, born of woman, born under the law. . . .

Psalms 75:1-2--We give thanks to thee, O God;
we give thanks; we call on thy name and recount the wondrous deeds. At the set time
which I appoint, I will judge with equity.

Luke 17:20--Being asked by the Pharisees when
the kingdom of God was coming, he answered
them, "The kingdom of God is not coming with
signs to be observed. . . ."

Aldersgate Street. In his journal, Wesley states
that on Wednesday evening, 20 September 1738, he "spoke
the truth in love at a society in Aldersgate Street.
Some contradicted at first, but not long; so that nothing
but love appeared at our parting." The exact location of that particular Church of England religious
society, as well as its composition, are unknown. It may
have been a Horneck or a newer Moravian society. Concerning the former, as early as 1678, "several young men
of the church of England, in the cities of London and
Westminster, inspired by the preaching of Dr. Anthony
Horneck in the Savoy Chapel, were touched with a very
affecting sense of their sins, and began to apply themselves in a very serious manner to religious thoughts
and purposes. Thus was launched the first of the
Anglican Religious Societies which Howell Harris was to
claim as the model for his own societies in the later
1730s, and which were to provide Whitefield, the Moravians, and the Wesleys with some of their earliest

audiences and their first converts" (Watts 423).

Anthony Horneck (1641-1696), a native of Bacharach,
in the Lower Palatinate, studied first at Heidelberg,
and then entered Queen's College, Oxford, in 1663. He
then became vicar of All Saints, Oxford (1663); prebendary of Exeter, of Westminster, of Wells; preacher of
the Savoy Chapel (1671). For a concise but clear discussion of Horneck and the early London religious societies, see Curnock, Wesley's Journal, 2:71-72, note 1.
His portrait may be found in the same volume, p. 236.

At any rate, John Wesley met with that particular
religious society at least once more, for prayer and
sermon, on Sunday afternoon (3:00), 11 February 1738.

Trinity Hall, Little Britain, Aldersgate Street.
Little Britain commemorates the mansion of John Duke of
Bretagne and Earl of Richmond, and is a tributary of
Aldersgate (on the left). During the reigns of the Stuarts
and until 1725, it served as a center for booksellers.
In 1711, in Little Britain, the Spectator papers
of Addison and Steele were first printed, and a year
later, 1712, a three year-old infant named Samuel
Johnson stayed there with John Nicholson, the printer.
Young Sam's father, Michael Johnson, himself a booksell-
er, perhaps had done business with Nicholson (Clifford,
Young Sam Johnson 11). During the greater part of 1739,
Wesley lodged at the house of Mr. John Bray, a brazier,
in Little Britain. Charles Wesley, who had lodged there
in 1738, referred to Bray as "an illiterate mechanic"
(Telford, Life of Charles Wesley 70), but, nonetheless,
held him in high regard as an honest and pious individual.

Trinity Hall exists as one of the two rival sites

claiming the honor as the scene of John Wesley's religious conversion, occurring on Wednesday, 24 May 1738
(see immediately below under Hall House, Nettleton
Court). Originally, Trinity Hall formed part of a religious house belonging to the French abbots of Clugni.
In 1738, the lower portion of the building did service
as a coffee-house, while the upper rooms functioned as
a chapel for a congregation of Nonjurors; they, in turn,
tranferred the building to the Church of England religious societies.

Hall House, Nettleton Court, Aldersgate Street.
Hall House, Nettleton Court, stood on the north side of
Aldersgate Street. In addition to Trinity Hall (see immediately above, pp. 129-130), it claims the honor as the
place of John Wesley's religious conversion on Wednesday,
24 May 1738. A religious society met there regularly,
and included James Hutton as one of its members. In May
1738, Wesley lived in Hutton's house, located at Great
Wild Street. Possibly, he accompanied his host to the
meeting in Nettleton Court instead of going to Trinity
Hall. Indeed, the entry in Wesley's journal for 24 May
1738 appears rather vague: "In the evening I went very
unwillingly to a society in Aldersgate Street, where one
was reading Luther's preface to the Epistle to the Romans
About a quarter before nine, while he was describing the change which God works in the heart through
faith in Christ, I felt my heart strangely warmed. I
felt I did trust in Christ, Christ alone, for salvation:
and an assurance was given me, that He had taken away my
sins --   even mine, and saved me from the the law of
sin and death."
     One must remember that Wesley's religious conver-

sion occurred less than four months after his return
from Georgia--his return from the failure of that mission and the abortive love affair with Sophia Christina
Hopkey. The experience at Aldersgate Street took place
but three days following Charles Wesley's religious conversion at John Bray's in Little Britain. In June 1738,
John Wesley left England to visit among Nicholaus von
Zinzendorf's Moravian Brethren.

St. Anne's Church, Gresham Street, Aldersgate.
Built by Wren between 1676 and 1687 at a cost of £ 2448
0s. 11d., St. Anne's had (previous to the Great Fire)
been known as St. Anne's near Aldersgate, St. Anne in
the Willows, St. Anne and St. Agnes within Aldersgate.
St. Anne's would have been the parish church of John
Bray (see pp. 129-130), the brazier in Little Britain
with whom Wesley lodged in late 1738 and throughout most
of 1739. Wesley preached at St. Anne's on Sunday morning, 14 May 1738, and was "quickly apprised that at St.
Anne's. . .I am to preach no more." He did attend there
early Sunday morning, 24 September 1738, for "prayers,
sermon, communion," and again for the same purposes on
Sunday morning, 29 October 1738. The Rev. Fifield Allen,
B.D., served as the incumbent of St. Anne's in 1738.

Old Jewry, Meeting-house Court. A noted Presbyterian
house of worship, Old Jewry sponsored several Nonconformist lectureships. There, Rev. Nathaniel Gardner
(1684-1768) presented, in 1723, "The Credibility of the
Gospel History." Between 1727 and 1757, the Old Jewry
lectures appeared, published in seventeen volumes. The
Presbyterian congregation remained until 1808, when it

moved to Jewin Street, Barbican.

On Sunday, 24 December 1786, John Wesley "was desired
to preach at the Old Jewry. But the church was cold,
and so was the congregation." He chose for his sermon
text on that occasions Acts 24:25--And as he argued
about justice and self-control and future judgment, Felix
was alarmed and said, "Go away for the present; when
I have an opportunity I will summon you."

Church of St. Lawrence Jewry, Guildhall Yard, Gresham Street. St. Lawrence Jewry, destroyed by the Great
Fire, rose again from the plans of Sir Christopher Wren
between 1671 and 1680. Built at a cost of £11,870, it
thus stood as the most expensive of all the London churches rebuilt by that noted architect.

John Wesley preached at St. Lawrence early on Sunday morning, 26 February 1738. More than two months later, on Sunday, 7 May 1738, he returned: "I was enabled
to speak strong words. . .and was therefore the less surprised at being informed I was not to preach any more"
at that church. Nonetheless, we find him there on Sunday, 8 October 1738; Sunday, 24 December 1738; and Sunday, 14 January 1739--on all instances for "prayers,
sermon, communion. . . ." Obviously, the incumbent held
forth in the pulpit on those occasions.

Church of St. Michael, Basingshall Street. St.
Michael, Basingshall (commonly pronounced Bassishaw) stood
as another of those London churches destroyed in the
Great Fire and rebuilt by Wren--on this instance between
1676 and 1679. Densely surrounded, it existed as the
only one of Wren's buildings with a decided deficiency

in the foundation. Constructed of brick, and with a
steeple one hundred and forty feet high, it eventually
got out of repair, closed its doors in 1893, and fell to
demolition in 1899. The parish then united with St.
Lawrence Jewry (p. 132).

Wesley preached at St. Michael's on five occasions:
Wednesday, 25 October 1738; Wednesday, 8 November 1738;
Wednesday, 27 December 1738; Wednesday, 3 January 1739;
and Wednesday, 10 February 1739.

St. Stephen's Church, Colman Street. Sir Christopher Wren rebuilt St. Stephen's in 1676, at a cost of
only £7652 13s. It stood as a plain building, without
aisles, measuring seventy-five feet in length and thirty-
five feet in breadth. The churchyard gate, adorned with
skulls, commemorated its having been one of the principal burial grounds for victims of the Great Plague of
1664-1665. Rev. Dr. John Hay served as the vicar from
1715 to 1753.

Between the autumns of 1739 and 1740, Wesley attended morning service at St. Stephen's on a fairly consis-
tent basis: Sunday, 16 September1739; Sunday, 20 July
1740; Sunday, 27 July 1740; Sunday, 10 August 1740; Sunday, 17 August 1740; Sunday, 24 August 1740; Sunday, 31
August 1740; Sunday, 14 September 1740; Sunday, 21 September 1740; and Sunday, 28 September 1740.

Church of St. Vedast, Foster Lane, Cheapside. Another of Wren's rebuildings (1670-1673) of a church destroyed by the Great Fire of 1666, St. Vedast achieved
status because of its distinguished tower, built between
1694 and 1697: a concave stage, a convex stage, and--
surmounting those--an obelisk-shaped spire, ball, finial

and vane. Internally, the church proved rather
small, measuring sixty-nine feet by twenty-one feet.
The incumbent, Rev. Thomas L. Barbault, invited Wesley
to preach at St. Vedast on Sunday, 10 November 1776.
The Methodist leader addressed the congregation "on
those words in the Gospel for the day (how little regarded even by men that fear God!), 'Render to Caesar
that things that are Caesar's, and to God the things
that are God's'" (Matthew 22:21).

    Hoxton. The district of Hoxton, beyond Shoreditch,
became known, in the eighteenth century, for its bal-
samic wells and gardens.   Hoxton Square, laid out
toward the end of the seventeenth century, housed one of
the earliest Dissenting academies. Prohibited from attending the universities, Presbyterian and Independent
(now known as Congregational) ministers received their
theological training there, and the sons of Dissenters
could gain some knowledge in the liberal disciplines.
The parish church, built in 1732, cost approximately
£12,980.
    John Wesley visited Hoxton on Friday, 6 October
1738, to converse with the Rev. Arthur Bedford (1668-
1745)--Chaplain to the Prince of Wales and to the Haberdashers' Hospital, theologian, promoter of church music,
astronomical theorist, Oriental scholar, and outspoken
opponent of the English stage. Bedford opposed, from
the pulpit, Wesley's doctrine of assurance on the ground
that it tended to foster spiritual pride. On that particular October afternoon, the latter "went to the Rev.
Mr. Bedford, to tell him, between me and him alone, of
the injury he had done both to God and his brother by
preaching and printing that very weak sermon on assurance,

which was an *ignoratio elenchi* from beginning to end;
seeing the assurance we preach is of quite another from
what he writes against. We speak of an assurance of our
present pardon; not as he does, of our final perseverance."

In the late summer and fall of 1740, Wesley made
four trips to Hoxton for what he termed prayer and conversation: Monday, 18 August; Monday, 25 August, Saturday, 30 September; and Wednesday, 1 October. Also, on
Sunday, 3 May 1741, he preached there (at Hoxton parish
church?) on **Philippians** 3--Finally, my brethren, rejoice
in the Lord. To write the same things to you is not irksome to me, and is safe for you.

Wesley spent the period between Monday, 16 December
1752, through Friday, 20 December 1762, at the home of
William Marriott in Hoxton; there he transcribed the names
of those belonging to the London Methodist societies,
entering them into notebooks. William Marriott--a successful London stockbroker, a generous donor, and a prominent London Methodist--appears in John Wesley's will
as an executor. The Marriotts did considerable writing
and transcription for Wesley; Thomas Marriott became one
of the earliest collectors of Wesley's letters and notebooks.

Charles Square, Hoxton. In the eighteenth century,
Charles Square presented to the eye a pleasant though
small tract, located south of Charles Street and near
the Hoxton market. George Whitefield conducted several
open-air meetings there, while John Wesley noted the following occasions upon which he preached in the square:
Sunday, 17 May 1741

John 14--"Let not your hearts be troubled;

believe in God, believe also in me. . . ."
Sunday, 7 June 1741. Wesley noted "A violent storm
began about the middle of the sermon. . . ."

> John 5:25--Truly, truly, I say to you, the
> hour is coming, and now is, when the dead
> will hear the voice of the Son of God, and
> those who hear will live.

Sunday, 28 June 1741. Wesley preached at Charles
Square late in the afternoon "to the largest congregation that I believe was ever seen there. . . . As soon
as I had done, I quite lost my voice.   But it was immediately restored. . . ."

> Acts 26:27--King Agrippa, do you believe the
> prophets? I know that you believe.

Sunday, 12 July 1741. In the midst of the sermon,
"a great shout began. Many of the rabble had brought up
an ox, which they were vehemently labouring to drive
among the people. But their labour was in vain: for in
spite of them all, he ran round and round, one way and
the other, and at length broke through the midst of them
clear away, leaving us calmly rejoicing and praising
God." He based his text upon

> Micah 6--Hear what the Lord says: Arise, plead
> your case before the mountains, and let the
> hills hear your voice.

When Wesley had no animals with which to contend,
he always found a plentiful supply of hecklers at
Charles Square. He preached there on Sunday, 20 September
1741, on "'This is life eternal, to know Thee, the only
true God, and Jesus Christ whom Thou hast sent [John 17:
3].' I trust God blessed His word. The scoffers stood
abashed, and opened not their mouth." When he preached
there on Sunday, 9 May 1742, to a large gathering, "Many
of the baser people would fain have interrupted; but they

found, after a time, that it was a lost labour. One,
who was more serious, was (as she afterwards confessed)
exceedingly angry at them. But she was quickly rebuked,
by a stone which light upon her forehead and struck her
down to the ground. In that moment her anger was at an
end, and love only filled her heart."

St. Leonard's Church, High Street, Shoreditch.
After a part of its tower gave way in 1716, during a
service, George Dance the elder rebuilt St. Leonard's
Church during 1736-1740. A double flight of stairs led
to a Doric portico, while the tower housed a series of
fine columns: two open stories, with a spire placed on
four balls above the upper one.

John Wesley preached at St. Leonard's on Sunday, 13
November 1785, noting in his journal that the "congregation was very numerous, and the collection unusually
large." He based his text upon 1 Corinthians 13:1--If
I speak in the tongues of men and angels, but have not
love, I am a noisy gong or a clanging cymbal. At the
invitation of the vicar, Rev. John Blake, he preached
a charity sermon there on Sunday, 15 November 1789, on
John 7:37--On the last day of the feast, the great day,
Jesús stood up and proclaimed, "If any one thirst, let
him come to me and drink. . . ."

Shoreditch Workhouse. On Tuesday, 24 June 1783,
Wesley, in the midst of one of his journeys to Holland,
viewed a new workhouse in Amsterdam. He remarked that
the building "much resembles Shoreditch Workhouse; only
it is considerably larger. . . ." Although neither the

diary nor the journal makes mention of a visit to the
workhouse at Shoreditch, Wesley obviously knew of and
had seen the structure. The problem, however, focuses
upon whether he meant to compare the institution in
Amsterdam with the old or the new Shoreditch Workhouse.
According to the Commons Journals for 21 January 1774,
earlier that month the parish of St. Leonard's, Shoreditch (see p. 137), had petitioned for a Bill to buy
ground for a new workhouse, as officials of the "old"
structure had been obliged to put thirty-nine children
into three beds, "by which means they contract disorders
from each other" (George 219).

Cock Lane, Shoreditch. Cock Lane, Shoreditch,
proves not at all the place made famous by the "Cock
Lane Ghost," with which Samuel Johnson became involved.
Those mysterious noises came from Number 33 Cock Lane,
off Giltspur Street, Smithfield.
Wesley's diary revealed that he twice visited Cock
Lane, York Street, for tea and conversation: Thursday,
18 September 1740; Tuesday, 7 October 1740.

City Road Chapel ("The New Chapel"), City Road. On
Friday, 1 March 1776, John Wesley recorded in his journal that, "As we cannot depend on having the Foundery
[see separate entry in this section, below] long, we met
to consult about building a new chapel. Our petition
to the City for a piece of ground lies before their committee. . . ." Thus began the arrangements for a new
Methodist house of worship in London. The lease on the
King's Foundery had not yet expired, but the entire district of Finsbury and Moorfields would be required by

the City for redevelopment. In fact, by summer 1776,
such building had already gone forward, and the leaders
of the London Methodist society thus considered the
construction of a new chapel a matter of urgency. The
committee of the society met again on Friday, 19 July
1776; three additional meetings (beginning Friday, 2
August 1776) produced subscriptions amounting to more
than one thousand pounds.

The land selected by the London Methodists formed
part of several plots of fields that functioned as ten-
ter grounds (ground occupied by tenters [or frames] for
stretching cloth). Located approximately two hundred
yards to the northwest of the King's Foundery, the new
site extended northwest to Old Street Road. Wesley chose
the portion nearest the Foundery as the actual building
site. Originally, the society trustees, yielding to
pressures from the City Corporation, planned to erect a
row of houses along the front of the property, leaving
an archway through which to approach the chapel. However, the City discovered that it required a strip of
land for the construction of a new City Road. The
Methodist trustees granted that issue, and the Corporation, in turn, struck from the lease its demand for the
row of houses. Not until 1779 did the society trustees
actually sign the land lease; the City set the duration
for the agreement at fifty-nine years.

On 18 October 1776, in a letter to his brother
Charles, John Wesley computed the cost of the project
(and at that time he included the houses and the chapel)
at"upward of six thousand pounds" (Telford, Letters 6:
235). By Friday, 29 November 1776, the trustees had
reached an agreement on the building plans. Thus, Monday, 21 April 1777, "was the day appointed for laying
the foundation of the chapel. The rain befriended us

much by keeping away thousands who purposed to be there.
But there were still great multitudes that it was with
great difficulty I got through them to lay the first
stone. Upon this was a plate of brass (covered with
another stone), on which was engraved, 'This was laid by
Mr. John Wesley, on April 21, 1777.'" Wesley further
informs us that, on Monday, 11 August 1777, "the building. . .is now ready for the roof"; Sunday, 1 November
1778, "was the day appointed for opening the new chapel
in City Road. It is perfectly neat, but not fine; and
contains far more people than the Foundery: I believe,
together with the morning chapel [see below, this sec-
tion], as many as the Tabernacle." For the opening sermon, Wesley addressed the congregation "on part of
Solomon's prayer at the dedication of the Temple [1 Kings
8]; and both in the morning and afternoon (when I
preached on the hundred forty and four thousand standing
with the Lamb on Mount Zion), God was eminently present
in the midst of the congregation."

A newspaper article, preserved in the Richmond
College interleaved edition of Wesley's Journal, yielded
this description of the first evening service at City
Road Chapel:

> The first quarter of an hour his [Wes-
> ley's] sermon was addressed to his numerous
> female auditory on the absurdity of the
> enormous dressing of their heads; and his
> religious labours have so much converted
> the women who attended at that place of wor-
> ship that widows, wives, and young ladies
> appeared on Sunday without curls, without
> flying caps, and without feathers; and our
> correspondent further says that the female
> sex never made a more pleasing appearance.
>
> (Journal 6:216)

Related to that account is the fact that for years, the
men sat on one side of the Chapel during public worship
service, while the women occupied the opposite side.

What follows constitutes a summary of John Wesley's
major activities , as well as the Scriptural sources of
his sermon texts, at City Road Chapel from the end of
1779 until his death in March 1791:

Monday, 13 December 1779. The first two persons
were interred in the City Road burial ground: Elizabeth
Fisher of Leicester Fields, whose grave was at the
northeast corner of the ground; and Susanna Debonair, a
French refugee.

Sunday, 5 November 1780. Wesley's sermon focused
upon Luke 9:55--But he turned and rebuked them. In his
text, he argued "that, supposing the Papists to be her-
etics, schismatics, wicked men, enemies to us, and to
our Church and nation; yet we ought not to persecute,
to kill, hurt, or grieve them, but barely to prevent
their doing hurt." Supposedly, he had at that time been
asked by Lord George Gordon (1751-1793) to visit him in
the Tower of London. Gordon, of course, had led the
riots in June 1780 against the Catholic Relief Act and
was then awaiting trial for high treason.

Tuesday, 1 January 1782. "in the evening," noted
Wesley, "many of us at the new chapel rejoiced in God
our Saviour."

Sunday, 6 July 1783. After his return from a jour-
ney to Holland, Wesley addressed members of the London
Methodist society, recounting the details of his visit.
City Road Chapel served as the principal site for
Methodist meetings and conferences, as well as a center
for public worship.

Saturday, 25 December 1784
       Matthew 1:21--. . .she will bear a son, and

you shall call his name Jesus; for he will
save his people from their sins.
Sunday, 7 August 1785
Hebrews 10:19--Therefore, brethren, since we
have confidence to enter the sanctuary by
the blood of Jesus. . . .
Monday, 5 December, through Saturday, 10 December
1985. Wesley spent the week soliciting funds for the
poor men who had been employed in finishing the City
Road Chapel. "It is true I am not obliged to do this;
but if I do it not, nobody else will."
Sunday, 5 February 1786
Isaiah 59:1-2--Behold, the Lord's hand is not
shortened, but it cannot save, or his ear
dull, that it cannot hear; but your iniquities have made a separation between you and
your God, and your sins have hid his face
from you so that he does not hear.
Monday, 1 January 1787
Genesis 17:1--When Abram was ninety-nine years
old the Lord appeared to Abram and said to
him, "I am God Almighty; walk before me and
be blameless.
Sunday, 25 February 1787
Ephesians 2:8--For by grace you have been saved
through faith; and this is not your own
doing, it is the gift of God. . . .
Sunday, 21 October 1787
Micah 6:8--And the remnant of Jacob shall be
among the nations, in the midst of many
peoples, like a lion among the beasts of
the forest, like a young lion among the
flocks of sheep, which, when it goes
through, treads down and tears in pieces,

and there is none to deliver.

Friday, 21 December 1787. Wesley received two proposals from the London Methodist societies concerning
the seating arrangements at both West Street and City
Road chapels: first, that families of men and women be
permitted to sit together; second, that persons be
given permanent rights to pews.He considered both of
those petitions as attempts to overthrow "the discipline
which I have been establishing for fifty years." In
the end, his rules held firm.

Monday, 24 December 1787. The group that had set
forth the proposals three days earlier met again and,
essentially, withdrew its requests. Those members
determined that the men and women would continue to sit
on opposite sides of the chapel and that no one could
lay claim to any pew as his own.

Sunday, 20 July 1788

> Hebrews 5:12--For though by this time you
> ought to be teachers, you need some one to
> teach you again the first principles of
> God's word. You need milk, not solid
> food. . . .

Thursday, 29 July, through Wednesday, 6 August 1788.
The forty-fifth conference of the Methodist societies
occurred during this period. Wesley preached at City
Road Chapel every evening of the Conference.

Sunday, 3 August 1788

> 2 Kings 5:10--And Elisha sent a messenger to
> him saying, "Go and wash in the Jordan
> seven times, and your flesh shall be
> restored, and you shall be clean."

> Hebrews 6:11--And we desire each one of you to
> show the same earnestness in realizing the
> full assurance of hope until the end. . . .

Sunday, 10 August 1788. Wesley preached in the
evening to a large audience on Hebrews 13:20--Now may
the God of peace who brought again from the dead our
Lord Jesus, the great shepherd of the sheep,by the blood
of the eternal covenant, equip you with everything good
that you may do his will, working with you that which is
pleasing in his sight, through Jesus Christ; to whom be
glory for ever and ever. The Methodist leader observed
that "It seems the people in general do not expect that
I shall remain long among them a great while sfter my
brother; and that, therefore, they are willing to hear
while they can." Charles Wesley had died on Saturday,
29 March 1788, at his house in Chesterfield Street,in
Marylebone; John Wesley, on that date, was preaching at
Madeley, Shropshire.

Saturday, 12 October 1788

　　　Ephesians 6:10--Finally, be strong in the Lord
　　　and in the strength of his might.

Thursday, 25 December 1788. "Notwithstanding the
severe frost, which has now lasted a month," wrote Wesley
in his journal for this Christmas day, "the congregation was uncommonly large."   That fact appears, indeed, an understatement, considering that the service
to which he refers took place at 5:00 a.m. At any
rate, he based his sermon texts upon--

　　　Haggai 2:7--. . .and I will shake all nations,
　　　so that the treasures of all nations shall
　　　come in, and I will fill this house with
　　　splendour, says the Lord of hosts.

　　　Isaiah 19:11--The princes of Zoan are utter-
　　　ly foolish; the wise counselors of Pharoah
　　　give stupid counsel. How can you say to
　　　Pharaoh, "I am a son of the wise, a son of
　　　ancient kings?"

Sunday, 1 March 1789. Wesley's journal for this
date indicates that "The new chapel was sufficiently
crowded both morning and afternoon. . . ." He based his
sermons on--

> 1 Corinthians 10:12--Therefore, let any one
> who thinks that he stands take heed,lest
> he fall.
>
> Hebrews 12:28--Therefore, let us be grateful
> for receiving a kingdom that cannot be
> shaken, and thus let us offer to God ac-
> ceptable worship with reverence and awe.

Sunday, 29 November 1789

> Romans 13:12--. . .the night is far gone, the
> day is at hand.   Let us then cast off the
> works of darkness, and put on the armour of
> light. . . .
>
> Romans 13:8--Owe no one anything, except to
> love one another; for he who loves his
> neighbour has fulfilled the law.

Thursday, 10 December 1789

> James 3:17--But the wisdom from above is first
> pure, then peaceable, gentle, open to
> reason, full of mercy and good fruits,
> without uncertainty or insincerity.

Friday, 25 December 1789

> Romans 6:1--What shall we say, then? Are we
> to continue to sin that grace may abound?
>
> Titus 2:12--. . .training us to renounce
> irreligion and worldly passions, and to live
> sober, upright, and godly lives in this
> world. . . .

Thursday, 31 January 1790. Wesley preached his
sermon from Revelation 3:1--And to the angel of the
church in Sardis write: "The words of him who has the
seven spirits of God and the seven stars. . . ."After the
service, he complained of a cramp.   "I am now an old man,

decayed from head to foot. My eyes are dim; my right
hand shakes much; my mouth is hot and dry every morning; I have a lingering fever almost every day; my motion is weak and slow. However. . .I can preach and
write still." At that point, we are reminded of
Wesley's comment of Thursday, 18 December 1783, when he
visited with Samuel Johnson at Bolt Court (see pp. 115-
117): "I spent two hours with that great man, Dr. Johnson,
who is sinking into the grave by a gentle decay."

Tuesday, 23 February 1790

> Galatians 6:15--For neither circumcision
> counts for anything, nor uncircumcision,
> but a new creation.

Sunday, 28 February 1790

> 1 Thessalonians 4:1--Finally, brethren, we
> beseech and exhort you in the Lord Jesus,
> that as you learned from us how you ought
> to live and to please God, just as you are
> doing, you do so more and more.

Sunday, 3 October 1790

> Matthew 22:37--And he said to him, "You shall
> love the Lord your God with all your heart,
> and with all your soul, and with all your
> mind.

> Matthew 22:39--And a second is like it, You
> shall love your neighbor as yourself.

Tuesday, 22 February 1791. Eight days before the
death of John Wesley:

> Galatians 5:5--For through the Spirit, by
> faith, we wait for the hope of righteous-
> ness.

Morning Chapel, City Road. As the name clearly

indicates, the Morning Chapel functioned principally for
early morning worship service. Physically, it was separated from the main City Road Chapel sanctuary by a
simple partition. Within four years after John Wesley's
death, the London Methodists abandoned the practice of
worship service at 4:30 or 5:00 a.m. During the lifetime
of their patriarch, however, a challenge to the practice
would have been unthinkable:

> Let the preaching at five in the morning
> be constantly kept up [commanded Wesley],
> wherever you can have twenty hearers.
> This is the glory of the Methodists! When-
> ever this is dropped, they will dwindle
> away into nothing. Rising early is equally
> good for the soul and body. It helps
> the nerves better than a thousand medi-
> cines; and, in particular, preserves the
> sight, and prevents lowness of spirits,
> more than can be well imagined.
>   (Tyerman 3:22)

In 1879, the original Morning Chapel was destroyed by
fire and a new building constructed on its site.

On Monday, 18 July 1785, Wesley preached in the
Morning Chapel on Colossians 3:10--. . .and have put on
the new nature, which is being renewed in knowledge
after the image of its creator. According to his journal
account for that day, the room was so crowded that "many
stood in the large chapel. . . ."

The Church of All-Hallows-on-the-Wall, London Wall.
All Hallows Church had its foundations on the old Roman
wall, and the vestry perpetuated the outline of a bas-
tion. A church stood on that site before the Norman

Conquest, and one built during 1528-1529 escaped serious damage during the Great Fire of 1666. However, by
1765, the building had fallen into disrepair, and an act
of Parliament provided for its rebuilding by George Dance
the younger, who carried out the work between 1765 and
1767, at a cost of £2941. In later life, Dance referred
to All Hallows as "my first child."

Wesley preached in the Church of All Hallows on
Sunday, 29 October 1738, perhaps at the invitation of
the incumbent, Samuel Smith. A graduate of Magdalene
Hall, Oxford, and trustee of the Georgia colony, Smith
wrote and published <u>A Sermon before the Trustees for
Establishing the Colony of Georgia</u>. <u>Isaiah 11:9</u> (London,
1733).

    <u>Gravel Lane</u>. During the 1740's and 1750's, four
separate "Gravel Lane" (s) existed in London: off Aldgate, Southwark; and Old and New Streets, Wapping. Thus,
one needs to look at Wesley's diary and journal for the
clues (if, indeed, any actually present themselves) to
the exact location:

    Monday, 12 February 1739. 8:00 p.m., "singing,
etc. . . ."

    Monday, 26 February 1739. 8:15 p.m., "singing,
etc. . . ."

    Monday, 19 March 1739. 8:00 p.m., "singing, etc
. . . ."

    Monday, 26 March 1739. 8:00 p.m., "many angry!!
singing, etc. . . ."

    Monday, 17 November 1755. "As we were walking
toward Wapping," recorded Wesley in his journal, "the
rain poured down with such violence that we were obliged
to take shelter till it abated. We then held on to
Gravel Lane, in many parts of which the waters were like

a river."

The consistency of the day of the week, Monday, and the time, 8:00 p.m., suggests strongly that Wesley visited only one Gravel Lane--perhaps (as on 17 November 1755) one of the two in Wapping.

Great St. Helen's Church, Bishopsgate Street. St. Helen's Church, which escaped serious damage from the Great Fire, occupied part of the site of an ancient nunnery founded (supposedly) in memory of Helena, mother of Constantine. The interior consisted of a nave divided into two aisles by pillars of pointed arches. On account of its large number of memorials to illustrious Londoners, St. Helen's has been termed the "Westminster Abbey of the City." The most notable monuments concern Sir Thomas Gresham (1519-15.79, financier, founder of the Royal Exchange, and formulator of "Gresham's Law"; Sir Julius Caesar (1558-1636), judge of the Admiralty Court, chancellor of the Exchequer, master of the rolls, and parliamentarian; Sir John Crosby and Lady Crosby (the former d. 1475); and Sir William Pickering.

John Wesley preached at Great St. Helen's Church on Tuesday, 21 February 1738, on the text "If any man will come after Me, let him deny himself, and take up his cross daily, and follow me [Luke 9:23]." At 2:30 p.m., Sunday, 23 April 1738, he returned there, to read prayers and to preach. Tuesday, 9 May 1738, found him there preaching "to a very numerous congregation, on 'He that spared not His own Son, but delivered Him up for us all, how shall He not with Him so freely give us all things? [Romans 8:32]'" Not until Sunday, 17 January 1790, did Wesley again preach at Great St.Helen's, "to a large congregation. It is, I believe, fifty

years since I preached there before   [9 May 1738].
What has God wrought since that time!" For his sermon
on that day, he spoke upon Hebrews 9:27--And just as it
is appointed for men to die once, and after that comes
judgment.

   Church of St. Ethelburga, Bishopsgate Street. St.
Ethelburga's, one of the smallest of the London parish
churches and dedicated to the daughter of King Ethelbert
(552-616), appears to have escaped serious damage from
the Great Fire. Formally known as St. Ethelburga-the-
Virgin within Bishopsgate,the church gained some attention
from Henry Hudson and his companions having received
communion there before setting out in the Hopeful
in 1607.
   John Wesley preached at St. Ethelburga's on Sunday afternoon, 20 February 1785, on Galatians 3:22--
But the scripture consigned all things to sin, that
what was promised to faith in Jesus Christ might be
given to those who believe. William Gilbank served as
the incumbent during that time.

   St. Botolph's Church, Bishopsgate. Although St.
Botolph's escaped serious damage from the Great Fire,
it had to be demolished in 1724 and then rebuilt during 1725-1728. George Dance the elder and his father-
in-law, James Gould, supervised the reconstruction,
completed at a cost of £10,000. At St. Botolph's, in
1795, the poet John Keats was christened (18 December).
   Early on Sunday morning, 5 December 1738, Wesley's
London Church of England religious society met and
appointed band leaders. Afterward, at 10:00 a.m., Wesley

preached at St. Botolph's perhaps because of the courtesy extended to him by the rector, William Crowe, D.D.
(d. 1743). Appointed to St. Botolph's in 1730, Crowe
served, also, as a chaplain-in-ordinary to King George
II; he proved a competent Greek scholar, published a
number of his occasional sermons, and left (at his death)
in excess of £5,000--bequeathed to the poor and to the
Church.

        London Workhouse, Bishopsgate Street. Established
in 1688 under provisions set forth in the Act of Settlement (1662)--calling for suitable places for putting able-
bodied (including mothers and children) persons to work--
the London Workhouse sought an ideal that it could not
possibly attain. Specifically, its sponsors hoped to
teach children and adult illiterates the catechism, reading, and writing, in addition to emphasizing their training in and for specific areas of occupation. However,
the Workhouse also attempted to be self-sufficient--
if not altogether profitable. That last purpose, of
course, came into direct conflict with the original
"ideals." Yet, the London Workhouse had one advantage
over similar institutions operated by individual London
parishes: it was generously endowed, and thus its inmates did not suffer from the filth and the crowded conditions found in the majority of the parish workhouses.
        According to one description of the London Work-
house, set down in 1708, "thirty or forty children were
put under the charge of one nurse in a ward, they lay
two together in bunks arranged around the walls in two
tiers, boarded and set one above the other. . .a flock
bed, a pair of sheets, two blankets and a rug to each."
Prayers and breakfast occurred from 6:30 a.m. to 7:00

a.m.; at 7:00, the children went off to work, twenty under a mistress, "to spin wool and flax, knit stockings,
to make their linnen, cloathes, shoes. . . ." They worked
until 6:00 p.m., with an hour (noon to 1:00) for dinner and play. Also, twenty children at a time were called
from their work for one hour each day to be taught
reading and some writing. Certain of the children earned
"a halfpenny, some a penny, and some four-pence a
day." At ages twelve, thirteen, or fourteen, the children were apprenticed, being permitted, at the master's
choice, either a "good ordinary suit of cloathes or 20s.
in money" (George, London Life 218-219).

By early 1771, conditions obviously remained on the
same "high" standard. On Thursday, 14 February of that
year, John Wesley visited "both the upper and lower
rooms" of the London Workhouse. "It contains," he noted, "about a hundred children, who are in as good order as any private family; and the whole house is as
clean, from top to bottom, as any gentleman's needs be.
And why is not every workhouse in London, yea, through
the kingdom, in the same order? Purely for want either
of sense, or of honesty and activity, in them that
superintend it." Twelve years later, on Tuesday, 30 December 1783, Wesley again visited the London Workhouse;
he noted that event in his diary, but did not set down
any commentary or reaction in the journal.

Moorfields. Known later as Finsbury Circus and
Finsbury Square, Moorfields existed, for the greater
part of the eighteenth century, as a large fen, or
moor, on the north side of London. It stretched, approximately, from Bishopsgate to Cripplegate, and from
London Wall to Finsbury Square. Londoners considered

that marshy ground a favorite place for Sunday strolling, since it was laid out in grass plots, intersected
by broad, gravel walks. Beneath a row of well grown
elms lay what the promenaders designated "the city mall,"
which, because of the smartness of its company, often
rivaled the mall of St. James Park. "Here might be seen
wives and daughters flaunting in all their finery and
displaying their charms to city maccaronis, whose hats
were cocked diagonally, and who gave themselves quite
as many airs as the aristocratic coxcombs in the royal
grounds. Under the trees were booths, whose fans, toys,
trinkets, and confectionary found ready purchasers; while
on the grass plots were erected mountebank diversions
for the amusement of the people" (Tyerman, Life of
Wesley 1:214).

Following the examples set by George Whitefield,
Wesley discovered the advantages of outdoor preaching--
particularly after the Establishment churches refused to
allow him access to their pulpits. Thus, between 1739
and 1777, we may observe his activities in that part of
London--although we must be aware that he tended to overestimate the numbers who constituted his outdoor congregations:

Sunday, 17 June 1739. "I preached, at seven [a.m.]
. . .to (I believe) six or seven thousand people, on 'Ho!
every one that thirsteth, come ye to the waters.'" That
text constitutes the opening of Isaiah 55.

Sunday, 9 September 1739. "I declared [at 7:00
a.m.] to about ten thousand, in Moorfields, what they
must do to be saved." He based that sermon on Acts 16:
31--Believe in the Lord Jesus, and you will be saved,
you and your household.

Sunday, 16 September 1739. "I preached [at 7:00
a.m.]. . .to about ten thousand. . .on those words of
the calmer Jews to St. Paul, 'We desire to hear of thee

what thou thinkest, for as concerning this sect, we know
that everywhere it is spoken against' [Acts 28:22]."

Sunday, 23 September 1739. "I declared [at 6:45
a.m.] to about ten thousand. . .with great enlargement
of spirit, 'The kingdom of God is not meat and drink;
but righteousness, and peace, and joy in the Holy Ghost'
[Romans 14:17]."

Sunday, 30 September 1739. Wesley preached at 7:00
a.m. to "15,000" persons on Matthew 11:28--Come to me,
all who labor and are heavy laden, and I will give you
rest. Again, we must be careful about placing too much
reliance upon Wesley's crowd estimates. He really had
no way of determining exactly (or even approximately)
how many actually attended a given open-air meeting--
how many constituted the faithful or how many were merely curious onlookers or even detractors. Therefore, his
figures tend to be inflated, particularly for the benefit of his published journals.

Sunday, 29 June 1740. "I preached [at 6:30 a.m.]
. . .on Titus iii.8, and endeavoured. . .to explain and
enforce the apostle's direction that those 'who have believed be careful to maintain good works.'"

Sunday, 20 July 1740. ". . .I preached [at 6:30
a.m.]. . .on the 'work and faith' and the 'patience of
hope,' and the labour of love' [1 Thessalonians 1:4]. A
zealous man was so kind as to free us from most of the
noisy, careless hearers (or spectators, rather), by reading, at a small distance, a chapter of The Whole Duty of
Man [1657]. I wish neither he nor they may ever read a
worse book; though I can tell them of a better--the
Bible." The book in question, a devotional tract, dis-
cusses man's duties in respect to God and his fellow human
beings. Contemporaries attributed the volume to Lady
Dorothy Pakington (d. 1679), but that person served
only as a copyist. Literary historians have since

assigned the piece to a divine acquainted with Hebrew,
Syriac, and Arabic. A prime candidate, Richard Allestree (1619-1681), served as a chaplain ordinary to King
Charles II, Regius professor of divinity at Oxford, and
provost of Eton College. At any rate, The Whole Duty of
Man gained immediate and wide acceptance and held its
popularity throughout the eighteenth century.

> Ascension Day, Thursday, 28 May 1747
>> Luke 24:49--And behold, I send the promise of
>> my Father upon you; but stay in the city,
>> until you are clothed with power from on
>> high.
>> Revelation 22--Then he showed me the river of
>> the water of life, bright as crystal, flow-
>> ing from the throne of God and of the Lamb.

Sunday, 31 May 1747. Wesley "preached at seven
[a.m.] to a large and well behaved congregation."

>> 1 John 1:3--. . .that which we have seen and
>> heard we proclaim also to you, so that you
>> may have fellowship with us; and our fellow-
>> ship is with the Father and with his son
>> Jesus Christ.

> Whitsunday, 7 June 1747
>> John 7:37--On the last day of the feast, the
>> great day, Jesus stood up and proclaimed,
>> "If any one thirst, let him come to me and
>> drink."

> Sunday, 27 September 1747
>> Galatians 6:16--Peace and mercy be upon all
>> who walk by this rule, upon the Israel of
>> God.
>> Acts 5:31--God exalted him at his right hand
>> as Leader and Saviour, to give repentance
>> to Israel and forgiveness of sins.

Psalms 138:7--Though I walk in the midst of
trouble, thou dost preserve my life; thou
dost stretch out thy hand against the wrath
of my enemies, and thy right hand delivers
me.

Wednesday, 1 June 1748

Matthew 3:10--Even now the axe is laid to the
root of the trees; every tree therefore
that does not bear good fruit is cut down
and thrown into the fire.

1 John 5:7--And the Spirit is the witness, because the Spirit is the truth.

Hosea 14:4--I will heal their faithlessness;
I will love them freely, for my anger has
turned from them.

Sunday, 5 June 1748. "I preached. . .both morning
and evening."

Sunday, 19 June 1748

Hebrews 8:11--And they shall not teach every
one his fellow or every one his brother,
saying, "Know the Lord," for all shall know
me, from the least of them to the greatest.

1 Timothy 3:16--Great indeed, we confess, is
the mystery of our religion; He was manifested in the flesh, vindicated in the Spirit,
seen by angels, preached among the nations,
believed on in the world, taken up
in glory.

Sunday, 4 September 1748

2 Corinthians 5:18--All this is from God,who
through Christ reconciled us to himself
and gave us the ministry of reconciliation.

John 14:22--Judas (not Iscariot)said to him,
"Lord, how is it that you will manifest

yourself to us, and not to the world?"

Galatians 5:22--Wives, be subject to your husbands, as to the Lord.

Saturday, 8 September 1750

Galatians 5:18--But if you are led by the Spirit,
you are not under the law.

Galatians 6:14--But far be it from me to glory
except in the cross of our Lord Jesus
Christ, by which the world has been crucified to me, and I to the world.

Sunday, 23 September 1750. "At five [p.m.] I called
the sinners in Moorfields to repentance."

Sunday, 26 May 1751

John 7:37--See above for Whitsunday, 7 June
1747 (p. 155).

Hebrews 7:15--This becomes even more evident
when another priest arises in the likeness
of Melchizedek. . . .

1 Kings 18:21--And Elijah came near to all the
people, and said, "How long will you go
limping with two different opinions? If
the Lord is God, follow him; but if Baal,
then follow him." And the people did not
answer him a word.

Sunday, 18 August 1751

Philippians 1:21--For me to live is Christ,
and to die is gain.

Luke 18:12--I fast twice a week, I give tithes
of all that I get.

Hebrews 7:25--Consequently, he is able for
time to save those who draw near to God
through him, since he always lives to make
intercession for them.

Sunday, 13 July 1755

Romans 6:23--For the wages of sin is death,
   but the free gift of God is eternal life
   in Christ Jesus our Lord.
Mark 9:44--. . .it is better for you to enter
   life maimed than with two hands to go to
   hell, to the unquenchable fire.
Sunday, 10 August 1755
   2 Kings 5:12--Are not Abna and Pharpar, the
      rivers of Damascus, better than all the
      rivers of Israel? Could I not wash in
      them, and be clean? So he turned and went
      away in a rage.
   Hebrews 9:27--And just as it is appointed for
      men to die once, and after that comes judg-
      ment. . . .
Sunday, 17 August 1755. "I took leave of the congregation in Moorfields by applying those awful words,
'It is appointed for men to die,' and early in the morning [Monday, 18 August] set out for Cornwall."
   Friday, 12 December 1755. "As I was returning from
Zoar [see under Section 3 below] I came as well as usual
to Moorfields; but there my strength entirely failed,
and such a faintness and weariness seized me that it was
with difficulty I got home."
   (?) September 1756
      Matthew 13:16--But blessed are your eyes, for
         they see, and your ears, for they hear.
      Ezekiel 18:31--Cast away from you all the
         transgressions which you have committed
         against me, and get yourselves a new heart
         and a new spirit! Why will you die, O
         house of Israel?
   Sunday, 10 October 1756. "I preached to a huge
multitude. . .on 'Why will ye die, O house of Israel?'

[Ezekiel] 18:31   It is field preaching which does the
execution still; for usefulness there is none compara-
ble to it."   At the outset of his grand evangelical mission, Wesley's sense of tradition and his commitment to
the Established Church had led him to doubt the validi-
ty and effectiveness of outdoor public worship and outdoor preaching.   Obviously, both necessity and practi-
cality caused him to see otherwise.   See, also, below,
for Sunday, 23 September 1759.

        Sunday, 12 August 1759
              1 Kings 18:21--See above for Sunday, 25 May
              1751 (p. 157).
              2 Kings 5:12--See above for Sunday, 10 August
              1755 (p. 158).
        Sunday, 23 September 1759.   "A vast majority of the
immense congregation in Moorfields were deeply serious,"
wrote Wesley in his journal.   "One such hour might convince any impartial man of the expediency of field-preaching
What building, except St. Paul's Church, would
contain such a congregation?   And if it would, what human voice could have reached them there?   By repeated
observations I find I can commend thrice the number in
the open air than I can under a roof.   And who can say
the time for field-preaching is over, while (1) greater
numbers than ever attend; (2) the converting as well as
convincing power of God is eminently present with them?"
        Sunday, 12 August 1764. "In the afternoon, I preached
. . .on those comfortable words, 'Believe in the
Lord Jesus Christ, and thou shalt be saved.'   Thousands
heard with calm and deep attention."
        Sunday, 7 October 1764.   "At five [p.m.] I preached
. . .to a huge multitude on 'Ye are saved through faith.'"
        Sunday, 25 July 1773. ". . .I preached. . .to (it
was supposed) the largest congregation that ever assem-

bled there [Moorfields]. But my voice was so strengthened that those who were farthest off could hear perfectly well. So the season for field-preaching is not yet
over. It cannot, while so many are in their sins and in
their blood." By the word season, Wesley had reference,
of course, not to the general season of the year, but to
the overall popularity and effectiveness of field preaching.

Sunday, 1 August 1773. At 9:00 p.m., Wesley preached
and administered the sacrament.

Sunday, 8 October 1775. Wesley preached to "a larger congregation than usual. Strange that their curiosity should not be satisfied yet, after hearing the
same thing near forty years!"

Sunday, 4 August 1776. "In the afternoon, I preached
. . .to a thousand on Acts 11. 32, 'This Jesus hath
God raised up, whereof we are all witnesses.'"

Sunday, 2 March 1777. "Being a warm sun-shiny day,"
wrote Wesley in his journal, "I preached in Moorfields,
in the evening. There were thousands upon thousands;
and all were still as night. Not only violence and
rioting, but even scoffing at field-preaching is now over."
Perhaps the Londoners were becoming accustomed to Methodism
but in the northern sections of England, particularly, Wesley and his Methodist preachers continued to
endure harassment from magistrates, press gangs,
Anglican bishops, and local citizens.

Sunday, 27 April 1777. "The sun breaking out, I
snatched the opportunity of preaching to many thousands
in Moorfields. All were still as night while I showed
how 'the Son of God was manifested to destroy the works
of the devil' [1 John 3:8]."

Sunday, 17 August 1777. Wesley noted that "In the
calm, fair evening, I took the opportunity to preach in

Moorfields. The congregation was at least as large as I
ever saw there. As yet I do not see any sign of the decay of the work of God in England." That may well have
been the last occasion upon which John Wesley preached
in Moorfields. During this period, the City had begun
to cover the upper grounds of Lower and Upper Moorfields
with streets and houses.

The King's Foundery, Windmill Street, Moorfields.
In 1739, a ruined building known as the King's Foundery
stood in what was then identified as Windmill Street
(later Tabernacle Street). Twenty-three years earlier,
in 1716, the Royal Artillery had determined to recast
the cannon that John Churchill, Duke of Marlborough
(1650-1722), had taken from the French during the War of
the Spanish Succession (1701-1714). Those pieces were
to be stored in the Foundery and on the adjacent artillery grounds. On the day the cannons stood ready to be
recast, a large audience gathered to view the process;
even temporary galleries had been erected for the
occasion.
     Among the throng roamed a young Swiss, Andrew
Schalch, of Schaffausen. Having been permitted to in-
spect the works, he had detected humidity in the molds,
and he warned Colonel Armstrong, the Surveyor-General of
the Ordnance, that a potential danger existed if the
workers poured hot metal into those molds. Armstrong,
however, refused to halt the proceedings--although he
did have the sense to quit the building, followed by
others persuaded by his and Schalch's arguments. When
the workers did pour the metal into the molds, the anti-
cipated danger did indeed result; part of the roof of
the Foundery was blown off, while spectators in the

galeries d workmen at the site suffered severely from
injuries and burns. For his sharp eyes, young Andrew
Schalch was commissioned by the Ordnance to uncover a
suitable location for a new Royal Foundery. He determined that the rabbit warren at Woolwich would do nice-
ly; the Government placed him in charge of the construction, and afterward appointed him Master Founder to the
Board of Ordnance. Thus, the Royal Army gained a new
arsenal and British Methodism secured its first London
home (see Wesley's Journal 2:316-319).

The building in Moorfields stood on the east side
of Windmill Street, sixteen or eighteen yards from
Providence Row. It measured approximately forty yards in
front (from north to south) and about thirty-three yards
in depth (from east to west). When John Wesley purchased the property and the structure in 1739 for £115, it
stood, obviously, in ruined condition. Nothing had been
done to the building since the explosion of 1716. In addition to the purchase price, money had to be expended
for repairs, in the construction of two galleries (one
each for men and women), and for enlargement of a room
for society meetings. Wesley borrowed the original £ 115
from friends; he then established subscriptions--at four,
six, and ten shillings per year--in an effort to liqui-
date the debt.   By 1742, the subscription amounted to
£480, leaving Wesley with a debt of nearly 300. Thus,
the total cost of the Foundery came to approximately
£800 (see Tyerman, Life of Wesley 1:271-272).

The first service at the Foundery occurred on Sunday, 11 November 1739. Wesley "preached. . .at five in
the even to seven or eight thousand, in the place
which had been the King's Foundery for cannon." From
that date until early August 1779, we may observe, by
way of the following summary, John Wesley's major

activities at the Foundery, including the Biblical texts
from which he developed his sermons:

Saturday, 26 April 1740

Mark 4:36--And leaving the crowd, they took
him with them, just as he was, in the boat.
And other boats were with him.

Monday, 28 April 1740

1 Kings 5:13--But his servants came near and
said to him, "My father, if the prophet had
commanded you to do some great thing,would
you not have done it? How much rather,
then, when he says to you, 'Wash and be
clean'?"

Thursday, 5 June 1740. From the diary entry on
this date, we may conclude that the Foundery became Wesley's
London residence until, in November 1778, he moved
to City Road Chapel.

Thursday, 19 June 1740

Ephesians 6--Children, obey your parents in
the Lord, for this is right.

Wednesday, 23 July 1740. "Our little company met
at The Foundery, instead of Fetter Lane." Thus, John
Wesley's separation from the Anglican religious society
at Fetter Lane had become complete. British Methodism
would now emerge as an entity.

Thursday, 18 September 1740. "The prince of the
air made another attempt," wrote Wesley, "in defense of
his tottering kingdom. A great number of men, having
got into the middle of the Foundery, began to speak big,
swelling words; so that my voice could hardly be heard
while I was reading the eleventh chapter of the Acts
[Now the apostles and the brethren who were in Judea
heard that the Gentiles also had received the word of
God.]. But immediately after, the hammer of the word

brake the rocks in pieces; all quietly heard the glad
tidings of salvation; and some, I trust, not in vain."
Acts 11, we may remember, begins--In the first book, O
Theophilus, I have dealt with all that Jesus began to
do and teach. . . .

Tuesday, 26 May 1741. "In the evening [6:45] I
preached at the Foundery. . .on 'Stand still, and see
the salvation of the Lord [Exodus 14:13]."

Sunday, 26 July 1741. "I. . .preached. . .on the
'liberty' we have 'to enter into the holiest by the
blood of Jesus [Hebrews 10:19]."

Thursday, 26 May 1743. "I. . .concluded the day by
enforcing those awful words at the Foundery, 'The Lord
hath proclaimed unto the end of the world: Say ye to the
daughters of Zion, Behold, thy Salvation cometh! Behold,
His reward is with Him, and His work before him.'"
[Isaiah 62:11].

Wednesday, 18 December 1745. This proved a national
fast day: the Pretender, Charles Edward, with his
army of Highlanders, had reached Derby. There, he proclaimed his father King of England. Wesley preached
at the Foundery at 4:00 a.m., on Joel 2:12--"Yet even
now," says the Lord, "return to me, with all your heart,
with fasting, with weeping, and with mourning. . . ."
At 5:00 p.m., he again preached on the text, "The Lord
sitteth above the water-floods" (Psalms 29:10).

Friday, 1 January 1748

> Romans 13:1--Let every person be subject to
> the governing authorities. For there is
> no authority except from God, and those
> that exist have been instituted by God.

> Luke 22:24--A dispute also arose among them,
> which of them was to be regarded as the
> greatest.

Wednesday, 6 January 1748

> Matthew 8:2-3--. . .and behold, a leper came
> to him and knelt before him, saying, "I
> will be clean." And immediately his lepro-
> sy was cleansed.

> Luke 22:31--Simon, Simon, behold, Satan demand-
> ed to have you, that he might sift you like
> wheat. . . .

> Psalms 42:10--As with a deadly wound in my body,
> my adversaries taunt me, while they say
> to me continually, "Where is your God?"

Wednesday, 1 June 1748

> John 1-3--In the beginning was the Word, and
> the Word was with God, and the Word was
> God. . . .

Monday, 17 October 1748

> Hebrews 12:19--. . .and the sound of a trum-
> pet, and a voice whose words made the hear-
> ers entreat that no further messages be
> spoken to them.

> John 4-9--Now when the Lord knew that the Phari-
> sees had heard that Jesus was making and
> baptizing more disciples than John. . . .

> John 4:13--Jesus said to her, "Every one who
> drinks of this water that I shall give him
> will never thirst; the water that I shall
> give him will never become in him a spring
> of water welling up to eternal life."

> Hebrews 4:12--For the word of God is living
> and active, sharper than any two-edged
> sword, piercing to the division of the soul
> and spirit, of joints and marrow, and dis-
> cerning the thoughts and tensions of the
> heart.

Ephesians 2:17--But if, in our endeavour to be
justified in Christ, we, ourselves, were
found to be sinners, is Christ then an
agent of sin?

Ephesians 2:11-13--But when Cephas came to Antioch I opposed him to his face, because he
stood condemned. For before certain men
came from James, he ate with the Gentiles;
but when they came he drew back and separated himself, fearing the circumcision party.
And with him the rest of the Jews acted
insincerely, so that even Barnabas was
carried away by their insincerity.

Luke 9:55--But he turned and rebuked them. And
they went on to another village.

Sunday, 1 November 1748

John 6:28--Then they said to him, "What must
we do, to be doing the works of God?"

John 6:38--For I have come down from heaven,
not to do my own will, but the will of him
who sent me. . . .

Philippians 3:20--But our commonwealth is in
heaven; and from it we wait a Saviour, the
Lord Jesus Christ. . . .

John 7:7--The world cannot hate you, but it
hates me because I testify of it that its
works are evil.

John 7:17--. . .if any man's will is to do his
will, he shall know whether the teaching is
from God or whether I am speaking on my own
authority.

1 Kings 19--Ahab told Jezebel all that Elijah
had done and how he had slain all the prophets with the sword.

Luke 3:8--Bear fruits that befit repentance,
and do not begin to say to yourselves,"We
have Abraham as our father"; for I tell
you, God is able from these stones to raise
up children to Abraham.

Romans 13:14--But put on the Lord Jesus Christ,
and make no provision for the flesh, to
gratify its desires.

Sunday, 4 December 1748

Luke 16:12--And if you have not been faithful
in that which is another's, who will give
you that which is your own?

Romans 15:5--May the God of steadfastness and
encouragement grant you to live in such harmony with one another, in accord with Christ
Jesus. . . .

Matthew 24:44--Therefore, you must also be ready
for the Son of man is coming at an hour
you do not expect.

Sunday, 1 January 1749

Isaiah 66:8--Who has heard such a thing? Who
has seen such things? Shall a land be born
in one day? Shall a nation be brought forth
in one moment? For as soon as Zion was in
labour she brought forth her sons.

Isaiah 49:22--Thus says the Lord our God: "Behold, I will lift up my hand to the nations
and raise my signal to the peoples' and they
shall bring your sons in their bosom, and
your daughters shall be carried on their
shoulders.

Romans 6:4--We were buried, therefore, with
him by baptism into death, so that as Christ
was raised from the dead by the glory of
the Father, we, too, might walk in the

newness of life.

John 10:12--He who is a hireling and not a
shepherd, whose own the sheep are not, sees
the wolf coming and leaves the sheep and
flees; and the wolf snatches them and scat-
ters them.

Sunday, 12 February 1749

Psalms 29--Ascribe to the Lord, O heavenly beings, ascribe to the Lord glory and

strength. . . .

Matthew 10:34--Do not think that I have come
to bring peace on earth; I have not come to
bring peace, but a sword.

Thursday, 8 March 1750. The following is an excerpt
from the journal of Charles Wesley for 8 March 1750:
"This morning, a quarter after five, we had another shock
of an earthquake, far more violent than that of February
8 [,] 1750. I was just repeating my text, when it shook
the Foundery so violently that we all expected it to
fall upon our heads. A great cry followed from the wom-
en and children. I immediately cried out, 'Therefore
will we not fear, though the earth be moved, and the
hills be carried into the midst of the sea: for the Lord
of hosts is with us; the God of Jacob is our refuge'
(Psalms 46:2-7). He filled my heart with faith, and my
mouth with words, shaking their souls as well as their
bodies."

John Wesley, in his journal, added to his brother·s
observations and reactions for that day. "The earth moved
westward, then east, then westward again, through
all London and Westminster. It was a strong and jarring
motion, attended with a rumbling noise, like that of dis-
tant thunder. Many houses were much shaken, and some
chimneys thrown down, but without any farther hurt." On
Friday, 9 March 1750, Charles Wesley delivered a sermon

at the Foundery entitled "The Cause and Cure of Earth-
quakes"; later that year, he published his Hymns Occasioned by the Earthquake, March 8, 1750 (London: Printed
in the Year MDCCL)--thirteen hymns on the subject, a sam-
ple of which may be seen in the following lines:

> Rising in Thy dreadful might
>   The wicked to rebuke,
> Thou hast with unwonted fright
>   Our sleeping bodies shook;
> Earth did to her centre quake,
> Convulsive pangs her bowels tore;
> Shake, our inmost spirits shake,
>   And let us sleep no more.
>   (Osborn, Poetical Works 6:20)

Saturday, 8 September 1750

> Luke 10:23--Then, returning to the disciples,
>   he said privately, "Blessed are the eyes
>   which see what you see!
> Psalms 116:12--What shall I render to the Lord
>   for all his bounty to me?
> Psalms 4:6-7--There are many who say, "O that
>   we might see some good! Lift up the light
>   of thy countenance upon us, O Lord!" Thou
>   hast put more joy in my heart than they
>   have when their grain and wine abound.

Tuesday, 11 September 1750

> Hebrews 9--Now the point in what we are saying
>   is this: we have such a high priest, one
>   who is seated at the right hand of the throne
>   of the Majesty in heaven. . . .

Wednesday, 12 September 1750

> Acts 26:8--Why is it thought incredible to any
>   of you that God raises the dead?
> Philippians 3:10--. . .that I may know him and

the power of his resurrection, and may
share his sufferings, becoming like him in
his death. . . .

Thursday, 1 November 1750

1 Corinthians 15:56--The sting of death is
sin, and the power of sin is the law.

Luke 16:9--And I tell you, make friends for
yourselves by means of uprighteous mammon,
so when it fails they may receive you into
the eternal habitations.

1 Peter 3:3--Let not yours be the outward
adorning with braiding of hair, decoration
of gold, and wearing of robes. . . .

1 Peter 2:2--Like newborn babes, long for the
pure spiritual milk, that by it you may
grow up to salvation. . . .

Exodus 32:10--. . .now therefore let me alone,
that my wrath may burn hot against them and
I may consume them; but of you, I will make
a great nation.

John 17:3--And this is eternal life, that they
know thee the only true God, and Jesus
Christ whom thou hast sent.

Ephesians 5:16--. . .making the most of the
time, because the days are evil.

Acts 22:16--And now, why do you wait? Rise
and be baptised, and wash away your sins,
calling on his name.

Isaiah 40:6--A voice says, "Cry!" And I said,
"What shall I cry?" All flesh is grass, and
all its beauty is like the flower of the
field.

Isaiah 40:8--The grass withers, the flower
fades; but the word of our God will stand
for ever.

Monday, 24 December 1750

Matthew 6:13--And lead us not into temptation,
but deliver us from evil.

Daniel 7:9--As I looked, thrones were placed,
and one that was ancient of days took his
seat; his raiment was white as snow, and
the hair of his head like pure wool; his
throne was fiery flames, its wheels were
burning fire.

Tuesday, 25 December 1750

Isaiah 9:6--For to us a child is born, to us
a son is given; and the government shall
be upon his shoulder, and his name will be
called "Wonderful Counselor, Mighty God,
Everlasting Father, Prince of Peace."

Titus 3:5--. . .he saved us, not because of
deeds done by us in righteousness, but in
virtue of his own mercy, by the washing of
regeneration and renewal in the Holy
Spirit. . . .

Monday, 7 January 1751

Hebrews 13:14--For here we have no lasting city,
but we seek the city that is to come.

Ephesians 1:10--. . .as a plan for the fulness of time, to unite all things in him,
things in heaven and things on earth.

Revelation 3:6--He who has an ear, let him
hear what the Spirit says to the churches.

Romans 15:9--. . .and in order that the Gentiles might glorify God for his mercy. As
it is written, "Therefore will I praise
thee among the Gentiles, and sing to thy
name."

John 15:21--I am the true vine, and my Father

is the vinedresser. . . .

Ecclesiastes 9:10--Whatever your hand finds to
    do, do it with your might; for there is no
    work or thought or knowledge or wisdom in
    Sheol, to which you are going.

Galatians 4:19--My little children, with whom
    I am again in travail until Christ be
    formed in you!

Hebrews 6:1--Therefore, let us leave the ele-
    mentary doctrines of Christ and go on to
    maturity, not laying again a foundation of
    repentance from dead works and of faith to-
    ward God. . . .

Friday, 1 February 1751

Luke 18:42--And Jesus said to him, "Receive
    your sight; your faith has made you well."

1 Corinthians 4:2--Moreover, it is required
    of stewards that they may be found trust-
    worthy.

Psalms 33:4--For the word of the Lord is up-
    right; and all his work is done in faith-
    fulness.

Psalms 33:6--By the word of the Lord the hea-
    vens were made, and all their host by the
    breath of his mouth.

James 2:12--So speak and so act as those who
    are to be judged under the law of liberty.

Psalms 118:28--Thou art my God, and I will
    give thanks to thee; thou art my God, I
    will extol thee.

Psalms 138:7--Though I walk in the midst of
    trouble, thou dost preserve my life; thou
    dost stretch out thy hand against the
    wrath of my enemies, and thy right hand

delivers me.

John 17:3--But now I am coming to thee; and
these things I speak in the world, that
they may have my joy fulfilled in themselves.

1 Thessalonians 4:7--For God has not called us
for uncleanliness, but in holiness.

John 18:13--First they led him to Annas; for
he was the father-in-law of Caiaphas, who
was high priest that year.

Thursday, 21 March 1751

Romans 11:33--O the depth of the riches and
wisdom and knowledge of God! How unsearchable are his judgments and how inscrutable
his ways!

Hebrews 9:13--For if the sprinkling of defiled
persons with the blood of goats and bulls
and with the ashes of a heifer sanctifies
for the purification of the flesh. . . .

John 18:36--Jesus answered, "My kingship is
not of this world; if my kingship were of
this world, my servants would fight, that
I might not be handed over to the Jews; but
my kingship is not from this world."

2 Peter 2:14-15--They have eyes full of adult-
ery, insatiable for sin. They entice
unsteady souls.They have hearts trained in
greed. Accursed children! Forsaking the
right way, they have gone astray; they have
followed the way of Balaam, the son of Beor,
who loved gain from wrongdoing.

1 Corinthians 2:5--. . .that your faith might
not rest in the wisdom of men, but in the
power of God.

Luke 16:31--He said to him, "If they do not
hear Moses and the prophets, neither will
they be converted if some one should rise
from the dead."

Sunday, 26 May 1751

John 14:16--And I will pray the Father, and
he will give you another Counselor, to be
with you for ever. . . .

Galatians 5;22--But the fruit of the Spirit is
love, joy, peace, patience, kindness, goodness faithfulness. . . .

John 14:21--He who has my commandments and
keeps them, he it is who loves me; and he
who loves me will be loved by my Father,
and I will love him and manifest myself to
him.

John 3:7--Do not marvel that I said to you,
"You must be born anew."

Thursday, 13 June 1751

John 19:5--So Jesus came out, wearing the
crown of thorns and the purple robe.
Pilate said to them, "Here is the man!"

Monday, 6 January 1752

Psalms 103:13--As a father pities his
children, so the Lord pities those who fear
him.

Philippians 3--Finally, my brethren, rejoice
in the Lord. To write the same thing to
you is not irksome to me, and is safe for
you.

Luke 15:7--Just so, I tell you, there will be
more joy in heaven over one sinner who repents than over ninety-nine righteous persons who need no repentance.

Matthew 18:15--If your brother sins against
you, go tell him his fault, between you and
him alone. If he listens to you, you have
gained your brother.

Colossians 1-2-- Paul, an apostle of Christ
Jesus by the will of God. . . . For I want
you to know how greatly I strive for you.

Matthew 18:35--So also my heavenly Father will
do to every one of you, if you do not forgive your brother from your heart.

James 2:4--. . .have not you made distinctions
among yourselves, and become judges with
evil thoughts?

Malachi 3:2--But who can endure the day of his
coming, and who can stand when he appears?

James 4:17--Whoever knows what is right to do
and fails to do it, for him it is sin.

1 Timothy 6:17--As for the rich in this world,
charge them not to be haughty, nor to set
their hopes on uncertain riches, but on God
who richly furnishes us with everything to
enjoy.

James 2:4--See directly above for this date
(p. 175).

Sunday, 5 November 1752

Colossians 3:4--When Christ who is our life
appears, then you also will appear with him
in glory.

Luke 9:55--See above for Monday, 17 October
1748 (p. 166).

1 Peter 4:12--Beloved, do not be surprised at
the fiery ordeal which comes upon you to
prove you, as though something strange were
happening to you.

1 <u>Peter</u> 1:13--Be subject for the Lord's sake
to every human institution, whether it be
to the emperor as supreme. . . .

Monday, 25 December 1752

1 <u>John</u> 3:8--He who commits sin is of the devil;
for the devil has sinned from the beginning.
The reason the Son of God appeared
was to destroy the works of the devil.

<u>Luke</u> 1:68--Blessed be the Lord God of Israel,
for he has visited and redeemed his people.

<u>Jude</u> 3--Beloved, being very eager to write to
you of our common salvation, I found it necessary to write appealing to you to contend for the faith which was once for all
delivered to the saints.

(?) December 1752

<u>Hebrews</u> 3:12--Take care, brethren, lest there
be in any of you an evil, unbelieving heart
leading you to fall away from the living
God.

Monday, 1 January 1753

2 <u>Peter</u> 3:10--But the day of the Lord will come
like a thief, and then the heavens will pass
away with a loud noise, and the elements
will be dissolved with fire, and the earth
and the works that are upon it will be
burned up.

1 <u>Thessalonians</u>--Chapter and verse not indicated.

<u>Revelation</u> 20:11--Then I saw a great white
throne and him who sat upon it; from his
presence earth and sky fled away, and no
place was found for them.

2 <u>Peter</u> 1:16--For we did not follow cleverly

devised myths when we made known to you the
power and coming of our Lord Jesus Christ,
but we were eyewitnesses of his majesty.

Matthew 15:20--These are what defile a man;
but to eat with unwashed hands does not defile a man.

Matthew 25:34--He also who had received the
one talent came forward, saying, "Master,
I knew you to be a hard man, reaping where
you did not sow, and gathering where you
did not winnow. . . ."

Mark 4:27--. . .and should sleep and rise night
and day, and the seed should sprout and
grow, he knows not how.

Tuesday, 9 October 1753

2 Thessalonians 2-3--Now concerning the coming
of our Lord Jesus Christ and our assembling
to meet him. . . .

Ephesians 4:1--I therefore, a prisoner for the
Lord, beg you to lead a life worthy of the
calling to which you have been called. . . .

Revelation 22:1--Then he showed me the river
of the water of Life, bright as crystal,
flowing from the throne of God and of the
Lamb. . . .

Luke 7:42--When they could not pay, he forgave them both. Now which of them will
love him more?

Psalms 115--Not to us, O Lord, not to us, but
to thy name give glory, for the sake of thy
steadfast love and thy faithfulness!

1 Timothy 1-3--. . .You then, my son, be
strong in the grace that is in Christ
Jesus. . . But understand this, that in

the last days there will come times of
stress.
Monday, 22 April 1754
    2 Peter 1:6--. . .and knowledge with self-
control, and self-control with steadfastness, and steadfastness with godliness.
Hebrews 3:13--But exhort one another every
as long as it is called "today," that none
of you may be hardened by the deceitfulness of sin.
1 Corinthians 9:27--. . .but I pommel my body
and subdue it, lest after preaching to
others I myself should be disqualified.

Whit Sunday, 2 June 1754. "I preached at the Foundery," noted the leader of the Methodists, "which I had
not done before in the evening. Still I have not re-
covered my whole voice or strength; perhaps I never may.
But let me use what I have." Since October 1753, Wesley
had been suffering from violent and regular attacks of
consumption; in fact, his friends thought he was dying
from that malady. The attacks, however, seem not to
have affected his rigorous schedule of activities--par-
ticularly the traveling. On this particular day, he based
his sermons on the following Scriptural texts:
    1 Thessalonians 5:19--Do not quench the
Spirit. . . .
    1 John 4:7--Beloved, let us love one another;
for love is of God, and he who loves is
born of God and knows God.
    1 John 5:7--And the Spirit is the witness, be-
cause the Spirit is the truth.
Sunday, 23 June 1754
    1 Corinthians 5:8--Let us, therefore, cele-
brate the festival, not with the old leaven,

the leaven of malice and evil, but with the
unleavened bread of sincerity and truth.

1 Corinthians 12:7--To each is given the mani-
festation of the Spirit for the common good.

Romans 8:21--. . .because the creation itself
will be set free from its bondage to decay
and obtain the glorious liberty of the children of God.

Genesis 6:3--Then the Lord said, "My spirit
shall not abide in man for ever, for he is
flesh, but his days shall be a hundred and
twenty years. '

Tuesday, 30 July 1754

Romans 6:23--For the wages of sin is death,
but the free gift of God is eternal life
in Christ Jesus our Lord.

Romans 8:13--. . .for if you live according to
the flesh you will die, but if by the Spirit
you put to death the deeds of the body,
you will live.

Mark 9:23--And Jesus said to him, "If you can!
All things are possible to him who
believes."

Philippians 3:17--Brethren, join in imitating
me, and mark those who so live as you have
an example in us.

Sunday, 13 October 1754

Genesis 27:38--Esau said to his father, "Have
you but one blessing, my father? Bless me,
even me also, O my father." And Easu
lifted up his voice and wept.

Revelation 21:4--. . .he will wipe away every
tear from their eyes, and death shall be no
more, neither shall there be mourning nor

crying nor pain any more, for the former
things have passed away.

Hebrews 13:1--Let brotherly love continue.

Monday, 23 December 1754

1 John 1:1--That which was from the beginning,
which we have heard, which we have seen with
our eyes, which we have looked upon and
touched with our hands, concerning the word of
life. . . .

Proverbs 4:23--Keep your heart with all vigilence; for from it flows the springs of life.

Tuesday, 31 December 1754

2 Peter 3:5--They deliberately ignore this
fact, that by the word of God, heavens existed long ago, and an earth formed out of
water and by means of water. . . .

Luke 10:42--. . .one thing is needful. Mary
has chosen the good portion, which shall
not be taken away from her.

Sunday, 5 January 1755

2 Peter 3:7--But by the same words the heaven
and earth that now exist have been stored
up for fire, being kept until the day of
judgment and destruction of ungodly men.

Romans 3:19--Now we know that whatever the law
says it speaks to those who are under the
law, so that every mouth may be stopped,
and the whole world may be accountable to
God.

1 Timothy 1:8--Now we know that the law is
good, if any one uses it lawfully. . . .

Psalms 10:4--In the pride of his countenance
the wicked does not seek him; all his
thoughts are, "There is no God."

Matthew 12:42--The queen of the South will
arise at the judgment with this generation
and condemn it; for she came from the ends
of the earth to hear the wisdom of Solomon,
and behold, something greater than Solomon
is here.

Jeremiah 5:29--Shall I not punish them for
these things? says the Lord, and shall I
not avenge myself on a nation such as this?

Mark 15:17--And they clothed him in a purple
cloak, and plaiting a crown of thorns, they
put it on him.

Mark 2:18--Now John's disciples and the Pharisees were fasting; and people came and said
to him, "Why do John's disciples and the
disciples of the Pharisees fast, but your
disciples do not fast?"

Monday, 3 February 1755

Titus 2:14--. . .who gave himself to us to
redeem us from all iniquity and to purify
for himself a people of his own who are
zealous for good deeds.

1 Corinthians 15:19--If for this life only we
have hoped in Christ, we are of all men
most to be pitied.

James 3:17--But the wisdom from above is first
pure, then peaceable, gentle, open to reason, full of mercy and good fruits, without
uncertainty or insincerity.

Sunday, 9 February 1755

1 Corinthians 5:18--All this is from God, who
through Christ reconciled us to himself and
gave us the ministry of reconciliation. . .

1 Thessalonians 5:16--Rejoice always. . . .

2 Corinthians 6:2--For he says, "At the
   acceptable time I have listened to you, and
   helped you on the day of salvation."
Monday, 17 February 1755
   Luke 9:23--And he said to all, "If any man
   would come after me, let him deny himself
   and take up his cross daily and follow me."
   Isaiah 58:10--. . .if you pour yourself out
   for the hungry and satisfy the desire of
   the afflicted, then shall your light rise
   in the darkness and your gloom be as the
   noonday.
   Micah 6:9--The voice of the Lord cries to the
   city--and it is sound wisdom to hear thy
   name: "Hear, O tribe and assembly of the
   city!
Sunday, 9 March 1755
   1 Corinthians 1:24--. . .but to those who are
   called, both Jews and Greeks, Christ the
   power of God and the wisdom of God.
   1 Timothy 4:1-8--Now the Spirit expressly says
   that in later times some will depart from
   the faith by giving heed to deceitful
   spirits and doctrines of demons. . .
Sunday, 16 March 1755
   Proverbs 23:23--Buy truth, and do not sell it;
   buy wisdom, instruction, and understanding.
   Acts 4:10--. . .be it known to you all, and to
   all the people of Israel, that by the name
   of Jesus Christ of Nazareth, who you crucified, whom God raised from the dead, by him
   this man is standing before you well.
   Colossians 2:6--As therefore you received
   Christ Jesus the Lord, so live in him. . .

Thursday, 1 January 1756

2 Timothy--Chapter and verse not indicated.

Hebrews 9:27--And just as it is appointed for
   men to die once, and after that comes judgment. . . .

John 13:28--Now no one at the table knew why
   he said this to him.

Isaiah 24:17--Terror, and the pit, and the
   snare are upon you, O inhabitants of the
   earth!

Isaiah 24:6--Therefore, a curse devours the
   earth, and its inhabitants suffer for their
   guilt; therefore, the inhabitants of the
   earth are scorched, and few men are left.

Acts 26:18--. . .to open their eyes, that they
   may turn from darkness to light and from
   the power of Satan to God, that they may
   receive forgiveness of sins and a place
   among those who are sanctified by faith in
   me.

Daniel 4:1--King Nebuchadnezzar to all peoples, nations, and languages, that dwell
   in all the earth: Peace be multiplied to
   you!

Matthew 8:19--And a scribe came to him and
   said to him, "Teacher, I will follow you
   wherever you go."

Sunday, 19 September 1756

2 Timothy--Chapter and verse not indicated.See
   also above for Thursday, 1 January 1756 (p.
   183).

Jeremiah--Chapter and verse not indicated.

Luke 7:16--Fear seized them all; and they glorified God, saying, "A great prophet has

arised among us!" and "God has visited his
people!"

Ephesians 2:13--But now in Christ Jesus you
who once were far off have been brought
near in the blood of Christ.

Ephesians 6:10-11--Finally, be strong in the
Lord and in the strength of his might. Put
on the whole armor of God, that you may be
able to stand against the wiles of the
devil.

John 6:69--. . .and we have believed, and have
come to know, that you are the Holy One of
God.

Luke 7:41--A certain creditor had two debtors;
one owed five hundred dinarii, and the
other fifty.

2 Thessalonians 2:7--For the mystery of law-
lessness is already at work; only he who
now restrains it will do so until he is out
of the way.

John 20:25--So the other disciples told him,
"We have seen the Lord." But he said to them,
"Unless I see in his hands the print of the
nails, and place my hand in his side, I will
not believe."

Romans 15:2--. . .let each of us please his
neighbor for his good, to edify him.

Hebrews 13:9--Do not be led away by diverse
and strange teachings; for it is well that
the heart be strengthened by grace, not by
foods, which have not benefited their adherents.

(?) December 1756

James 4:4--Unfaithful creatures!   Do you not

know that friendship with the world is en-
mity with God? Therefore, whoever wishes
to be a friend of the world makes himself
an enemy of God.

Ecclesiastes 4:1-2--Again, I saw all the op-
pressions that are practiced under the sun.
And behold the tears of the oppressed, and
they had no one to comfort them! On the
side of their oppressors there was power,
and there was no one to comfort them. And
I thought the dead who are already dead
more fortunate than the living who are
still alive. . . .

1 John 1:7--. . .but if we walk in the light,
as he is in the light, we have fellowship
with one another, and the blood of Jesus
his Son cleanses us from all sin.

(?) January 1757

Hosea 14:4--I will heal their faithfulness; I
will love them freely, for my anger has
turned from them.

Joshua 10:12--Then spoke Joshua to the Lord
in the day when the Lord gave the Amorites
over to the men of Israel; and he said in
the sight of Israel, "Sun, stand thou still
at Gibeon, and thou Moon in the valley of
Aijalon."

Romans 12:2--Do not be conformed to this world
but be transformed by the renewal of your
mind, that you may prove what is the will
of God, what is good and acceptable and perfect.

Psalms 144--Blessed be the Lord, my rock, who
trains my hands for war and my fingers for

battle. . .

Mark 6:12--So they went out and preached that
    men should repent.

Matthew 10:13--And if the house is worthy, let
    your peace come upon it; but if it is not
    worthy, let your peace return to you.

1 Corinthians 13:13--So faith, hope, love,
    abide, these three; but the greatest of
    these is love.

1 Corinthians 13:10--. . .but when the perfect
    comes, the imperfect will pass away.

2 Corinthians 6:2-3--For he says, "At the ac-
    ceptable time I have listend to you, and
    helped you on the day of salvation." Be-
    hold, now is the acceptable time; behold,
    now is the day of salvation. We put no ob-
    stacle in any one's way, so that no fault
    may be found with our ministry. . . .

Luke 17:6--And the Lord said, "If you had
    faith as a grain of mustard seed, you could
    say to this sycamine tree, 'Be rooted up,
    and be planted in the sea,' and it would
    obey you.

John 11:26--. . .and whosoever lives and
    believes in me shall never die. Do you
    believe this?

John 14:27--Peace I leave with you; my peace
    I give to you. Let not your hearts be
    troubled, neither let them be afraid.

Isaiah 1:3--The ox knows its owner, and the
    ass its master's crib; but Israel does not
    know, my people does not understand.

John 7:17--See above for Sunday, 1 November
    1748 (p. 166).

Philippians 2:5--Have this mind among
yourselves, which you have in Christ Jesus. . .
Mark 1:5--And there went out to him all the
country of Judea, and all the people of
Jerusalem; and they were baptized by him
in the River Jordan, confessing their sins.
Psalms 16:4--Those who choose another god multiply their sorrows; their libations of
blood I will not pour out and take their
names upon my lips.
1 Peter 4:2--. . .so as to live for the rest
of the time in the flesh no longer by human passions but by the will of God.

Thursday, 4 August 1757

Titus--Chapter and verse not indicated.
Luke 16:3--And the steward said to himself,
"What shall I do, since my master is taking the stewardship away from me? I am not
strong enough to dig, and I am ashamed to
beg.
Psalms 71:4--But I will hope continually, and
will praise thee yet more and more.
Luke 18:4--I tell you, this man went down to
his house justified rather than the others;
for every one who exalts himself will be
humbled, but he who humbles himself will be
exalted.
Matthew 10:21--Brother will deliver up brother
to death, and the father his child, and the
children will rise against parents and have
them put to death. . . .

Saturday, 12 November 1757

John 5:25--Truly, truly, I say to you, the
hour is coming, and now is, when the dead

will hear the voice of the Son of God, and
those who hear will live.

1 Peter 5:8--Be sober, be watchful. Your adver-
sary the devil prowls around like a roaring
lion, seeking some one to devour.

Psalms 96:1-2--O sing to the Lord a new song;
sing to the Lord, all the earth! Sing to
the Lord, bless his name; tell of his salvation from day to day.

1 Peter 1:14--As obedient children, do not be
conformed to the passions of your former
ignorance. . . .

Sunday, 25 December 1757

Revelation 1:8--"I am the Alpha and the Omega,"
says the Lord God, who is and who was
and who is to come, the Almighty.

1 Peter 1:2--. . .chosen and destined by God
the Father and sanctified by the Spirit for
obedience to Jesus Christ and for sprinkling with his blood: May grace and peace be
multiplied to you.

Monday, 26 December 1757

Haggai 2:7--. . .and I will shake all nations,
so that the treasures of all nations shall
come in, and I will fill this house with
splendor, says the Lord of hosts.

Matthew 20:12--. . .saying, "These last worked
only one hour, and you have made them
equal to us who have borne the burden of
the day and the scorching heat."

Romans 12:21--Do not be overcome by evil, but
overcome evil with good.

Saturday, 28 January 1758

Luke 18:41--"What do you want me to do for

you?" He said, "Lord, let me receive my
sight."

1 Thessalonians 4:1--Finally, brethren, we beseech and exhort you in the Lord Jesus, that
as you learned from us how you ought to live
and to please God, just as you are doing,
you do so more and more.

Luke 21--He looked up and saw the rich putting
their gifts into the treasury. . . .

Sunday, 26 February 1758

Ephesians 3:1--For this reason, I, Paul, a
prisoner for Christ Jesus on behalf of you
Gentiles. . . .

Luke 10:11--Even the dust of your town that
clings to our feet, we wipe off against
you; nevertheless, know this, that the
kingdom of God has come near.

John 4:34--Jesus said to them, "My food is to
do the will of him who sent me, and to ac-
complish his work.

Sunday, 22 October 1758

Philippians 1:9-12--And it is my prayer that
your love may abound more and more. . . .

1 Peter 3:8--Finally, all of you, have unity
of spirit, sympathy, love of the brethren,
a tender heart and a humble mind.

1 Peter 3--Likewise you wives, be submissive
to your husbands. . . .

1 Peter 5--So I exhort the elders among you,
as a fellow elder and a witness of the sufferings of Christ. . . .

Sunday, 26 November 1758

Isaiah 40:1--Comfort, comfort my people, says
your God.

Genesis 49:4--Unstable as water, you shall not
have pre-eminence because you   went to
your father's bed; then you defiled it--
you went up to my couch!

Sunday, 31 October 1738

1 Peter 4:7--The end of all things is at hand;
therefore, keep sane and sober for your
prayers.

Isaiah 24:4--The earth mourns and withers, the
world languishes and withers; the heavens
languish together with the earth.

Sunday, 14 January 1759

Matthew 12:22--Then a blind and dumb demoniac
was brought to him, and he healed him, so
that the dumb man spoke and saw.

1 Peter 4:8--Above all, hold unfailing your
love for one another, since love covers a
multitude of sins.

1 Peter 5--So I exhort the elders among you,
as a fellow elder and a witness of the sufferings of Christ, as well as a partaker of
the glory that is to be revealed. . . .

Sunday, 21 January 1759

Matthew 19:22--When the young man heard this,
he went away sorrowful; for he had great
possessions.

Matthew 26:46--Rise, let us be going; see, my
betrayer is at hand.

Psalms 119:137--Righteous art thou, O Lord,
and right are thy judgments.

Daniel 4:27--Therefore, O king, let my counsel
be acceptable to you; break off your sins
by practicing righteousness, and your iniquities by showing mercy to be oppressed,

that there may perhaps be a lengthening of
your tranquillity.

Friday, 16 February 1759. On this day the British
nation celebrated a public fast--a time of panic throughout the island-kingdom because of an expected invasion by
the French and rumors that only 11,000 British troops remained to defend Great Britain. John Wesley preached at
the Foundery at 8:30 p.m. Among the congregation sat
Selina Shirley, Countess of Huntingdon, the patroness of
Rev. George Whitefield and the sponsor of the Calvinist
Methodists.

Sunday, 18 February 1759

> Genesis 3:19--In the sweat of your face you
> shall eat bread till you return to the
> ground, for out of it you were taken; you
> are dust, and to the dust you shall return.

> Luke 10:28--And he said to him, "You have
> answered right; do this and you will live."

> Mark 13--And as he came out of the temple,one
> of his disciples said to him, "Look,
> Teacher, what wonderful stones and what
> wonderful buildings!"

> Acts 17:10--The brethren immediately sent
> Paul and Silas away by night to Beroea;
> and when they arrived they went into the
> Jewish synagogue.

Thursday, 9 August 1759

> Luke 1:6--And they were both righteous before
> God, walking in all the commandments and
> ordinances of the Lord blameless. . . .

> Luke 22:19--And he took bread, and when he had
> given thanks he broke it and gave it to
> them, saying, "This is my body. . . ."

> John 5:39--You search the scriptures, because

you think that in them you have eternal
life; and it is they who bear witness to
me. . . .

Ephesians 5:29--For no man ever hates his own
flesh, but nourishes and cherishes it, as
Christ does the Church. . . .

Friday, 10 August 1759

Psalms 9:17--The wicked shall depart to Sheol,
all the nations that forget God.

2 Peter--Chapter and verse not indicated.

Galatians 5:22--See above under Sunday, 26 May
1751 (p. 174).

Jeremiah 8:20--The harvest is past, the summer
is ended, and we are not saved.

Matthew 22:12--. . .and he said to him,"Friend,
how did you get in here without a wedding
garment?" And he was speechless.

Ephesians 6:12--For we are not contending
against flesh and blood, but against the
principalities, against the powers, against
the world rulers of this present darkness,
against the spiritual hosts of wickedness
in heavenly places.

Proverbs 2:1-5--My son, if you receive my words
and treasure up my commandments with you,
making your ear attentive to wisdom and in-
clining your heart to understanding; yes,
if you cry out for insight and raise your
voice for understanding, if you seek it
like silver and search for it as for hidden
treasures; then you will understand the
fear of the Lord and find the knowledge of
God.

Sunday, 18 November 1759

Nehemiah 13:16--Men of Tyre, also, who lived
in the city, brought in fish and all kinds
of wares and sold them on the sabbath to
the people of Judah, and in Jerusalem.

Psalms 62:1--For God alone my soul waits in
silence; from him comes my salvation.

Psalms 103:2--Bless the Lord, O my soul, and
forget not all his benefits. . . .

Tuesday, 4 December 1759

2 Peter 3:8--But do not ignore this one fact,
beloved, that with the Lord one day is as
a thousand years, and a thousand years as
one day.

2 Peter 3:10--See above for Monday, 1 January
1753 (p. 176).

Acts 9:31--So the church throughout all Judea
and Galilee and Samaria had peace and was
built up; walking in the fear of the Lord
and in the comfort of the Holy Spirit, it
was multiplied.

Tuesday, 8 January 1760

Acts 14:22--. . .strengthening the souls of
the disciples, exhorting them to continue
in the faith, and saying that through many
tribulations we must enter the kingdom of
God.

Romans 3:28--For we hold that a man is justified by faith apart from works of law.

Romans 12:5--. . .so we, though many, are one
body in Christ, and individually members
one of another.

Isaiah 51:16--And I have put my words in your
mouth, and hid you in the shadow of my hand,
stretching out the heavens and laying the

foundations of the earth, and saying to
Zion, "You are my people."

1 Corinthians 3:12--Now if any one builds on
the foundation with gold, silver, precious
stones, wood, hay, stubble. . . .

James 3:2--For we all make many mistakes, and
if any one makes no mistakes in what he
says, he is a perfect man, able to bridle
the whole body also.

Matthew 20:16--So the last will be first, and
the first last.

1 Corinthians 7:35--I say this for your own
benefit, not to lay any restraint upon you,
but to promote good order and to secure
your undivided devotion to the Lord.

Tuesday, 5 February 1760. Wesley noted, "I baptized
a gentlewoman. . .and the peace she immediately found
was a fresh proof that the outward sign, daily received,
is always accompanied with the inward grace."

Sunday, 22 February 1761

Luke 5:13--And he stretched out his hand, and
touched him, saying, "I will; be clean."And
immediately the leprosy left him.

Galatians 5--For freedom, Christ has set us
free. . . .

Ephesians 2:9--. . .not because of works, lest
any man should boast.

1 John 1:9--If we confess our sins, he is
faithful and just, and will forgive our sins
and cleanse us from all unrighteousness.

Matthew 5:48--You, therefore, must be perfect,
as your heavenly Father is perfect.

1 Corinthians 9:22--To the weak, I became weak,
that I might win the weak. I have become

all things to all men, that I might by all
means save some.

Romans 10:4--For Christ is the end of the law,
that every one who has faith may be justified.

Psalms 102:7--Let the redeemed of the Lord say
so, whom he has redeemed from trouble. . .

1 Peter 4:10--As each has received a gift, employ it for one another, as good stewards of
God's varied grace. . . .

Ephesians 4:30--And do not grieve the Holy
Spirit of God, in who you were sealed for
the day of redemption.

Mark 9:23--See above for Tuesday, 30 July 1754
(p. 179).

Tuesday, 3 November 1761

1 Peter 1:9--For whosoever lacks these things
is blind and shortsighted and has forgotten
that he was cleansed from his old sins.

1 Samuel 17--Now the Philistines gathered their
army for battle. . . .

1 Peter 1:9--See directly above, first entry,
under this date.

Friday, 20 November 1761

Galatians 5:5-For through the Spirit, by faith,
we wait for the hope of righteousness.

John 14:6--Jesus said to him, "I am the way and
the truth and the life; no one comes to the
Father but by me.

Zechariah 4:7--What are you, O great mountain?
Before Zerubbabel you shall become a plain;
and he shall bring forward the top   stone
amid shouts of "Grace, grace to it!"

Philippians 3:13--Brethren, I do not consider

that I have made it my own; but one thing
I do, forgetting what lies behind and
straining forward to what lies ahead. . . .
Sunday, 6 December 1761

Mark 9:23--See above for Tuesday, 30 July 1754
(p. 179) and for Sunday, 22 February 1761
(p. 195).

1 John 2:1--My little children, I am writing
this to you so that you may not sin; but if
any one does sin, we have an advocate with
the Father, Jesus Christ, the righteous. . .

James 3:17--See above for Monday, 3 February
1755 (p. 181).

Thursday, 10 December 1761

Romans 10:4--See above for Sunday, 22 February
1761 (p. 195).

Romans 7:4--Likewise, my brethren, you have
died to the law through the body of Christ,
so that you may belong to another, to him
who has been raised from the dead in order
that we may bear fruit for God.

1 Corinthians 9:22--See above for Sunday, 22
February 1761 (pp. 194-195).

Revelation 20:1--Then I saw an angel coming
down from heaven, holding in his hand the
key of the bottomless pit and a great chain.

Revelation 20:8--. . .and will come out to deceive the nations which are at the four corners of the earth, that is, Gog and Magog,
to gather them for battle.

Wednesday, 16 December 1761

Romans 3:10--. . .as it is written:"None is
righteous, no, not one. . . ."

1 Timothy 1:5--. . .whereas the aim of our

charge is love that issues from a pure heart
and a good conscience and sincere faith.

Ephesians 2:12--. . .remember that you were at
that time separated from Christ, alienated
from the commonwealth of Israel, and strangers to the covenants of promise, having no
hope and without God in the world.

Monday, 21 December 1761

James 3:2--For we all make many mistakes, and
if any one makes no mistakes in what he says,
he is a perfect man, able to bridle the whole
body also.

Matthew 22:27--After them all, the women died.

Revelation 1:5--. . .and from Jesus Christ the
faithful witness, the first born of the
dead, and the ruler of kings on earth. To
him who loves us and has freed us from our
sins by his blood. . . .

Friday, 25 December 1761

John 3:16--For God so loved the world that he
gave his only Son, that who ever believes
in him should not perish, but have eternal
life.

Dueteronomy 29:12--. . .that you may enter into
the sworn covenant of the Lord your God,
which the Lord your God makes with you this
day. . . .

2 Kings 23:3--And the king stood by the pillar
and made a covenant before the Lord, to walk
after the Lord and keep his commandments and
his testimonies and his statutes, with all
his heart and all his soul, to perform the
words of this covenant that were written in
this book. . . .

Thursday, 13 January 1763. Wesley noted that he
"strongly enforced, on a large congregation. . . the
words of Isaiah (never more needful): 'He that believeth shall not make haste.'"

Thursday, 2 February 1764. "I preached again at the
Foundery, which has been repairing for several weeks. It
is not only firm and safe (whereas before the main timbers were quite decayed) but clean and decent, and capa-
ble of receiving several hundreds more." In a letter to
his wife, dated 7 June 1764, Charles Wesley stated that
he preached in the Foundery "to above five thousand lis-
tening souls. Five or six hundred more it is supposed
to hold since the alterations." Unfortunately, there appears no clear or reasonable means by which to validate
the younger Wesley's figures. He, as did brother John,
tended to overestimate the sizes of congregations   at
both indoor and outdoor public worship services.

Wednesday, 1 January 1766. "A large congregation," noted John Wesley, "met in the Foundery at four o'
clock a.m., and ushered in the New Year with the voice of
praise and thanksgiving."

Sunday, 8 August 1779. "This was the last night
which I spent at the Foundery," wrote Wesley in his journal. "What hath God wrought there in one and forty years."

The Hospital of St. Mary of Bethlehem ("Bedlam"),
Moorfields. The original St. Mary's Hospital, in Bishopsgate, was founded as a priory in about 1247, with the
special duty of receiving and entertaining the clergy of
St. Mary of Bethlehem, the mother church, as often as
they might come to England. In about 1330, the priory
became a hospital, and by 1402 it served to accommodate
lunatics. The original structure gave way to a new

hospital, built in 1675 in Moorfields, to be replaced   in
1815 by a still   newer building   located on the Lambeth
Road.   The governors finally relocated the hospital at
Monks Orchard, Eden Park, Beckenham.

Until around 1770, "Bedlam" stood as one of the regular tourist stops of London. For the sum of one   penny,
the tourist could gaze upon the poor maniacs,   naked and
chained to the walls of their dungeons.   Public viewing
thus brought approximately £ 400 annually into the hospital coffers.   In his Life of Samuel Johnson   (p. 1225),
Boswell   records   a conversation (for Friday,   18 April
1783) between Dr. Johnson and the wife of the musicolo-
gist, Dr. Charles Burney (1726-1814).   The latter "wondered that some very beautiful new buildings would be
erected in Moorfields, in so shocking a situation as between Bedlam and St. Luke's Hospital (see immediately below); and said she could not live there." Johnson replied, "Nay, Madam, you see nothing there to hurt   you.
You no more think of madness by having windows that look
to Bedlam, than you think of death by having windows that
look to a church-yard." He commented further that "a
very moral use may be made of these new buildings: I
would have those who have heated imaginations live there,
and take warning."

On Wednesday, 15 August 1744, John Wesley went to
St. Mary's "at the request of Mr. S-----, who had been
confined there above two years.   This   was   the person
who, while he was speaking against my brother [Charles]
and me to the society at Kingswood [outside Bristol],
was in a moment struck raving mad.   But it seems God is
at length entreated for him, and has restored to him a
sound mind." More than five years later, on Thursday,
22 February 1750, Wesley returned: "Having been sent for
several times, I went to see a young woman in Bedlam. But

I had not talked with her long before one gave me to
know that none of these preachers were to   come there.
So we [Methodists] are forbid to go to Newgate, for fear
of making them wicked; and to Bedlamd, for fear of driv-
ing them mad!"

St. Luke's Hospital, Moorfields. Located on the
northern boundary of Moorfields, St. Luke's was instituted in 1751 to receive poor, insane persons.   In 1790,
the governors removed the facility to Old Street.

Upon visiting the hospital on Tuesday, 21 December 1762, and perusing the register, Wesley expressed
surprise in observing "three or four (at least) of
those who are admitted receive a cure. I doubt this is
not the case of any other lunatic hospital either in
Great Britain or Ireland."

Spitalfields. Spitalfields takes its name from
having been the property of the Priory and Hospital of
St. Mary's (thus "'spital"), founded in about 1197 by Walter Brune and Rosia, his wife, for Canons regular. French
Protestant silk weavers settled in that London district
after the revocation (1685) of the Edict of Nantes; thus
began the great British silk industry that reached its
height in the eighteenth century. In 1719, for example,
over £300,000 worth of silk scarves and hoods for women
were manufactured in London. During the reign of Anne
(1702-1714), the Spitalfields weavers numbered approximately 50,000--the majority being men and women (English)
working under the guidance and direction of Huguenots--
and the number of looms varied between 14,000 and 20,000
(See Davey 2:314-315). Ironically, the white silk cas-

socks of the Roman Popes continued to be woven by those
French and English Protestants until the last quarter of
the nineteenth century.

Between January 1739 and February 1791, John Wesley
made frequent visits to the district of Spitalfields--
most certainly a fertile orchard in which to plant the
social and theological seeds of Methodism. Unfortunately,
however, his diary and journal entries are not always
clear as to specific places within the district. In
other words, we may observe numerous references merely
to "Spitalfields," rather than to a particular church,
chapel, public or residential building, or even street.
Thus, we would do well to follow his major activities in
the area in strict chronological order, identifying specific places when Wesley, in turn, clearly identifies
them in the diary or the journal. As usual, Biblical
references identify sources upon which the Methodist
leader based his sermon addresses.

Thursday, 25 January 1739. At 3:00 p.m., Wesley
heard a sermon delivered by George Whitefield for the
"Orphan House."

Sunday, 18 February 1739. Wesley preached at 10:00
a.m. at Sir George Wheeler's Chapel. Wheeler (1650-
1723), canon and rector of Houghton-le-Spring, built
his chapel in 1693 for his tenantry and--by his will--
secured a provision for the minister officiating. In
1842, the original building underwent modernization and
became known as St. Mary's, Spital Square.

Wednesday, 21 March 1750. "I preached in the old
French [Protestant] church in Grey Eagle Street, Spitalfields. It was extremely full, and many of the hearers
were greatly moved." The London Methodists obtained possession of that church early in 1750. Eventually, the
building and the site became a part of Truman, Bixton,

and Hanbury Brewery. Wesley's sermons on this day came
from the following Biblical texts:

> Galatians 5:6--For in Christ Jesus neither cir-
> cumcision nor uncircumcision is of any avail,
> but faith working through love.
>
> Hebrews 8:11--And they shall not teach every
> one his fellow or every one his brother,
> saying, "Know the Lord," for all shall
> know me, from the least of them to the
> greatest.
>
> Matthew 11:28--Come to me, all who labour and
> are heavy laden, and I will give you rest.
>
> Galatians 6:14--But far be it from me to glory
> in the cross of our Lord Jesus Christ, by
> which the world has been crucified to me,
> and I to the world.
>
> 1 Peter 2:12--Like newborn babes, long for
> the pure spiritual milk, that by it you may
> grow up to salvation. . . .
>
> Mark 2:26--. . .how he entered the house of
> God, when Abiathur was high priest,and ate
> the bread of the Presence, which is not
> lawful for any but the priests to eat, and
> also gave it to those who were with him?

Friday, 21 September 1750. "We had a watch-night
at Spitalfields [in the French Protestant chapel, Grey
Eagle Street]." Simply, the watch-night proved an occasion on which a group spent the greater part of the
night in prayer, praise, and thanksgiving. Wesley had
begun the custom in 1742 among the Kingswood colliers,
outside Bristol.

Sunday, 27 January 1751. Wesley preached a charity
sermon "for the use of our poor children. The church
[perhaps the French Protestant chapel] was extremely

crowded; but not many rich, not many. . .'well-born,'
were there." Simply stated, the charity sermon produced
little for charity!

Sunday, 24 February 1751. He preached both morning and evening at Spitalfields, "where many who had been
wandering from God for several years seemed at length to
have fresh desires of returning to Him."

Sunday, 3 November 1751. On this day, John Wesley
delivered five sermons at one of the dissolved French
churches in Spitalfields. During the general period under discussion, at least seven French Protestant churches existed in the district. Thus, through the religious societies or by temporary occupancy of abandoned
or partially occupied buildings, the early London Methodists struck a relationship with Hugenot exiles and their
descendants in both east and west London. At any rate,
Wesley based his sermons upon the following texts from
Scriptures:

> Philippians 1:4--. . .always in every prayer
> of mine for you all, making my prayer with
> joy. . . .
>
> Isaiah 11:9--They shall not hurt or destroy in
> all my holy mountain; for the earth shall be
> full of the knowledge of the Lord as the
> waters cover the sea.
>
> Isaiah 1-3--The vision of Isaiah, the son of
> Amoz, which he saw concerning Judah and
> Jerusalem. . . .
>
> Philippians 3:3--For we are the true circumci-
> sion, who worship God in spirit, and glory
> in Christ Jesus, and put no confidence in
> the flesh.
>
> Philippians 1:29--For it has been granted to
> you that for the sake of Christ you should

not only believe in him, but also suffer
for his sake. . . .

    <u>Psalms</u> 77:3--I think of God, and I moan; I med-
itate, and my spirit faints.

Sunday, 18 November 1753. Wesley "preached at
Spitalfields, and administered the sacrament to a large
congregation."

Monday, 11 August 1755. At 6:00 p.m., Wesley addressed a meeting of the French Protestant church on the
means of "increasing serious religion, which had been frequently practised by our forefathers and attended with
eminent blessing, namely, the joining in a covenant to
serve God with all our heart and with all our soul." He
estimated the congregation at "about eighteen hundred
persons."

Sunday, 6 February 1757. "The number of communicants at Spitalfield made this Lord's Day a little more
laborious than the former." On the preceding Sunday (30
January), Wesley had conducted a service at West Street
Chapel that lasted "between four and five hours" (see
above, p. 78).

Friday, 17 February 1758. On this public fast-day,
Wesley preached at Spitalfields sometime in the afternoon.

Friday, 16 February 1759. This being another fast-
day, the result of a threatened French invasion and rumors that only 11,000 British troops remained to defend
England (see above, p. 191, for the same date under <u>The
Foundery</u>), Wesley preached at 9:00 a.m. and at 3:00 p.m.
"in the church at Spitalfields." He based his sermons
on the following texts:

    <u>Isaiah</u> 58:5-12--Is such the fast that I choose,
a day for a man to humble himself? Is it
to bow down his head like a rush. . . .

Genesis 3:19--In the sweat of your face you
shall eat bread till you return to the
ground, for out of it you were take; you
are dust, and to dust you shall return.

Acts 17:27--. . .that they should seek God,
in the hope that they might feel after him
and find him. Yet, he is not far from each
one of us. . . .

Galatians 5:18--But if you are led by the
Spirit, you are not under the law.

Saturday, 24 February 1759

Ephesians 1:13--In him you also, who have heard
the word of truth, the gospel of your salvation, and have believed in him, were
sealed with the promised Holy Spirit. . . .

Luke 8:10--Two men went up to the temple to
pray, one a Pharisee and the other a tax
collector.

James 1:27--Religion that is pure and undefiled before God and the Father is this: to
visit orphans and widows in their affliction, and to keep oneself unstained from
this world.

Psalms 62:1--For God alone my soul waits in
silence; from him comes my salvation.

1 Peter 3:18--For Christ also died for sins
once for all, the righteous for the
unrighteous, that he might bring us to God,
being put to death in the flesh, but made
alive in the spirit. . . .

Acts 17:8--And the people and the city author-
ities were disturbed when they heard this.

1 Corinthians 13:13--So faith, hope, love abide,
these three; but the greatest of these is

love.

Sunday, 28 October 1759. "I found," proclaimed
Wesley, "the ancient spirit in the congregation. . .at
Spitalfields. . . ."

Monday, 29 October 1759

> Ephesians 5:15--Look carefully, then, how you
> walk, not as unwise men but as wise. . . .
>
> Luke 20:34--And Jesus said to them, "The sons
> of this age marry and are given in
> marriage. . . .
>
> Philippians 1:9--And it is my prayer that your
> love may abound more and more, with know-
> ledge and all discernment. . . .
>
> John 8:12--Again Jesus spoke to them, saying,
> "I am the light of the world; he who fol-
> lows me will not walk in darkness, but will
> have the light of life."

Friday, 29 February 1760. ". . .at six in the evening we met at the church in Spitalfields to renew our
covenant with God."

Friday, 1 January 1762. "We had, I believe, pretty
near two thousand of the society in Spitalfields in the
evening, where Mr. Berridge, Maxfield, and Colley assisted me." Rev. John Berridge (1716-1793) served as vicar
of Everton, Bedfordshire; Thomas Maxfield functioned, for
more than twenty years, as one of Wesley's principal as-
sistants, both in London and in the rural counties; and
Rev. Benjamin Colley, ordained in the Church of England
and officiated as a clergyman in Methodist chapels, came
from Tollerton, Yorkshire.

Sunday, 28 February 1762. "We had a peculiar blessing at Spitalfields while I was enforcing 'Now is the
day of salvation [2 Corinthians 6:2].' Indeed, there is
always a blessing when we cut off all delay, and come to
God now by simple faith."

Saturday, 25 December 1762. The Society met "at
the chapel in Spitalfields, to renew our covenant with
God. . . ."

Monday, 28 February 1763. "preaching in the evening
at Spitalfields on 'Prepare to meet thy God [Amos 4:12],'
I largely showed the utter absurdity of the supposition
that the world was to end that night. But. . .many were
afraid to go to bed, and some wandered about in the
fields, being persuaded that, if the world did not end,at
least London would be swallowed by an earthquake. I went
to bed at my usual time, and was fast asleep about ten
o'clock." The man responsible for the prophecy, George
Bell--a native of Barningham, near Barnard Castle, York-
shire--had been a corporal in the Life Guards. He converted to Methodism in 1758; in March 1761, he announced
himself to be sanctified. Then, joined by Thomas
Maxfield (see above for Friday, 1 January 1762 [p. 206]),
he formed an independent society based upon the doctrine
that the sanctified do not require self-examination or
private prayer, that they cannot be taught by anyone not
in the same state as themselves. On 27 February 1763,
Bell and his followers ascended a mound near St. Luke's
hospital (see above, p. 200). There, the magistrates
arrested him, brought him to trial, and committed him to
prison--where he eventually awaited the outcome of his
prediction relative to the end of the world (see Tyerman
2:433-441, 460, 462).

Sunday, 10 March 1765. In the old French Protestant Church, Grey Eagle Street, Wesley took up a collection for the impoverished, unemployed weavers of Spi-
Spitalfields. He collected "about forty pounds." In the
evening, he managed to collect   "fourteen pounds more."
Throughout its history, as a center for the British silk
industry, Spitalfields suffered from extreme degrees of

trade fluctuation. Simply, the industry tended to be
overstocked with workers, except during periods of exceptional prosperity. And, throughout the major part
of the eighteenth century, weaving proved to be one of
the worst paying of the London trades. "The wages of
weavers in general are but poor," noted The Parents'
Director in 1761, a time of extended prosperity in the
silk trade, "the best hands among the journeymen being
seldom able to get above 15s. a week," while a journeyman brocade weaver (an art requiring considerable skill
and ingenuity) "cannot earn above 12s. or 15s. a week"
(George 176-195).

Wednesday, 1 January 1766. "In the evening we met,
as usual, at the church in Spitalfields, to renew our
covenant with God. This is always a refreshing season,
at which some prisoners are set at liberty."

Wednesday, 1 January 1767. Again, the society met
in the evening in "Spitalfields church. . . ."

Sunday, 1 January 1768. Here we may observe another New Year's Day meeting of the society at "Spitalfields Chapel. . . ."

Sunday, 5 March 1769. Wesley preached "at Spitalfields in the morning. . . ."

Sunday, 15 October 1769. Both John and Charles
Wesley "had such a congregation at Spitalfields as has not
been there since the covenant night." See above for Wednesday, 1 January 1766 (this page).

Sunday, 25 July 1773. Wesley considered this a "day
of strong consolation, particularly at Spitalfields."

Sunday, 25 February 1781. "My brother [Charles],
Mr. Richardson, and Mr. Buckingham being ill, I went
through the service at Spitalfields alone. The congregation was much larger than usual, but my strength was
as my day. . . ." John Richardson, curate of Emhurst,

Sussex, came (in 1762) to assist Wesley in London; he
served the London society until his death in 1792--one
year following the passing of Methodism's founder and
leader. Rev. William Buckingham, who often preached in
the Calvinist Methodist chapels of Selina Shirley, Countess of Huntingdon, worked with Wesley for two years before he abandoned his Methodist activities--until at
least 1781. On Monday, On Monday, 15 September 1766,
John Wesley wrote in his journal, "Here [Port Isaac,
Cornwall] Mr. Buckingham met me, who, for fear of of-
fending the Bishop, broke off all commerce with the
Methodists. He had no sooner done this than the Bishop
rewarded him by turning him out of his curacy; which, had
he continued to walk in Christian simplicity, he would
probably have had to this day."

    Sunday, 15 December 1782

        2 Timothy 3:4--. . .treacherous, reckless,
           swollen with conceit, lovers of pleasure
           rather than lovers of God. . . .

    Sunday, 19 January 1783

        Matthew 17:20--He said to them, "Because of
           your little faith. For truly, I say to
           you, if you have faith, as a grain of
           mustard seed, you will say to this moun-
           tain, 'Move hence to yonder place,' and it
           will move; and nothing will be impossible
           to you."

    Sunday, 16 February 1783

        Mark 16:6--And he said to them, "Do not be
           amazed; you seek Jesus of Nazareth, who was
           crucified. He has risen; he is not here;
           see the place where they laid him.

    Sunday, 19 October 1783

        Matthew 22:39--And a second is like it: You
           shall love your neighbor as yourself.

Sunday, 16 November 1783

John 8:12--Again Jesus spoke to them, saying,
"I am the light of the world; he who follows me will not walk in darkness, but will
have the light of life."

Sunday, 21 December 1783

Matthew 24:17--For as the lightning comes from
the east and shines as far as the west, so
will be the evening of the Son of man.

Sunday, 18 January 1784

Matthew 16:23--But he turned and said to
Peter, "Get behind me Satan! You are a hind-
rance to me; for you are not on the side of
God, but of men."

Sunday, 15 February 1784

John 15:7--If you abide in me, and my words
abide in you, ask whatever you will, and it
shall be done for you.

Sunday, 17 October 1784

Daniel 3--King Nebuchadnezzar made an image of
gold. . . .

Sunday, 21 November 1784

1 Peter 1:18--You know that you were ransomed
from the futile ways inherited from your
fathers, not with perishable things such as
silver or gold. . . .

Sunday, 16 January 1784

Matthew 14:31--Jesus immediately reached out
his hand and caught him, saying to him, "O
man of little faith, why did you doubt?"

Sunday, 20 February 1785

1 Thessalonians 4:3--For this is the will of
God, your sanctification: that you abstain
from immorality. . . .

Sunday, 30 October 1785
> Luke 16:31--He said to him, "If they do not
> hear Moses and the prophets, neither will
> they be convinced if some one should rise
> from the dead."

Sunday, 18 December 1785
> Isaiah 30:18--Therefore, the Lord waits to be
> gracious to you; therefore, he exalts him-
> self to show mercy to you. For the Lord
> is a God of justice; blessed are all those
> who wait for him.

Sunday, 15 January 1786
> Matthew 13:3--And he told them many things in
> parables, saying: "A sower went out to sow.

Sunday, 19 February 1786
> Luke 8:18--Take heed, then, how you hear; for
> to him who has will more be given, and from
> him who has not, even what he thinks that
> he has will be taken away.

Sunday, 15 October 1786
> Luke 1:72--. . .to perform the mercy
> promised to our fathers, and to remember his
> holy covenant. . . .

Sunday, 17 December 1786
> Acts 17:30--The times of ignorance God over-
> looked, but now he commands all men every-
> where to repent. . . .

Sunday, 21 January 1787
> Matthew 19:21--Jesus said to him, "If you
> would be perfect, go, sell what you pos-
> sess and give to the poor, and you will
> have treasure in heaven; and come, follow
> me."

Sunday, 18 February 1787

1 <u>Corinthians</u> 13:3--If I give away all I have,
and if I deliver my body to be burned, but
have not love, I gain nothing.

Sunday, 21 October 1787

<u>Ephesians</u> 5:15--Look carefully, then, how you
walk, not as unwise men, but as wise. . . .

Sunday, 18 November 1787. "We had, as usual, a large
congregation and comfortable opportunity at Spitalfields." Wesley preached on <u>John</u> 11:48--If we let him
go on thus, every one will believe in him, and the Romans
will come and destroy both our holy places and
our nation.

Sunday, 16 December 1787

<u>Acts</u> 16:31--And they said, "Believe in the
Lord Jesus, and you will be saved, you and
your household."

Sunday, 20 January 1788

1 <u>Corinthians</u> 7:24--So, brethren, in whatever
state each was called, there let him remain with God.

Sunday, 17 February 1788

1 <u>Thessalonians</u> 4:3--See above for Sunday, 20
February 1785 (p. 210).

Sunday, 19 October 1788

<u>Philippians</u> 1:9--And it is my prayer that your
love may abound more and more, with knowledge and all discernment. . . .

Sunday, 16 November 1788

<u>Isaiah</u> 55:1--Ho, every one who thirsts, come
to the waters; and he who has no money
come, buy and eat! Come, buy wine and milk
without money and without price.

Sunday, 21 December 1788

<u>Philippians</u> 4:7--And the peace of God, which

passes all understanding, will keep your

hearts and your minds in Christ Jesus.

Sunday, 18 January 1789

Psalms 90:4--For a thousand years in thy

sight are but as yesterday when it is past,

or as a watch in the night.

Sunday, 15 February 1789

Luke 8:14--And as for what fell among the

thorns, they are those who hear, but as

they go on their way they are choked by

the cares and riches and pleasures of life,

and their fruit does not mature.

Sunday, 15 February 1789. "We had, as usual, a

large congregation and a solemn opportunity at Spital-

fields. . . ." Notice the close parallel in wording

between that statement and the one recorded by Wesley

in his journal for Sunday, 18 November 1787 (see above,

p. 212). At any rate, he preached on Philippians 3:20--

But our commonwealth is in heaven, and from it we await

a Savior, the Lord Jesus Christ. . . .

Sunday, 20 December 1789

Matthew 22:12--. . .and he said to him,

"Friend, how did you get in here without

a wedding garment?" And he was speech-

less.

Sunday, 21 February 1790

2 Corinthians 6:1--Working together with him,

then, we entreat you not to accept the grace

of God in vain.

Sunday, 24 October 1790. "I explained, to a numer-

ous congregation in Spitalfields church 'the whole ar-

mour of God [Ephesians 6:11].'" Hester Ann Rogers--one

of the Methodist patriarch's most devoted female assis-

tants and whose picture appears in Marshall Claxton's

painting, The Death Bed of John Wesley—noted that Wesley preached with great liberty and related the story
of a general who, though harassed by the enemy on all
sides, was shot in the armpit by a musketball while
holding up his arm and pronouncing a boastful oath (see
Curnock, Journal 8:110 + note).

Sunday, 21 November 1790

Job 6:27—You would even cast lots over the
fatherless, and bargain over your friend.

Sunday, 19 December 1790

Isaiah 3:10—Tell the righteous that it shall
be well with them, for they shall eat the
fruit of their deeds.

Sunday, 16 January 1791—less than two months before the death of the eighty-nine year-old Wesley—

Revelation 21:6—And he said to me, "It is
done! I am the Alpha and the Omega, the
beginning and the end. To the thirsty I
will give water without price from the
fountain of the water of life.

"St. George's, Spitalfields." Wesley noted, in
his journal for Sunday, 31 December 1738, that he preached
"to many thousands in St. George's, Spitalfields."
That particular church becomes extremely difficult to
identify, specifically since there exists no evidence
of a "St. George's, Spitalfields," having been in operation at that time. There may well be an error here;
perhaps Wesley actually meant Sir George Wheeler's Chapel (see above, under Spitalfields, for Sunday, 18 February 1739, p. 201),or even another Anglican church in
Spitalfields—Christ Church, rebuilt in 1723. At any
rate, neither Christ Church nor Wheeler's Chapel could

have accommodated "many thousands." Again, both John
and Charles Wesley tended to overestimate (and thus to
overstate) the sizes of their congregations--those attending outdoor services as well as indoor exercises in
public worship.

Bethnal Green. Beyond Spitalfields, to the east,
lay the district of Bethnal Green, consisting mainly of
open land, except where it merged with Spitalfields. At
that point, it existed as a section densely built and
obviously industrial. By 1667, the actual Green had
dwindled to seven acres. The silk-weaving industry of
Spitalfields overflowed into Bethnal Green, whose
southwest end became continuous with London. Descendants of Huguenot refugees formed part of the population, which numbered 15,000 in 1742. Those persons
crowded into narrow streets and courts in the south and
west sections; in certain instances, three or four families could be found occupying a single house! The
poverty of Bethnal Green was known throughout the City
and existed because of the large numbers of journeyman
weavers. Until 1743, the area stood as a separate hamlet; in that year, it became incorporated into St.
Matthew parish.

    John Wesley preached at Bethnal Green on Thursday,
23 September 1764, and again on Sunday, 12 November 1775.
On the latter date, he was "desired to preach, in Bethnal
Green [St. Matthew's], a charity sermon for the widows and orphans of the soldiers that were killed in
America. Knowing how many would seek occasion of offence, I wrote down my sermon." Wesley had actually
written the tract earlier in the week (7 November), basing his text on 2 Samuel 24:17--Lo, I have sinned, and

I have done wickedly: but these sheep, what have they
done? Although he focused upon the topic of "National
Sins and Miseries," Wesley published the piece as A
Sermon Preached at St. Matthew's, Bethnal-Green, on
Sunday, Nov. 12, 1775. For the Benefit of the Widows
and Orphans of the Soldiers Who Lately Fell near Boston,
in New England (London: E. Hawes, n.d.). The bat-
tles at Lexington, Concord, and Bunker Hill occurred,
of course, during April 1775. For the text of this sermon see Outler, Sermons 3:564-576.

During the winter of 1776-1777, a severe cold spell
gripped London. Thus, on Wednesday and Thursday, 15-
16 January 1777, Wesley moved among the members of the
Methodist society who lived in Bethnal Green. "Many of
them I found in such poverty as few can conceive without seeing it. . . . Such another scene I saw the next
day [16 January], in visiting another part of the society. I have not found any such distress, no, not in
the prison of Newgate. One poor man was just creeping
out of his sick-bed to his ragged wife and three little children, who were more than half naked, and the
very picture of famine; when, one bringing in a loaf of
bread, they all ran, seized upon it, and tore it to
pieces in an instant."

He returned to St. Matthew's Church--built during
1743-1746 from the design of George Dance the elder--on
Sunday, 20 November 1785, where he "spoke as plain as I
possibly could on 'having a form of godliness, but denying the power thereof' [2 Timothy 3:5]. And this I
judged to be far more suitable to such a congregation
than talking of justification by faith." Indeed, Wesley
took advantage of every opportunity to outline the
differences between himself and his Anglican colleagues.
At any rate, more than two years later (Sunday, 27 July

1788), he delivered a sermon at St. Matthew's on "our
Lord's lamentation over Jerusalem [Amos 5]. I believe
the word did not fall to the ground." Finally, Wesley
came to St. Matthew's on Sunday, 5 December 1790; he based
his sermon text on Proverbs 22--A good name is to
be chosen, rather than great riches. . . .

   Bonner's House (or Bishop's Hall), Bonner Road,
Bethnel Green. On a portion of the site that later became the Victoria Park Chest Hospital (or the London
Chest Hospital, built in 1851)--and not far from the
Children's Home buildings on Bonner Road--stood Bishop's
Hall (or Bishop Bonner's House), an old manor-house and
palace of the bishops of London. Edmund Bonner (1500-
1569) was the last Bishop of London to die in communion
with the Papacy. Appointed Bishop of Hereford in 1538
and of London in 1539, he refused to compromise his defence of traditional Church doctrines. Thus, Edward VI
deprived him of his office, Mary restored him to it; under Elizabeth I he refused to take the oath to the Act
of Supremacy, and so the Queen sent him to the Marshalsea
Prison, where he died.
   John Wesley retired to Bishop's Hall on Monday, 7
October 1754, and remarked, "Here I was in college.
Twice a day we joined in prayer. The rest of the day
(allowing about an hour for meals, and another for walking before dinner and supper), I spent quietly in my
study." Two years later, Thursday, 16 September 1756,
he "preached to a large and serious congregation. I
found some faintness, the sun being extremely hot. . ."
   From the Sermon Register, we can determine the biblical texts from which Wesley developed his sermons, delivered either in Bonner's House or in the vicinity of

Bonner Road:

    (?) November 1754

        Isaiah 55:7--. . .let the wicked forsake his
        way, and the unrighteous man his thoughts;
        let him return to the Lord, that he may
        have mercy upon him, and to our God, for he
        will abundantly pardon.

        1 Corinthians 13:13--So faith, hope, love abide,
        these three; but the greatest of these is
        love.

        John 4:24--God is spirit, and those who worship
        him must worship in spirit and truth.

    (?) December 1754

        John 17:3--So his brother said to him, "Leave
        here and go to Judea, that your disciples
        may see the works you are doing.

        John 11:48--If we let him go on thus, every
        one will believe in him, and the Romans
        will come and destroy both our holy place
        and our nation.

        Psalms 147:3--He heals the broken-hearted, and
        binds up their wounds.

        Psalms 81:1--Sing aloud to God our strength;
        shout for joy to the God of Jacob!

    Saturday, 5 July 1755

        Luke 13:27--But he will say, "I tell you, I do
        not know where you come from; depart from
        me, all you workers of iniquity!"

    Thursday, 10 July 1755

        Acts 11:26--. . .and when he had found him, he
        brought him to Antioch. For a whole year
        they met with the church, and taught a large
        company of people; and in Antioch the dis-
        ciples were for the first time called Chris-
        tians.

2 Timothy 2:4--No soldier on service gent en-
tangled in civilian pursuits, since his aim
is to satisfy the one who enlisted him.

Luke 2:42--And when he was twelve years old,
they went up according to custom. . . .

Thursday, 7 August 1755

Hebrews 4:12--For the word of God is living
and active, sharper than any two-edged
sword, piercing to the division of soul and
spirit, of joints and marrow, and discern-
ing the thoughts and attention of the heart.

Hebrews 4:14--Since we then have a great high
priest who has passed through the heavens,
Jesus, the Son of God; let us hold fast our
confession.

1 Timothy 6:6--There is a great gain in godliness with contentment. . . .

Thursday, 30 October 1755

1 Thessalonians 5:16--So then let us not sleeep,
as other do, but let us keep awake and be
sober.

Romans 3:1--Then what advantage has the Jew?
Or what is the value of circumcision?

Luke 21:34--But take heed to yourselves, lest
your hearts be weighed down with dissipa-
tion and drunkenness and cares of this life,
and that day comes upon you suddenly like a
snare. . . .

Thursday, 15 January 1756

Hebrews 9:27--And just as it it appointed for
men to die once, and after that comes judgment. . . .

John 13:28--Now no one at the table knew why
he said this to him.

Jeremiah 4:1-2--If you return, O Israel, says
the Lord, to me you should return. If you
remove your abominations from my presence,
and do not waver, and if you swear, "As the
Lord lives," in truth, in justice, and in
uprightness, then nations shall bless themselves in him, and in him shall they glory.

Ezekiel 37:1--The hand of the Lord was upon
me, and he brought me out by the Spirit of
the Lord, and set me down in the midst of
the valley; it was full of bones.

John 4:24--God is spirit, and those who worship him must worship in spirit and truth.

Saturday, 17 January 1756

Genesis 32--Jacob went on his way and the
angels of God met him. . . .

Matthew 16:23--But he turned and said to
Peter, "Get behind me, Satan! You are a hindrance to me; for you are not on the side
of God, but of men."

1 Corinthians 6:9--Do you not know that the unrighteous will not inherit the kingdom of
God? Do not be deceived; neither the immoral, nor idolaters, nor adulterers, nor
homosexuals. . . .

Acts 22:16--And now, why do you wait? Rise and
be baptized, and wash away your sins, calling on his name.

Psalms 147:20--He has not dealt thus with any
other nation; they do not know his ordinan-
ces. Praise the Lord!

Isaiah 24:6--Therefore, a curse devours the
earth, and its inhabitants suffer for their
guilt; therefore, the inhabitants of the

earth are scorched, and few men are left.

Mark 8:38--For whoever is ashamed of me and my
words in this adulterous and sinful generation, of him will the Son of man also be
ashamed, when he comes in the glory of his
Father with the holy angels.

Ephesians 5:15--Look carefully, then, how you
walk, not as unwise men, but as wise. . . .

Sunday, 18 January 1756

Isaiah 51:12--I, I am he that comforts you; who
are you that are afraid of man who dies, of
the Son of man who is made like grass. . . .

Luke 13:4--Or those eighteen upon whom the tower in Siloam fell and killed them; do you
think that they were worse offenders than
all the others who dwelt in Jerusalem?

Matthew 13:9--He who has ears, let him hear.

Sunday, 1 February 1756

Mark 1:1--The beginning of the gospel of Jesus
Christ, the Son of God.

Isaiah 26:20--Come, my people, enter your chambers, and shut your doors behind you; hide
yourselves for a little while until the
wrath is past.

Jeremiah 4:1-2--See above for Thursday, 15 January 1756 (p. 220),

Friday, 6 February 1756

Luke 13:4--See above for Sunday, 18 January
1756 (this page).

2 Timothy 2:4--See above for Thursday, 10 July
1755, p.219)

Jeremiah 4:1-9--If you return, O Israel, says
the Lord. . . .

Luke 5:32--I have not come to call the righteous, but sinners, to repentance.

Thursday, 15 February 1756

Matthew 20:16--So the last will be the first,
and the first last.

Isaiah 24:15-16--Therefore, in the east, give
glory to the Lord; in the coastlands of the
sea, to the name of the Lord, the God of
Israel. From the ends of the earth we hear
songs of praise, of glory to the Righteous
One. But I say, "I pine away, I pine away.
Woe is me! For the treacherous deal treach-
erously, the treacherous deal very treacher-
ously."

Jeremiah 4:1-9--See above for Thursday, 15 January 1756 (p. 220); Sunday, 1 February 1756
(p. 211); Friday, 6 February 1756 (p. 221).

Galatians 5:1--For freedom, Christ has set us
free; stand fast, therefore, and do not sub-
mit again to a yoke of slavery.

Saturday, 11 September 1756

Micah 6:8--He has showed you. O man, what is
good; and what does the Lord require of you
but to do justice, and to love kindness, and
to walk humbly with your God?

Thursday, 16 September 1756

John 4:24--See above for Thursday, 15 January
1756 (p. 220).

Psalms 34:8--O taste and see that the Lord is
good! Happy is the man who takes refuge in
him!

Luke 23:43--And he said to him, "Truly, I say
to you, today, you will be with me in
Paradise."

Colossians 1:4--. . .in whom we have redemption, the forgiveness of sins.

1 John 1:7--. . .but if we walk in the light,
we have fellowship with one another, and
the blood of Jesus his Son cleanses us from
all sin.

(?) March 1757

1 Corinthians 2:14--The unspiritual man does
not receive the gifts of the Spirit of God,
for they are folly to him, and he is not
able to understand them because they are
spiritually discerned.

Malachi 3:3--. . .he will sit as a refiner and
purifier of silver, and he will purify the
sons of Levi and refine them like gold and
silver, till they present right offerings
to the Lord.

Thursday, 8 December 1757

Revelation 22:17--The Spirit and the Bride say,
"Come." And let him who hears say, "Come."
And let him who is thirsty, come; let him
who desires take water of life without
price.

Mark 4:26--And he said, "The kingdom of God is
as if a man should scatter seed upon the
ground. . . ."

1 Peter 1:9--As the outcome of your faith you
obtain the salvation of your souls.

(?) December 1758

1 John 4:3--and every spirit which does not
confess Jesus is not of God. This is the
spirit of antichrist, of which you heard
that it was coming, and now it is in the
world already.

Luke 16:31--He said to him, "If they do not
hear Moses and the prophets, neither will

they be convinced if some one whould rise
from the dead."
Acts 11:26—See above for Thursday, 10 July
1755 (p. 218).

Whitechapel. As with its neighboring districts of
Spitalfields and Bethnal Green, Whitechapel, in the eighteenth century, existed as a highly industrialized but
equally poverty-stricken area. The district had the reputation as one of the worst localites in London, both
in terms of its narrow, filthy streets and disreputable
inhabitants. The parish church, St. Mary's (or St. Mary
Matfelon), managed to escape destruction in the Great
Fire. Although John Wesley never mentioned the church
by name, he probably preached there on the following occasions (Biblical text indicated):
Sunday, 31 December 1738. "I preached. . .to a. . .
crowded congregation at Whitechapel in the afternoon
[and] I declared those glad tidings (oh, that they should
know the things which make for their peace!). 'I will
heal their backslidings; I will love them freely [Hosea
14:4]."
Saturday, 21 June 1740
    Matthew 5:2-4—And he opened his mouth and
    taught them, saying, "Blessed are the poor
    in spirit, for theirs is the kingdom of heav-
    en. Blessed are those who mourn, for they
    shall be comforted."
Saturday, 5 July 1740
    Luke 13:12—And when Jesus saw her, he called
    to her and said to her, "Woman, you are
    freed from your infirmity."

Goodman's Fields, Whitechapel. Goodman's Fields
covered the site of Leman Street, East, and derived its
name from a farmer named (of course) Goodman, who owned
the property at the end of the sixteenth century. Since
funeral urns were discovered in the area, speculation
has arisen that the field once existed as the site of a
Roman burial ground. Henry Gifford (1699-1772), actor
and manager, owned a theatre in Goodman's Fields that had
to close its doors in 1737 as a result of the Licensing
Act--particularly that provision requiring the acting of
a legitimate drama to be sanctioned by a Royal patent.
In July 1740, he sought permission from the Lord Chamberlain
to re-open the playhouse. Upon failing to obtain
the license, Gifford nonetheless re-opened his theatre
under the pretense of performing a play and afterpiece
gratis and charging admission only for the concert that
preceded and followed the main entertainment. On 19 October 1741, David Garrick made his debut at the Goodman
Fields Theatre in Richard III. Gifford's theatre eventually came down in 1746, but it was soon rebuilt. Fire
destroyed the new structure in 1802.

Wesley's single recorded visit to Goodman's Fields
occurred on Friday, 22 December 1738. At 11:30 a.m., he
visited a Mr. Jones there for prayer and conversation.

Great Gardens, Whitechapel Road. According to
Wesley's own description (Journal 3:45), Great Gardens existed as an "open place. . .lying between Whitechapel on
the north side of Whitechapel Road and Coverlet Fields."
He preached there on Sunday, 12 September 1742, "where I
found a vast multitude gathered together. Taking knowledge that a great part of them were little acquainted
with the things of God, I called upon them in the words

of our Lord, 'Repent, ye, and believe the gospel [Mark
1:15].' Many of the beasts of the people laboured much
to disturb those who were of a better mind. They endeavoured to drive in a herd of cows among them; but the
brutes were wiser than their masters. They then threw
whole showers of stones, one of which struck me just between the eyes: but I felt no pain at all; and when I had
wiped away the blood, went on testifying with a loud
voice that God hath given to them that believe 'not the
spirit of fear, but of power, and of love, and of a
sound mind [1 Timothy 1:7].'"

On Trinity Sunday, 29 May 1743, Wesley preached
again at Great Gardens, "to an immense congregation on
'Ye must be born again [John 3:7].'"

Greyhound Lane, Whitechapel. From Wesley's notations in the diary and also from remarks in his journal,
we may conclude that, between October 1740 and early September 1741, a religious society existed somewhere in
Greyhound Lane (Biblical texts indicated):
Wednseday, 1 October 1740
    Acts 11:26--. . .and when he had found them,
        he brought him to Antioch. For a whole year
        they met with the church, and taught a large
        company of people; and in Antioch the dis-
        ciples were for the first time called Christ-
        ians.
Wednesday, 15 October 1740
    Ephesians 4--I therefore, a prisoner for the
        Lord, beg you to lead a life worthy of the
        calling to which you have been called. . .
Wednesday, 5 November 1740
    Matthew 12:26--. . .and if Satan casts out
        Satan, he is divided against himself; how,
        then, will his kingdom stand?

Saturday, 14 February 1741
>   1 John 5:11--And this is the testimony, that
>   God gave us eternal life, and this life is
>   in his Son.

Wednesday, 15 April 1741."I was so weak in body that
I could hardly stand; but my spirit was much strengthened. On that day he based his sermon on Ephesians
4 (see above for Wednesday, 15 October 1740 (p. 226).

Wednesday, 29 April 1741
>   Ezekiel 36:25--I will sprinkle clean water up-
>   on you, and you shall be clean from all your
>   uncleanliness; and from all your idols I
>   will cleanse you.

Wednesday, 6 May 1741
>   Luke 7--After he had ended all his sayings in
>   the hearing of the people,he entered Caper-
>   naum.

Wednesday, 27 May 1741
>   Luke 16:2--And he called him and said to him,
>   "What is this that I hear about you? Turn
>   in the account of your stewardship, for you
>   can no longer be a steward."

Wednesday, 3 June 1741
>   2 Corinthians 6:1--Working together with him,
>   then, we entreat you not to accept the grace
>   of God in vain.

Wednesday, 29 July 1741
>   Luke 18:18--And a ruler asked him, "Good Tea-
>   cher, what shall I do to inherit eternal
>   life?"

Wednesday, 5 August 1741
>   John 9--As he passed by he saw a man blind
>   from his birth. And his disciples asked
>   him, Rabbi, who sinned, this man or his

parents, that he was born blind?"
Wednesday, 9 September 1741

> Psalms 107--O give thanks to the Lord, for he
> is good; for his steadfast love endures for
> ever!

St. Dunstan's Church, High Street, Stepney. The
parish church of Stepney, St. Dunstan's dates to the
fourteenth century, while its parish registers begin at
1568. John Colet (1467-1519)--dean of St. Paul's, founder of St. Paul's School, and a friend of Erasmus--ser-
ved as vicar there. Apart from Bow Church (see below,
this section), St. Dunstan's stood as the only medieval
church in East London. Perhaps the most tragic note associated with the building concerns the selling of its
Renatus Harris organ, built in 1678, to Drury Lane
Theatre.

Wesley, who termed St. Dunstan's "one of the largest parish churches in England," preached there on Sunday, 27 February 1785. He based his sermon text upon 1
Corinthians 13:1--If I speak in the tongues of men and
of angels, but have not love, I am a noisy gong or a
clanging cymbal.

Old Ford. John Wesley preached at the church of
Old Ford--a district lying east of the City center (and,
in the eighteenth century, an industrial hamlet situated
in the parish of Bow)--on Friday, 21 February 1766."Part
of the congregation," he observed and then noted in his
journal, "were deeply serious; the other part wild and
stupid enough. ₅But the bridle was in their mouth, so
that they made no noise; nay, and were, in a manner, attentive.

Bow. Lying five miles east-northeast of Charing
Cross, and just about southeast of Old Ford, Stratford-
le-Bow (or, merely, Bow) was known in the eighteenth century for the manufacture of chinaware, as well as for cal-
ico printing and scarlet dyeing. By the end of the
century, the population of Bow stood at approximately
2000; in 1901, the district could claim more than 42,000
inhabitants! St. Mary's Church, dating from 1311, stood
as the principal house of worship in the district.

Wesley preached at Bow on the following occasions
(Biblical text indicated):

Thursday, 12 Februay 1784

1 John 4:19--We know that we are of God, and
the whole world is in the evil one.

Friday, 12 November 1784

Galatians 3:22--But the scripture consigned
all things to sin, that what was promised
to faith in Jesus Christ might be given to
those who believe.

Friday, 10 February 1786

Acts 16:31--And they said, "Believe in the Lord
Jesus, and you will be saved, you and your
household."

ILLUSTRATIONS

Charterhouse School

Fetter Lane Chapel

St. Bartholomew the Great; St. Ann, Aldersgate;
St. Lawrence Jewry; and St. Katherine Cree

Old St. Mary, Islington; St. Michael Bassishaw;
and St. George's-in-the-East

St. Botolph, Bishopsgate; St. Mary-le-Bow;
St. Antholin; and St. Clement Danes

King's Foundery, Moorfields

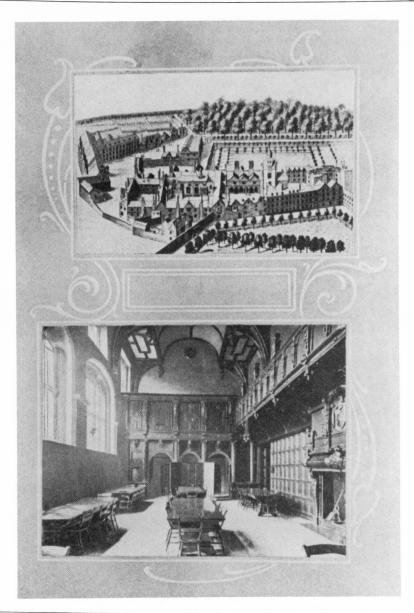

Charterhouse School (p. 101)

Reproduced from N. Curnock's edition
of John Wesley's *Journal*

Fetter Lane Chapel (p. 106)

Reproduced from N. Curnock's edition
of John Wesley's *Journal*

St. Bartholomew the Great (p.113), St. Ann, Aldersgate (p.131), St. Lawrence Jewry (p. 132), and St. Katherine Cree (p. 329)

Old St. Mary, Islington (p. 349), St. Michael Bassishaw (p.132),
and St. George's-in-the-East (p. 352)

Reproduced from N. Curnock's edition
of John Wesley's *Journal*

St. Botolph, Bishopsgate (p. 150), St. Mary-le-Bow (p.272),
St. Antholin (p. 271), and St. Clement Danes (p. 250)

Reproduced from N. Curnock's edition
of John Wesley's *Journal*

King's Foundery, Widmill Street, Moorfields (p. 161)

Reproduced from N. Curnock's edition
of John Wesley's *Journal*

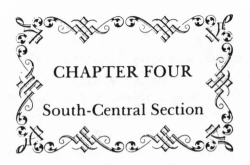

CHAPTER FOUR

South-Central Section

If any one thinks he is religious, and
does not bridle his tongue, but deceives
his heart, this man's religion is vain.
Religion that is pure and undefiled before
God and the Father is this: to visit orph-
and and widows in their affliction, and to
keep oneself unstained from this world.

James 2:26-27

Kensington Gardens. King William III began the construction of Kensington Gardens near Kensington Palace;
Queen Anne enlarged the project by giving thirty acres
from the park near Nottingham House. Those two actions occurred between 1690 and 1708. In 1726-1728, Queen Caroline
of Anspach made the round ponds and planted the avenues,
each of which has a distinctive name--such as "Old
Pond Walk" and "Bayswater Walk." The groves were filled
with squirrels, and a large number of tortoises, presented
to Caroline by the Doge of venice, were distributed about
the grounds. Deer abounded, and even certain favored
gentlemen received permits to hunt foxes on the public
grounds. After the Court removed to Richmond, George
II opened the gardens to the public on Saturdays, provided that strollers appear in full, formal dress. In fact,
until 1795, no one who wore a silk necktie or leathern
breeches without topboots could gain admission. Thus,
soldiers, sailors, and livery servants found themselves
excluded from Kensington Gardens. Certainly, accurate
accounts of the activities within Kensington Gardens may

be found in Joseph Addison's Spectator 477 or Thomas
Tickell's poem, Kensington Gardens (1722).

When James Boswell walked through Kensington Gardens
on Monday, 23 May 1763, he thought the area "delightful."
In his London Journal (265), he described the site as "a
glorious thing for the King to keep such walks so near
the Metropolis, open to all his subjects." John Wesley,
however, seemed not impressed, and he noted the following in his own journal for Saturday, 6 July 1754: "I
spent two hours in the gardens at Kensington. They are
just fit for a king, far more grand than pleasant; and
yet nothing so grand as many parts of the Peak in
Derbyshire."

Brompton. Brompton lay south of Kensington Gardens
and north of Chelsea. The area gained reputation for
its market gardens and nursery grounds. In 1681, for
instance, George London founded Brompton Park Nursery
in partnership with Henry Wise, one-time superintendent
of the Royal Gardens.

Wesley came to Brompton on Thursday morning, at 8:15,
12 February 1789, where he took tea, engaged in conversation, and conducted prayer.

Tyburn, Hyde Park. At the northeastern corner of
Hyde Park stood the famous "Tyburn Tree"--sometimes referred to as the "Three-Legged Mare," being a triangle
on three legs. There, public executions occurred until,
in 1783, officials transferred such activities to Newgate
Prison. The manor of Tyburn (or Ey-burn) took its
name from the Eye bourne (brook), which rose under Primrose
Hill and flowed south to the Thames through what are

now the dips in Oxford Street and Picadilly, west of
Bond Street. The gallows of Tyburn, which originally
stood further east, were moved in the sixteenth century
to a post northwest of the present position of Marble
Arch. There, the Tyburn Road turned off from Watling
Street and, following approximately the line of Oxford
Street and Holborn, reached the City at Newgate.

The condemned prisoners were brought to Tyburn from
Newgate Prison, usually carrying nosegays. By custom,
the malefactors received their flowers on the steps of
St. Sepulchre's Church. Then followed bowls of ale at
St. Giles. The cart bearing the prisoner was driven
underneath the the gallows and the noose adjusted; then,
Jack Ketch, the hangman, drove the cart away quickly,
leaving the condemned person suspended. Naturally, death
by such a method proved slow and, at times, uncertain,
for the more sophisticated "drop" had not yet been
developed.

Around the area of the gallows stood raised galleries that spectators could rent. In 1758, a mob, disappointed by the reprieve of a Dr. Henesey, destroyed that
structure. On the house at the corner of Upper Bryanston
Street and Edgware Road stood--until 1785--the iron
balconies from which the sheriffs could witness the executions. On 7 November 1783, John Austin became the last
person to be hanged at Tyburn.

John and Charles Wesley witnessed an execution at
Tyburn on Wednesday, 8 November 1738, at noon. After
the hanging, Charles "took that occasion of declaring
the gospel of peace to a large assembly of publicans
and sinners."

Knightsbridge. Knightsbridge, in the eighteenth
century a suburb of the City of London, skirted the

southern portion of Hyde Park. Supposedly, it derives its
name from two knights who quarrelled on their way to receive the Bishop of London's blessing. Fighting, they
killed each other by the bridge over the West Bourne,
which stood on the site later occupied by Albert's Gate.

Knightsbridge stood as a lonely district, one infes-
ted by highwaymen. On 2 April 1740, according to a re-
port in the Gentleman's Magazine, the British mail from
London was robbed a little distance beyond Knightsbridge
by a man on foot who made off with the Bath and Bristol
bags. Mounting the post-boy's horse, he rode off toward
London. As late as 30 November 1774, two men named Lane
and Trotman were executed at Tyburn for that robbery of
the Knightsbridge stagecoach. Also in 1774, Richard
Tatersall, stud-groom to the Duke of Kingston, established,
at Brompton Road crossway, the celebrated auction market
for horses and the headquarters of the horse racing
trade. Sales occurred every Monday throughout the year
and every Thursday during the racing season.

On Sunday, 14 January 1750, John Wesley preached at
Knightsbridge "in the afternoon for the benefit of the
poor children. The little church was quite full when I
came. Knowing it to be the greatest charity to awaken
those that sleep in sin, I preached on 'What is man pro-
fited if he shall gain the whole world and lode his own
soul?' [Matthew 16:26]" He preached there again on Sunday, 9 March 1766; again on Sunday, 23 January 1785, basing his text upon John 4:24--God is spirit, and those
who worship him must worship in spirit and truth. Regarding that last occasion, he remarked. "I preached. . .in
the evening in the chapel at Knightsbridge. I think it
will be the last time; for I know not that I have ever
seen a worse behaved congregation." A Mr. John Walsh, a
member of the London Methodist society, lived in Knights-

bridge, and Wesley seems to have lodged with him on Sunday, 9 March 1766, prior to a journey to Bristol.

St. George's Hospital, Hyde Park Corner, Grosvenor Place. St. George's, close by the original site of Tat-Tatersall's (see p. 234), came into being in 1733 through the efforts of seceding governors of Westminster Hospital. The original building, Lanesborough House, functioned merely as a small infirmary of approximately sixty beds. By 1740, it stood as a handsome building of brick, situated--as most hospitals of the period--away from other houses. In 1750, the hospital could accommodate as many as 273 in-patients. Surgeons were always in attendance, but physicians came one once each week, unless specifically required. St. George's maintained an almost exceptional record of 3073 cures for the year of 1753, despite imperfect hygiene--a trademark of the day. To guard against the "evils" from varying temperatures, attendants kept windows shut for extended periods; visiting physicians carried vinaigrettes (or eighteenth-century versions of smalling salts) in their cases as deodorants. After 1753, a proper ventilation system was installed in the building (see Phillips, Mid-Georgian London 74-75).

Some thirty yards west of St. George's lay the cottage of a man named Huggitt, a cow-keeper, who supplied the hospital with milk. The full diet for patients included--

> Breakfast, one pint milk pottage
> Dinner: eight ounces of meat (four days),
>   one pint pease pottage (three days)
> Supper: two ounces of cheese or one and one-
>   half ounces of butter or one pint of

           broth
     daily: fourteen ounces of bread and one
     quart of small beer
Finally, patients who died received burial at the church
of St. George Hanover Square. Perhaps the most significant name associated with the institution, John Hunter
(1728-1793)--the noted surgeon and biologist--received
his appointment in 1768. He suffered from angina and
supposedly stated that if his temper were roused, he
might die--which he did at a hospital governors' meeting!
(see Weinreb and Hibbert 710)

     John Wesley spent an hour at St. George's Hospital
on Friday, 20 November 1761. According to his journal
notation, "The behaviour of two or three patients there
had done unspeakable good. Deep prejudice was torn up
by the roots, and much good will to the truth had succeeded it. Oh what may not a single believer do, who
seeks nothing but the glory of God?"

     Chapel of the Lock Hospital, Grosvenor Place. Lo-
cated in relatively isolated but green fields, where, at
present, Chester Street meets Grosvenor Place, the Lock
Hospital first opened its doors in 1747. It served for
the cure of venereal disease of women--and particularly
female children--who had contacted such affliction inno-
cently under circumstances of rape. Curiously enough,
there existed a popular falacy that men could rid themselves of the disease by passing it on to a child. The
reader of American novelist Michael Crichton's The Great
Train Robbery (New York: Alfred A. Knopf, 1975)--a work
of fiction well known for its historical accuracy--will
discover that the practice of men attempting to rid themselves of venereal disease through intercourse with teen-

age (or less) virgins continued well into the nineteenth
century.

At any rate, on 27 April 1749, a magnificent fireworks display occurred at Green Park to celebrate the
peace of Aix-la-Chapelle and the end of the War of the
Austrian Succession (1741-1748). A large wooden pavi-
lion was constructed of wood and painted to resemble
stone; the structure measured 410 feet in length and
stood 114 feet in height. One Thomas Piddock built the
principal grandstand for spectators in front of the Lock
Hospital.

On Wednesday, 29 March 1764, John Wesley went to
the Lock Hospital chapel to see and hear a performance
of Judith , the second oratorio of Thomas Augustine Arne
(1710-1778). Originally performed at Drury Lane Theatre
on 27 February 1761, the piece was presented at this
time for the benefit of charity. Wesley thought that
"Some parts of it were exceeding fine; but there are two
things in all modern pieces of music which I could never
reconcile to common sense. One is singing the same
words ten times over; the other, singing different words
by different persons, at one in the same time. And this
is the most solemn address to God, whether by way of
prayer or thanksgiving. This can never be defended by
all the musicians in Europe, till reason is quite out of
date." For more on Wesley's (so-called) music criticism,
see his tract On the Power of Music (1779) and Routley's
Musical Wesleys.

On Wednesday, 13 February 1765, Wesley heard another oratorio at the Lock Hospital--this one entitled
Ruth, a cooperative effort by Charles Avison (1710-1779),
Felice de Giardini (1716-1796), and William Boyce (1710-
1779). His reaction appears more positive than that of
the previous year: "The sense was admirable throughout;

and much of the poetry not contemptible. This, joined
with exquisite music, might possibly make an impression
upon rich and honourable sinners." Selina Shirley, Countess of Huntingdon, and her Calvinist Methodist chaplains
also attended the performance.

    Carnaby Market, Carnaby Street. John Wesley
preached--probably at a meeting of an Anglican religious
society on Monday evening, 13 December 1740. Carnaby
Street itself was situated near the present Great Marlborough Street and the Church of St. John. Laid out in
the 1680's, the street and market took their name from
Karnaby House, a structure built on the east side of the
street in 1683 by Richard Taylor, a bricklayer. The
early inhabitants of the area proved to be Huguenots.

    On that night of 13 December 1740, Wesley based his
sermon text on 1 John 5:11-12--And this is the testimony, that God gave us eternal life, and this life is in
his Son. He who has the Son has life; he who has not
the Son of God has not life. In the autumn of the previous year (Monday, 24 September 1739), Wesley had been
at Carnaby Market for "singing, etc. . . . ."

    Queen's House, St. James Park. In 1666, on the
present site of Buckingham Palace, Bennet, Earl of
Arlington, purchased Goring House and renamed it Arlington
House. John Sheffield (1648-1721), Duke of Buckingham,
bought the place in 1698; in 1703, he had a new
structure built for him by a Dutch architect of Bergen
and changed the name to (of course!) Buckingham House.
That same John Sheffield had nominated the eight-year
old John Wesley , "the son of Dr. [Samuel] Wesley, my

chaplain," to be a poor scholar of Sutton's Hospital and
to study at Charterhouse School. George II, when Prince
of Wales, wished to purchase the residence from Buckingham's third wife (the daughter of James II by Catherine
Sedley), but she demanded too high a price. Finally, in
1761, King George III purchased the property from Sir
Charles Sheffield for £21,000, paid in four separate in-
stallments at five percent interest. In 1774, the King
settled the house upon Queen Charlotte, in place of
Somerset House, and named it Queen's House. In 1825, the
same Queen's House was pulled down and the present
Buckingham Palace erected on that site (1837).

John Wesley toured Queen's House on Thursday, 22
December 1774, "with one that belongs to the family."
He seemed not overly impressed. "The apartments are
nothing so rich as those in Blenheim House [Blenheim
Palace, Oxford, seat of the Duke of Marlborough], but full
as elegant. Nor is anything in Blenheim itself more
grand than the staircase and saloon. But I was quite
disappointed in the Cartoons. They are but the shadow
of what they were; the colours are so entirely faded that
you can hardly distinguish what they were once." In this
instance, the term cartoon referred to a preparatory
drawing or painting for a fresco.

The Adelphi, Adelphi Terrace, the Strand. Between
the Strand and the River Thames lay the Adelphi Terrace,
one of the most ambitious of eighteenth-century London
residential architectural projects. In 1768, John,
Robert (1728-1792), James (1730-1794), and William Adam--
the most respected of Scottish architects--leased Durham
Yard, between the Strand and the River Thames, from the
Duke of St. Albans. The following year they commenced

to build the Adelphi (the name symbolizing the fraternal
partnership), conceived of as a vast construction of
arches on which roads were to be laid and twenty-four houses to be built. The architects made provisions for
wharfage and storage on the shores of the Thames, with
access from the Strand, completely separated from the
streets and the terrace above. They even imported
Scottish laborers from Glasgow, who worked to the accompa-
niment of Scottish pipers. However, the project, though
partially completed, failed commercially. By 1773, the
Adam brothers obtained a bill of sanction concerning the
disposal of the property by lottery.

David Garrick (1717-1779)--the actor/manager/ poet/
playwright--moved to Number 5 Adelphi Terrace in March
1772; he died there on 20 January 1779. On Friday, 20
April 1781, Mrs. Garrick had, for the first time since
her husband's death, "a select party of his friends to
dine with her": James Boswell, Samuel Johnson, Sir Joshua
Reynolds, Dr. Charles Burney, and Mrs. Hannah More
(Boswell's Life of Johnson 1139-1141).

John Wesley paid a visit to the Adelphi on Wednesday, 10 December 1783, at 5:00 p.m. Exactly whom he visited there remains unknown; his diary for that day contains this brief entry: ". . .5 tea, within, the Adelphi;
9:30 chaise. . ."

St. Paul's Church, Covent Garden. When the Church
of St. Martin-in-the-Fields became too small for its pa-
rishioners, Francis, fifth Earl of Bedford and virtual
owener of the entire parish area, desired that Inigo
Jones build for him a chapel in Covent Garden. Bedford
declared that he would not spend a large sum on the project, that the result be little more than a barn. Thus,

in 1633, Jones built, on the west side of the Market,
the handsomest "barn" in all of England. He gave to
London its first Protestant church since the Reformation
--at a cost of £5000. Nonetheless, it proved bare
and generally featureless in form. Notable eighteenth-
century figures buried in St. Paul's include William
Wycherley (1641-1715), Susannah Centlivre (1669-1723),
Robert Wilkes, John Armstrong (1709-1779), Tom Davies the
bookseller (1712-1785), and Charles Macklin (1699-1797).
Under the northwest wall lies Samuel Butler (1613-1680).

On Sunday, 28 November 1784, the eighty-one year-
old John Wesley preached a charity sermon at St. Paul's
Covent Garden. "It is," he observed in his journal,
"the largest and best constructed parish church that I
have preached in for several years, yet some hundreds
were obliged to go away, not being able to get in.   I
strongly enforced the necessity of that humble, gentle,
patient love which is the essence of true religion." He
based his sermon text upon 1 Corinthians 13:1--If I
speak in the tongues of man and angels, but have not
love, I am a noisy gong or a clanging cymbal. Most probably Wesley preached upon the invitation of the incumbent of St. Paul's, Richard Bullock, D.D., whose own
sermons were published in 1754 and 1789.

Cox's Museum, Spring Gardens, Charing Cross. James
Cox, jeweler and clockmaker in Shoe Lane, owned a museum
in Spring Gardens that housed unique pieces of mechanism
and jeweled ornaments. His catalogues for 1772 and 1774
figure in the Catalogue of the British Museum. At one
point, the East India Company ordered two clocks from
Cox to be sent to the Emperor of China, and Cox himself
estimated the value of his entire stock at £197,000.

However, the museum did not prosper, and its owner had to
dispose of the stock by lottery.

Mention of the museum appears in Fanny Burney's
Evelina (1778) and Richard Brinsley Sheridan's The Rivals
(1775). In the latter's play, Sir Anthony Absolute tells
his son, ". . .the lady shall be as ugly as I choose;
she shall have a lump on each shoulder; she shall be as
crooked as the Crescent [a semi-ellipse of fashionable
houses in Bath]; her one eye shall roll like the Bull's
in Cox's Museum. . ." (Act 2, scene 1). In 1772, on the
recommendation of Samuel Johnson, James Boswell toured
Cox's Museum and found the mechanisms there a wonder and
the jewels rather pleasing. According to the Gentlemen's
Magazine for March 1772, "The objects [at Cox's] that
first strike the eye are two-and-twenty pieces of mechanism, some nine, some ten, some twelve, and some sixteen
feet high, each blazing with a profusion of the most
costly gems. . . . An elephant, richly caparisoned,
supports a pedestal on which is a triumphal car, drawn
by doves round a magnificent temple of mother-of-pearl
. . . . Pagodas, pouring all Golcanda upon the sight of
the beholder, rise to the music of their own chimes. . .
The various flowers of the year bloom in jewels. . .
Storks, dragons, lizards, dolphins. . .present themselves
. . .in gold, silver, agate, amber, lapis lazuli,and
aventurine. . . " (see Wimsatt and Pottle, Boswell 54,
98).

As one would expect, however, Wesley's reaction to
Cox's Museum proved quite different. He received an
invitation to visit the place on Wednesday, 3 March 1773,
after which he remarked in his journal, "I cannot say my
expectation was disappointed; for I expected nothing, and
I found nothing but a heap of pretty, glittering, trifles,
prepared at an immense expense. For what end? To please

the fancy of fine ladies and pretty gentlemen."

   Church of St. John the Evangelist, Milbank, Westminster. The year 1728 witnessed the consecration of a
new parish church of Westminster, St. John the Evangelist,
begun in 1716 by Thomas Archer (d. 1743). After
the consecration had gone forward, the foundation demon-
strated a tendency to sink into the swampy soil. Archer
then conceived the device of four equal towers at the
corners to ensure that any sinking would at least be
uniform. Fire gutted the structure in 1742, but repairs
came forth with assistance from the House of Commons.
   Wesley preached at St. John's on Sunday afternoon,
5 February 1738, and based his text upon "those strong
words, 'If any man be in Christ, he is a new creature'
(2 Corinthians 5:17). I was afterwards informed, many
of the best in the parish were so offended, that I was
not to preach there any more."

   Westminster. The present City of Westminster, constituted a municipality in 1900 (although its royal char-
ter goes back centuries), extends from the River Thames
to Oxford Street, and from Temple Bar to Kensington. Its
eighteenth-century boundaries proved not significantly
different from the present, as can be determined by the
parishes included within the City: St. Anne, St. Clement
Danes, St. George (Hanover Square), St. James, St. Margaret,
St. John, St. Martin's-in-the-Fields, St. Mary le
Strand, St. Paul (Covent Garden), the Verge of the Palaces
of Whitehall and St. James. The estimated combined
population of those parishes stood at 125,954 in 1710/
1711 and at 153,272 in 1801 (see George, London Life

414). Supposedly, the preaching room for the London
Methodists at Westminster occupied the site of the
Wesleyan Methodist Central Hall, opposite Westminster Abbey
That hall was dedicated on 3 October 1912 (see Journal,
4:47 + Note 2).

The following summarizes John Wesley's major activities within the general area of Westminster between
late 1738 and 1791. Once again, Biblical citations refer to the sources for his sermon addresses:

Friday, 20 October 1738. Wesley "met a society (of
soldiers chiefly) at Westminster." That note may well
stand as the first reference to the work of the early
religious societies with and for soldiers.

Monday, 4 January 1748

> Romans 3:23--. . .since all have sinned and
> fall short of the glory of God. . . .
>
> Romans 9:32--Why? Because they did not pursue
> it through faith, but as if it were based
> on works. They have stumbled over the stum-
> bling stone. . . .
>
> Romans 12:1--I appeal to you, therefore, bre-
> thren, by the mercies of God, to present
> your bodies as a living sacrifice, holy and
> acceptable to God, which is your spiritual
> worship.

Sunday, 5 November 1752. Of more than passing interest is the knowledge (gained from the Sermon Register)
that on this day, Wesley preached at five different places: Snowsfield, the Foundery, West Street Chapel, Spitalfields, and Westminster. At the last named, he based
his sermon upon Hebrews 10:36--For you have need of endurance, so that you may do the will of God and receive
what is promised.

Thursday, 16 September 1756. "I found some faintness,

noted Wesley, "the sun being extremely hot; but
more in walking from thence [Bishop Bonner's House, see
pp. 217-114] to Westminster, where I preached at seven."
    Thursday, 11 February 1783
        2 Corinthians 4:18--. . .because we look not
           to the things that are seen, but to the
           things that are unseen; for the things that
           are seen are transient, but the things that
           are unseen are eternal.
    Tuesday, 3 February 1784
        Hebrews 12:14--Strive for peace with all.men,
           and for the holiness without which no one
           will see the Lord.
    Monday, 7 August 1786
        Hebrews 10:36--For you have no need of endu-
           rance, so that you may do the will of God
           and receive what is promised.
    Tuesday, 27 November 1787
        Hebrews 2:1--Therefore, we must pay the closer
           attention to what we have heard, lest
           we drift away from it.
    Tuesday, 15 February 1791. "Westmr., tea, conversed,
class, society, coach. . . ." Wesley entered that notation in his diary only two weeks before his death on 2
March 1791.

    Westminster Abbey. There exists such a quantity of
available written material describing the history of
Westminster Abbey that any form of of summary here would but
prove impractical and unnecessary. We really have no
clear idea as to the number of occasions upon which John
Wesley visited the Abbey; the journal, itself, contains
but two references, and those are limited to the tombs.

of additional interest is the fact that the cloisters
contain a plain stone recording the deaths of the
infant children of Ursula and Samuel Wesley the younger
(1690-1739): Netty (1725), Susanna (1726), Ursula (1727),
and Samuel (1731). Samuel Wesley the younger was, of
course, the eldest of the three surviving sons born to
Susanna and Samuel Wesley the elder.

When thinking of reactions to the tombs of Westminster Abbey, we almost immediately turn to the comments
of the essayist Joseph Addison (1672-1719), as recorded in Spectator No. 26 for Friday, 30 March 1711:"When
I am in a serious humour, I very often walk by myself in
Westminster Abbey; where the gloominess of the place,
and the use to which it is applied, with the solemnity
of the building, and the condition of the people who lie
in it are apt to fill the mind with a kind of melancholy,
or rather thoughtlessness, that is not disagreeable" (Addison 1:78). However, when John Wesley went to the tombs
on Thursday, 16 February 1764, he had other thoughts:
"I took. . .a serious walk through the tombs in Westminster Abbey. What heaps of unmeaning stone and marble!   But there was one tomb which showed common sense:
that beautiful figure of Mr. Nightingale, endeavouring
to screen his lovely wife from Death.   Here indeed the
marble seems to speak, and the statutes appear only not
alive."

Wesley had directed the preceding reference to the
monument by Louis Francois Roubillac (1702-1762), that
French sculptor's last work. The "lovely wife" was Lady
Elizabeth Nightingale--interestingly enough the eldest
sister of the patroness of Calvinist Methodism, Selina
Shirley, Countess of Huntingdon.   Lady Elizabeth had
married Joseph Gascoigne Nightingale of Manhead, in De-
Devonshire, and she died in 1731.   The monument, erected

in 1758, actually memorializes her husband, who died in
1752. The tomb itself represents the skeleton figure of
Death bursting upon the iron doors of the grave and aim-
ing a dart at the lady, who shrinks back into the arms
of her horror-stricken husband. He, in turn, eagerly
but vainly attempts to defend her. In his fury, Death
has grasped the dart at the end, by the feathers. The
tomb was placed in the chapel formed by the three chapels
of St. John, St. Michael, and St. Andrew.

Wesley noted another visit to the tombs on Monday,
25 February 1771. "I showed a friend coming out of the
country the tombs in Westminster Abbey. The two with
which I still think none of the others worthy to be compared are that of Mrs. Nightingale and that of the Admiral rising out of his tomb at the resurrection. But the
vile flattery inscribed on many of them reminded me of
that just reflection:

> If on the sculptured marble you rely,
> Pity that worth like his should ever die.
> If credit to the real life you give,
> Pity a wretch like him should ever live!"

The sculpture of the admiral rising from his tomb proved
the work of Nathaniel Read, a pupil of Roubillac;
the subject, Admiral Richard Tyrell, who died in 1766,
distinguished himself in action agains the French while
commander of the Buckingham. He was buried at sea. The
sculptor Read represented the ascent of the admiral--a
naked figure--from the waves into heaven. Beneath the
figure he recreated, in wild confusion, the coralline
depths of the sea, several allegorical figures, and the
Buckingham jammed into a rock. The monument--positioned
in the oak gallery opening from the deanery and above
the the south aisle of the nave--was partially destroyed
in 1882 and the figure removed. Further, the four lines

of verse cited at the end of Wesley's journal entry for
25 February 1771 constitute an epigram by his brother,
Samuel Wesley the younger.

Medallions of both John and Charles Wesley, by J.
Adams Acton, were placed on the South Choir Aisle of
Westminster Abbey.

.

Westminster School, Little Dean's Yard, Westminster
Abbey. Originally founded by King Henry VIII and richly
endowed by Elizabeth I in 1560, Westminster School,by
the early eighteenth century, had become one of the most
famous educational institutions in England. When Charles
Wesley entered there in 1716, at the age of eight, the
enrollment stood at more than four hundred boys, almost
equally divided between the upper and the lower schools.
Samuel Wesley the younger had preceded his youngest brother there in 1704; by 1716, he had become an usher (or
an assistant master).   In 1715, Samuel the younger married Ursula Berry, daughter of the Rev. John Berry, who
maintained a boarding house for Westminster scholars.

In 1716, the old dormitory for the King's scholars
(of which Charles Wesley was one, having been elected in
1721) still stood in Dean;s Yard; a row of three houses
stretched into the Green opposite the headmaster's house.
The dormitory--erected as early as 1380--spread across
the Green from the archway of Little Dean's Yard and
toward the terrace on the south side of the enclosure.
It was a two-storied building, with a tower at its western end, and with pointed windows.   In 1708, an old
scholar left £1000 toward the rebuilding of the residence,
which (understandably) stood in ruinous condition. After long debate, with an appeal to the House of Lords,
the trustees determined to construct a new dormitory from

designs submitted by the Earl of Burlington; it would
stand in the College Gardens. George I subscribed £1000
and the Prince of Wales added another £500; Parliament
granted an additional £1200. The foundation stone was
laid on 24 April 1722 (see Telford, Charles Wesley 22-
31). In that dormitory, the so-called "Westminster
Plays"--Andria, Adelphi, and Phormio of Terence, and
Trinummus of Plautus--were acted by the young scholars
during the month of December. David Garrick usually designed the scenery for those performances.

Thus, on Wednesday, 1 December 1762, James Boswell
"went to a play of Terence's (The Eunuch) performed by
the King's Scholars at Westminster School. There was a
very numerous audience, but none of whom I knew except
[Charles] Churchill, and him only by sight. Although I
seldom understand them, yet I was entertained to see the
boys play and hear them speak Latin with an English ac-
cent [since in Boswell's native Scotland, the Continen-
tal pronunciation of Latin was taught]. When Dr. [William]
Markham the Master came in, the scholars gave a
loud clap. My mind was filled with many ideas of
London, which relieved me from care" (Pottle, London
Journal 63).

Six years later, on Wednesday, 14 December 1768,
John Wesley "saw the Westminster scholars act the Adelphi
of Terence, and entertainment not unworthy of a Christian. Oh how do these heathens shame us! Their very
comedies contain both excellent sense, the liveliest pic-
tures of mane and manners, and so fine strokes of genu-
ine morality as are seldom found in the writings of
Christians." Unlike young Boswell, Wesley had no difficulty with the actors' pronunciation, although his
comments were, interestingly enough, directed to the text
rather than to the actual dramatic performance.

St. Anne's Lane, Westminster. St. Anne's Lane takes
its name from one of the two chapels connected with the
Almonry, where William Caxton (1422-1491) established
his printing press in 1746 or 1477.   In Spectator 125,
for Tuesday, 24 July 1711, Joseph Addison relates Sir
Roger de Coverley's adventure when, "but a stripling,
[he] had occasion to inquire which was the way to St.
Anne's Lane, upon which the person whom he spoke to. . .
called him a young popish cur, and asked him who had
made St. Anne a saint! The boy being in some confusion,
inquired of the next he met, which was the way to St.
Anne's-Lane; but was. . .told, that she had been a saint
before he was born, and would be one after he was hanged.
Upon this, says Sir Roger, I did not think fit to repeat
the former question, but going into every lane of the
neighbourhood, asked what they called the name of that
lane. By which ingenious artifice he found out the
place he inquired after, without giving offence to any
party" (Addison 1:380).

Wesley noted a visit to St. Anne's Lane on Friday
evening, at 7:45, 5 January 1739, for "singing, etc."
Undoubtedly, there existed a Church of England religious
society there at that time. Otherwise, the place will
continue to be remembered as the street in which the poet Robert Herrick (1591-1674) lived from 1647 to 1660,
as well as the street where the younger Henry Purcell
was born in 1658.

The Church of St. Clement Danes, the Strand.   In
1682, Edward Pierce, working under the supervision of
Sir Christopher Wren, headed the reconstruction of St.
Clement's. Thus, as with the majority of Wren's parish
churches, the structure depended entirely for its repu-

tation upon the merits of its steeple. For all purposes,
St. Clement's served as Samuel Johnson's church; he occupied pew number 18, in the north gallery. Boswell re-
ports that on Good Friday, 9 April 1773, Johnson "carried me with him to the church of St. Clement Danes,
where he had his seat; and his behaviour was, as I
had imagined to myself, solemnly devout. I shall never
forget the tremulous earnestness with which he pronounced
the awful petition in the Litany, 'In the hour of death,
and at the day of judgement, good Lord deliver us'" (Boswell, Life of Johnson 510).

John Wesley preached at the Church of St. Clement
Danes at 6:00 p.m., Sunday, 5 November 1738, "to such a
congregation as I never saw before. . . . As this was
the first time of my preaching here, I suppose it is to
be the last." He proved in error, however, for he preached
there again forty-four years later, on Sunday 24
November 1782, agian "to an immense congregation. I
fully discharged my own soul. . . .

The Chapel Royal, Savoy, the Strand. The Savoy Chapel
derives its name from Peter of Savoy, seventh son of
Thomas, Count of Savoy, who came to England in 1241 and
gave his name to the manor bestowed upon him by King Henry
III. Henry married Thomas's niece, Eleanor of Provence.
Land lying on the southeast side of the Strand,
over and against Exeter Exchange, was conferred upon
Peter in 1246. During the reign of William III (1688-
1702), the area around the chapel (built by Henry VII in
1505) and subsequent hospital became a disreputable quarter, as ill-doers claimed the rights of sanctuary. Thus,
in 1702, the hospital (built also by Henry VII) was dissolved, the rents confiscated to the Crown, and a receiver

appointed to administer the estates. However, the
Chapel remained. Various religious groups met in the
precinct; Charles II founded a Huguenot chapel there,
while George I (in 1723) granted a warrant for a German
Lutheran church. The Savoy Chapel became a chapel royal
by order of George III, a title it retained until 1925.

On Sunday, 14 May 1738, John Wesley preached in the
afternoon at the Savoy Chapel on what he termed "free
salvation by faith in the blood of Christ." He returned
there at 7:45 p.m. on Thursday, 21 September 1738, to
"declare the mighty works of God. . .in all simplicity.
And the word did not return empty."

Lambeth. In Wesley's day, Lambeth appeared as a
small but thriving suburban village. A scattering of
houses stood along the river bank between Westminster
and Nine Elms, with additional dwellings along Kennington
Road. During the reign of William III and Mary (1688-
1694; 1688-1702), Lambeth Wells served as a source of med-
icinal water for Labeth Walk. The northern section of
Lambeth tended to attract a number of industries: the
Vauxhall Plate Glass Works (1670-1780), Coade's artifi-
cial stone factory (established in 1769), Doulton's Pottery at the end of the century.

Wesley's general activities in Lambeth may be sum-
marized as follows--including the sources (when known)
of Biblical sources for sermon texts:

Sunday, 9 September 1739. "7[:00 p.m.] Lambeth
Marsh, singing, etc. . . ."

Sunday, 16 September 1739. At 7:00 p.m., he "found
our congregation considerably increased; and exhorted
them to cry mightily to our Lord, that He might say unto
them, as unto the sick of the palsy, 'Be of good cheer;

thy sins are forgiven thee [Matthew 9:2].'"

Sunday, 23 September 1739. At 6:30 p.m. "I went to Lambeth and showed (to the amazement, it seemed, of many who were present) how 'he that is born of God doth not commit sin [1 John 3:9].'"

Wednesday, 30 October 1751. After preaching in the evening at West Street Chapel, Wesley walked to Lambeth to see a "Miss Sm---, who had for several days expressed and earnest desire to see either my brother or me." Upon his arrival, the woman's sister informed Wesley that "her senses were gone, and that she had not spoke for several hours. But she spoke as soon as I took her by the hand, and declared a hope of full immortality. I prayed with her, and praised God on her behalf. An hour or two after her spirit returned to God."

(?) January 1757

> Luke 16--He also said to the disciples, "There was a rich man who had a steward, and charges were brought to him that this man was wasting his goods. And he called him. . .

Friday, 11 December 1778. Wesley noted in his journal for this day that he "preached at Lambeth, in the chapel prepared by Mr. Edwards, whose wife has seventy-five boarders." According to the Methodist Record (4 December 1913), this Mr. Edwards built a small chapel in Lambeth Marsh, its dimensions being twenty-three feet wide and twenty-two feet deep. The first Methodist service in Lambeth occurred in Edwards' dining room. However, his new chapel proved too small, and he enlarged the building at his own expense. During the owner's lifetime, he housed boarders at no charge; afterward, his wife maintained and educated more than twelve Methodist preachers' daughters, charging them only a modest rental.

Wednesday, 19 February 1783
    Romans 14:7--None of us lives to himself,and
    none of us dies to himself.
Thursday, 13 November 1783
    Micah 2:10--Arise and go, for this is no place
    to rest; because of uncleanliness that des-
    troys with grievous destruction.
Wednesday, 11 February 1784
    Luke 10:42--. . .one thing is needful. Mary
    has chosen the good portion which shall not
    be taken away from her.
Thursday, 11 November 1784
    1 Peter 1:24--. . .for "All flesh is like
    grass and all its glory like the flower of
    grass. The grass withers and the flower
    falls. . . .
Thursday, 10 February 1785
    Revelation 20:12--And I saw the dead, great
    and small, standing before the throne, and
    books were opened. Also another book was
    opened, which is the book of life. And the
    dead were judged by what was written in the
    books, by what they had done.
Thursday, 10 November 1785
    1 Corinthians 15:55--O death, where is thy
    victory? O death, where is thy sting?
Thursday, 9 February 1786
    1 Peter 4:18--And "If the righteous man is
    scarcely saved, where will the impious and
    sinner appear?"
Thursday, 8 February 1787
    Matthew 20:16--So the last will be the first,
    and the first last.
Thursday, 8 November 1787
    Psalms 31:1--In thee, O Lord, do I seek refuge;

let me never be put to shame; in thy righteousness deliver me!

Tuesday, 29 November 1787. Wesley preached at approximately 6:30 a.m., at Mr. Edwards' chapel (see above
for Friday, 11 December 1778, p. 253) on Isaiah 5:6--I
will make it a waste; it shall not be pruned or honed,
and briars and thorns shall grow up; I will also command
the clouds that they rain no rain upon it. He remarked,
in his journal, "How wonderfully does God fit people for
their work! Here Mrs. Edwards, a person of no extraordi-
nary natural abilities, teaches near a hundred children
and keeps them in as good, if not better, order than most
school-mistresses in the kingdom!"

Friday, 8 February 1788

> Galatians 6:14--But far be it from me to glo-
> ry, except in the cross of our Lord, Jesus
> Christ, by which the world has been
> crucified to me, and I to the world.

Thursday, 13 November 1788

> Colossians 3:4--When Christ who is our life
> appears, then you will also appear with
> him in glory.

Thursday, 19 February 1789

> Hebrews 12:28--Therefore, let us be greatful
> for receiving a kingdom that cannot be sha-
> ken, and thus let us offer to God accepta-
> ble worship, with reverence and awe. . . .

Thursday, 18 November 1790

> John 6:27--Do not labour for the food which
> perishes, but for the food which endures
> to eternal life, which the Son of man will
> give to you; for on him has God the Father
> set his seal.

If nothing else, Wesley's visits to Lambeth reveal

the degree--almost the rigidity!--by which the Methodist
patriarch maintained a regular schedule for preaching to
the London Methodists. After 1740, that regularity became almost a necessity as the demands from the outlying
counties of Great Britain (including Ireland, Scotland,
Wales, and the Channel Islands) took away more and more
of his time from the London societies.

Blackfriars. According to one major social histo-
rian of the eighteenth century, Blackfriars, at mid-
century (c. 1756), could be observed as a panorama of
"laystalls and bawdy houses, obscure pawnbrokers, gin-
shops and alehouses; the haunts of strolling prostitutes,
thieves, and beggars, who nestling thus in the heart
of the City, became a nuisance. . . ." One cause for
such a condition may have been the nearness of Blackfriars
to the prisons of the Fleet, Ludgate, and Newgate;
to the House of Correction at Bridewell; and, until the
Fleet was built over in 1747, to that terrible sewer
known as the Fleet ditch (George, London Life 348).
     There may well have been a religious society in the
vicinity of Blackfriars. Wesley recorded in his diary
for Thursday, 14 December 1738, that after reading George
Whitefield's sermons, at 8:00 p.m. he went to Blackfriars
for (the usual) "singing, prayers, etc. . . ."

     St. Benet's Church, Paul's Wharf. Destroyed by the
Great Fire and rebuilt by Sir Christopher Wren in 1683
at a cost of £3,328 18s. 10d., St. Benet's consisted of
red brick, relieved by stone quoins and by stone festoons
over the windows. Included among the noteworthy figures
buried there are Inigo Jones (1652), Mary de la Riviere

Manley (1724), and William Oldys (1761). Henry Fielding
married his second wife (the maid of his first wife),
Mary Daniel, there in 1747.

John Wesley preached at St. Benet's Paul's Wharf
only once-- Whitsunday evening, 21 May 1738. His comment in the journal appears similar to others set down
during this early period in his evangelical career: "At
these churches [e.g. St. Benet's and St. John's, Wapping]
I am to preach no more."

St. Paul's Cathedral, Ludgate Hill. As is the case
with Westminster Abbey (see above, pp. 245-248), there
exists such quantity of written history, description, observation, and commentary concerning St. Paul's Cathedral
that space here could not justify even a summary. However, one cannot allow the subject to pass without at
least observing the effect of the structure, as well as
the principal activity for which it had been constructed,
upon the eighteenth-century mind. Thus, on Sunday, 15
May 1763, we may observe the Lord's Day as practiced by
one Scotsman, James Boswell:

> I was in an excellent calm and serious
> mood. I attended divine service in
> Ludgate Church with patience and satisfac-
> tion, and was much edified. I then dined
> at honest Cochrane's, after which he and
> I and two other gentlemen went to Dr.
> Fordyce's meeting in Monkwell Street and
> heard Dr. Blair preach. I thought this
> would have done me good. But I found the
> reverse. Blair's New Kirk delivery and
> the Dissenters roaring out the Psalms sit-
> ting on their backsides, together with the

extempore prayers, and in short the whole
vulgar idea of the Presbyterian worship
made me very gloomy. I therefore hastened
from the place to St. Paul's, where I heard
the conclusion of the service, and had my
mind set right again.

(Pottle, Boswell London Journal 259)

Wesley's opinion of St. Paul's Cathedral--in his
day the most significant architectural tribute to
Protestantism--fell, understandably, far short of Boswell's
mental and spiritual realignment. For example, on Sunday, 28 August 1748, while traveling to his home county
of Lincoln, he paused to reflect upon "those who still
talk so loud of the indecency of field preaching. The
highest indecency is in St. Paul's Church Cathedral,
when a considerable part of the congregation are asleep,
or talking, or looking about, not minding a word the
preacher says."

From John Wesley's diary, we may note the following
occasions between 1739 and 1741 upon which he went to St.
Paul's:

Saturday, 6 January 1739. 3:30 p.m.; prayers
Sunday, 7 January 1739. 3:15 p.m.; prayers, ser-
   mon
Sunday, 14 January 1739. 10:00 a.m.; prayers,ser-
   mon, communion
Sunday, 18 March 1739. 3:15 p.m.; prayers
Sunday, 23 September 1739. 9:45 a.m.
Sunday, 27 April 1740. 10:00 a.m.
Sunday, 8 June 1740. 10:00 a.m.; communion; "one
   ordained"
Sunday, 15 June 1740. 9:45 a.m.
Sunday, 22 June 1740. 10:00 a.m.

Sunday, 29 June 1740.   10:00 a.m.

Sunday, 13 July 1740.   9:45 a.m.

Thursday, 7 August 1740.   4:00 p.m.

Thursday, 9 October 1740.   4:00 p.m.

Sunday, 12 October 1740.   10:00 a.m.

Sunday, 19 October 1740.   10:00 a.m.; communion

Sunday, 30 November 1740.   9:45 a.m.; communion

Sunday, 25 January 1741.   9:45 a.m.; communion

Sunday, 8 February 1741.   9:45 a.m.

Sunday, 15 February 1741.   9:45 a.m.

Sunday, 5 April 1741.   10:00 a.m.

Sunday, 12 April 1741.   10:00 a.m.

Sunday, 19 April 1741.   10:00 a.m.

Sunday, 26 April 1741.   10:00 a.m.; communion

Sunday, 31 May 1741.   10:00 a.m.; communion

Sunday, 7 June 1741.   10:00 a.m.; communion

Sunday, 28 June 1741.   10:00 a.m.

Saturday, 1 August 1741.   4:00 p.m.

Southwark. Beginning in about the twelfth century,
Southwark existed as a second-class London, lying south
of the River Thames. Of course, every student of British
literature can recite those lines (19-22) from the
General Prologue of Geoffrey Chaucers's Canterbury Tales:
        Bifel that in that seson on a day,
        In Southwerk at the Tabard as I lay,
        Redy to wenden on my pilgrimage
        To Canterbury with ful devout corage. . . .
Although not officially incorporated until 1554, the
area long had close association with the town of London.
The borough sheltered the dregs of the City, but people
of all classes visited there in search of diversion. By
1748, Southwark could be described as "a quarter of the

town ill-built, having but two streets in its breadth,
and almost entirely occupied by tanners and weavers."
One could find little evidence of fine clothes or fashion, but rather mostly of "rags and filth" covering "de-
formed and twisted bodies and noses eaten away by disease."
The buildings in Southwark stood, generally, in
sad state of repair; instead of gutters, for instance,
"a narrow ditch runs through the middle of the floun-
dering street into which filth of every description, offal,
dead cats and dogs, and night soil is heaped. There
are no sidewalks here, but footways. . .marked off from
the road by posts placed at intervals" (Lewis, Three
Tours 7-11).

Early in the seventeenth century (perhaps even before), Southwark became, through the convenience of the
church by the bridgehead, not only a habitat of clerics,
but of debtors, criminals, and prostitutes. After the
Reformation, the church, built on the site of a Roman
structure, became known as St. Saviour's--a name that remained until it became, in 1905, Southwark Cathedral. A
medieval church stood east of the bridgehead, known as
St. Olive's in Tooley Street and dedicated to the warrior
king of Norway. Henry Flitcroft (1679-1769) rede-
signed and rebuilt St. Olive's in 1740, and that structure remained until 1928.

Aside from the specific places described and discussed
under the headings below, we may note those activities of John Wesley as they pertained to and occurred
within the general vicinity of Southwark:

Friday, 15 December 1738. "7[:00 p.m.] in Southwark,
prayer, singing, etc. . . ."

Monday, 3 September 1739. "4.45 [p.m.] Southwark,
visited. . ." until 6:45 p.m.

Monday, 30 June 1740. "5.45 [p.m.] Southwark. . ."

Monday, 14 July 1740. "7[:00 p.m.] Southwark. . ."
Saturday, 10 September 1748. Wesley visited the
classes in Southwark, "the only part of the society in
London which increases daily. This I chiefly impute to
the zeal and vigilence of the leaders, who do indeed labour in the work, and spare no care or pains to seek and
save that which is lost."

Zoar Chapel, Zoar Street, Southwark. Zoar Chapel
stood on the north side of the street, near the west end.
Originally a Presbyterian meeting house in which (supposedly) John Bunyan (1628-1688) once preached, the building evolved into a brewery, then a factory, and finally
underwent demolition--to be replaced by a block of
model dwellings!
    In his journal (4:140), Wesley informs us that
Samuel Larwood, one of the Wesleyan Methodist preachers in
Ireland, had bought and repaired the old meeting house
sometime in 1755. Larwood died on Sunday, 2 November
1755, and Wesley buried him on Wednesday, 5 November.
"His [Larwood's] executor offering it [Zoar Chapel] to
me on the evening of Friday the 7th [November 1755],that
solemn day which we observed with fasting and prayer for
our King and country, I preached there to a large and
quiet congregation; but most of them appeared wild enough:
and such were we, till grace made the difference." Eleven
days later (Tuesday, 18 November), he noted "a solemn
watch-night at Zoar." He preached there again on
Friday, 12 December 1755, and on Monday, 12 November
1759. One remembers, of course, that in 1755, the
British army suffered defeat at the hands of the French at
Fort Duquesne (now Pittsburgh, Pennsylvania), and the
Anglo-Austrian alliance came to an end during that same
year.

From the Sermon Register, we may take note of a
more complete record of John Wesley's preaching at Zoar
Chapel between 1756 and 1760, including Biblical sources
for the sermons:

Friday, 9 February 1756

> John 17:3--And this is eternal life, that they
> know thee the only true God, and Jesus
> Christ whom thou hast sent.

> Hebrews 9:27--And just as it is appointed for
> men to die once, and after that comes judg-
> ment. . . .

> Hebrews 12:28--Therefore, let us be grateful
> for receiving a kingdom that cannot be sha-
> ken, and thus let us offer to God accepta-
> ble worship, with reverence and awe. . . .

Friday, 24 September 1756

> 2 Timothy 3:5--. . .holding the form of reli-
> gion, but denying the power of it. Avoid
> such people.

(?) September 1756

> Psalms 34:8--O taste and see that the Lord is
> good! Happy is the man who takes refuge in
> him!

> Psalms 37:1--Fret not yourself because of the
> wicked; be not envious of wrongdoers!

> 1 Corinthians 6:19--Do you not know that your
> body is a temple of the Holy Spirit within
> you, which you have from God? You are not
> your own. . . .

> Romans 3:22--. . .the righteousness of God
> through faith in Jesus Christ for all who
> believe.

> Acts 11:26--. . .and when he had found him, he
> brought him to Antioch. For a whole day

they met with the church, and taught a large
company of people; and in Antioch the disciples were for the first time called Christians.

(?) March 1757

Hosea 14:4--I will hear their faithlessness; I
will love them freely, for my anger has
turned from them.

Matthew 11:12--From the days of John the
Baptist until now, the kingdom of heaven has
suffered violence, and men of violence take
it by force.

Luke 7:42--When they could not pay, he forgave
them both. Now, which of them will love
him more?

(?) April 1757

John 20:18--Mary Magdalene went and said to the
disciples, "I have seen the Lord"; and she
told them that he had said these things to
her.

Matthew 10:32--So every one who acknowledges
me before men, I also will acknowledge before my Father who is in heaven. . . .

Isaiah 1:3--The ox knows its owner, and the
ass its master's crib; but Israel does not
know, my people does not understand.

John 11:47--So the chief priests and the Pharisees gathered the council, and said,
"What are we to do? For this man performs
many signs."

Matthew 22:4--Again he sent other servants,
saying, "Tell those who are invited, 'Behold, I have made ready my dinner, my oxen
and my fat calves are killed, and every-

thing is ready; come to the marriage feast.'"
Thursday, 18 August 1757

    2 Corinthians 5:19--. . .that is, God was in
    Christ reconciling the world to himself,
    not counting their trespasses against them,
    and entrusting to us the message of
    reconciliation.

    Matthew 10:21--Brother will deliver up brother
    to death, and the father his child, and childre
    will rise against parents and have them
    put to death. . . .

    Hebrews 13:20--Now may the God of peace who
    brought again from the dead our Lord Jesus,
    the great shepherd of the sheep, by the
    blood of the eternal covenant. . .

Thursday, 1 December 1757

    1 Timothy 3:16--Great indeed, we confess, is
    the mystery of our religion: He was
    manifested in the flesh, vindicated in the
    Spirit, seen by angels, preached among the
    nations, believed on in the world, taken up
    in glory.

    Romans 10:4--For Christ is the end of the law,
    that every one who has his faith may be
    justified.

    Hebrews 3:14--For we share in Christ, only if
    we hold our first confidence firm in the
    end. . . .

    1 Peter 1:9--As the outcome of your faith you
    obtain the salvation of your souls.

Thursday, 16 January 1758

    Titus 2:14--. . .who gave himself for us to
    redeem us from all iniquity and to purify
    for himself a people of his own who are

zealous for good deeds.

1 John 3:8--He who commits sin is of the devil;
    for the devil has sinned from the beginning.
    The reason the Son of God appeared was to
    destroy the works of the devil.

1 John 5:12--He who has the Son has life; he
    who has not the Son of God has not life.

John 6:37--All that the Father gives me will
    come to me; and him who comes to me I will
    not cast out.

Monday, 20 November 1758

1 Timothy 1:8--Now we know that the law is
    good, if any one uses it lawfully. . . .

Thursday, 7 December 1758

Romans 13--Let every person be subject to the
    governing authorities. For there is no
    authority except from God. . .

Thursday, 6 December 1759

Romans 3:19--Now we know that whatever the law
    says, it speaks to those who are under the
    law, so that every mouth may be stopped, and
    the whole world may be held accountable to
    God.

2 Peter 3:10--But the day of the Lord will come
    like a thief, and then the heavens will pass
    away with a loud noise, and the elements
    will be dissolved with fire, and the earth
    and the works that are upon it will be
    burned up.

1 Peter 3:17-18--You therefore, beloved, know-
    ing this beforehand, beware lest you be car-
    ried away with the error of lawless men and
    lose your own stability. But grow in the
    grace and knowledge of our Lord and Savior

Jesus Christ. To him be the glory, both
now and the day of eternity.
Monday, 4 February 1760
Romans 14:7--None of us lives to himself,and
none of us dies to himself.
James 3:2--For we all make many mistakes, and
if any one makes no mistakes in what he says
he is a perfect man, able to bridle the
whole body, also.
1 Corinthians 6:9--Do you not know that the
unrighteous will not inherit the kingdom
of God? Do not be deceived; neither the
immoral, nor idolators,nor adulterers nor
homosexuals. . . .
Acts 1:25--. . .to take the place in this
ministry and apostleship from which Judas
turned aside, to go to his own place.

St. George the Martyr's Church, Southwark. The present St. George's, known by Dickensians as the church of
"Little Dorritt" (Little Dorritt, 1855-1857), dates from
as early as the twelfth century, although rebuilt on
several occasions. John Price, who also designed Chandos
House in 1720, rebuilt St. George's between 1733 and
1736; the Skinners', Grocers', Fishmongers', and Drapers'
companies contributed significantly to defray the cost
of the project.
     John Wesley preached in St. George the Martyr's on
Sunday afternoon, 25 January 1784, and he described the
building as "a very large and commodious church." He
based his sermon for that day upon Acts 26:8--Why is it
thought incredible to any of you that God raises the
dead? He preached there again on Sunday afternoon, 8

February 1784, this time on 1 Corinthians 13:1--If I
speak in the tongues of men and of angels, but have not
love, I am a noisy gong or a clanging cymbal.

All Hallows Church, Lombard Street. Although All
Hallows suffered severely from the Great Fire, government officials held some hope that it might simply be
restored. Workers immediately coped the walls with straw
and lime to arrest further decay. In fact, in 1679, a
bell was actually mounted from the steeple. However,
the damage proved too considerable for reparation, and
Sir Christopher Wren completely rebuilt the structure between 1686 and 1694 at a cost of £8058 15s. 6d.

Early in 1735, John Wesley preached at All Hallows
Church "at the earnest request of the churchwarden, to
a numerous congregation, who came, like me, to hear Dr.
[John] Heylyn [1685-1759, then rector of St. Mary-le-
Strand and lecturer of All Hallows]. This was the first
time that, having no notes about me, I preached extempore" (Journal 6:96). According to one popular source
(Kent, Encyclopaedia 126), Wesley had arrived without
his manuscript, which disturbed him considerably. After
telling his troubles to the caretaker, the latter re-
sponded, "What, can't you trust God for a sermon?" Rev.
Luke Tyerman, the nineteenth-century biographer of John
Wesley, offered a slightly different version (Life of
Wesley 3:563): On the last Sunday in December 1788 (see
immediately below, under this entry, for "Sunday, 28 December 1788") Wesley said to his attendant, while putting
on his clerical gown, "Sir, it is above fifty years since
I first preached in this church; I remember it from a
particular circumstance. I came without a sermon [manu-
script]; and going up the pulpit stairs, I hesitated,

and returned into the vestry, under much mental confusion
and agitation. A woman, who stood by, noticed my
concern, and said, 'Pray, sir, what is the matter?' I
replied, 'I have not brought a sermon with me.' Putting
her hand on my shoulder, she said, 'Is that all? Cannot
you trust God for a sermon?' The question had such an
effect upon me, that I ascended the pulpit, preached
extempore, with great freedom to myself, and acceptance
to the people; and have never since taken a sermon with me
to the pulpit."

Forty-one years after that initial experience, on
Sunday, 28 January 1776, John Wesley preached a charity
sermon at All Hallow's Church. Afterward, he returned
there on the following occasions:

Sunday, 26 January 1777. "I preached. . .morning
and afternoon. I found great liberty of spirit; and the
congregation seemed to be much affected. How is this?
Do I yet please men? Is the offense of the Cross ceased?
It seems, after being scandalous near fifty years,
I am at length growing into an honorable man!" Wesley
refers, of course, to all of those years (1742-1770)
during which he could not gain access to Church of
England pulpits.

Sunday, 22 October 1786. "I preached. . .at All-
Hallows Church in the evening. It was much crowded; and
God gave us so remarkable a blessing as I scarce ever
found at that church." Wesley based his sermon text on
Ephesians 2:8--For by grace you have been saved through
faith; and this is not your own doing; it is the gift of
God. . . .

Sunday, 28 December 1788. Wesley preached in the
afternoon "on those words [from 1 John 5:3] in the
Service, 'His commandments are not grievous.' The
congregation was exceeding large, and seemed to taste

the good word." He preached the sermon for the benefit of
forty-eight poor children belonging to the St. Ethelburga
society.

Sunday, 25 October 1789. At 3:00 p.m., Wesley ·
preached "to a crowded audience" on Micah 6:8--He has showed
you, O man, what is good; and what does the Lord require
of you but to do justice, and to love kindness, and to
walk humbly with your God?

Sunday, 28 November 1790. Wesley preached at 3:00
p.m. on Hebrews 13--Let brotherly love continue.

Crooked Lane. Crooked Lane, situated in the
general area between Fish Street and the present Arthur
Street--and beyond the Cannon Street Station--housed St.
Michael's Church (see imeediately below, next entry). A
London religious society obviously held meetings there,
for Wesley noted in his diary for Sunday, 13 December
1738, "6[:00 a.m.] Singing, Crooked Lane, prayer, communion. . . ." The last item--"communion"-- may well
identify the site as St. Michael's, although one can
only speculate here.

Church of St. Michael, Crooked Lane. Dating from
about 1271, St. Michael's suffered from the Great Fire,
and thus Sir Christopher Wren rebuilt the structure during 1684-1689. He did not complete the tower, however,
until 1698. On 21 November 1703, (the year of John Wes-
Wesley's birth), a violent storm struck London, and vases
from the steeple of St. Michael's came tumbling to the
ground. In 1831, under an act of Parliament (1830) for
the formation of the new approaches to the London Bridge,
the church was removed to make way for King William

Street.

In addition to the strong likelihood of Wesley attending St. Michael's on Sunday, 31 December 1738 (see above under Crooked Lane, p. 269), he had attended there on Sunday, 17 December 1738, at 6:45 a.m., for meditation and prayer and communion.

Dowgate Hill. A steep street of Walbrook, Dowgate Hill lay off New Queen Street and Old Swan Street, running directly to the River Thames. A religious society no doubt held forth in that area, for Wesley, in his diary, noted "singing, etc." at Dowgate Hill at 7:30 p.m., Tuesday, 13 February 1739. He repeated that notation for Tuesday, 20 February 1739, at 8:00 p.m. Further meetings or gatherings occurred at the home of a "Mr. Crouch" at Dowgate Hill: first on Tuesday, 4 September 1739, at 8:00 p.m.; second, at 7:00 p.m., Tuesday, 6 November 1739, when John Wesley preached on Matthew 12--At that time Jesus went through the grainfields on the sabbath; his disciples were hungry. . .

Friday Street, Cheapside. Friday Street, in the eighteenth century, lay (north and south) between Cheapside and Watling Street, and West of Bread Street. Pri to the Great Fire, three churches stood there: St. Margaret Moses, St. John the Evangelist, and St. Matthew. All fell to the flames, but St. Matthew was rebuilt-- although it no longer stands.

In his diary for Sunday, 2 March 1783, Wesley noted, ". . .8[:00 p.m.] Fri Str. . . ." Afterward, he took the coach for Bath.

St. Antholin Church, Watling Street and Size Lane.
Dating from about 1119, St. Antholin was destroyed in the
Great Fire. Wren completed its reconstruction in 1678;
architectural historians have long considered it one of
his finest buildings. Officials ordered the church destroyed in 1875; they sold the site for £44,990 and dis-
posed of Wren's spire for the sum of £5!

John Wesley preached at St. Antholin in the early
morning of Friday, 21 April 1738. Dr. Richard Venn (d.
1739), whose son Henry (1725-1797) became associated with
George Whitefield and Selina Shirley, Countess of
Huntingdon, then served as rector. Wesley returned on
Thursday, 25 May 1738; Friday, 6 October 1738, at 7:00
a.m.; at 7:00 a.m. on Friday, 3 November 1738; Thursday
morning (7:00?), 9 November 1738; and at 7:00 a.m., Friday, 15 December 1738. On the following Thursday, 15
December 1738, Dr. Venn announced that Methodists would
no longer be permitted to preach at St. Antholin. However, Wesley managed to return to the church almost exactly forty years later--on Sunday evening, 15 November
1778--at the invitation of the incumbent, Jerome De Salis,
who served there between 1774 and 1810. The Methodist
patriarch noted in his journal for that date that
the church "was extremely hot; but this I soon forgot;
for it pleased God to send a gracious rain upon his inheritance." On Sunday, 25 March 1781, Wesley once again
preached at St. Antholin, noting that the service "lasted
till near nine [p.m.]. . . ." His final appearance there
came about on Sunday evening, 30 January 1785, when he
preached on 1 Corinthians 13:1--If I speak in the tongues
of men and of angels, but have not love, I am a
noisy gong or a clanging cymbal.

St. Benet Fink, Threadneedle Street. Dating from
about 1216, St. Benet Fink suffered severe damage from
the Great Fire. Wren supervised its replacement during
1670-1681--a ten-sided structure built at a cost of £4129
16s. 10d., that stood until demolition in 1842-1844 to
make way for the new Royal Exchange. John Wesley attended St. Benet Fink--named after Robert Finch (or Fink),
the individual who paid for the original building--on
Sunday, 14 September 1740, at 2:30 p.m. He returned later in the week--at 4:00 p.m. (?), Thursday, 18 September.

Threadneedle Street. Lying north of Cornhill, between the Poultry and Bishopsgate Street, Threadneedle
Street at one time housed the New-England Coffee-House
(or, the American Coffee-House), where gathered merchants
and businessmen interested in the trade with the colonies. There, American loyalists (not Tories) received
news of the Declaration of Independence; that group gathered regularly to read their letters from home and to
express their sentiments that the colonials would teach
the British a lesson (Lewis, Three Tours 79).
On Sunday, 10 February 1751, John Wesley suffered
from a fall on the ice while crossing London Bridge. He
spent the remainder of the week at Threadneedle Street,
"partly in prayer, reading and conversation, partly in
writing an Hebrew Grammar and Lessons for Children." The
specific titles to which he referred he published as Lessons
for Children, Part IV (London: Henry Cock, 1754) and
A Short Hebrew Grammar (London: William Bowyer, 1765).

The Church of St. Mary-le-Bow, Cheapside. Dating

from about 1091, the Church of St. Mary-le-Bow burned to
the ground in the Great Fire; Wren began its reconstruction in 1670, basing his design upon the Basilica of
Maxentius in Rome. The project cost £15,500--a larger
amount by over £3000 than was expended on any other of
Wren's parish churches. In dimension, the building measured sixty-five by sixty-three feet; its spire, 221
feet nine inches high and surpassed only by that of St.
Bride's Church in Fleet Street, was built of Portland
stone and cost £7388--or almost one-half of the total
cost of the entire edifice. James Boswell, attending
service there on Sunday, 10 July 1763, termed the Bow
Church "the true centrical temple of the bluff citizens"
(London Journal 299).

Special services were held during the year at St.
Mary-le-Bow for the Society for Promoting Christian
Knowledge (SPCK) and for the Society for the Propagation
of the Gospel (SPG). The SPCK, founded in 1698 by Thomas
Bray (1656-1730), set out to promote and encourage
the establishment of charity schools in England and
Wales, to distribute Bibles and religious tracts in
Britain and abroad, and generally to promote Christian
knowledge. Bray also founded the SPG in 1701 to provide the ministrations of the Church of England for
Britons overseas and to evangelize non-Christian people
living under the jurisdiction of the Crown. John Wesley
belonged to both organizations. Thus, on Wednesday evening, 27 September 1738, he read prayers at one
of those services.

Church of St. Mary Somerset, Upper Thames Street,
Queenhithe Ward. St. Mary Somerset, dating from the
reign of Richard III (1189-1199), burned in the Great

Fire. Wren supervised its reconstruction between 1686
and 1695; it then united with the parish of St. Mary
Mountshaw. An act of Parliament caused it to be pulled
down in 1872, providing for a new St. Mary Somerset
church to be built in Hoxton.

Wesley read prayers at the Church of St. Mary
Somerset at 10:00 a.m., Sunday, 7 January 1739. The incumbent, Dr. Samuel Croxall the younger (d. 1752)--a
pseudo-literary scholar, minor poet, editor of some miscellaneous fiction, and collector of fables--preached on
that day. A cleric who owed his appointments to his political connections, Croxall served as prebend of Hinton,
prebend of Morton Magna, archdeacon of Salop (Shropshire),
chancellor of Hereford, and vicar of Hampton. And, of
course, he continued to hold his incumbency of the joint
parish of St. Mary Somerset and St. Mary Mountshaw in
London. In essence, Croxall represented that element of
the Anglican clergy that John Wesley sought to reform--
to redirect its energy and attention from political to
human concerns.

Church of St. Stephen, Walbrook. Dating from about
1096, St. Stephen's can be numbered among those London
parish churches destroyed by the Great Fire and later
(1672-1679) rebuilt by Sir Christopher Wren. In that
reconstruction, he tested a number of architectural the-
ories that later came into actuality with the building
of St. Paul's Cathedral--principally the combination of
a cross-in-square plant with a large, centralized dome.
The test of Wren's art and skill came, in 1940, when St.
Stephen's fittings, font, pulpit, sounding board, altar
piece and communion rails all survived German bombs.

Oblong in shape, the building measured 59 feet, six

inches, with four rows of Corinthian columns elevated on
bases--almost all of which could be seen from the southwest corner. Richard Boyle, third Earl of Burlington
(1695-1753), when in Italy, saw a church that he admi-
red and was told that it had been copied from Wren's St.
Stephen's. Thus, upon his return to London, Burlington
supposedly rushed immediately to St. Stephen's and viewed that structure by candlelight.

In his journal for Monday, 4 December 1758, John
Wesley noted that "I was desired to step into the little
church behind the Mansion House, commonly called St.
Stephen's Walbrook. It is nothing grand, but neat and elegant beyond expression. So that I do not wonder at the
speech of the famous Italian architect, who met Lord
Burlington in Italy:'My lord, go back and see St. Stephen's
in London. We have not so fine a piece of architecture
in Rome.'"

St. Swithin's Church, London Stone, Cannon Street.
Located in Cannon Street, at the corner of St. Swithin's
Lane, the church of St. Swithin's dates from approximately 1236. Destroyed in the Great Fire and rebuilt by
Wren in 1677-1678, the building boasts of a fine octagonal domed roof. Built into the south wall was a stone
that, according to tradition, preceded the founding of
London by the Romans. At one time, the church stood as
one of the three surviving ancient City landmarks that
helped to define the old place on the map and to determine the original limits of the small town in the Thames
Marshes destined to become the capital of an empire. The
stone itself may well have been the actual Roman milli-
arium (central milestone) from which the outgoing roads
and distances were measured. The incumbent of St.

Swithin's between 1729 and 1765 was Dr. William Ayerst,
whose sermon on The Duty and Motives of Praying for
Peace (based on Psalms 122:6-9) reached publication in
1712. In 1941, German bombs destroyed the structure.

The following summarizes John Wesley's visits to
St. Swithin's Church--first in late 1738, then between
1781 and 1787:

Sunday, 17 December 1738. Wesley preached there in
the evening (5:30) "for the last time." His absence from
that pulpit would last some forty-three years.

Sunday, 2 December 1781. "I preached. . .at St.
Swithin's in the evening. The tide is now turned; so
that I have more invitations to preach in churches than
I can accept of." He based his sermon for the 6:00 p.m.
service on 1 Corinthians 1:14--The unspiritual man does
not receive the gifts of the Spirit of God, for they are
folly to him, and he is not able to understand them
because they are spiritually discerned.

Sunday, 14 December 1783, 5:30 p.m.

  1 Peter 3:22--. . .who has gone into heaven
       and is at the right hand of God, with
       angels, authorities, and powers subject
       to him.

Sunday, 21 December 1783, 6:00 p.m.

  1 John 1:3--. . .that which we have seen and
       heard we proclaim also to you, so that you
       may have fellowship with us; and our fellow-
       ship is with the Father and his Son, Jesus
       Christ.

Sunday, 8 February 1784, 6:00 p.m.

  2 Corinthians 4:5--For what we preach is not
       ourselves, but Jesus Christ as Lord, with
       ourselves as your servants for Jesus' sake.

Sunday, 18 December 1785, 3:00 p.m.

> Matthew 7:24--Every one, then, who hears these
> words of mine and does them will be like a
> wise man who built his house upon the rock.

Sunday, 21 January 1787. Wesley preached at 6:00
p.m. to "a numerous congregation" on 1 Corinthians 3:11--
For no other foundation can any one lay than that which
is laid, which is Jesus Christ.

Sunday, 14 October 1787, 6:00 p.m.

> Matthew 9:5--For which is easier to say, "Your
> sins are forgiven," or to say, "Rise and
> walk"?

Guy's Hospital, St. Thomas Street, Southwark. Thomas
Guy (1644-[27 December] 1724) kept a bookshop on the
corner of Little Lombard Street and Cornhill between 1688
and 1724. He and his brother, John, bought from the Stationers' Company large stocks of Bibles, which the Company
had seized on the London wharves; the Guys proceeded
to sell those volumes in direct competition with the Universities. As early as 1678, Thomas Guy had founded, at
Tamworth (in northern Warwick), an almhouse for six poor
women, which he enlarged in 1693 to accommodate fourteen
men and women. In 1704, he became governor of St. Thomas's
Hospital (see below, in this section); three years
later, he built and furnished three new wards. Noticing
that many patients could not gain admission to St.
Thomas's, or were quickly discharged as incurables, Guy
leased, in 1721, from the governors of St. Thomas a piece
of ground directly opposite that institution. After
pulling down a number of small houses on the property,
he began the construction of a new hospital that would
bear his name. Guy's Hospital cost £ 18,793, and the
founder and builder lived just long enough to see it

roofed (1724). Thomas Guy's will, proved on 4 January
1725, provided the hospital with an endowment of over
£200,000. Perhaps the most noted association with Guy's
Hospital is that of the Romantic poet John Keats (1795-
1821); in 1815, he cancelled his fifth year of apprenticeship to an apothecary-surgeon and entered medical
school at Guy's. He qualified for an apothecary's
license, but he abandoned that profession for poetry.

John Wesley visited Guy's Hospital at 4:00 p.m.,
Saturday, 6 December 1740, in company with a "Mr.
Chandler" and one known only as "S[ister] Lincoln," for the
purpose of prayer and conversation. On Monday, 6 April
1741, between 5:30 p.m. and 6:30 p.m., he stopped first
at St. Thomas's Hospital and then at Guy's. One month
later--Monday, 4 May 1741, at 6:00 p.m.--he visited one
"Betty Patrick" there. Finally, we may note this journal
entry for Saturday, 24 December 1748: "I buried the
body of William Turner, who, towards the close of a long
illness, had been removed into Guy's Hospital, though
with small hope of recovery. The night before his death
he was delirious, and talked loud and incoherently,which
occasioned many in the ward to gather round his bed, in
order to divert themselves."

Marshalsea Prison, Southwark. Marshalsea Prison,
closed in 1842, existed as an accurate image of the
suffering and abuse endured by those eighteenth-century
Londoners in prison for various (and not always legitimate) reasons. The British Museum houses a copy of a
poem entitled Hell in Epitome, or a Description of the
M--sh--sea, published in 1738 by one imprisoned therein.
It reads, in part,
            . . .an old pile most dreadful to the view,
          Dismal as wormwood or repenting rue.

> Thither the graduates in sin resort
> And take degrees becoming Satan's court,
> There are instructed in the Paths of Vice,
> There sell good Linen, there they purchase
>   Lice.
>
> (see Kent, _Encyclopaedia_ 529)

In 1714, Marshalsea contained seven or eight hundred prisoners, with two or three commonly perishing in a single
day because of the miserable and wasting conditions. A
Parliamentary committee reported, as early as 1719, that
three hundred persons had died there in less than three
months, while another committee formed by General James
Oglethorpe (the settler of the Georgia colony) in 1729
found that more than 350 prisoners were literally dying
from starvation. The government adopted measures to feed
those people, but nonetheless "a day seldom passed without a death, and upon the advancing of spring not less
than eight or ten usually died every twenty-four hours"
(George 307). Late in the century, the Marshalsea was
removed to a site north of St. George's Church; in 1811,
when the government purchased the White Lion--the old
county jail standing on an adjacent site that had been
superseded by the jail in Horsemonger Lane--a new
Marshalsea Prison underwent construction.

John Wesley visited Marshalsea Prison on three
occasions: He read prayers there and preached on Sunday,
25 March 1739, at 2:45 p.m. On Saturday, 3 February
1753, he "visited one in the Marshalsea Prison--a nursery of all manner of wickedness. Oh shame to man that
there should be such a place, such a picture of Hell upon earth! And shame to those who bear the name of Christ
that there should need any prison at all in Christendom!"
Then, on Saturday, 2 January 1768, Wesley "called on a
poor man in the Marshalsea whose case appeared to be
uncommon. He is by birth a Dutchman,a chemist by profession.

Being but half-employed at home, he was advised
to come to London, where he doubted not of having full
employment. He was recommended to a countryman of his
to lodge, who after six weeks arrested him for much more
than he owed, and hurried him away to prison, having a
wife near her time, without money, friend, or a word of
English to speak. I wrote the case to Mr. T-------
[Thornton (?)], who immediately gave fifteen pounds; by
means of which, with a little addition, he was set at
liberty, and put in a way of living. But I never saw
him since; and reason good; for he could now live without me."

     St. Saviour's Church, Southwark. By an act of 1540,
the Church of St. Mary Magdalene and St. Margaret's
Church became unified into a single parish under the title of St. Saviour's. The chief interest of the Church
for others lies in its literary associations: buried
there were John Gower (1330-1408), Edmund Shakespeare
(1580-1607), Philip Massinger (1583-1640), and John Fletcher
(1579-1625). Also, John Harvard (1607-1638), founder of the American university that bears his name, was
baptized there on 29 November 1607, his father then being a church warden. In 1905, the diocese of Rochester
was divided, and St. Saviour's Church became Southwark
Cathedral.

     John Wesley, in his diary for Sunday, 27 April 1740,
noted his attendance at St. Saviour's Church at 3:00 p.m.
However, he did not indicate whether he preached there
(although most likely he did not) or merely attended an
afternoon service.

St. Thomas's Hospital, Borough Street, Southwark.
The second oldest hospital in London, St. Thomas's came
into being early in the thirteenth century, founded by
the canons of St. Mary Overy's Priory, apparently to tend
to the victims of a great fire in Southwark (in 1207,
1212, or 1213). In 1871, the hospital was transferred
to a site on the Albert Embankment; the railway company
that acquired the Southwark site paid approximately
£300,000 for land bought for £31 in 1507. According to
one source, in 1685, the deaths at St. Thomas's stood at
a ratio of one in seven; in 1689, one in ten; one in ten
in 1741; one in fourteen between 1773 and 1783; one in
fifteen over the next ten years. Also, between 1770 and
1775, approximately six hundred patients (or one in thirteen) of all admitted died annually (George 50-51).
      John Wesley visited St. Thomas's Hospital at 5:00
p.m., Monday, 6 April 1741, and again on Monday, 7 September 1741. On the latter occasion, he "visited a
young man. . .who, in a strong pain, was praising God
continually. At the desire of many of the patients, I
spent a short time with them in exhortation and prayer.
Oh what a harvest there might be, if any lover of souls
who has time upon his hands would constantly attend these
places of distress, and, with tenderness and meekness of
wisdom, instruct and exhort those on whom God has laid
His hands to know and improve the day of their visita-
tion!" One must remember that during the period of
Wesley's fellowship at Lincoln College, Oxford (1726-1735),
he spent considerable time (especially in his capacity
as the leader of the Oxford Holy Club) visiting the sick
in hospitals and the prisoners in the jails. Certainly,
the activities of the London Methodists originated during
that Oxford period--prior to the Georgia mission and the
Aldersgate conversion.

St. Thomas's Church, Borough High Street, Southwark.
St. Thomas's, a relatively small parish church, extended
from the Borough High Street to the Maze (a network of
streets: the Maze, and Maze Pond) in St. Olave's. The
church, originally a part of St. Thomas's Hospital (see
above, p. 281), dated from the thirteenth century and
underwent rebuilding in 1702. In 1902, it became merely
the charterhouse of Southwark Cathedral, the parish of
St. Thomas having been abolished.

John Wesley preached at St. Thomas's Church on Sunday afternoon (2:30), 19 January 1783, on 1 Corinthians
1:30--He is the source of your life in Christ Jesus,
whom God made our wisdom, our righteousness and sanctification and redemption. . . .

Snowsfields, Southwark. On Saturday, 6 August 1743,
Wesley announced that "a convenient chapel was offered
me at Snowsfields, on the other side of the water. It
was built on purpose, it seems, by a poor Arian misbeliever, for the defence and propagation of her faith.
But the wisdom of God brought that device to nought; and
ordered, by His overruling providence, that it should be
employed, not for 'crucifying the Son of God afresh,'but
for call all to believe on His name." The Unitarian Chapel
in Snowsfields thus became the third building acquired in London by John Wesley--the other two being the
chapels at West Street and City Road. It served for the
Methodist society formed at Long Lane, and was the pre-
decessor of Long Lane Chapel and the Bermondsey Mission.
Charles Wesley's first service at the "new" chapel in
Snowsfields occurred on Saturday, 20 August 1743; however, he had preached there as early as 27 May 1740.
The "poor Arian misbeliever" to whom Wesley referred, a
Madame Ginn, seceded from Maze Pond Chapel and built the

Snowsfields Meetinghouse. Mr. Thomas Day, an original
trustee of City Road Chapel, described three Southwark
religious societies meeting in the area bounded by the
Borough on the east and Blackfriars Road on the west:
Clink Street, College Graveyard, The Great Hall (once a
part of Winchester Palace) appear to have been the locales
of Day's three societies. However, there also existed a room on Long Lane, another in Snowsfields (other
than the Unitarian Chapel), and one at Zoar Street (see
Wesley's Journal 3:82 + note 3).

On Saturday, 8 August 1764, John Wesley "preached,
for the first time, in our new chapel at Snowsfields, on
'Oh how amiable are Thy tabernacles, Thou Lord of hosts!'"
[Psalms 84:1] That "new" structure thus became the second
Methodist chapel in Southwark--an octagon building
not far from Long Lane; as late as 1910, it continued to
survive, transformed into a warehouse! The chief agent
in erecting that second chapel, Samuel Butcher, functioned
as a leather-seller in Crucifix Lane, Bermondsey. He
and Wesley were on intimate terms; for years, the Methodist leader dined at Butcher's house for Christmas day,
in company with a number of the less fortunate members
of the Snowsfields society (see Wesley's Journal 5:92 +
note 1). Thus, after August 1764, Wesley's activities
in Snowsfields focus upon the octagonal chapel near the
Long Lane.

Wesley noted, in his journal for Monday, 8 August
1743, that upon mentioning his intention to preach at
Snowsfields Chapel, a zealous woman "warmly replied,
'What! At Snowsfields! Will Mr. W. preach at Snowsfields?
Surely he will not do it! Why, there is not such another
in all the town. The people there are not men, but dev-
ils!' However, I resolved to try if God was not stronger among them: so this evening [8 August] I preached

there on that scripture, 'Jesus said, They that be whole
need not a physician; but they that are sick. I come
not to call the righteous, but sinners to repentance'"
[Matthew 9:11-13, Mark 2:17, Luke 5:31]. The following
Sunday, 14 August 1743, a Rev. Mr. Garden assisted him
at Snowsfields, "one who had then a deep sense of the
goodness of God, in lifting him up from the gates of
death and delivering him out of all of his troubles."
From that point, the following will summarize John
Wesley's activities at the two Snowsfields chapels (not always identified specifically in the journal or diary) between 1744 and 1790:

Saturday, 25 March 1744. After preaching in the evening "at the corner of Joyner Street [running at right
angles out of Tooley Street, southward]," Wesley reported
that "the coach wherein five of us were, was overturned;
but without any one's being hurt, although the shock was
so great as not only to dash the fore-windows in pieces,
but to break the axle-tree in two."

Monday, 24 December 1744. While reading prayers at
the Chapel, "I found such light and strength as I never
remember to have had before. I saw every thought, as
well as action or word, just as it was rising in my heart;
and whether it was right before God, or tainted with
pride or selfishness. I never knew before (I mean not
as at this time) what it was 'to be still before God.'"

Saturday, 9 January 1748

> Romans 7--Do you not know, brethren--for I am
> speaking to those who know the law--that
> the law is binding on a person only during
> his life?

Saturday, 11 June 1748

> Psalms 61:2-4--. . .from the end of the earth
> I call to thee, when my heart is faint.

Lead thou me to the rock that is higher
than I; for thou art my refuge, a strong
tower against the enemy. Let me dwell in
thy tent forever! Oh to be safe under the
shelter of thy wings.

Galatians 2:17--But if, in our endeavor to be
justified in Christ, we ourselves were found
to be sinners, is Christ then an agent of
sin? Certainly not!

Saturday, 10 September 1748

Romans 2:23--You who boast in the law, do you
dishonor God by breaking the law?

Monday, 31 October 1748

Ephesians 2:2--. . .in which you once walked,
following the course of this world, following the prince of the power of the air,
the spirit that is now at work in the sons
of disobedience.

Philippians 3:3--For we are the true circumcision, who worship God in spirit, and glory
in Christ Jesus, and put no confidence in
the flesh.

Monday, 7 November 1748

2 Timothy 2:19--But God's firm foundation
stands, bearing this seal: "The Lord knows
those who are his," and "Let every one who
names the name of the Lord depart from iniquity."

Hebrews 2:13--And again, "I will put my trust
in him." And again, "Here am I, and the
children of God hath given me."

Saturday, 3 December 1748

Hebrews 9:13--For if the sprinkling of defiled
persons with the blood of goats and bulls

and with the ashes of a heifer sanctifies
for the purification of the flesh. . .

Isaiah 30:20--And though the Lord give you the
bread of adversity and the water of affliction, yet your Teacher will not hide himself any more, but your eyes shall see your
Teacher.

Jude 3--Beloved, being very eager to write to
you of your common salvation, I found it
necessary to write appealing to you to contend for the faith which was once for all
delivered to the saints.

Monday, 30 January 1749

Exodus 3:14--God said to Moses, "I am who I
am." And he said, "Say this to the people
of Israel, 'I am has sent me to you.'"

Saturday, 11 February 1749

2 Corinthians 7:1--Since we have these promi-
ses, beloved, let us cleanse ourselves from
every defilement of body and spirit, and
make holiness perfect in the fear of God.

2 Thessalonians 2--Now concerning the coming
of our Lord Jesus Christ and our assembling
to meet him, we beg you, brethren. . .

John 14:1--Let not your hearts be troubled; believe also in me.

Isaiah 55:7--Let the wicked forsake his way,
and the unrighteous man his thoughts; let
him return to the Lord, that he may have
mercy upon him, and to our God, for he will
abundantly pardon.

Friday, 10 November 1749

Hebrews 10:36--For you have need of endurance,
so that you may do the will of God and

receive what is promised.

Psalms 78:9--The Ephraimites, armed with the
bow, turned back on the day of battle.

John 11:48--If we let him go on thus, every
one will believe in him, and the Romans
will come and destroy both our holy places
and our nation.

Monday, 13 November 1749

John 15:1--I am the true vine, and my Father
is the vinedresser.

Hebrews 12:28--Therefore, let us be grateful
for receiving a kingdom that cannot be shaken, and thus let us offer to God acceptable
worth, with reverence and awe. . .

Saturday, 2 December 1749. Wesley found "still
greater blessing at Snowsfields, where it seemed as if all
would then 'know the Lord, from the least even to the
greatest.'" He preached on--

Hebrews 8:10--This is the covenant that I will
make with the house of Israel after those
days, says the Lord: I will put my laws into their minds, and write them on their
hearts, and I will be their God, and they
shall be my people.

James 2:14--What does it profit, my brethren,
if a man says he has faith but has not works?
Can his faith save him?

1 Peter 4:7--The end of all things is at hand;
therefore, keep sane and sober for your
prayers.

Sunday, 3 December 1749

Hebrews 12:2--. . .looking to Jesus, the pioneer and perfecter of our faith, who for
the joy that was set before him endured the

cross, despising the shame, and is seated
at the right hand of the throne of God.
Psalms 90:12--So teach us to remember our days
that we may get a heart of wisdom.
Acts 17:23--For as I passed along, and observed
the objects of your worship, I found
also an altar with this inscription,"To an
unknown god." What therefore you worship
as unknown, this I proclaim to you.

Saturday, 23 December 1749

1 John 3:1--See what love the Father has given
us,that we should be called the children of
God; and so we are. The reason why the world
does not know us is that it did not know him.
1 John 2:3--And by this we may be sure that we
know him, if we keep his commandments.

Sunday, 14 January 1750. Wesley "read prayers and
preached. . .to a crowded congregation at seven in the
morning."

Saturday, 20 January 1750

1 Corinthians 2:14--The unspiritual man does
not receive the gifts of the Spirit of God,
for they are folly to him, and he is not
able to understand them because they are
spiritually discerned.
Isaiah 60:18--Violence shall no more be heard
in your land, devastation or destruction
within your borders; you shall call your
walls Salvation, and your gates Praise.
Psalms 69:30--I will praise the name of God
with a song; I will magnify him with thanksgiving.
Psalms 130:1--Out of the depths I cry to Thee,
O Lord!

Matthew 20--For the kingdom of heaven is like
a householder who went out early in the
morning to hire laborers for his vineyard.

Matthew 25:1--Then the kingdom of heaven shall
be compared to ten maidens who took their
lamps and went out to meet the bridegroom.

Saturday, 3 February 1750

1 Corinthians 15:33--Do not be deceived: "Bad
company ruins good morals."

2 Corinthians 6--Working together with him,
then, we entreat you not to accept the grace
of God in vain.

Matthew 11--And when Jesus had finished in-
structing his twelve disciples, he went on
from there to teach and preach in their
cities.

Numbers 23:10--Who can count the dust of Jacob,
or number the fourth part of Israel?
Let me die the death of the righteous, and
let my end be like his!

Luke 1:58--And her neighbors and kinsfolk
heard that the Lord had shown great mercy
to her, and they rejoiced with her.

Galatians 6:14--But far be it for me to glory,
except in the cross of our Lord Jesus Christ,
by which the world has been crucified to me,
and I to the world.

Luke 7:36--One of the Pharisees asked him to
eat with him, and he went into the Pharisee's
house, and sat at table.

Romans 13:10--Love does no wrong to a neighbor; therefore, love is the fulfilling of
the law.

1 Corinthians 6:19--Do you not know that your

body is a temple of the Holy Spirit within
you, which you have from God? You are not
your own. . .

Saturday, 17 February 1750. After preaching   at
Snowsfields, Wesley went to a friend's house.

Thursday, 1 November 1750

Hebrews 12:22--But you have come to Mount Zion
and to the city of the living God, the heavenly Jerusalem, and to innumerable angels
in festal gathering. . .

Philippians 3:10--. . .that I may know him and
and the power of his resurrection, and may
share his sufferings, becoming like him in
his death.

Hebrews 12:1-3--Therefore, since we are surrounded by so great a cloud of witnesses,
let us also lay aside every weight. . .

Hebrews 12:5-6--And have you forgotten the exhortation which addresses you as sons?

1 Peter 2:2--Like newborn babes, long for the
pure spiritual milk, that by it you may
grow up to salvation. . .

John 17:3--And this is eternal life, that they
know thee the only true God,and Jesus Christ
whom thou hast sent.

Acts 16:22--The crowd joined in attacking them;
and the magistrates tore the garments off
them and gave orders to beat them with rods.

1 John 2:13--I am writing to you, fathers, because you know him who is from the beginning. I am writing to you, young men, because you have overcome the evil one. I
write to you, children, because you know
the Father.

1 John 5:5--Who is it that overcomes the world
but he who believes that Jesus is the Son
of God?

Saturday, 5 January 1751

Romans 4:7--Blessed are those whose iniquities
are forgiven, and whose sins are covered. . .

Romans 10:13--For, "every one who calls upon
the name of the Lord will be saved."

1 Corinthians 1:30--He is the source of your
life in Christ Jesus, whom God made our wisdom, our righteousness and sanctification
and redemption. . .

Exodus 34:6--The Lord passed before him and
proclaimed, "The Lord, the Lord, a God merciful and gracious, slow to anger, and abounding in steadfast love and faithfulness."

John 16:27--. . .for the Father himself loves
you, because you have loved me and have believed that I come from the Father.

Philippians 1:9--And it is my prayer that your
love may abound more and more, with knowledge and all discernment. . .

Saturday, 10 February 1751. Wesley preached at
Snowsfield at 5:00 p.m.

Tuesday, 21 March 1751

2 Timothy 1:7--. . .for God did not give us a
spirit of timidity, but a spirit of power
and love and self-control.

John 18:11--Jesus said to Peter, "Put your
sword into its sheath; shall I not drink
the cup which the Father hath given to me?"

Saturday, 25 May 1751

Nehemiah 1:10--They are thy servants and thy
people, whom thou hast redeemed by thy

great power and by thy strong hand.

John 16:22--So you have sorrow now, but I will
    see you again and your hearts will rejoice,
    and no one will take your joy from you.

Job 28:28--And he said to man, "Behold, the
    fear of the Lord, that is wisdom; and to
    depart from evil is understanding."

Saturday, 10 August 1751

John 20:29--Jesus said to him,"Have you be-
    lieved because you have seen me? Blessed
    are those who have not seen and yet believe."

1 Peter 2:1--So put away all malice and all
    guile and insincerity and envy and all slan-
    der.

Philippians 1:27--Only let your manner of life
    be worthy of the gospel of Christ, so that
    whether I come and see you or am absent, I
    may hear of you that stand firm in one spirit,
    with one mind striving side by side for
    the faith of the gospel. . .

Philippians 2:1-2--So if there is any encour-
    agement in Christ, any incentive of love,
    any participation in the Spirit, any affec-
    tion and sympathy, complete my joy by being
    of the same mind, having the same love, be-
    ing of full accord and of one mind.

1 Thessalonians 5:19--Do not quench the
    spirit. . .

Psalms 50:22--Mark this, then, you who forgot
    God, lest I rend, and there be none to
    deliver!

John 9--As he passed, he saw a man blind from
    his birth.

2 Timothy 1:7--See above for Thursday, 21 March

1751 (p. 291).

Titus 2:14--. . .who gave himself for us to redeem us from all iniquity and to purify for
himself a people of his own who are zealous
for good deeds.

Saturday, 26 October 1751

Ephesians 6:10--Finally, be strong in the Lord
and in the strength of his might.

John 16--I have said all this to you to keep
you from falling away.

Hebrews 6:4-5--For it is impossible to restore
again to repentance those who have once
been enlightened, who have tasted the heavenly gift, and who have become partakers
of the Holy Spirit, and have tasted of the
goodness of the word of God and the powers
of the age to come. . .

Sunday, 1 December 1751

Acts 2:28--Thou has made known to me the ways
of life; thou will make me full of gladness in thy presence.

Acts 8:5--Philip went down to the city of
Samaria maria, and proclaimed to them the Christ.

Philippians 3:3--See above for Monday, 31 October 1748 (p. 285).

Acts 5:18--. . .they arrested the apostles and
put them in the common prison.

1 John 1:3--. . .that which we have seen and
heard we proclaim also to you, so that you
may have fellowship with us; and our fellowship is with the Father and with his Son,
Jesus Christ.

Acts 22:16--And now, why do you wait? Rise and
be baptized, and wash away your sins,

calling on his name.

1 John 5:20--And we know that the son of God
has come and has given us understanding,
to know him who is true, in his Son Jesus
Christ. This is the true God and eternal
life.

Acts 26:25--But Paul said, "I am not mad, most
excellent Festus, but I am speaking the sober truth.

Saturday, 4 January 1752

Romans 3:22--. . .the righteousness of God
through faith in Jesus Christ for all who
believe. For there is no distinction. . .

Matthew 3:22--And the tempter came and said to
him, "If you are the Son of God, command
these stones to become loaves of bread."

Romans 9--I am speaking the truth in Christ,
I am not lying; my conscience bears me witness in the Holy Spirit. . .

Philippians 4:7--And the peace of God which
passes all understanding will keep your
hearts and your minds in Christ Jesus.

Matthew 17--And after six days Jesus took with
him Peter and James and John his brother,
and led them up a high mountain apart.

1 Corinthians 6:9--Do you not know that the
unrighteous will not inherit the kingdom
of God? Do not be deceived; neither the immoral, nor idolators, nor adulterers, nor
homosexuals. . .

Matthew 23--Then said Jesus to the crowds and
to his disciples, "The scribes and the Pharisees sit on Moses' seat. . .

Colossians 1:12--. . .giving thanks to the Father

who has qualified us to share in the
inheritance of the saints in light.

1 Corinthians 13:13--All the saints greet you.

Sunday, 8 March 1752

Colossians 2:10--. . .and you have come to
fulness of life in him, who is the head of
all rule and authority.

Luke 19:1--He entered Jericho and was passing
through.

1 Thessalonians 5:19--See above for Saturday,
10 August 1751 (p. 292).

Sunday, 15 March 1752

John 3:8--The wind blows where it wills, and
you hear the sound of it, but you do not
know whence it comes or whither it goes;
so it is with every one who is born of the
Spirit.

1 Corinthians 13:13--So faith, hope, love
abide, these three; but the greatest of
these is love.

2 Thessalonians 2:1--See above for Saturday,
11 February 1749 (p. 286).

Friday, 3 November 1752

1 Thessalonians 5:19--See above for Saturday,
10 August 1751 (p. 292) and for Sunday, 8
March 1752 (p. 295).

Colossians 3:11--Here there cannot be Greek
and Jew, circumcised and uncircumcised,
barbarian, Scythian, slave, free man, but
Christ is all, and in all.

John 11:48--See above for Friday, 10 November
1749 (p. 287).

Sunday, 5 November 1752

1 Timothy 6:17--As for the rich in this world

charge them not to be haughty, nor to set
their hopes on uncertain riches, but on God
who richly furnishes us with everything to
enjoy.

Malachi 3:2--But who can endure the day of his
coming, and who can stand when he appears?
For he is like a refiner's fire and like
fuller's soap. . .

Luke 9:55--But he turned and rebuked them.

2 Thessalonians 1--Paul, Sylvanus, Timothy, To
the church of the Thessalonians in God our
Father and the Lord Jesus Christ. . .

John 4:14--. . .but whoever drinks of the water
that I shall give him will never thirst;
the water that I shall give him will become
in him a spring of water welling up to eternal life.

Saturday, 18 November 1752

Colossians 3:11--See above for Friday, 3 November
1752 (p. 295).

John 11:25--Jesus said to her, "I am the resurrection and the life. . . ."

Hebrews 1:14--Are they not all ministering spirits
sent forth to serve, for the sake of
those who are to obtain salvation?

Hebrews 2:3--. . .how shall we escape if we
neglect such a great salvation? It was declared at first by the Lord, and it was
attested to us by those who heard him. . .

Colossians 3:16--Let the word of Christ dwell
in you richly, as you teach and admonish one
another in all wisdom, and as you sing
psalms and hymns and spiritual songs with
thankfulness in your hearts to God.

Tuesday, 26 December 1752

> 1 Peter 4:18--And "If the righteous man   is
> scarcely saved, where will the impious and
> sinner appear?"
>
> Acts 24:26--At the same time he hoped that money
> would be given him by Paul. So he sent
> for him often and conversed with him.
>
> Isaiah 62:11--Behold, the Lord has proclaimed
> to the end of the earth: Say to the daughter
> of Zion, "Behold, your salvation comes;
> behold, his reward is with him, and his re-
> compense before him."
>
> 1 John 3:1--See above for Saturday, 23 Decem-
> ber 1749 (p. 288).
>
> Acts 28:22--But we desire to hear from   you
> what your views are;   for with regard to
> this sect we know that everywhere it   is
> spoken against.

Monday, 5 January 1753.   "We had our first watch-
night at Snowsfields," noted Wesley.   "Scarce any went
away till between twelve and one. How is it that never
any one, in England or Ireland, has been hurt for   all
these years in going to all parts at the dead of night?
Are not the hairs of our head all numbered?"

Tuesday, 30 January 1753

> Psalms 34:10--The young lions suffer want and
> hunger; but those who seek the Lord lack no
> good thing.
>
> Matthew 5:20--For I tell you, unless your right-
> eousness exceeds that   of the   scribes and
> Pharisees, you will   never enter the king-
> dom of heaven.
>
> Matthew 12:43--When   the   unclean spirit has
> gone out of a man, he passes through water-

less places seeking rest, but finds none.

1 Corinthians 2:2--For I decided to know nothing among you except Jesus Christ and him
crucified.

Matthew 19:29--And every one who has left houses or brothers or sisters or father or
mother or children or lands, for my name's
sake will receive a hundred-fold, and inherit eternal life.

Matthew 25:1--See above for Saturday,20 January 1750 (p. 289).

Colossians 3:10--. . .and have put on the new
nature, which is being renewed in knowledge
after the image of its creator.

Saturday, 3 February 1753

1 Corinthians 15:19--If for this life only we
have hoped in Christ, we are of all men most
to be pitied.

Mark 4:1--Again he began to teach beside the
sea. And a very large crowd gathered about
him, so that he got into a boat and sat in
it on the sea; and the whole crowd was beside the sea on the land.

2 Corinthians 1:22--. . .he has put his seal
upon us and given us his Spirit in our
hearts as a guarantee.

2 Timothy 3:16--All scripture is inspired by
God and profitable for teaching, for re-
proof, for correction, and for training in
righteousness. . .

Galatians 6:14--But far be it from me to glory
except in the cross of our Lord Jesus Christ,
by which the world had been crucified to me,
and I to the world.

2 Corinthians 6:1--See above for Saturday, 3
February 1750 (p. 289)

Numbers 23:10--See above for Saturday, 3 February 1750 (p. 289).

Luke 1:72--. . .to perform the mercy promised
to our fathers, and to remember his holy
covenant. . .

Saturday, 24 February 1753

Galatians 6:15--For neither circumcision counts
for anything, nor uncircumcision, but a new
creation.

Luke 8:25--He said to them, "Where is your
faith?" And they were afraid, and they
marveled, saying to one another, "Who, then,
is this, that he commands even wind and water, and they obey him?"

2 Corinthians 12:7--And to keep me from being
too elated by the abundance of revelations,
a thorn was given me in the flesh, a messenger of Satan, to harass me, to keep me from
being too elated.

Colossians 1:9--And so, from the day we heard
of it, we have not ceased to pray for you,
asking that you may be filled with the knowledge of his will in all spiritual wisdom
and understanding. . .

Sunday, 18 November 1753

Psalms 90:12--See above for Sunday, 3 December 1749 (p. 288).

Saturday, 20 April 1754

Matthew 11:12--From the days of John the Baptist
until now the kingdom of heaven has
suffered violence, and men of violence take
it by force.

Acts 24:27--But when two years had elapsed,
Felix was succeeded by Porcius Festus; and
desiring to do the Jews a favor, Felix left
Paul in prison.

1 Corinthians 9:27--. . .but I pommel my body
and subdue it, lest after preaching to others
I, myself, should be disqualified.

Monday, 20 May 1754

2 Kings 5:11--But Naaman was angry, and went
away, saying, "Behold, I thought that he
would surely come out to me, and stand,and
call on the name of the Lord his God, and
wave his hand over the place, and cure the
leper.

1 Peter 1:4--. . .and to an inheritance which
is imperishable, undefiled, and unfading,
kept in heaven for you. . .

2 Corinthians 6:1--See above for Saturday, 3
February 1753 (p. 289), and for Saturday,
3 February 1753 (p. 299).

Saturday, 15 June 1754

Hebrews 3:13--But exhort one another every day,
as long as it is called "Today," that none
of you may be hardened by the deceitfulness
of sin.

Galatians 6:15--See above for Saturday, 24
February 1753 (p. 299).

1 Corinthians 12:7--To each is given the mani-
festation of the Spirit for the common good.

Saturday, 6 July 1754

Isaiah 42:19--Who is blind but my servant, or
deaf as my messenger whom I send? Who is
blind as my dedicated one, or blind as the
servant of the Lord?

Genesis 6:3--Then the Lord said, "My spirit
shall not abide in man for ever,for he is
flesh, but his days shall be a hundred and
twenty years."

Hebrews 5:13--. . .for every one who lives on
milk is unskilled in the word of righteousness, for he is a child.

Job 22:21--Agree with God and be at peace;
thereby, good will come to you.

Saturday, 5 October 1754

1 Corinthians 4:7--For who sees anything different in you? What have you that you did
not receive? If then you received it, why
do you boast as if it were not a gift?

2 Corinthians 13:14--The grace of the Lord Je-
Jesus Christ and the love of God and the fellowship of the Holy Spirit be with you all.

Galatians 5:1--For freedom, Christ has set us
free; stand fast, therefore,and do not sub-
mit again to a yoke of slavery.

Sunday, 20 October 1754

Luke 6--On a sabbath,while he was going through
the grainfields, his disciples plucked and
ate some ears of grain, rubbing them in
their hands.

Ephesians 6:11--Put on the whole armour of God,
that you may be able to stand against the
wiles of the devil.

Luke 13:1--There were some present at that very
time who told him of the Galileans whose
blood Pilate had mingled with their sacrifi-
ces.

Colossians 2:6--As therefore you received Christ
Jesus the Lord, so live in him. . . .

Sunday, 3 November 1754

Luke 19--See above for Sunday,8 March 1752
(p. 295).

1 Thessalonians 5:19--See above for Saturday,
10 August 1751 (p. 292), and for Sunday, 8
March 1752 (p. 295).

Hebrews 13:1--Let brotherly love continue.

Sunday, 17 November 1754

John 9--See above for Saturday, 10 August 1751
(p. 292).

Titus 2:14--See above for Saturday, 10 August
1751 (p. 293).

Hebrews 6:4--See above for Saturday, 26 October 1751 (p. 293).

Acts 2--When the day of Pentecost had come,
they were all together in one place.

Saturday, 7 December 1754

Hebrews 13:20--Now may the God of peace who
brought again from the dead our Lord Jesus,
the great shepherd of the sheep, by the
blood of the eternal covenant. . .

1 Peter 2:2--See above for Thursday, 1 November 1750 (p. 290).

Acts 15:18--. . .says the Lord, who has made
these things known from of old.

Saturday, 21 December 1754

1 John 1:1--That which was from the beginning,
which we have heard, which we have seen
with our eyes, which we have looked upon
and touched with our hands, concerning the
word of life. . .

1 John 5:19--We know that we are of God,and the
whole world is in the power of the evil one.

Saturday, 4 January 1755

Psalms 23--The Lord is my shepherd, I shall

not want. . .

Matthew 4:7--Jesus said to him, "Again it is
written, 'You shall not tempt the Lord your
God.'"

Psalms 93--The Lord reigns; he is robed in
majesty. . . .

Sunday, 19 January 1755

Matthew 27--When morning came, all the chief
priests and the elders of the people took
counsel against Jesus to put him to death.

Psalms 8--O Lord, our Lord, how majestic is
thy name in all the earth!

Mark 2:8---And immediately, Jesus, perceiving
in his spirit that they thus questioned
within themselves, said to them, "Why do
you thus question in your hearts?"

Saturday, 8 February 1755

Psalms 42--As a hart longs for flowing streams,
so longs my soul for thee, O God.

Galatians 5:16--But I say, walk by the Spirit,
and do not gratify the desires of the flesh.

Luke 6:1--See above for Sunday, 20 October 1754
(p. 301).

Saturday, 1 March 1755

Psalms 2:12--Blessed are all who take refuge
in him.

Micah 6:9--The voice of the Lord cries to the
city--and it is sound wisdom to fear thy
name: "Hear, O tribe and assembly of the
city!

Luke 20:1--One day, as he was teaching the
people in the temple and preaching the gospel, the chief priests and the scribes with
the elders came up. . .

Saturday, 15 March 1755

> 1 _Timothy_ 4:7--Have nothing to do with godless
> and silly myths. Train yourself in godli-
> ness. . . .
>
> _Galatians_ 5:23--. . .gentleness, self-control;
> against such there is no law.
>
> _Luke_ 6:22--Blessed are you when men hate you,
> and when they exclude you and revile you,
> and cast out your name as evil, on account
> of the Son of man!

Sunday, 26 October 1755. Wesley read prayers,
preached, and gave the sacrament in the morning.

Sunday, 12 September 1756

> 2 _Timothy_ 1:6--Hence I remind you to rekindle
> the gift of God that is within you through
> the laying on of my hands. . .
>
> _Romans_ 8:13--. . .for if you live according to
> the flesh you will die, but if by the Spirit
> you put to death the deeds of the body,
> you will live.
>
> _Matthew_ 9:5--For which is easier to say, "Your
> sins are forgiven," or to say, "Rise and
> walk?"

Friday, 24 September 1756

> _Micah_ 6:8--He has showed you, O man, what is
> good; and what does the Lord require of
> you but to do justice and to love kindness,
> and to walk humbly with your God?
>
> _Matthew_ 13:27--And the servants of the house-
> holder came and said to him, "Sir, did you
> not sow good seeds in your field? How then
> has it weeds?"
>
> _Matthew_ 20:27--. . .and whoever would be first
> among you must be your slave. . .

2 Timothy 3:16--See above for Saturday, 3 February 1753 (p. 298).

2 Corinthians 1:22--See above for Saturday, 3 February 1753 (p. 298).

Mark 13:27--And then he will send out the angels, and gather his elect from the four winds, from the ends of the earth to the ends of heaven.

Galatians 2:20--I have been crucified with Christ; it is no longer I who live, but Christ who lives in me; and the life I now live in the flesh I live by faith in the Son of God, who loved me and gave himself for me.

Luke 10:42--. . .one thing is needful. Mary has chosen the good portion,which shall not be taken away from her.

Sunday, 3 October 1756. My disorder returned as violent as ever; but I regarded it not while I was performing the service at Snowsfields in the morning. . . ." That illness may well have been a form of consumption, from which Wesley suffered at regular periods during his life.

(?) October 1756

Ephesians 1:12--. . .we who first hoped in Christ have been destined and appointed to live for the praise of his glory.

Luke 17:20--Being asked by the Pharisees when the kingdom of God was coming, he answered them, "The kingdom of God is not coming with signs to be observed. . . ."

Luke 23:39--One of the criminals who were hanged railed at him, saying, "Are you not the Christ? Save yourself and us!"

(?) November 1756

Psalms 69:33--For the Lord hears the needy,
    and does not despise his own that are in
    bonds.

John 6:29--Jesus answered them, "This is the
    work of God, that you believe in him whom
    he sent."

2 Timothy 3:12--Indeed, all who desire to live
    a godly life in Christ Jesus will be perse-
    cuted. . . .

John 13:27--Then, after the morsel, Satan en-
    tered into him. Jesus said to him, "What
    you are going to do, do quickly."

Psalms 130:7-8--O Israel, hope in the Lord!
    For with the Lord, there is steadfast love,
    and with him is plenteous redemption. And
    he will redeem Israel from all his iniqui-
    ties.

John 20--Now on the first day of the week Mary
    Magdalene came to the tomb early, while it
    was still dark, and saw that the stone had
    been taken away from the tomb.

Hebrews 10:36--See above for Friday, 10 Novem-
    ber 1749 (pp. 286-287).

Acts 6:1--Now in these days, when the disci-
    ples were increasing in number, the Hellenists
    murmured against the Hebrews because
    their widows were neglected in the daily
    distribution.

Psalms 62:1--For God alone my soul waits in silenc
    from him comes my salvation.

James 4:14--. . .whereas you do not know about
    tomorrow. What is your life? For you are
    a mist that appears for a little time and

then vanishes.

Psalms 93:1--See above for Saturday, 4 January
(p. 303)

2 Peter 1:16--For we did not follow cleverly
devised myths when we made known to you the
power and the coming of our Lord Jesus
Christ, but we were eyewitnesses of his
majesty.

Acts 6:8--And Stephen full of grace and power,
did great wonders and signs among the
people.

Sunday, 30 January 1757. Wesley officiated at
Snowsfield "as usual. . . ."

Friday, 11 February 1757

2 Corinthians 7:1--See above for Saturday, 11
February 1749 (p. 286).

Galatians 1:4--. . .who gave himself for our
sins to deliver us from the present evil
age, according to the will of our God and
Father. . .

Luke 2--In those days a decree went out from
Caesar Augustus that all the world should
be enrolled.

Friday, 25 February 1757

Ephesians 2:1--And you he made alive when you
were dead through the trespasses and sins
. . .

Philippians 3:3--See above for Monday, 31
October 1748 (p. 285) and for Sunday, 1
December 1751 (p. 293).

John 4:14--See above for Sunday, 5 November
1752 (p. 296).

Sunday, 13 March 1757

Matthew 1:21--. . .she will bear a son, and

you shall call his name Jesus, for he will
save his people from their sins.

Romans 6:23--For the wages of sin is death,
but the free gift of God is eternal life in
Jesus Christ our Lord.

Matthew 7:16--You will know them by their fruits
Are grapes gathered from thorns, or figs
from thistles?

Genesis 28:20--Then Jacob made a vow, saying,
"If God will be with me, and will keep me
in this way that I go, and will give me
bread to eat and clothing to wear. . .

1 Corinthians 2:14--See above for Saturday, 20
January 1750 (p. 288).

1 Corinthians 10:12--Therefore, let any one who
thinks that he stands take heed lest he
fall.

Psalms 144--Blessed be the Lord, my rock, who
trains my hands for war, and my fingers for
battle. . .

2 Corinthians 3--Are we beginning to commend
ourselves again? Or do we need, as some
do, letters of recommendation to you, or
from you?

Mark 6:12--So they went out and preached that
men should repent.

2 Corinthians 7:1--See above for Saturday, 11
February 1749 (p. 286) and for Friday, 11
February 1757 (p. 307).

Numbers 23:10--See above for Saturday, 3 February 1750 (p. 289).

Deuteronomy 10:12--And now, Israel, what does
the Lord your God require of you, but to
fear the Lord your God, to walk in all his

ways, to love him, to serve the Lord your
God with all your heart and with all your
soul. . . .

Luke 10:23--Then turning to the disciples, he
said privately, "Blessed are the eyes which
see what you see!

1 Thessalonians 3:11-12--Now may our God and
Father himself, and our Lord Jesus, direct
our way to you; and may the Lord make you
increase and abound in love to one another
and to all men, as we do to you. . . .

Luke 24:25--And he said to them, "O foolish
men, and slow of heart to believe all that
the prophets have spoken!

1 Timothy 3:16--Great, indeed, we confess, is
the mystery of our religion:
He was manifested in the flesh,
vindicated in the Spirit,
seen by angels,
preached among the nations,
believed on in the world,
taken up in glory.

John 7:37--On the last day of the feast, the
great day, Jesus stood up and proclaimed,
"If any one thirsts, let him come to me and
drink.

Wesley noted, in his journal for this day, that, "finding myself weak at Snowsfields, I prayed (as if He saw
good) that God would send me help at the chapel, and I
had it. A clergyman whom I never saw before came and offered me his assistance, and as soon as I had done preaching,
Mr. Fletcher [Rev. John William de la Flechere
(1729-1785)] came, who had just then been ordained priest
[in the Church of England], and hastened to the chapel

on purpose to assist, as he supposed me to be alone."
There exists some ambiguity in the above passage that
may lead us to believe that Fletcher came to John Wesley
at Snowsfields Chapel; however, having been ordained at
Whitehall on this date (13 March), Fletcher could not
possibly have reached Snowsfields in time for the communion service. In all probability, he came to the
Methodist founder and leader at West Street Chapel (see
Wesley's Journal, 5:198 + note 1).

Friday, 18 March 1757. Wesley returned to London
from Canterbury, and then preached at Snowsfields.

(?) April 1757

2 Timothy 4:5--As for you, always be steady,
endure suffering, do the work of an evangelist, fulfil your ministry.

John 14:2--In my Father's house are many rooms;
if it were not so, would I have told you
that I go to prepare a place for you?

Hebrews 3:9--. . .where your fathers put me to
the test and saw my works for forty years.

John 21:15--When they had finished breakfast,
Jesus said to Simon Peter, "Simon, son of
John, do you love me more than these?" He
said to him, "Yes, Lord; you know that I
love you." He said to him, "Feed my lambs."

Hebrews 4:13--And before him no creature is
hidden, but all are open and laid bare to
the eyes of him with whom we have to do.

Luke 24:8--And they remembered his words. . .

Sunday, 7 August 1757

Acts 5:32--And we are witnesses to these things,
and so is the Holy Spirit whom God has
given to those who obey him.

Psalms 71:14--But I will hope continually, and

will praise thee yet   more   and   more.

Philippians 3:19--Their end is   destruction,
    their god is the belly, and they glory in
    their shame with minds set on earthly things.

Acts 19:2--And he said to them, "Did you   re-
    ceive the Holy Spirit when you believed?"
    And they said, "No, we have never even heard
    that there is a Holy Spirit."

John 19:10--Pilate therefore said to him, "You
    will not speak to me? Do you not know that I
    have power to release you, and power to cru-
    cify you?"

Acts 18:17--And they all seized Sosthenes, the
    ruler of the synagogue, and beat him in
    front of the tribunal. But Gallio paid no
    attention to this.

1 Corinthians 3:8--He who plants and he who wa-
    ters are equal, and each shall receive his
    wages according to his labor.

Saturday, 12 November 1757

1 Thessalonians 3:5--For this reason, when I
    could bear it no longer, I sent that I might
    know your faith, for fear that somehow the
    tempter had tempted you and that our labour
    would be in vain.

Isaiah 26:8--In the path of thy judgments, O
    Lord, we wait for thee; thy memorial name
    is the desire of our soul.

1 John 4:13--By this we know that we abide in
    him and he in us, because he has given us
    of his own Spirit.

John 5:25--Truly, truly, I say to you,the hour
    is coming, and now is, when the dead will hear
    the voice of the Son of God, and those who

hear will live.

1 Peter 1:1-3--. . .By his great mercy we have
been born anew to a living hope through the
resurrection of Jesus Christ from the
dead. . . .

Matthew 20:12--These last worked only one hour,
and you have made them equal to us who have
borne the burden of the day and the scorching heat.

Saturday, 3 December 1757

Hebrews 9:12--. . .he entered once for all
into the Holy Place, taking not the blood of
goats and calves, but his own blood, thus
securing an eternal redemption.

1 Peter 5:8--Be sober, be watchful. Your ad-
versary the devil prowls around like a roaring lion, seeking some one to devour.

Exodus 14:16--Lift up your rod, and stretch
out your hand over the sea and divide it
that the people of Israel may go on dry
ground through the sea.

Mark 4:26--And he said, "The kingdom of God is
as if a man should scatter seed upon the
ground. . . ."

Sunday, 22 October 1758

Luke 8:48--And he said to her, "Daughter, your
faith has made you well; go in peace."

2 Timothy 2:6--It is the hard-working farmer
who ought to have the first share of the
crops.

Jeremiah 23:6--In his days, Judah will be
saved, and Israel will dwell securely. And
this is the name by which he will be
called: "The Lord is our righteousness."

James 1:27--Religion that is pure and undefiled before God and the Father is this: to
visit orphans and widows in their affliction,
and to keep oneself unstained from
the world.

Saturday, 25 November 1758

Hebrews 1:14--See above for Saturday, 18 November
1752 (p. 296).

Hebrews 8:10--See above for Saturday, 2 December 1849 (p. 287).

Acts 4:2--. . .annoyed because they were teaching the people and proclaiming in Jesus the
resurrection from the dead.

1 Peter 4:3--Let the time that is past suffice
for doing what the Gentiles like to do, living
in licentiousness, passions, drunkenness, revels, carousing, and lawless
idolatry.

Sunday, 31 December 1758

Acts 28:22--See above for Tuesday, 26 December
1752 (p. 297).

James 2:14--See above for Saturday, 2 December
1749 (p. 287).

James 2:22--You see that faith was active along
with his works, and faith was completed by
works. . .

Sunday, 12 August 1759. On Tuesday, 7 August, Wesley
returned to London, "thoroughly tired [,] having rode
in seven months above four-and-twenty hundred miles."
Thus, on the 12th, he complained of being "exceeding weak
at Snowsfields in the morning. . . ."

Sunday, 25 August 1759

1 John 2:12--I am writing to you, little children
because your sins are forgiven for

his sake.

Acts 24:27--See above for Saturday, 20 April
1754 (p. 300).

Romans 16:16--Greet one another with a holy
kiss. All the churches of Christ greet you.

Sunday, 16 September 1759

Matthew 17:20--He said to them, "Because of
your little faith. For truly, I say to
you, if you have faith as a grain of mus-
tard seed, you will say to this mountain,
'Move hence to yonder place,' and it will
move. . . ."

Ecclesiastes 9:10--Whatever your hand finds to
do, do it with your might; for there is no
work or thought or knowledge or wisdom in
Sheol, to which you are going.

Matthew 24:37--As were the days of Noah, so
will be the coming of the Son of Man.

Sunday, 28 October 1759

Luke 14:20--And another said, "I have married
a wife, and therefore I cannot come."

1 Peter 5:12--By Sylvanus, a faithful brother
as I regard him, I have written briefly to
you, exhorting and declaring that this is
the true grace of God; stand fast in it.

John 3:7--The sick man answered him, "Sir, I
have no man to put me into the pool when the
water is troubled, and while I am going,
another steps down before me."

Hebrews 7:19--. . .(for the law made nothing
perfect); on the other hand, a better hope
is introduced, through which we draw near
to God.

Saturday, 8 December 1759

Isaiah 30:18--Therefore, the Lord waits to be
gracious to you; therefore he exalts himself to show mercy to you.   For the   Lord
is a God of justice; blessed are those who
wait for him.

2 Peter 3:8--But do not ignore this one fact,
beloved, that with the Lord one day is as
a thousand years, and a thousand years as
one day.

Saturday, 19 January 1760

Romans 10:4--For Christ is the end of the law,
that every one who has faith may be justified.

1 Corinthians 1:24--. . .but to those who are
called, both Jews and Greeks, Christ the
power of God and the wisdom of God.

Genesis 49:4--Unstable as water, you shall not
have pre-eminence because you went up to
your father's bed; then you defiled it--
you went up to my couch!

1 Corinthians 13:13--See above for Saturday, 4
January 1752 (p. 295).

Saturday, 2 February 1760

2 Corinthians 5:17--Therefore, if any one is
in Christ, he is a new creation; the old
has passed away, behold, the new has come.

2 Corinthians 11:3--But I am afraid that as
the serpent deceived Eve by his cunning,
your thoughts will be led astray from a sincere and pure devotion to Christ.

Matthew 20:15--Am I not allowed to do what I
choose with what belongs to me? Or do you
begrudge my generosity?

Saturday, 1 March 1760

Ephesians 5:24--And those who belong to Christ
Jesus have crucified the flesh with its passions and desires.

Isaiah 40:28--Have you not known?   Have you
not heard? The Lord is the everlasting God,
the Creator of the ends of the earth. He
does not faint or grow weary; his understanding is unserachable.

Acts 14:22--. . .strengthening the souls of the
disciples, exhorting them to continue in the
faith, and saying that through many tribulations we must enter the kingdom of God.

Saturday, 29 November 1760

Hebrews 5:12--For though by this time you ought
to be teachers, you need some one to teach
you again the first principles of God's
word. You need milk, not solid food. . .

Isaiah 53:5--But he was wounded for our transgressions; he was bruised for our iniquities; upon him was the whole chastisement
that made us whole, and with his stripes we
are healed.

Acts 21:14--And when he would not be persuaded,
we ceased, and he said, "The will of the
Lord be done."

Saturday, 20 December 1760. Wesley preached again
at Snowsfields, in the evening.

Saturday, 3 January 1761

Romans--For he is not a real Jew who is one
outwardly, nor is true circumcision something external and physical.

Matthew 3:12--His winnowing for is in his
hand, and he will clear his threshing floor
and gather his wheat into the granary, but

the chaff he will burn with unquenchable
fire.

Psalms 74:20--Have regard for thy covenant;
for the dark places of the land are full of
the habitations of violence.

Sunday, 15 February 1761

Psalms 77:3--I think of God, and I moan; I me-
ditate and my spirit faints.

Galatians 5:6--For in Christ Jesus neither circumcision nor uncircumcision is of any avail,
but faith working through love.

Luke 5:13--And he stretched out his hand and
touched him, saying, "I will; be clean."
And immediately the leprosy left him.

Luke 12:13--One of the multitude said to him,
"Teacher, bid my brother divide the inheritance with me."

Ephesians 5:12--For it is a shame even to speak
of the things that they do in secret.

Colossians 3:5--Put to death, therefore, what
is earthly in you: immorality, impurity,
passion, evil desire, and covetousness,
which is idolatry.

1 John 5:19--See above for Saturday, 21 December 1754 (p. 302).

Jude 22--And convince some, who doubt. . .

(?) September 1761

Matthew 7:8--For every one who asks receives,
and he who seeks finds, and to him who
knocks it will be opened.

Romans 13:10--See above for Saturday, 3 February 1750 (p. 289).

Psalms 68:1--Let God arise, let his enemies be
scattered; let those who hate him flee before him!

Zechariah 4:7--What are you, O great mountain? Before Zerubbabel you shall become a plain; and h
shall bring forward the top stone amid shouts c
"Grace, grace to it!"

John 21:19--(This he said to show by what death he
was to glorify God.) And after this, he said t
him, "Follow me."

Acts 15:27--We have therefore sent Judas and Silas
who themselves will tell you the same things by
word of mouth.

Psalms 103:3--. . .who forgives all your iniquity,
who heals all your diseases. . .

Hebrews 12:1--See above for Thursday, 1 November
1750 (p. 290).

1 Peter 1:9--As the outcome of your faith you obtain the salvation of your souls.

Luke 24:48--You are witnesses of these things.

Saturday, 14 November 1761

Romans 10:4--See above for Saturday, 19 January
1760 (p. 315).

1 Timothy 3:16--See above for Sunday, 13 March 175
(p. 309).

John 7:37--See above for Sunday, 13 March 1757 (p.
309).

1 John 2:1--My little children, I am writing this
to you so that you may not sin; but if any one
does sin, we have an advocate with the Father,
Jesus Christ the righteous. . .

Psalms 107:2--Let the redeemed of the Lord say so,
whom he has redeemed from trouble. . .

Saturday, 12 February 1763. "I visited the classes at
Snowsfields, where I was told many would go away; but the
time was not come. As yet we have lost none, though some are
held as by a single hair."

Sunday, 7 October 1764. Wesley preached in the
morning at Snowsfields.

Thursday, 27 December 1764. Wesley preached and administered the sacrament at the new chapel. "How well
does God order all things! By losing the former chapel
we have gained both a better house and a larger congregation."

Saturday, 28 October 1769. He preached at
Snowsfields in the evening.

Saturday, 23 February 1771. "We had the greatest
number of communicants. . .that we have had since the
[new] chapel was built. It seems as if God were about
thoroughly to heal the wound which we received here in
the house of our friends."

Saturday, 1 February 1772. "I found an increase of
the work of God even in Southwark. Those who so furiously
opposed us some years ago, as though they would have
swallowed us up quick, are now crumbled to nothing. Only
the old chapel subsists as a dull, useless, dissenting
meeting-house."

Saturday, 14 November 1772. For the first time,
Wesley saw the chapel at Snowsfields filled to capacity,
"a pressage, I hope, of a greater work there than has
been since the deadly breach was made."

Saturday, 16 December 1775. In the evening, Wesley
preached "a kind of funeral sermon" for one June Binknell,
who died from "an incurable and painful disorder. . . ."

Saturday, 21 December 1782, 5:45 p.m.

    1 John 1:9--If we confess our sins, he is
        faithful and just, and will forgive our sins
        and cleanse us from all unrighteousness.

Saturday, 15 November 1783. 7:00 a.m., class;
6:00 p.m., 1 Timothy 4:8--. . .for while bodily training

is of some value, godliness is of value in every way, as
it holds promise for the present life and also for the
life to come.

Friday, 26 December 1783. 10:00 a.m., Acts 7:55--
But he, full of the Holy Spirit, gazed into heaven and
saw the glory of God, and Jesus standing at the right
hand of God. . .   6:00 p.m. John 4:24--God is spirit,
and those who worship him must worship in spirit and
truth.

All Saints Day, Saturday, 1 November 1788. At 6:00
p.m., Wesley preached on Revelation 14:1 (Then I looked,
and lo, on Mount Zion stood the Lamb, and with him a hundred
and forty-four thousand who had his name and his Father's
name written on their foreheads.), "a comfortable
subject; and I always find this a comfortable day."

Saturday, 2 January 1790. Wesley preached "to the
largest congregation I have seen there [Snowsfields] this
year, on 'I am not ashamed of the gospel of Christ"
(Romans 1:16).

Saturday, 27 February 1790. At 6:00 p.m., Wesley
preached on Ephesians 3:13 (So I ask you not to lose
heart over what I am suffering for you, which is your
glory.) to "such a congregation at Snowsfields as has
not been seen there before for many years. Afterwards I
met the penitents for the last time. They quite filled
the room, and God was in the midst of them."

Saturday, 13 November 1790. According to Wesley's
diary, he met the class at 3:00 p.m., and at 6:00 p.m
preached on 1 Timothy 1:5--. . .whereas the aim of our
charge is love that issues from a pure heart and a good
conscience and sincere faith.

Winchester Yard, Southwark. Winchester Yard lay as

an open space between St. Saviour's Church and what was
to become Barclay and Perkin's Brewery.   Abutting upon
it stood the town house of the Bishops of Winchester; a
part of that manor, an old Gothic hall,survived into the
nineteenth century when, in 1814, a fire almost destroyed
the entire structure.   The hall had been divided into
small tenements; as far back as 1738, a Dissenters' meeting house was registered in one of those.

John Wesley preached in Winchester Yard at 8:00 p.m.,
Tuesday, 25 September 1739,   "where it was believed were
present eleven or twelve hundred persons;   to whom I declared, if 'they had nothing to pay,' God would 'frankly
forgive them all' [Luke 7:42]." He addressed a gathering
there again on Sunday, 4 November 1739,   at 5:00   p.m.,
basing his sermon   upon   John 5:5-6--One man   was there,
who had been ill for thirty-eight years.   When Jesus saw
him and knew that he had been lying there a long time,He
said to him, "Do you want to be healed?"

Long Lane, Bermondsey.   Long Lane ran   between St.
George's Church, Southwark,   and the Church   of St. Mary
Magdalen, Bermondsey.   Before the establishment of Long
Lane Chapel and the Bermondsey Mission--and even before
John Wesley parted company with the Moravians--the
Methodist societies in London had meeting-rooms there. The
following summarizes Wesley's   activities   in Long   Lane
from the middle of 1740 until early 1742:

Monday, 7 July 1740.   7:00 p.m., 1 Peter 1:9--As the
outcome of your faith   you   obtain the salvation of your
souls.

Saturday, 19 July 1740.   6:30 p.m.

Monday, 21 July 1740.   7:00 p.m.

Saturday, 26 July 1740.   6:30 p.m.   Acts 2:8--And

how is it that we hear, each of us in his own native
language?

Monday, 28 July 1740. 7:00 p.m. Acts 2--When the
day of Pentecost had come, they were all together in one
place.

Saturday, 2 August 1740. 6:30 p.m. Acts 2--See
immediately above.

Monday, 4 August 1740. 7:00 p.m. Wesley preached
on Acts 2 (see immediately above). At that service,
"many were gathered together. . .on purpose to make a
disturbance; having procured a woman to begin, well known
in these parts, as neither fearing God nor regarding man.
The instant she broke out I turned full upon her and declared the love of our Lord for her soul. She was struck
to the heart, and shame covered her face. From her I
turned to the rest, who melted away like water, and were as
men that had no strength."

Monday, 11 August 1740. 7:00 p.m. Acts 4--And as
they were speaking to the people, the priests and the
captain of the temple and the Sadducees came upon them
. . .

Saturday, 16 August 1740. 6:30 p.m. Acts 4--See
immediately above.

Monday, 18 August 1740. 7:00 p.m. Acts 4--See
immediately above.

Saturday, 23 August 1740. 6:15 p.m. Acts 5--But a
man named Ananias with his wife Sapphira sold a piece of
property. . .

Saturday, 30 August 1740. 8:15 p.m. Acts 6--Now in
these days when the disciples were increasing in number,
the Hellenists murmured against the Hebrews because their
widows were neglected in the daily distribution.

Saturday, 13 September 1740. 6:30 p.m. Acts 7--
And the high priest said, "Is this so?"

Monday, 15 September 1740.   7:00 p.m.

Saturday, 20 September 1740.   6:00 p.m.   Acts 8--
And Saul was consenting to his death. And on that day a
great persecution arose against the church in Jerusalem;
and they were all scattered throughout the region of
Judea and Samaria, except the apostles.

Saturday, 27 September 1740.   6:00 p.m.

Monday, 29 September 1740.   6:45 p.m.

Saturday, 4 October 1740.   6:00 p.m.

Saturday, 29 November 1740.   6:00 p.m.   Acts 14--
Now at Iconium they entered together into the Jewish
synagogue, and so spoke that a great company believed, both
of Jews and of Greeks.

Saturday, 6 December 1740.   6:00 p.m.

Saturday, 31 January 1741.   6:00 p.m.   Acts 16:31--
And they said, "Believe in the Lord Jesus, and you will
be saved, you and your household."

Monday, 2 February 1741.   6:00 p.m.   Acts 17--Now
when they had passed through Amphipolis and Apollonia,
they came to Thessalonica, where there was a synagogue
of the Jews.

Saturday, 7 February 1741.   6:00 p.m.   Acts 17--
See immediately above.

Monday, 9 February 1741.   7:00 p.m.   Acts 17--See
immediately above.

Monday, 16 Febraury 1741.   At 7:00 p.m., Wesley
preached on Acts 18--After this he left Athens and went
to Corinth. During the sermon "the host of the aliens
gathered together; and one large stone (many of which
they threw) went just over my shoulder. But no one was
hurt in any degree; for 'Thy kingdom ruleth over all'
[Psalms 103:19]."

Saturday, 4 April 1741.   6:00 p.m.   Acts 19--While
Apollos was at Corinth, Paul passed through the upper

country and came to Ephesus.

Saturday, 11 April 1741. 6:00 p.m. Acts 20--After
the uproar ceased, Paul sent for the disciples, and having
exhorted them took leave of them and departed for
Macedonia.

Monday, 13 April 1741. 6:30 p.m. Acts 20--See
immediately above.

Saturday, 18 April 1741. 6:00 p.m. Acts 21--And when
we had parted from them and set sail, we came by a straight
course to Cos, and the next day to Rhodes, and from there
to Patara.

Monday, 20 April 1741. 6:30 p.m. Acts 22--Brethren
and fathers, hear the defense which I now make before
you.

Saturday, 25 April 1741. 6:45 p.m. Acts 23--And
Paul, looking intently at the council, said, "Brethren,
I have lived before God in all good conscience up to
this day."

Saturday, 9 May 1741. 6:00 p.m. 1 Corinthians 15--
Now I would remind you, brethren, in what terms I preached
to you the gospel, which you received, in which you
stand. . . .

Monday, 11 May 1741. 6:15 p.m. Acts 26--Agrippa
said to Paul, "You have permission to speak for yourself." Then Paul stretched out his hand and made his
defense.

Saturday, 30 May 1741. 6:00 p.m. Acts 26:24--And
as he thus made his defense, Festus said with a loud
voice, "Paul, you are mad; your great learning is turning you mad."

Monday, 1 June 1741. 6:30 p.m. Acts 26--See above
(this page) for Monday, 11 May 1741.

Saturday, 6 June 1741. 6:00 p.m. Acts 28--After
we had escaped, we then learned that the island was

called Malta.

Saturday, 1 August 1741. 6:00 p.m. 1 _John_ 1--That
which was from the beginning, which we have heard, which
we have seen with our eyes, which we have looked upon and
touched with our hands, concerning the word of life. . .

Saturday, 26 December 1741. In the evening, Wesley
preached before "a crowded audience. . .from those words,
'Oh the depth of the riches both of the wisdom and the
knowledge of God! How unsearchable are His judgments,
and His ways past finding out!'" [_Romans_ 11:33]

Saturday, 9 January 1742. As Wesley preached, "a
rude rout lifted up their voices on high. I fell upon
them without delay. Some pulled off their hats, and
opened their mouths no more; the rest stole out, one after
another. All that remained were quiet and attentive."

Monday, 18 January 1742. "We greatly rejoiced in
the Lord. . .even in the midst of those that contradicted
and blasphemed. Nor was it long before many of them
also were touched, and blasphemies were turned into praise."

Minories, Aldgate High Street. Minories takes its
name from the community of the _Sorores Minores_, established in 1293 just outside the walls of the City of
London. The group owed its beginnings to the influence of
Edmund, Earl of Lancaster, and his wife. The community
belonged to the second order of St. Francis. In 1563,
the Marquis of Winchester sold the property and the mo-
nastery to the Crown. Then followed its conversion into
a storehouse and workshops for the Ordnance Department,
and further as assigned residences for lieutenant-gener-
als of the Army. A considerable part of the abbey buildings remained until their destruction by fire in 1797.

The name _Minories_ seems to have been given to the

street at the end of the sixteenth century--or, perhaps,
at the outset of the seventeenth century. On that rather
unattractive thoroughfare leading southward to the
Tower of London lived, in 1702, the Dissenter poet, hymnodist, and preacher, Isaac Watts (1674-1748).

On Sunday, 17 September 1738--almost immediately upon his return from Herrnhut (an absence of three months'
duration)--John Wesley expounded "the Holy Scripture to
a large company in the Minories." Peter Sims (b. 1716),
a butcher in Paved Alley, Leadenhall Street, either lived
in or owned a building in the Minories, and there one
of the most important of the London religious societies
met. Wesley appeared at Sims' shop in the late afternoon
of Friday, 22 September 1738, and he preached there on
the following Sunday (24 September) at 6:00 p.m.   We
must not always assume that the Minories society met at
Sims' house, for Wesley's diary entry for 24 September
1738 reads, "5.30 [p.m.] Mr. Sims,' tea, conversed; 6
[:00 p.m.] in the Minories. . . ." Thus, the society may
have met in a workshop or in some other building near or
adjacent to Sims' actual residence.

The following entries recount John Wesley's activities in the Minories between October 1738 and February
1741:

Sunday, 1 October 1738. "7:15 [p.m.] Mrs. Sims,
singing, supper, prayer [until 8:45 p.m.]." Throughout
the diary, Wesley tends to identify the house in which
a religious society met by noting the name of the occu-
pant's wife, even though the husband may well have been
a member of that group and at home with his wife at the
time of the visit.

Monday, 2 October 1738. "Later than usual, "Wesley
drank tea with Mrs. Sims, who appears to have been ill.
Then followed the usual "singing and prayer."

Thursday, 19 October 1738. At 11:00 a.m., John and
Charles Wesley engaged in prayer and singing at Mrs. Sims'
house; John had dinner there at 2:00 p.m.

Sunday, 22 October 1738. "5:15 [p.m.] Mr. Sims,'
singing, etc." until 7:00 p.m.

Thursday, 7 November 1738. "11 [:00 a.m.] at Mr.
Sims's in talk" until 11:45 a.m.

Wednesday, 20 December 1738. The diary entry for
this day reads, "10.30 [a.m.] at Mr. S--'s, conversed"
until 11:00 a.m. The reference obviously focuses upon
Peter Sims.

Saturday, 6 January 1739. Wesley visited with Mr.
Sims from 12:30 p.m. until 1:15 p.m. and said a prayer
for his host's child.

Sunday, 14 January 1739. The Methodist leader spent
between 5:45 p.m. and 8:15 p.m. expounding "twice at Mr.
Sims's in the Minories."

Sunday, 21 January 1739. He devoted two hours (from
5:00 p.m. until 7:00 p.m.) at Peter Sims', "singing, etc."

Monday, 22 January 1739. Between 11:00 a.m. and
3:00 p.m., Wesley conversed at Sims' house with a "Mrs.
Randal"; he ate dinner there and apparently continued
the conversation.

Sunday, 4 February 1739. Wesley spent the time between 6:15 p.m. and 7:30 p.m. at Sims', again "singing,
etc."

Thursday, 8 February 1739. "5 [p.m.] at Mrs. Sims's,
singing, etc." until 6:00 p.m.

Saturday, 10 February 1739. Sometime after 10:00
a.m., Wesley visited at Mrs. Sims' house for conversation and prayer; he remained there until noon.

Sunday, 11 February 1739. "5 [:00 p.m.] Mr. Sims's,
singing, etc.' until 6:30 p.m.

Thursday, 22 February 1739. Wesley remained at Mrs.

Sims' between 5:00 p.m. and 6:30 p.m., "singing, etc."

Sunday, 25 March 1739. ". . .at Mr. Sims's, singing, etc; 6.45 [p.m.] tea, conversed," until 7:15 p.m.

Thursday, 27 September 1739. Wesley visited with
Peter Sims (the diary entry reads "P. Syms's") for two
hours, from 1:00 p.m. until 3:00 p.m., and then he remained for dinner.

Tuesday, 22 July 1740. "2[:00 p.m.] at Peter Sims's,
Chapman there! dinner." He remained at the Sims' until
3:30 p.m. According to Wesley's journal for the same
date, "Mr. Chapman, just come from Germany, gave me a
letter from one of our (once) brethren there; wherein,
after denying the gift of God which he received in
England, he [the writer of the letter] advised my brother
[Charles] and me no longer to take upon us to teach and
instruct poor souls, but to deliver them up to the care
of the Moravians, who alone were to instruct them." Thus,
we can begin to understand the reasons for the exclama-
tion point after Chapman's name in the diary entry cited
above. As to the identity of Chapman himself, there
exist three possibilities: Mr. Chapman of Pembroke; Rev.
William Chapman of Bath; or George Chapman, a butcher in
Lime Street. The second name appears as the most likely
candidate.

Tuesday, 2 December 1740. "2[:00 p.m.] at Bro.
Sym's, Marschall there, dinner, conversed," until 3:30
p.m. Variously spelled Marshall and Marschall, the individual in question was born near Dresden and had at
times connections with the University of Leipzig.   He
apparently occupied a prominent position within the
Fetter Lane religious society.

Saturday, 7 February 1741. Between 2:00 p.m. and
3:30 p.m., Wesley had dinner and enjoyed some conversation at the home of Peter Sims.

St. Katherine Coleman Church, Fenchurch Street.
St. Katherine Coleman dates from about 1301; the name
Coleman may well refer to a builder or restorer. The
church did manage to escape the Great Fire; however,
although general repair and restoration went forward in
1703, the structure came down in its entirety in 1734,
and a majority of its monuments transferred to St.
Olave's Church, Hart Street (the church that Samuel
Pepys attended throughout his career in the Navy Office).
In 1739, James Horne rebuilt the church on its original
site, but it claimed no features of architectural or an-
antiquarian interest. According to George Godwin in his
Churches of London (1838), St. Katherine Coleman could
be termed "most ugly and inelegant," an example "to
serve as evidence of the improvement which has taken
place in public taste" (Weinreb and Hibbert 727). Another
source claimed that "It may be confidently stated
that no parish in the metropolis would now [c. 1930]
allow such a piece of ugliness to be erected" (Kent 119).
The last service held in the church occurred 1921; by
1925, the structure had been demolished and the parish
united with St. Olave's, Hart Street.
     George Whitefield preached at St. Katherine Coleman
Church at 10:15 a.m., Sunday, 17 December 1738. Preceding the sermon, Wesley read the prayers. On Sunday
morning, between 9:45 and 1:00 p.m., Wesley meditated,
read prayers, and preached there.

St. Katharine Cree Church, Leadenhall Street. Originally known (about 1280) as St. Katherine de Christ
church at Aldgate, and later (about 1303) as Sancte
Katerinae Trinitatis, St. Katharine Cree underwent rebuilding between 1628 and 1630, its design being attributed

to Inigo Jones. The font of the church bears the arms
of Sir John Gayer, Lord Mayor of London in 1646, whose
escape from a lion in Africa has been, since that year,
commemorated by the "Lion Sermon," delivered annually
on 16 October. Marshall Sisson restored the building in
1962, although it suffered only minor damage from German
bombs during World War II.

John Wesley preached at St. Katherine Cree Church
at 10:00 a.m., Sunday, 26 February 1738, and again on
Sunday, 7 May 1738. Regarding the latter occasion, the
Methodist leader stated that he was "enabled to speak
strong words. . .and was therefore the less surprised
at being informed I was not to preach [there] any more
. . . ." In his diary for Sunday, 7 January 1739,
Wesley noted that he spent the hours from 5:15 p.m. to
7:00 p.m. at "Creed Ch[urch] Society, prayers, singing,
etc." During that period, there could possibly have
been a London Anglican religious society in one of the
old buildings close by St. Katharine Cree Church--or
even under it. For example, the London bookseller
Peter Parker, Sr. did business, between 1667 and 1672,
under Creed Church near Aldgate.

St. Katharine near the Tower, St. Katharine's Way.
Formerly the Chapel of the St. Katharine's Royal Hospital, established in 1148 by Matilda, wife of King Stephen
and located near the Tower of London, St. Katharine
stood as one of the earliest ecclesiastical foundations in all of England. In 1672, a fire destroyed
a hundred houses in the precincts; another blaze during
a great storm in 1734 destroyed thirty buildings in the
area surrounding the chapel. During the "No Popery riots" of 1780, a Protestant mob, armed with swords, was

about to destroy the church--since it remained as a re-
lic of Popish times--when the gentlemen of the London
Association arrived and prevented such action. Three
leaders of that attack were hanged on temporary gallows
on Tower Hill. In 1825, the church came down to make
way for the St. Katharine Docks; three years later, in
1828, a new chapel arose in Regent's Park, which came
to be known as St. Katharine's Royal Chapel.

John Wesley preached at the chapel of St. Katharine's
near the Tower at 10:15 a.m., Sunday, 25 February
1739, "to a numerous congregation." The Hon. John
Berkeley served as incumbent of St. Katharine's between
1738 and 1746.

St. Margaret Pattens Church, Rood Lane, Eastcheap.
In existence since at least as far back as 1067, St.
Margaret Pattens underwent rebuilding in 1530; further
repairs went forward between 1614 and 1632. Having suffered from the Great Fire, the church benefitted from rebuilding by Sir Christopher Wren in 1687, specifically to
serve the united parish of St. Gabriel, Fenchurch Street,
and St. Margaret Pattens. Its lofty spire, some two
hundred feet high, appears largely Gothic in conception
and more like a medieval church spire than any other designed by Wren. Beside the pulpit, an hour-glass stood
as a timing device for the sermons. Since 1954, the
Church has stood as one of the London Christian study
centers.

Two distinguished rectors of St. Margaret Pattens
require at least brief mention. Dr. Thomas Burch (1705-
1766), secretary of the Royal Society and the author of
its history, became one of the principal contributors
to the General Dictionary, Historical and Critical (1734-

1741). A biographer of Henry, Prince of Wales (the el-
dest son of James I), Birch edited The Faeries Queene,
Walter Raleigh's Works and Bacon's Letters and
 Speeches, and Milton's prose works. His successor, Peter
Whalley, M.A., D.D. (d. 1791), served for eight years as
the headmaster of Christ Hospital. He published An Inquiry into the Learning of Shakespeare, with Remarks on
Several Passages of His Plays. Miss Eliza Wesley, daughter
of Samuel Wesley (1766-1837), granddaughter of Charles
Wesley (1707-1788)--and thus the grand-niece of the
founder and leader of British Methodism--and sister of
Samuel Sebastian Wesley (1810-1876), served as organist
of St. Margaret Pattens for forty years (1846-1886).

John Wesley preached a charity sermon at St. Margaret
Pattens Church on Sunday, 16 November 1777. "In
the morning I desired my friends not to come; in the afternoon it was crowded sufficiently, and I believe many
of them felt the word of God sharper than any two-edged
sword." He preached there again at 7:00 p.m., Sunday,
29 December 1778, to a "crowded" congregation.

Church of St. Peter, Gracechurch Street, Cornhill.
Dating perhaps as far back as 179 A.D., St. Peter's burned
to the ground in the Great Fire; Wren rebuilt it during
1680-1681. The steeple, one hundred and forty feet
high, the architect crowned with representation of St.
Peter's key; the chancel, on the north and south of
which stood side chapels, separated itself from the nave
by a carved wooden screen. Such a plan could have been
found only in one other of Wren's churches--All Hallows
the Great. J.D. Wyatt restored the building in 1872.
During the late eighteenth century, John Thomas (1744-
1797) served as incumbent.

John Wesley attended the Church of St. Peter, Cornhill, on Saturday, 26 October 1740, at 10:00 p.m., for
communion. He appeared again for the same purpose on
Sunday, 9 November 1740 (10:00 a.m.), and on Sunday, 23
November 1740 (10:00 a.m.). Almost forty years later,
on Sunday, 28 March 1779, he "declared to a crowded
congregation, 'God hath given us His Holy Spirit,'". He
preached a charity sermon at St. Peter's on Sunday, 28
November 1779, and he delivered still another pulpit
address on Friday, 4 February 1780--a national fast-day,
principally as the result of the government's inclina-
tion to legislate on behalf of Catholic relief.

Tower of London. For several centuries, the most
entertaining aspect of the Tower of London focused upon
its menagerie, which came into existence during the reign
of Henry III (1216-1272). In 1235, Emperor Frederick II
presented the King with three leopards, symbolic of Henry's
coat of arms. A single lion came to the Tower in
1604, several more in 1609, and two others in 1682--
brought over from Tunis and named "Charles" and
"Katherine"(obviously after Charles II and his queen,
Catherine of Braganza). By the eighteenth century, the
number of lions had increased to eleven, five having
come as gifts from the Emperor of Morocco to Queen Anne,
and another as a gift to the British nation from the
consul of Algiers. In 1775, the government of Senegal
presented still another beast to George III. By 1835,
the entire menagerie had been removed to Regent's Park.
        On Monday, 31 December 1764, John Wesley determined
to conduct an "odd experiment." Having remembered,
during one of his journeys to Edinburgh, a lion supposedly
fond of music, the Methodist patriarch set out "to

try whether this was the case with all animals of the
same kind." Thus, he ventured to the Tower with a companion "who plays on the German Flute." The latter began
to play within hearing distance of four or five lions;
only one appeared at all interested. However, "a tiger
in the same den started up, leaped over the lion's back,
turned and ran under his belly, leaped over him again,
and so to and fro incessantly. Can we account for this
by any principle of mechanism? Can we account for it at
all?"

In a context totally aside that of lions, Wesley
noted, in his journal for Thursday, 5 November 1767, that
at noon he preached at Northiam, in Kent, and was "surprised, at one [1:00 p.m.], to hear the Tower guns so
plain at above fifty miles' distance." His last visit
to the Tower occurred on Thursday, 9 December 1790; he
visited there for over an hour (2:00 to before 3:30 p.m.);
yet, neither his journal nor his diary indicate why he
went there or what he did during that interval.

Church of St. John Horsleydown, Tower Bridge Road.
An act of Parliament in 1711 provided for a tax to be
levied on coal to pay for the building of fifty new
churches in or near the City of London and the City of
Westminster, or their suburbs. John James built the most
fashionable of those structures--St. George's, Hanover
Square, and also, in 1732, St. John's Horsleydown. German
bombs destroyed the latter building in 1939-1940.

John Wesley preached at the Church of St. John
Horsleydown at 3:00 p.m., Sunday, 19 February 1786, on
Revelation 20:12--And I saw the dead, great and small,
standing before the throne, and books were opened. Also
another book was opened, which is the book of life. And

the dead were judged by what was written in the books,
by what they had done. Wesley seemed not surprised that
"no man, woman, or child seemed to know me either by face
or by name! But before I had done, many of the numerous
congregation knew that God was there of a truth."

Rosemary Lane, Whitechapel. Now known as Royal Mint
Street, located northeast of the Tower of London, Rosemary
Lane lay in a dangerous neighborhood of old wooden houses
and wretched inhabitants. Specifically, a number of
Jews established and operated a place known as Rag Fair;
itinerant collectors gathered discarded or even stolen
clothes and rags, which they handed over to the local
inhabitants.

A meeting-house of the London Methodist society was
undoubtedly located on Rosemary Lane, for John Wesley
preached there at 6:45 p.m., Friday, 29 August 1740, on
1 John 5:11--And this is the testimony, that God gave us
eternal life, and this life is in His Son. He preached
there again at 6:45 p.m., Friday, 12 September 1740, on
Romans 1:16--For I am not ashamed of the gospel: it is
the power of God for salvation to every one who has faith,
to the Jew first, and also to the Greek. Again, on Friday, 5 December 1740, at 6:45 p.m., Wesley preached at
Rosemary Lane on Romans 10:7--. . .or "Who will descend
into the abyss" [that is, to bring Christ up from the
dead]?

Rag Fair, Rosemary Lane. Rosemary Lane, in the eighteenth century, housed an old-clothes market known as Rag
Fair, noted for the poor condition and the cheapness of
the goods sold there. According to Alexander Pope's own
note to line 27, Book I, of the 1728 version of The Dunciad,

ciad, the sacred dome of Dulness stands firmly at Rag
Fair, "a place near the Tower of London, where old
cloathes and frippery are sold."

On Friday, 27 June 1740, Wesley noted in his diary,
"5[:00 p.m.] Rag Fair, Eph. ii, 8 [For by grace you have
been saved through faith; and this is not your own doing,
it is the gift of God. . . .]." Was that yet another
meeting-house at Rosemary Lane (see above, p. 335), or
was it the same house where, on three occasions between
late August and early December 1740, Wesley preached?
At any rate, he went again to Rag Fair on Friday, 19 September 1740; he spent the time between 5:00 p.m. and
6:30 p.m. at the home of a Mrs. Burton, where he conversed, prayed, and visited with friends.

Wapping. In the eighteenth century, the riverside
parish to Wapping contained a fluctuating population of
seafaring men, mostly lodging in alehouses. They spent
considerable time fending off the wares and the services
of a number and variety of parasites representing both
sexes. One contemporary source described the area as a
place of "dirt and filth and rubbish and old miserable
houses and noise and tumult and riot, drunkenness and
obscenity. . ." (George 354). On Saturday, 12 April 1783,
Samuel Johnson advised James Boswell "of the wonderful
extent and variety of London, and observed, that men of
curious inquiry might see it in such modes of life as
very few could imagine." The London sage then recommended that the man in search of such varying modes ex-
plore Wapping, which Boswell resolved to do. However, the
exploration did not come about until October 1792: Boswell
and William Windham (1750-1810) "carried our scheme into
operation. . .but whether from that uniformity which has

in modern times, in a great degree, spread throughout
every part of the Metropolis, or from our want of sufficient exertion, we were disappointed" (Boswell, Life of
Johnson 1219). Thus, Wapping, at the end of the century,
represented a general lessening in peculiarity of classes
and localities.

The following chronology (with Scriptural references to indicate themes of sermon addresses) summarizes
John Wesley's activities in Wapping between 1739 and
1791:

Friday, 9 February 1739. An unidentified person
hands a note to Wesley "in nearly these words: 'Sir,
Your prayers are desired for a child that is a lunatic,
and sore vexed day and night, that our Lord would be
pleased to heal him, as He did in the days of His flesh,
and that He would give his parents faith and patience
till his time is come.'" Perhaps Wesley received this
message during a meeting of a religious society.

Friday, 16 March 1739. Between 6:00 p.m. and 9:00
p.m., he prayed and sang at "Wapping Room," undoubtedly
at a meeting of one of the London Anglican religious societies.

Friday, 15 June 1739. At 6:00 p.m., Wesley attended a meeting at Wapping Room, "weary in body and faint
in spirit." Intending to speak on Romans 3:19 (Now we
know that whatever the law says, it speaks to those who
are under the law, so that every mouth may be stopped,
and the whole world may be accountable to God.), Wesley
"could not tell how to open my mouth." Throughout the
singing of the hymn, his mind focused on Hebrews 10:19-
22: "Having therefore, brethren, boldness to enter into
the holiest, by the blood of Jesus; by a new and living
way which He hath consecrated for us, through the veil,
that is to say, His flesh. . .let us draw near with a

true heart, in full assurance of faith; having our hearts
sprinkled from an evil conscience, and our bodies washed
with pure water." There followed a scene of considerable
demonstration of emotions. "Some sunk down, and there
remained no strength in them; others, exceedingly trembled
and quaked; some were torn with a kind of convulsive
motion in every part of their bodies, and that so violently
that often four or five persons could not hold one of
them. I have seen many hysterical epileptic fits; but
none of them were like these in any respects." Twenty-
six of those so affected promised to call upon Wesley the
next day, but only eighteen actually returned. That meeting lasted until 11:00 p.m.

Friday, 6 June 1740. Wesley preached at Wapping,
at 6:30 p.m., on 1 Peter 4--Since therefore Christ suffered in the flesh, arm yourselves with the same thought,
for whoever has suffered in the flesh has ceased from
sin. . . . A notation in the diary reads, ". . .many
ill!"

Friday, 20 June 1740, 7:40 p.m.

> Mark 3:8--. . .and Jerusalem and Idumea and
> from beyond the Jordan and from about Tyre
> and Sidon a great multitude, hearing all
> that he did, came to him.

Friday, 11 July 1740, 6:30 p.m.

> Matthew 5:4--Blessed are the meek, for they
> shall inherit the earth.

Friday, 18 July 1740, 6:30 p.m. Wesley first preached
on John 16:9--. . .of sin, because they do not believe
in me. . . . He also visited, until 8:00 p.m.,
with three persons who were ill.

Friday, 25 July 1740, 6:15 p.m.

> Zechariah 13--On that day there shall be a foun-
> tain opened for the house of David and the

inhabitants of Jerusalem to cleanse them
from sin and uncleanness.

Friday, 1 August 1740

Matthew 7:8--For every one who asks receives,
and he who seeks, finds, and to him who
knocks it will be opened.

Friday, 8 August 1740

John 15--I am the true vine, and my Father is
the vinedresser.

Friday, 15 August 1740, 5:30 p.m.   Wesley preached
on Hosea 13--When Ephraim spoke, men trembled; he was
exalted in Israel; but he incurred guilt through Baal
and died. The diary entry for that date contains the
cryptic notation, "three ill."

Friday, 19 September 1740, 6:30 p.m.

John 6:40--For this is the will of my Father,
that every one who sees the Son and believes
in him should have eternal life; and I
will raise him up at the last day.

Friday, 3 October 1740, 6:15 p.m.

Luke 24--But on the first day of the week, at
early dawn, they went to the tomb, taking
the spices which they had prepared.

Monday, 3 February 1755. Wesley preached on

1 Corinthians 15:19--If for this life only we
have hoped in Christ, we are of all men most
to be pitied.

1 Corinthians 1:24--. . .but to those who are
called, both Jews and Greeks, Christ the
power of God and the wisdom of God.

The reference for this day and all others that fail to
indicate the time of day, or further details, come from
the Sermon Register, wherein the entries read merely
"Wapping." Thus, after October 1740, one cannot easily determine the exact places in Wapping where Wesley preached.

Monday, 21 July 1755

2 Timothy 2:4--No soldier on service gets en-
tangled in civilian pursuits, since his aim
is to satisfy the one who enlisted him.

Monday, 3 November 1755

Luke 12:7--Why, even the hairs of your head
are all numbered. Fear not; you are of more
value than many sparrows.

Luke 21:34--But take heed to yourselves lest
your hearts be weighed down with dissipa-
tion and drunkenness and cares of this life,
and that day come upon you suddenly like a
snare. . .

(?) January 1756

Hebrews 9:27--And just as it is appointed for
men to die once, and after that comes judgment. . .

John 18:28--Then they led Jesus from the house
of Caiaphas to the praetorium. It was early.
They, themselves, did not enter the praetorium, so that they might not be defiled, but
might eat the passover.

Isaiah 24:17--Terror, and the pit, and the snare
are upon you, O inhabitants of the earth!

Monday, 13 September 1756

2 Timothy 2:11--The saying is sure: If we have
died with him, we shall also live with
him. . . .

2 Timothy 3:5--. . .holding the form of religion but denying the power of it. Avoid
such people.

(?) September 1756

Hosea 14:4--I will heal their faithlessness;
I will love them freely, for my anger has

turned from them.

> Hebrews 12:24--. . .and to Jesus, the mediator
> of a new covenant,and to the sprinkled
> blood that speaks more graciously than the
> blood of Abel.

Thursday, 10 February 1757. Wesley inserted into his journal for this date a note that "was given into my hands at Wapping: 'John White, master-at-arms aboard his Majesty's ship <u>Tartar</u>, now at Plymouth, desires to return Almighty God thanks for himself and all the ship's company for their preservation in four different engagements they have had with four privateers which they have taken, particularly the last, wherein the enemy first boarded them. They cleared the deck, boarded in their turn, and took the ship, thirty of the enemy being killed, and fifty more wounded. Only two of our crew were wounded, who, it is hoped, will recover.'" As with the note handed to him on 9 February 1739 (see p. 337) at Wapping, Wesley did not offer a reaction to the message.

> (?) March 1757

> > <u>James</u> 4:16--As it is, you boast in your arro-
> > gance. All such boasting is evil.

> > 1 <u>Corinthians</u> 13:13--So faith, hope, love
> > abide, these three; but the greatest of
> > these is love.

> > 2 <u>Corinthians</u> 10:5--We destroy arguments and
> > every prous obstacle to the knowledge of
> > God, and take every thought captive to obey
> > Christ. . .

> > <u>Hebrews</u> 6:1--Therefore, let us leave the ele-
> > mentary doctrines of Christ and go on to
> > maturity, not laying again a foundation of
> > repentance from dead works and of faith to-
> > ward God. . .

Monday, 28 November 1757

 Luke 16:3--And the steward said to himself,
  "What shall I do, since my master is taking the stewardship away from me? I am not
  strong enough to dig, and I am ashamed to beg.

 Isaiah 9:11--So the Lord raises adversaries
  against them, and stirs up their enemies.

 1 Corinthians 6:19--Do you not know that your
  body is a temple of the Holy Spirit within
  you, which you have from God? You are not
  your own. . .

Monday, 5 December 1757

 Hebrews 11:1--Now faith is the assurance of
  things hoped for, the conviction of things
  not seen.

 1 Peter 2:1--So put away all malice and all
  guile and insincerity and envy and all slan-
  der. . .

 1 Corinthians 13:1--If I speak in the tongues
  of men and of angels, but have not love, I
  am a noisy gong or a clanging cymbal.

Monday, 16 January 1758

 Genesis 28:22--. . .and this stone, which I
  have set up for a pillar, shall be God's
  house; and of all that thou givest me I will
  give the tenth to thee.

 1 Peter 2:14--. . .or to punish governors sent
  by him to punish those that do wrong and to
  praise those who do right.

 1 Timothy 1:8--Do not be ashamed, then, of
  testifying to our Lord, nor of me his
  prisoner, but take your share of suffering for
  the gospel in the power of God. . .

Sunday, 26 November 1758

Hebrews 3:7--Therefore, as the Holy Spirit says,
"Today, when you hear his voice. . . ."
Hebrews 12:28--Therefore, let us be grateful
for receiving a kingdom that cannot be shaken,
and thus let us offer to God acceptable
worship, with reverence and awe. . .
Monday, 15 January 1759
Hebrews 11:1--See above for 5 December 1757
(p. 342).
1 Corinthians 2:12--Now we have received not
the spirit of the world, but the Spirit which
is from God, that we might understand the
gifts bestowed upon us by God.
Matthew 12:22--Then a blind and dumb demoniac
was brought to him, and he healed him, so
that the dumb man spoke and saw.
Leviticus 26:11--And I will make my abode among
you, and my soul shall not abhor you.
John 3:7--Do not marvel that I said to you,
"You must be born anew."
Matthew 22:20--And Jesus said to them, "Whose
likeness and inscription is this?"
Psalms 10:12--Arise, O Lord; O God, lift up
thy hand; forget not the afflicted.
Monday, 3 December 1759
Hebrews 9:14--. . .how much more shall the
blood of Christ, who through the eternal
Spirit offered himself without blemish to
God, purify your conscience from dead works
to serve the living God.
Isaiah 35:8--And a highway shall be there, and
it shall be called the Holy Way; the unclean
shall not pass over it, and fools shall not
err therein.

1 <u>Peter</u> 5:8--Be sober, be watchful. Your ad-
versary the devil prowls around like a roaring lion, seeking some one to devour.

Sunday, 13 January 1760

<u>Romans</u> 12:1--I appeal to you, therefore, breth-
ren, by the mercies of God, to present
your bodies as a living sacrifice, holy and
acceptable to God, which is your spiritual
worship. . .

1 <u>Corinthians</u> 3:12--Now if any one builds on
the foundation with gold, silver, precious
stones, wood, hay, stubble. . .

1 <u>Corinthians</u> 9:27--. . .but I pommel my body
and subdue it, lest after preaching to others I myself should be disqualified.

<u>Numbers</u> 23:10--Who can count the dust of
Jacob, or number the fourth part of Israel?
Let me die the death of the righteous, and
let my end be like his!

Monday, 25 February 1760

<u>Ephesians</u> 2:8--For by grace you have been
saved through faith; and this is not your
own doing; it is the gift of God. . .

<u>Isaiah</u> 62:11--Behold, the Lord has proclaimed
to the end of the earth: Say to the daughter of Zion, "Behold your salvation comes;
behold, his reward is with him, and his re-
compense before him."

<u>Galatians</u> 4:10--You observe days, and months,
and seasons, and years!"

<u>Galatians</u> 5:6--For in Christ Jesus neither cir-
cumcision nor uncircumcision is of any avail,
but faith working through love.

Friday, 7 November 1760

Galatians 1:3--Grace to you and peace from God
the Father and our Lord Jesus Christ. . .
Acts 22:16--And now, why do you wait? Rise and
be baptized, and wash away your sins, calling on his name.
Monday, 9 February 1761
2 Corinthians 5:18--All this is from God, who
through Christ reconciled us to himself and
gave us the ministry of reconciliation. .
Ecclesiastes 12:13--The end of the matter; all
has been heard. Fear God and keep his commandments; for this is the whole duty of
man.

Monday, 21 February 1763. "Observing the terror
occasioned by that wonderful prophecy to spread far and
wide, I endeavoured to draw some good therefrom by strongly
exhorting the congregation at Wapping, 'to seek the
Lord while He might be found' [Isaiah 55:6]. But at the
same time I thought it incumbent upon me to declare (as
indeed I had done from the hour I heard it) that 'it must
be false, if the Bible be true.'" George Bell, whom Wesley
had expelled from the Foundery in December 1762, had
prophesied the end of the world on 28 February 1763.

Monday, 6 February 1764. On this date Wesley opened
a new chapel at Wapping, "well filled with deeply attentive hearers."

Wednesday, 20 February 1771. "We never, that I remember, before had such a congregation at Wapping, either
of hearers or communicants; and very seldom such an
outpouring of the Spirit."

Monday, 24 November 1785. In his diary for this date,
Wesley noted the following activities at Wapping, where he
spent the hours between 2:30 p.m., and 8:00 p.m.: ". . .
class, tea, class. . .read prayers, Rev xiv. 1 [Then I

looked and lo, on Mount Zion, stood the Lamb, and with
him a hundrend and forty-four thousand who had his name
and his Father's name written on their foreheads], etc.,
coach."

Wednesday, 24 February 1790. At 6:00 p.m., Wesley
preached to "a crowded audience" on Ephesians 1:13--In
him you also, who have heard the word of truth, the gospel of your salvation, and have believed in him, were
sealed with the promised Holy Spirit. . .

Wednesday, 29 December 1790. At 6:00 p.m.,
Wesley preached on 2 John 8--So we ought to support such
men, that we may be fellow workers in the truth.

Monday, 7 February 1791. Wesley spent five hours
in Wapping (from 2:30 p.m. until 7:30 p.m.); in the evening (6:00), he preached there on Colossians 3:23--What-
ever your task, work heartily, as serving the Lord and
not men. . .   That demonstrates the extent to which the
Methodist patriarch labored in his final years. Some
three weeks later, on 2 March 1791, he died.

Huguenot Chapel, Great Hermitage Street, Wapping.
On Sunday, 2 August 1741, at 10:00 a.m., "after having
been long importuned by Dr. Deleznot," John Wesley preached
at the Huguenot Chapel, Wapping, on 1 Kings 21--Now
Naboth the Jezreelite had a vineyard in Jezreel, beside
the palace of Ahab, King of Samaria. The Chapel, at that
time, seems to have been in use by the Huguenots; however, perhaps as early as two months later (September
1741), the London Methodists appropriated the site, and
the societies met there regularly. On five consecutive
Sundays (6, 13, 20, and 27 September, and on 4 October)
in 1741, Wesley preached in the Huguenot Chapel, administering the sacrament to five successive batches--each

of two hundred members--until all in the Society had received it. Rev. John Meriton (d. 1753), a clergyman
from the Isle of Man, read prayers on that first Sunday
(2 August); he spent the last two years of his life accompanying both John and Charles Wesley on their preaching excursions throughout the British Isles, assisting
the brothers in administering services at the chapels
they had established. On Wednesday, 24 April 1742, Wesley
"preached for the last time in the French chapel at
Wapping, on 'If ye continue My word, then are ye My disciples indeed' [John 8:31]."

     Church of St. John, Wapping. The parish church of
St. John stood just outside the northern boundary of
Wapping, on the east side of Church Street. Its founders
established it as a chapel-at-ease in 1617. Joel Johnson
rebuilt the structure in 1756. The Rev. Francis Willis,
M.D. (1718-1807), who attended George III in his first
madness, served as the rector here; he authored treatises
on mental derangement and insanity.
     John Wesley preached at the Church of St. John,
Wapping, in the afternoon of Sunday, 26 February 1738; he
read prayers and preached there again on Sunday morning,
at 10:00, 23 April 1738. On Whit Sunday, 21 May 1738,
he preached there at 3:00 p.m., and indicated in his journal for that date, "I am to preach [at St. John's and
at St. Benet's, Paul's Wharf] no more." However, almost
forty-three years later, on Sunday, 14 January 1781, he
returned to St. John's. "Although the church was extremely crowded, yet there was not the least disorder while I
besought them all, by the mercies of God, to present
themselves a living sacrifice, holy, acceptable to God."
Finally, Wesley preached there on Sunday, 18 November
1781, where, in his words, "God was present both to wound

and to heal."

German bombs destroyed the church early in World
War II, although the tower survived and became part of
the restoration.

St. Paul's Church, Shadwell. A small parish by the
riverside between Ratcliff (see below) and Wapping (see
immediately preceding, above), Shadwell separated   from
Stepney parish in 1670. The   parish church,   dedicated
to St. Paul, was built in 1656. John Nash served as the
incumbent between 1736 and 1740; in 1741, Bishop Joseph
Butler (1692-1752) nominated as rector his nephew, also
named Joseph Butler. The younger Butler   disliked   his
appointment to such a degree that he preached his first
sermon at St. Paul's from Psalms 120:5--Woe is me, that
I sojourn in Mesech, that I dwell in the house of Kedar!"
Nevertheless, the younger Butler remained at   Shadwell
until 1798 (see Kent, Encyclopaedia of London 609).   The
old church underwent demolition in 1817, and a   new one
rose in its place in 1821--only that structure appeared
on the south side of Shadwell High Street.

John Wesley preached at St. Paul's, Shadwell,   on
Sunday afternoon, at 2:45, 22 October 1738,   and again
on Sunday afternoon, 14 December 1777.   He preached a
charity sermon there on Sunday, 24 October 1779, speaking "with all possible plainness; and surely some, out of
an immense multitude, will receive the truth, and bring
forth fruit and patience." Luke 10:42 (. . .one thing is
needful. Mary has chosen the good portion, which shall
not be taken away from her) provided the basis for his
sermon text on Sunday, at 3:00 in the afternoon, 24
October 1784; on that date, the church "was exceedingly
crowded with rich and poor, who all seemed to receive

the truth in love." Wesley's final recorded appearance
at St. Paul's came about on Sunday, 24 October 1790, at
3:00 p.m. Speaking before a crowded congregation on
Luke 10:42 (see p. 348), "he enforced that important
truth, 'One thing is needful'; and I hope many, even
then, resolved to choose the better part."

    Rotherhithe (Redriff). Rotherhithe--long popularly
known as "Redriff"--comprised approximately 754 acres
of mostly commercial docks. The parish church of the district, St. Mary's located by the riverside, underwent
construction in 1715 and opened its doors three years later
(1718). Launcelot Dowbiggin designed the stone spire
and erected it in 1739,while the last major restoration
came about through the efforts of William Butterfield in
1876. Finally, a charity school, built some time during
the eighteenth century to the south end of the church,
still stands.
    Between June 1740 and the end of February 1790,
Wesley preached and held society meetings in the rooms of
several buildings and in various chapels throughout Rotherhithe. As far as possible, those instances can be identified through the following summary of his activities in
that section of the City, as noted in the diaries:
    Friday, 6 June 1740
        Ezekiel 33--The word of the Lord came to me:
    Friday, 13 June 1740, 5:30 p.m.-8:00 p.m.
        Romans 4:5--And to one who does not work but
           trusts him who justifies the ungodly, his
           faith is reckoned as righteousness.
    Friday, 20 June 1740, 5:00 p.m.-7:30 p.m.
        John 3:7--Do not marvel that I said to you,
           "You must be born anew."

Friday, 11 July 1740, 5:00 p.m.-6:30 p.m.

Matthew 5:20--For I tell you, unless your
righteousness exceeds that of the Scribes
and Pharisees, you will never enter the
kingdom of heaven.

Friday, 18 July 1740, 5:15 p.m.-6:30 p.m.

1 Corinthians 13--If I speak in the tongues of
men and of angels, but have not love, I am a
noisy gong or a clanging cymbal.

Friday 25 July 1740, 5:00 p.m.-6:30 p.m.

1 John 3:1--See what love the Father has given
us, that we should be called children of
love; and so we are.

Friday, 1 August 1740, 5:15 p.m.-6:15 p.m.

Hebrews 3--Therefore, holy brethren, who share
in a heavenly call, consider Jesus, the apostle and high priest of our confession.

Friday, 3 October 1740, 5:00 p.m.-6:15 p.m.

1 John 1--That which was from the beginning,
which we have heard, which we have seen with
our eyes, which we have looked upon and
touched with our hands, concerning the word
of life. . .

Friday, 10 October 1740, 5:00 p.m.-6:30 p.m.

Hebrews 2:4--. . .while God also bore witness
by signs and wonders and various miracles
and by gifts of the Holy Spirit distributed
according to his own will.

Friday, 17 October 1740, 5:00 p.m.-8:15 p.m.

Matthew 3:2--Repent, for the kingdom of
heaven is at hand.

Wednesday, 24 March 1768. Wesley preached in "a
large room, which is taken at Redriff, above three miles
from London." Although the people were strangely squeezed

together, "ye they appeared to be all attention. Not
a cough was to be heard. I strongly exhorted them to
'call upon the Lord while he is near' [Isaiah 55:6]. And
when I had concluded, no one offered to move, but every
one stood still in his place till I had passed through
them."

Tuesday, 7 December 1779. He preached in a chapel
in Rotherhithe, "a cold, uncomfortable place, to a handful of people, who appeared to be just as much affected
as the benches they sat upon."

Friday, 3 November 1786. "Taking advantage of a
moonlight evening, I went down to the chapel in Rotherhithe. I never saw it so well filled before, nor with
such serious and attentive hearers. Is anything too hard
for God? Shall this wilderness blossom and bud as the
rose?" He preached on Hebrews 12--Therefore, since we
are surrounded by so great a cloud of witnesses, let us
lay aside every weight, and sin which clings so closely,
and let us run with perseverance the race that is set
before us. . .

Friday, 16 February 1768. "I went to Rotherhithe,
which used to be one of the most uncomfortable places in
England. But it was far otherwise now. Many of the people
seemed much alive to God, and His presence was manifested
in the congregation in a very uncommon manner."
Preaching at 6:30 p.m., Wesley based his sermon upon
Matthew 20:16--And about the eleventh hour he went out and
found others standing; and he said to them, "Why do you
stand here idle all day?"

Thursday, 15 November 1787, 4:00 p.m.-8:00 p.m.
2 Corinthians 5:19--. . .that is, God was in
Christ reconciling the world to himself,
not counting his trespasses against them,
and entrusting to us the message of reconciliation.

Friday, 26 February 1790. Wesley preached at 6:00
p.m. on 2 Corinthians 6--Working together with him, then,
we entreat you not to accept the grace of God in vain.
He noted that in Rotherhithe "there is lately a remarkable
revival in the work of God."

Church of St. George's-in-the-East, Cannon Street,
Ratcliff. St. George's-in-the-East, designed by Nicholas
Hawksmoor and built in 1715, stood as a large building of Portland stone, with something resembling a mini-
ature castle, rather than a traditional steeple, on top
of its square tower. Sir Joshua Reynolds (1723-1792)
decorated the east windows. Although the church suffered
serious interior burning from German bombs, Arthur Bailey
restored the structure during 1960-1964. William
Simpson, D.D., who published collections of his Sermons
in 1732 and 1738, served as incumbent from 1729 to 1764.
    On Sunday morning, at 10:00, 1 October 1738, John
Wesley read prayers, preached, and administered the communion at the Church of St. George's-in-the-East. He
returned there in the afternoon, where he read prayers,
preached, and baptized several persons. At 10:00 a.m.,
Sunday, 4 February 1739, he heard George Whitefield
preach there before a congregation of one thousand persons (according to Wesley's own estimate). The next and
last recorded visit of Wesley to this church occurred on
Sunday, 15 January 1786, at 3:00 p.m., when he preached
a sermon on Romans 13:10--Love does no wrong to a neighbor; therefore, love is the fulfilling of the law.

Ratcliff Highway. East Smithfield, beginning from
the north end of Tower Bridge, became extended by

Ratcliff Highway (in the parish of St. George-in-the-East).
A lengthy street, it contained old wooden dwellings and
held the reputation for its drinking dens frequented,
mostly, by seamen. In fact, by the end of the eighteenth
century, the street embraced more public houses than any
other London thoroughfare of proportionate length. In
December 1811, one John Williams supposedly murdered se-
seven persons in two separate incidents at Ratcliff
Highway.

There no doubt existed a meeting-room (or meeting-
house) of a London religious society in Ratcliff Highway.
John Wesley preached there at 7:00 p.m., Saturday, 16
May 1741, basing his sermon text upon Acts 2--When the
day of Pentecost had come, they were all together in one
place.

Ratcliff Cross, Ratcliff. Ratcliff Cross constituted that part of Butcher Row, between Broad Street and
the Thames. The area, which presently crosses the entrance to Rotherhithe Tunnel, served as the most important station for watermen east of the Tower of London.
For example, Samuel Pepys, on more than one occasion,
hired a boat from there to cross the river.

At 7:15 a.m., Tuesday, 25 November 1740, Wesley no-
noted that he walked through Ratcliff Cross, perhaps to attend an open-air service, in company with a "Sister
Jackson and a "Sister Weldron."

Ratcliff Square, Stepney. Later to be known as
Albert Square, Ratcliff Square lay directly off (south)
Commercial Road East, west of Stepney Causeway and Bower
Street, and east of Havering Street. Wesley preached at

the Square, perhaps at an open-air service, at 5:00 p.m.,
Sunday, 25 April 1742, on the text, "I came not to call
the righteous, but sinners to repentance" (Matthew 9:13).

Poplar. A metropolitan borough in the extreme east
of London, Poplar takes its name from the poplar trees
that flourished there in considerable quantity,a number
of which still stood in 1720. The borough originally
existed as one of the hamlets in Stepney parish; in 1817,
it became a separate parish. Naturally, during the eighteenth century, this poor district containing comparatively
few buildings catered principally to the shore require-
ments of sailors. For example, in 1737, the combined
total number of houses for the hamlets of Poplar and Blackwel
well stood at 497; by 1801, that figure had risen to 756,
in addition to thirty unoccupied dwellings. The combined
population of Poplar and Blackwell numbered 5136 in
1710/1711; that figure, by 1801, had decreased to 4493
(see George 413).
     On Friday, 28 February 1772, John Wesley opened the
"new preaching-house in Poplar." A "Mrs. Clippingdale,"
who had joined the Methodist society at Swalwell, near
Newcastle-upon-Tyne, when only thirteen years of age,
eventually settled in Poplar; there she became known as
"a lovely pattern of holiness." However, Poplar contained
few Methodists--and those proved extremely poor. The
cause had declined to such a degree that, at the regular
Sunday morning breakfast, the London Methodist preachers
proposed to abandon further work in the hamlet. Wesley,
upon learning that Mrs. Clippingdale still resided in
Poplar, determined to continue his efforts there. A driv-
ing force in Methodism's mission, Mrs. Clippingdale lived
to see the Poplar chapel erected and the society increased

from a mere handful to almost 250 members (see
Curnock, Journal 5:447 + note 7).

In his journal for that Friday (28 February 1772),
Wesley noted (concerning the opening of Poplar chapel)
that "One might say consecrated it; for the English law
(notwithstanding the vulgar error) does not require, nay,
does not allow, any other consecration of churches than
by performing public service therein." At any rate, he
preached in the new chapel at noon on Friday, 13 February 1784, on Acts 26:18--. . .to open their eyes, that
they may turn from darkness to light, and from the power of Satan to God, that they may receive forgiveness
of sins and a place among those who are sanctified by
faith in me. He returned there on Thursday evening, at
6:00, 15 November 1787, preaching on 2 Corinthians 5:19,
. . .that is, God was in Christ reconciling the world to
himself, not counting their trespasses against them, and
entrusting to us the message of reconciliation. Of the
latter occasion, he remarked that "Even at Poplar I
found a remarkable revival of the work of God. I never
saw the preaching-house so filled before; and the power
of the Lord seemed to rest on many of the hearers."

CHAPTER FIVE

Southern Section

If to the city sped--what waits him there?
To see profusion that he must not share;
To see ten thousand baneful arts combined
To pamper luxury and thin mankind;
To see each joy the sons of pleasure know
Extorted from his fellow creature's woe.
Here while the courtier glitters in brocade,
There the pale artist plies the sickly trade;
Here while the proud their long drawn pomps
    display,
There the black gibbet glooms beside the way.
  (Goldsmith, The Deserted Village 1770)

Chelsea. In 1724, Daniel Defoe labeled Chelsea "a
town of palaces, and which by its new extended buildings
seems to promise itself to be made one time or another a
part of London, I mean London in its new extended capacity, which if it should once happen, what a monster must
London be. . . " (Tour 345-346) Indeed, throughout the
eighteenth century, Chelsea existed as a fashionable place
for those who sought occasional or prolonged escape from
the smell and the smoke of London to the neighboring countryside. Sir Robert Walpole (1676-1745), shortly after
leaving the office of prime minister in 1742, bought a
house and garden there as his rural estate for £ 1100.
Prior to that, we may take note of other retirees to the
Chelsea "suburbs": Sir Richard Steele (1672-1729) rented
a house by the water for £ 14 per year; Sir Hans Sloane

(1660-1753), the physician and president of the Royal Society, bought the manor house from Lord Cheyne in 1712
and retired there thirty years later. Eighteenth-century
observers of the Chelsea scene could complement their
view of the fine houses there by strolling through the
equally fashionable garden at Ranelagh, opened in 1742.
The price of entry to that park stood at two shillings
and six pence (including tea and coffee); the entrance
fee rose to five shillings on fireworks nights. Although
one could not dine or wine there, the Gardens did possess, as its principal attraction, a rotunda: one hundred and fifty feet in diameter, an orchestra in the center, and tiers of boxes all around (see Rude, Hanoverian
London 50-51, 73).

In spite of (or, perhaps, because of) its overall
affluence, Chelsea played no small part in the rise of
Methodism during the eighteenth century. Selina
Shirley, Countess of Huntingdon (1707-1791), lived in the
district for a time, as did Count Nicholas von Zinzendorf
(1700-1760). In fact, the latter desired to establish a
Moravian Brethren settlement there. James Hutton (1715-
1795) acquired Lindsay House (formerly the property of
the Duke of Ancaster) on 15 June 1750 from Sir Hans Sloane
for that purpose, and by 1763 residents of Chelsea could
claim to have seen the completion of a dwelling-house,
with a garden and a burial-ground. In that plot were buried, in addition to Hutton, such prominent early English
Moravians as Peter Bohler and Mrs. John Gambold.

The following comprises a summary of John Wesley's
activities in Chelsea for almost half a century (1741-
1791):

Tuesday, 4 August 1741. Wesley preached at Chelsea,
perhaps at a London religious society meeting-house, at
6:00 p.m. on Ephesians 2:8--For by grace you have been

saved through faith; and this is not your own doing; it
is the gift of God. . . .

Tuesday, 25 August 1741. At Chelsea, Wesley explained
"the nature and necessity of the new birth. One (who
I afterwards heard, was a Dissenting teacher) asked me
when I had done, 'Quid est tibi nomen?' and, on my not
answering, said, 'Aye, I told you he did not understand
Latin!'"

Tuesday, 26 January 1742. He explained at Chelsea
"the faith which worketh by love [Galatians 5:6]. I was
very weak when I went into the room; but the more 'the
beasts of the people' increased in madness and rage, the
more I was strengthened, both in body and soul; so that
I believe few in the house, which was exceedingly full,
lost one sentence of what I spoke. Indeed, they could
not see me, or one another at a few yards' distance, by
reason of the exceeding thick smoke, which was occasioned
by the wild fire, and things of that kind, continually thrown into the room. But they who could praise
God in the midst of the fires were not to be affrighted
by a little smoke."

Wednesday, 7 September 1748. For some time, Lady
Huntingdon had been applying pressure upon Wesley to
preach in her Methodist chapel in Chelsea. On the previous Saturday (3 September), George Whitefield, who had
been holding regular services for the nobility at Lady
Huntingdon's house, left London on the first of his so-
journs into Scotland. Obviously, the Countess desired
that Wesley continue Whitefield's work (or entertainment, if one believes Horace Walpole) among persons of
rank. In his journal for 7 September, John Wesley observed that "Our pew at the chapel in the evening was so
full I could hardly stir. Col. Hilliard, Lord Townsend,
and many others were there, who came with Lady Bath,

Lady Townsend [one of Whitefield's earliest admirers],
and Lady Charlotte Edwin [one of the attendants of the
Princess of Wales' children and the wife of Charles Edwin,
M.P.]. I scarce ever spake stronger in my life than
I did to-night from those words in the Second Lesson,
'Who shall lay anything to the charge of God's elect'&c.
[Romans 8:33]. Perhaps even the rich may be witness to
these things."

Friday, 9 September 1748. Under further pleading
from Lady Huntingdon, Wesley returned to her house in
Chelsea. In the congregation sat Lady Huntingdon, Lady
Bath, Lady Townsend, and Baron Zulendahl, the Danish am-
bassador's brother. The Methodist leader preached on
"'Thou art not far from the kingdom of God' [Mark 12:34].
Yet I cannot find that any one of the audience was of-
fended. What is this which God is working on earth?"
Before departing, he promised the Countess that he would
return on Sunday.

Sunday, 11 September 1748. After open-air services
at 7:00 a.m. and 5:00 p.m., and an additional service at
10:00 a.m. in West Street Chapel, Wesley arrived in Chelsea at 8:00 p.m.. Present at the service were Lord and
Lady Huntingdon, Lady Betty, Lady Townsend, Lady Thanet
(daughter of the Marquis of Halifax and wife to Sackville,
Earl of Thanet), Lady Gertrude Hotham (a daughter
of the Earl of Chesterfield and wife to Sir Charles
Hotham, Bart.), and Lady Bath. The last named lady proved
to have been the daughter of Colonel Gurnley of Bath,
whose wife gave Charles Wesley the lease of her house in
the Marylebone section of London; her husband, William
Pulteney, Earl of Bath (1682-1764), regularly attended
Whitefield's Tabernacle in Tottenham Court Road. Wesley
spoke "much closer than on Friday [9 September] from
those words, 'God is a Spirit,' &c. After preaching they

gathered round me on every side, and I was enabled to
speak to their hearts.   They all stood without either
speech or motion, till Lady Th[anet] sank down into a
chair.   Surely, I am not come to this warfare on my own
cost.   Now let God do as seemeth in His own eyes."

Thursday, 10 February 1774. Wesley "was desired by
that affectionate man, Mr. P-----," to deliver a sermon
in Chelsea.   "Every corner of the room was thoroughly
crowded, and all but two or three gentlewomen (so called)
were deeply serious while I strongly enforced, 'Strait
is the gate, narrow the way, that leadeth unto life'
[Matthew 7:14]."

Thursday, 12 February 1789. Early in the evening,
Wesley preached at Chelsea on Job 22:21--Agree with God,
and be at peace; thereby good will come to you. Concerning the state of his labors there, he noted that "there
is a length a fair and promising prospect." At that
period, the Methodists had been worshiping in an upper
room of a dwelling located in Upper Hospital Row.Wesley's
optimism undoubtedly sprung from the Society having recently secured, at an annual rate of ten guineas, one
of the dancing-rooms in the recently closed Ranelagh Gardens.

Friday, 19 February 1790. At 6:00 p.m.,Wesley
preached to a "large audience at Chelsea, and examined
little society, who do not decrease, but rather grow in
grace and strengthen each other's hands." He based his
sermon upon Hebrews 9:27--And just as it is appointed
for men to die once, and after that comes judgment. . . .

Friday, 18 February 1791. He arrived at Chelsea
sometime after 2:00 p.m, at which time he took tea and
conversed. At 6:00 p.m., he preached on 1 Samuel 21:18,
And David said to Ahimelech, "And have you not here a
spear or a sword at hand? For I have brought neither my

sword nor my weapons with me, because the king's business required haste."

The Royal Hospital, Royal Hospital Road, Chelsea.
In 1682, Charles II established the Royal Hospital (known
as Chelsea Hospital or Chelsea College) for veteran and
invalid soldiers. The establishment of a standing army
during the Commonwealth had also set forth the provision
for a hospital, rather than retaining the system of pen-
sions or poor relief for soldiers. However, the inspira-
tion for that type of an institution came from the Hotel
des Invalides, Paris (founded in 1670 by Louis XIV), not
from Charles II's mistress, Nell Gwyn, as had long been
popularly supposed. The buildings, mainly of brick, were
designed by Sir Christopher Wren; they consisted of three
ranges enclosing a quadrangle, two hundred feet square,
open toward the River Thames, with wings extending on the
east and west.

     Built on the site of an unsuccessful theological
college founded by James I in 1609, the Royal Hospital
owed its inception to Sir Stephen Fox, a former paymaster-
general, who contributed the bulk of the funds and
undertook the responsibility for its management. John
Evelyn (1620-1706) supported the scheme and Wren chose
the site (M.S. Briggs, Wren 194-200). First opened in
1692, the hospital admitted five hundred patients or,
more accurately, pensioners--all armed, clothed, and or-
ganized under a governor and rankings of lower officers.
Under William III, nearly a third of the original forty-
two acre tract was granted to the Earl of Ranelagh, the
treasurer. Slight alterations and additions to the buildings came about under the direction of the architect
Robert Adam between 1765 and 1782, and afterward by Sir
John Soane. However, the main block remained essentially

unchanged from Wren's original scheme.

John Wesley viewed the Royal Hospital at Chelsea on
Friday, 13 February 1789, at 12:30 p.m. In his mind, the
structure stood as a "noble building. . .designed to
lodge five hundred old soldiers, who are furnished with
all things needful for life and godliness." However, he
never received an invitation to attend to any of the
residents' godliness.

Chelsea Physic Garden, Swan Walk, Chelsea Embankment. In 1673, the Society of Apothecaries leased the
land that would eventually become Chelsea Physic Garden
and sold it, in 1712, to Sir Hans Sloan. Two years later
ter (1714), Sir Hans leased the land back to the Royal
Society for an annual rent of five pounds. In 1737,
the Flemish sculptor John Michael Rysbrack (1693-1770)
finished a sculpture of Sloane, which presently stands
in the center of the Garden. Of particular interest,
one recalls the fact that in 1732, three years prior to
John Wesley's departure for Georgia, scientists sent
cotton seed from the Chelsea Garden to that colony,thus
establishing the major product of that future state.

On Saturday, 22 November 1748, John Wesley spent
"an hour in observing the various works of God" in the
Physic Garden. He seemed hardly impressed. "It would
be a noble improvement of the design if some able and in-
dustrious person were to make a full and accurate inquiry into the uses and virtues of all these plants. Without this, what end does the heaping them thus together
answer, but the gratifying an idle curiosity?"

Battersea. In the eighteenth century, Battersea,

as with neighboring Chelsea, existed as a fashionable
section for temporary or permanent retirement. Perhaps
its most famous family proved to be that of St. John,
and certainly the best known member of that great clan
was Henry St. John (1678-1751)--Secretary of War, Secretary of State, and otherwise identified as Viscount
Bolingbroke. He, of course, holds a niche in literary
history as the principal idea behind Alexander Pope's
poetic Essay on Man (1733-1734).

No doubt a Methodist society had been established
in Battersea, and certainly John Wesley--within the limits of his exhausting schedule--visited the district as
often as he could. However, he related to his contemporaries almost nothing of his activities there. For
Tuesday, 4 November 1766, he noted in his journal merely that he preached at Battersea and "examined" the society.

Kennington Common, Lambeth. St. Mark's, the parish
church of Kennington, stood on what had been a part of
Kennington Common, a popular place for executions. The
most noted and notorious of those social exercises occurred after the Battle of Culloden (April 1746). Thirty-
eight Jacobite prisoners were drawn on hurdles (wooden
frames) to Kennington Common, hanged there for six minutes, cut down while still alive, decapitated and dis-
emboweled, and their heads placed on Temple Bar. The last
of those momentos from the 1745 Jacobite rebellion could
still be seen as late as 1772 (Rude 76)!

John Wesley held open-air meetings regularly at
Kennington Common between June 1739 and September 1740. As
such, the area proved one of the early training grounds
for British Methodism. The following summarizes those
meetings:

Sunday, 15 June 1739. At 5:00 p.m., Wesley preached
on Isaiah 45:22 ("Look unto Me and be ye saved, all
ye ends of the earth") before "about fifteen thousand
people." As usual, one needs to be cautious about accep-
ting those unqualified attendance figures provided, in
their journals and letters, by both John and Charles
Wesley. Both tended to overestimate the numbers in their
audiences, especially at open-air meetings.

Sunday, 2 September 1739. Wesley preached at 5:15
p.m., to "eight or ten thousand people cn Psalms 40:16--
"Innumerable troubles are come about me; my sins have
taken hold upon me that I am not able to look up; yea,
they are more in number than the hairs of my head, and
my heart hath failed me." In that sermon, Wesley expressed
his reaction to one he had heard earlier in the day
(at 3:00 p.m.) delivered by John Heylyn, D.D. (d. 1760),
prebendary of Westminster and rector of St. Mary-le-
Strand.

Sunday, 9 September 1739. Wesley preached at 5:00
p.m. before a gathering of "twenty thousand people" on
Acts 16:31. "I again insisted on that foundation of all
our hope, 'Believe in the Lord Jesus, and thou shalt be
saved.'" Susanna Wesley, then in her seventieth year,
accompanied her son to this meeting.

Sunday, 16 September 1739. Wesley preached to "near
twenty thousand" persons at 5:00 p.m. on Acts 28:22--"We
desire to hear of thee what thou thinkest; for as concerning this sect, know that everywhere it is spoken
against."

Sunday, 23 September 1739. Before "about twenty
thousand," at 5:00 p.m., he spoke on Luke 10:42--"One
thing is needful." If we permit ourselves to believe
the figures set for in the journals, then during the month
of September 1739, between 68,000 and 70,000 people heard

John Wesley preach on Kennington Common.

Sunday, 27 April 1740. He preached at 5:00 p.m. on
Job 5:18--For he wounds, but he binds up; he smites, but
his hands heal.

Sunday, 22 June 1740, 5:00 p.m.

> 1 Peter 1:9--As the outcome of your faith, you
> obtain the salvation of your souls.

Sunday, 29 June 1740. At 5:15 p.m., Wesley preached
on Titus 3:8, endeavoring to "explain and enforce the
apostle's direction that those 'who have believed be careful to maintain good works.' The works I particularly
mentioned were praying, communicating, searching the Scriptures; feeding the hungry, clothing the naked, assisting
the stranger, and visiting or relieving those that are
sick or in prison."

Sunday, 20 July 1740, 5:00 p.m.

> Galatians 6--Brethren, if a man is overtaken in
> any trespass, you who are spiritual should
> restore him in a spirit of gentleness. Look
> to yourself, lest you, too, be tempted.

Sunday, 27 July 1740, 5:00 p.m.

> 2 Corinthians 3:17--Now the Lord is the Spirit,
> and where the Spirit of the Lord is,
> there is freedom.

Sunday, 3 August 1740, 5:00 p.m.

> Zechariah 12:10--And I will pour out on the
> house of David and the inhabitants of
> Jerusalem a spirit of compassion and supplica-
> tion, so that, when they look on him whom
> they have pierced, they shall mourn for him,
> as one mourns for an only child, and weep
> bitterly over him, as one weeps over a first-
> born.

Sunday, 24 August 1740, 5:15 p.m.

Hosea 11--When Israel was a child, I loved him,
and out of Egypt I called my son.
Sunday, 31 August 1740, 5:00 p.m.
1 John 5:11--And this is the testimony, that
God gave us eternal life, and this life is
in his Son.
Sunday, 14 September 1740, 5:00 p.m.
Romans 11:6--But if it is by grace, it is no
longer on the basis of works; otherwise,
grace would no longer be grace.
Sunday, 21 September 1740, 5:00 p.m.
Romans 8:15--For you did not receive the spirit of slavery to fall back into fear, but
you have received the spirit of sonship.
Sunday, 28 September 1740. At 5:00 p.m., Wesley
preached on Acts 13--Now in the church at Antioch there
were prophets and teachers, Barnabas, Symeon, who was
called Niger, Lucius of Cyrene, Manaen, a member of the
court of Herod the tetrarch, and Saul. He "described,
to a numerous congregation. . .the life of God in the
soul. One person who stood on the mount made a little
noise at first; but a gentleman, whom I knew not, walked
up to him, and, without saying one word, mildly took
him by the hand and led him down. From that time he was
quiet till he went away."

Camberwell. Present Camberwell lies south of Walworth, east of Brixton, west of Peckham, and north of
Herne Hill. In the eighteenth century, it existed as a
mere village surrounded by fields and known for its flowers
and fruit trees. Among those lying in Camberwell
churchyard may be counted the remains of Molly Vazielle
Wesley, the shrewish but unfortunate wife of Methodism's
founder and leader, who died in 1781. In 1724, Daniel

Defoe had described the area as a pleasant village, "with
some of the finest dwellings about London" (Tour 176).

   By the end of the eighteenth century, Camberwell had
not changed radically, and John Wesley found the place to
his liking for brief periods of respite from his busy
schedule. Thus, we find him there on Monday, 22 December
1783, where he spent the day reading and conversing--and
in particular at work on his Arminian Magazine. He spent
Wednesday, 20 February 1788, and Thursday, 15 January 1789,
at Camberwell, reading and conversing. On that last-men-
tioned day, he also worked on his journal, "probably as
far as I shall live to write it." Undoubtedly, at that
juncture in his life, Wesley understood that his days on
earth were approaching their end. He returned to Camberwell twice more: on Thursday, 14 January 1790, and on Wednesday, 22 December 1790, where he visited at "sister
Ford's."

   Peckham. Another of Defoe's pleasant villages containing fine dwellings, Peckham stood, throughout the
eighteenth century, as a rural area of pasture land and
market gardens. Cattle drovers, before proceeding to
the London markets, paused at Peckham--setting their herds
out to graze and stopping to take refreshment at the near-
by inns and public houses. The student of literature recalls that Oliver Goldsmith once taught at Dr. Milner's
Academy in Peckham.

   Peckham proved another of John Wesley's favorite
places of retirement, especially during his late years.
He spent three days there--from Monday, 27 January 1783,
to Friday, 31 January--working on his journal and preparing the Arminian Magazine. Between Thursday, 1 January 1784, and Saturday, 3 January, he again retired to

Peckham to work on the Arminian Magazine. He returned,
on Thursday, 21 July 1785, to write in his journal and,
principally, to prepare for the firty-second Methodist
Conference, which began on Tuesday, 26 July 1785. We
find him there again on Thursday, 26 January 1786, and
once more on Wednesday, 13 December 1786. On the following evening (14 December), at 7:00, he preached "to
as many as the house would well contain, and found much
liberty of spirit in enforcing upon them the glorying
only in the cross of Christ." He based his sermon on
Galatians 6:14--But far be it from me to glory except in
the cross of our Lord Jesus Christ, by which the world
has been crucified to me, and I to the world.

Wesley preached at Peckham on Tuesday, 11 December
1787, at 6:30 p.m., on James 3:17--So faith by itself,
if it has no works, is dead. He addressed "a more awa-
kened congregation than ever I observed there before."
On Thursday, 8 January 1789, he retired to the village
to write his will--leaving "no money to any one. . .be-
cause I had none." Also, on that day, at 5:30 p.m., he
preached on 1 John 3:8 (He who commits sin is of the devil; for the devil has sinned from the beginning. The
reason the Son of God appeared was to destroy the works
of the devil.) "to a very serious congregation, although
many of them were of the better rank. But rich and poor
seemed equally determined to work out their own salvation." A week later, Thursday, 15 January 1789, he again
preached at Peckham and "did not withhold from them that
had ears to hear, the whole counsel of God" (Acts 30:27).

On Monday, 28 December 1789, Wesley once again retired to Peckham, where he remained at least until Friday, 1 January 1790. During the greater part of his stay
there, he read An Apology for Her Life written by Herself
(six volumes, 1785), authored by the actress George Anne
Bellamy (1733-1788). That lady's work, as well as her

life, he thought to have been "lively and elegant. . . .
She has a fine imagination, a strong understanding, an
easy style, improved by much reading; a fine, benevolent
temper, and every qualification that could consist with
a total ignorance of God. But God was not in all her
thoughts. Abundance of anecdotes she inserts, which may
be true or false." A resident of Covent Garden, Miss
Bellamy, a courtesan of royalty and men of fashion, proved
a popular actress and a practitioner of high styled
living. Her Apology (actually her memoirs) created a
mild sensation because of its frankness.

At 6:30 p.m., Tuesday, 29 December 1789, John Wesley
preached at Peckham "to a crowded congregation, some
of whom seemed a good deal affected." He based his sermon on Mark 12:32--And the scribe said to him, "You are
right, Teacher; you have truly said that he is one, and
there is no other but he. . . ." Wesley's last recorded
appearance at Peckham appears to have been on Thursday,
3 February 1791; he probably remained there through the
following day.That visit occurred almost exactly a month
prior to his death (2 March).

Deptford. Throughout the eighteenth century, Deptford remained known for its naval dockyard, founded by
Henry VII in 1485 and closed in 1869. The Emperor Peter
the Great worked as a shipwright there in 1698, and he
occupied the residence of John Evelyn at Sayes Court. The
site of the dockyard presently houses a series of store-
rooms, located to the southeast of the former Royal
Naval Victualling Yard--that area having opened in 1745
and shut down in 1961. In 1730, the larger part of Deptford came into being as a separate parish, St. Paul's.
According to Defoe, Deptford "was formerly reckoned, at

least two miles off from Redriff, and that over the marshes too, a place unlikely ever to be inhabited; and yet
now [c. 1724], by the increase of buildings in that town
itself, and the many streets erected at Redriff, and by
the docks and building-yards on the riverside, which stand
between both the town of Deptford, and the streets of
Redriff. . .are effectually joined, and the buildings daily
increasing; and were the town of Deptford now separated,
and rated by itself, I believe it contains more people,
and stands upon more ground, than the city of Wells" (Tour
287).

The following summarizes John Wesley's activities
in Deptford between 1739 and 1789:

Thursday, 27 September 1739. Wesley attended a
meeting of a religious society at 3:00 p.m.

Wednesday, 20 February 1740. To the society at Dept-
Deptford, Wesley explained "the nature of Christian faith
and salvation. Many seemed to receive the word with joy.
Others complained, 'Thou bringest strange things to our
ears' [Acts 17:20]; though some of them had not patience
to hear what this new doctrine was."

Thursday, 19 June 1740. In the late afternoon (sometime between 4:15 and 6:00), Wesley "discovered another
snare of the devil. The woman of Deptford had spoke plain
to Mr. Humphreys, ordering him not to preach, to leave
off doing good, and, in a word, to be still. We talked
largely with her, and she was humbled in the dust, under
a deep sense of the advantage Satan had gained over her."
Joseph Humphreys, who as early as 1738 had been employed
by Wesley as a Moravian lay preacher, was at that time acting as Moravian minister at Deptford. In May 1741, Humphreys
broke with Wesley and cast his lot with George
Whitefield and the Calvinist Methodists. A year and a
half later, on 5 January 1743, he joined with Whitefield,

John Cennick (the earliest of Wesley's lay preachers),
Daniel Rowlands, Howell Harris, and others to pray, and
then to organize the Calvinist Methodists in Wales.

Wednesday, 25 June 1740. At 3:00 p.m., Wesley walked
to Deptford, where he had tea at "Sister Church's,"
met with the society, and then preached on Hebrews 4:11--
Let us therefore strive to enter that rest, that no one
fall by the same sort of disobedience.

Wednesday, 23 July 1740. He took tea (at 3:45 p.m.)
at "Sister Clavel's" and later (5:00) preached at the
"Barn" on Romans 3:21--But now the righteousness of God
has been manifested apart from law, although the law and
the prophets bear witness to it. . . .

Wednesday, 20 August 1740. At 5:15 p.m., Wesley
preached at "Deptford Room" on Acts 13--Now in the church
of Antioch there were prophets and teachers. . . . He
"offered remissions of sins to a small serious congregation. . . . Towards the end, a company of persons came
in, dressed in habits fit for their work, and laboured
greatly either to provoke or to divert the attention of
the hearers. But no man answering them a word, they were
soon weary, and went away."

Monday, 22 September 1740, 6:45 a.m.

Matthew 7--Judge not, that you be not judged.

Wednesday, 24 September 1740. Wesley went to Deptford
at 3:00 p.m.; after "conversation" at "Brother Church's,"
he preached at the "Barn" on Matthew 1:22--. . .
she will bear a son, and you shall call his name Jesus,
for he will save his people from their sins.

Wednesday, 8 October 1740. After tea with Brother
Church at 4:00 p.m., he preached at the Barn on 2 Corinthians 4:1--Therefore, having this ministry by the mercy
of God, we do not lose heart.

Wednesday, 28 January 1741. 5:00 p.m.

> Psalms 23--The Lord is my shepherd, I shall
>   not want. . . .

Wednesday, 4 February 1741. Wesley preached on John
11:36--So the Jews said, "See how he loved him!" He noted that the congregation consisted of "Many poor wretch-
es. . .[who] got together, utterly void both of common
sense and common decency. They cried aloud, as if just
come from 'among the tombs'; but they could not prevail
agains the Holy One of God. Many of them were altogether
confounded, and, I trust, will come again with a better
mind."

Wednesday, 8 April 1741. At 4:00 p.m., Wesley christened a child at Deptford.

Saturday, 25 April 1741, 4:45 p.m.

> Philippians 3:13--Brethren, I do not consider
>   that I have made it my own; but one thing I
>   do, forgetting what lies behind and strain-
>   ing forward to what lies ahead. . . .

Tuesday, 5 May 1741. After dinner at "Brother
Giles's" (3:00 p.m.), he preached at 3:45, in "the dancing
room" on 2 Corinthians 5:17--. . .for we walk by faith,
not by sight.

Monday, 1 June 1741. He spent the hours between
9:00 p.m. and 11:30 p.m. with the society at Deptford.

(?) January 1748

> Romans 10:4--For Christ is the end of the law,
>   that every one who has faith may be justi-
>   fied.

(?) June 1748

> John 14:22--Judas (not Iscariot) said to him,
>   "Lord, how is it that you will manifest
>   yourself to us, and not to the world?"

Saturday, 29 October 1740

> Hebrews 5:12--For by this time you ought to be

teachers; you need some one to teach you
again the first principles of God's word.

(?) January 1749

Romans 6:3-4--Do you not know that all of us
who have been baptized into Christ Jesus
were baptized into his death? We were buried, therefore, with him by baptism into
death, so that as Christ was raised from the
dead by the glory of the Father, we, too,
might walk in newness of life.

John 14:1--Let not your hearts be troubled; believe in God, believe also in me.

Hebrews 10:36--For you have need of endurance,
so that you may do the will of God and receive what is promised.

Saturday, 2 December 1749. At 3:00 p.m., Wesley arrived in Deptford from Bexley, and "found a more than ordinary blessing. . . ."

Tuesday, 8 January 1751

Hebrews 12:2--. . .looking to Jesus, the pioneer and perfecter of our faith, who for the
joy that was set before him endured the cross,
despising the shame, and is seated at the
right hand of the throne of God.

Philippians 1:27--Only let your manner of life
be worthy of the gospel of Christ, so that
whether I come and see you or am absent, I
may hear of you that you stand firm in one
spirit, and one mind striving side by side
for faith of the gospel. . . .

Tuesday, 28 January 1752

Philippians 4:7--And the peace of God, which
passes all understanding, will keep your
hearts and your minds in Christ Jesus.

Matthew 18:15--If your brother sins against
  you, go and tell him his fault, between you
  and him alone. If he listens to you, you
  have gained your brother.

Tuesday, 6 February 1753

  1 Thessalonians 3:3--. . .that no one be moved
    by these afflictions. You, yourselves, know
    that this is to be your lot.

  John 18:11--Jesus said to Peter, "Put your sword
    into its sheath; shall I not drink the cup
    which the Father has given me?"

Wednesday, 15 May 1754

  2 Corinthians 5:8--We are of good courage, and
    we would rather be away from the body and
    at home with the Lord.

  Matthew 16:23--But he turned and said to Peter,
    "Get behind me, Satan! You are a hindrance
    to me; for you are not on the side of God,
    but of men."

  Genesis 6:5--The Lord saw that the wickedness
    of man was great in the earth, and that every
    imagination of the thoughts of his heart was
    only evil continually.

Tuesday, 5 August 1755

  Hebrews 3:7--Therefore, as the Holy Spirit says,
    "Today, when you hear his voice. . . ."

  Micah 6:9--Can I forget the treasures of wick-
    edness in the house of the wicked, and the
    scant measure that is accursed?

  Psalms 84:11--For the Lord God is a sun and
    shield; he bestows favor and honor. No good
    thing does the Lord withhold from those who
    walk uprightly.

Tuesday, 17 February 1756

1 <u>Peter</u> 2:7--To you, therefore, who believe,
he is precious, but for those who do not
believe, "The very stone which the builders
rejected has become the head of the corner,"
. . . .

<u>Hebrews</u> 9:27--And just as it is appointed for
men to die once, and after that comes judgment. . . .

<u>Hebrews</u> 3:14--For we share in Christ, if only
we hold our first confidence firm to the
end. . . .

<u>Philippians</u> 4:7--See above for Tuesday, 28 Jan-
uary 1752 (p. 374).

(?) September 1756

<u>Psalms</u> 34:8--O taste and see that the Lord is
good! Happy is the man who takes refuge in
him!

<u>Psalms</u> 130:7-8--O Israel, hope in the Lord! For
with the Lord there is steadfast love, and
with him is plenteous redemption. And he
will redeem Israel from all his iniquities.

<u>James</u> 4:14--. . .whereas you do not know about
tomorrow. What is your life? For you are a
mist that appears for a little time and then
vanishes.

Tuesday, 22 February 1757. In his journal for this
date, Wesley noted that "Even in this wilderness [Dept-
ford] does at length 'bloom and bud as the rose.' Never
was there such life in this little flock before, nor such
an increase in the number of hearers."

(?) April 1757

<u>Hosea</u> 14:4--I will heal their faithlessness;
I will love them freely, for my anger has
turned from them.

Matthew 10:32--So every one who acknowledges
me before men, I will acknowledge before my
Father who is in heaven. . . .

(?) November 1758

John 4:24--God is Spirit, and those who worship him must worship in spirit and truth.

1 John 3:1--See what love the Father has given
us, that we should be called the children
of God; and so we are.

Monday, 12 February 1759. The diary entry for this
date indicates, simply, that Wesley preached at Deptford
in the evening.

Tuesday, 30 October 1759. He preached at Deptford
and "rejoiced to find an increasing work there. . . ."

Tuesday, 12 February 1760. Before riding to Welling,
Wesley preached at Deptford.

Tuesday, 15 September 1761

Matthew 8:2--. . .and behold a leper came to
him and knelt before him, saying, "Lord,
if you will, you can make me clean."

1 Samuel 17--Now the Philistines gathered their
army for battle; and they were gathered at
Socoh, which belongs to Judah, and encamped
between Socoh and Azekah, in Ephesdammim.

Matthew 15:28--Then Jesus answered her, "O woman, great is your faith! Be it done for you
as you desire." And her daughter was healed
instantly.

Tuesday, 10 November 1761. Wesley "found the society at Deptford more alive than ever, a sure consequence
of which is their increasing number."

(?) November-December 1761. He preached at Deptford
sometime between 30 November and 2 December 1761
(see Curnock, Journal 4:480).

Tuesday, 9 February 1762. Wesley preached at Deptford; neither diary nor journal entry for this date indicates the place or the text upon which he based his sermon.

Tuesday, 16 November 1762. Again, he merely indicated in his journal that "I preached at Deptford. . . ."

Tuesday, 15 February 1763. Wesley found the society "united in faith and love. During the sermon in the afternoon one poor mourner found peace with God."

(?) February 1764. Wesley preached at Deptford sometime between Friday, 17 February, and Thursday, 23 February (see Curnock, Journal 5:46).

Tuesday, 4 November 1766. He preached at Deptford and "examined" the society there.

Friday, 10 February 1769. Wesley went to Deptford specifically to see "honest William Brown, worn out with age and pain, and long confined to his bed, without the use of either hand or foot. But he has the use of his understanding and his tongue, and testifies that God does all things well; that he has no doubt or fear, but is cheerfully waiting till his change shall come." That may well have been the same "Brother Brown" at whose home Wesley had dinner on Tuesday, 12 May 1741.

Wednesday, 2 January 1771. In the evening, Wesley preached "a kind of funeral sermon for Mr. Whitefield. In every place I wish to show all possible respect for the memory of that great and good man." George Whitefield had died on 30 September 1770, at Newburyport, Massachusetts, in the fifty-sixth year of his age.

Tuesday, 2 November 1784. Wesley remained at Deptford between 4:00 p.m. and 9:30 p.m. At 6:30 he preached a sermon on Matthew 8:13--And to the centurion Jesus said, "Go; be it done for you as you have believed." And the servant was healed at that very moment.

Tuesday, 15 February 1785. Wesley spent the hours
from 1:00 p.m. to 10:00 p.m. at Deptford. At 6:30 he
preached on <u>Matthew</u> 21:21--And Jesus answered them,"Truly
I say to you, if you have faith and never doubt, you will
not only do what has been done to the fig tree, but even
if you say to this mountain, 'Be taken up and cast into
the sea,' it will be done.

Thursday, 27 October 1785. He arrived, at 4:30 p.m.,
wrote letters, took tea, wrote more letters, ate supper,
and conversed until 9:30 p.m.

Tuesday, 24 October 1786. Wesley met the classes
in Deptford at 4:00 p.m., and was "violently importuned
to order the Sunday service in our room at the same time
with that of the church [the parish church of Deptford].
It is easy to see that this would be a formal separation
from the Church [of England]. We fixed both our morning
and evening service, all over England, at such hours as
not to interfere with the Church; with this very design--
that those of the Church, if they chose it, might attend
both the one and the other. But to fix it at the same
hour is obliging them to separate either from the Church
or us; and this I judge to be not only inexpedient, but
totally unlawful for me to do." After the classes, he
preached on <u>Ephesians</u> 2:8--. . .(for he who worked through
Peter for the mission to the circumcised worked through
me also for the Gentiles). . . .

Tuesday, 2 January 1787. The controversy over separation from the Church of England continued. "Most of
the leading men of the [Deptford] society were mad for
separating from the Church," wrote Wesley in his journal.
"I endeavoured to reason with them, but in vain; they had
neither sense or even good manners left. At length, after
meeting the whole society [at 6:30 p.m.], I told them:
'If you are resolved, you may have your service in church

hours; but remember, from that time you will see my face
no more.' This struck deep; and from that hour I have
heard no more of separating from the Church." The problem that Wesley described illustrates well the control
and influence he had over his societies. Such influence
appears even more remarkable when we realize that during
this Deptford "crisis," John Wesley had almost reached
his eighty-fourth year!

Thursday, 15 February 1787. After the sermon, he
seemed "agreeably surprised to find the threatening storm
[the controvery over the Methodists' attempts to separate
from the Church of England] blown over, and all our brethren in peace and love with each other."

Tuesday, 12 February 1788. Wesley visited with the
Deptford society between 2:00 p.m. and 10:00 p.m. At 6:30
p.m., he preached on Hebrews 10:35--Therefore, do not
throw away your confidence, which has a great reward
. . .

Tuesday, 17 February 1789. Wesley examined the society and preached, at 6:30 p.m., on Mark 12:32--And the
scribe said to him, "You are right, Teacher; you have
truly said that he is one, and there is no other but he
. . . ."

Monday, 30 November 1789. Wesley found the Deptford society "in peace, but nearly at one stay. I endeavoured to stir up both them and the congregation, in the
evening, to go on to perfection." The sermon, delivered
at 6:30 p.m., focused upon Ephesians 5:14--Stand before,
having girded your loins with truth, and having put on
the breastplate of righteousness. . .

Clapham. According to Daniel Defoe (Tour 176), from
the hills about Clapham, one could see Peckam, Camberwell,

and, "to crown all, a fair prospect of the whole city of
London itself. . . ." Clapham constituted still another
of the pleasant villages outside the City that became fashionable during the middle and late eighteenth century.
A tablet on the south wall of Holy Trinity Church--built
in 1775 by Kenton Couse--commemorates the Clapham Sect,
an Anglican group that [according to the tablet] "in the
latter part of the xviiith and early part of the xixth
centuries laboured so abundantly for the increase of National Righteousness and Conversion of the Heathen and
rested not until the curse of slavery was swept away from
all parts of the British dominions." On the site of the
present Number 29 North Side, Clapham, Samuel Pepys (born
in 1633) died in 1703.

   The only record of John Wesley's activities in Clapham
comes to us from his Sermon Register. Sometime in
October 1756, he preached in that village on the following texts:

> Luke 21:34--But take heed to yourselves lest
> your hearts be weighed down with dissipa-
> tion and drunkenness and cares of this life,
> and that day come upon you suddenly like a
> snare. . . .

> Hebrews 8:11--And they shall shall not teach
> every one his fellow or every one his brother,
> saying, "Know the Lord," for all shall
> know me, from the least of them to the
> greatest.

> 1 Corinthians 1:30--He is the source of your
> life in Christ Jesus, whom God made our wis-
> dom, our righteousness and sanctification
> and redemption. . . .

APPENDICES

A. A Chronology of Important Events
B. Eighteenth-Century Archbishops of Canterbury
C. Eighteenth-Century Bishops of London
D. Sir Christopher Wren's London Churches

A. A Chronology of Important Events

So that the reader may more easily relate John Wesley's actions, reactions, and opinions found in the main body of this text to certain of the larger literary, historical, and biographical events of eighteenth-century Britain, the following chronology has been prepared for consultation and consideration:

1662. 17 December. Birth of Samuel Wesley the elder, father of John Wesley

1669. January. Birth of Susanna Annesley, wife of Samuel Wesley the elder and mother of John Wesley

1680. Samuel Wesley the elder enters the academy of Charles Morton of Newington Green, London

1683. August. Samuel Wesley the elder enters Exeter College, Oxford

1685. Samuel Wesley the elder, Maggots: or, Poems on Several Subjects

1688. 19 June. Samuel Wesley the elder graduates B.A. from Oxford

7 August. Samuel Wesley the elder ordained deacon at Bromley

1690. 24 February. Samuel Wesley the elder ordained priest at St. Andrew's, Holborn

Marriage of Samuel Wesley the elder and Susanna Annesley

1691. 10 February. Birth of Samuel Wesley the younger

1692. Birth of Emilia Wesley

1693. Samuel Wesley the elder, The Life of Our Blessed Lord and Saviour, Jesus Christ: an Heroic Poem

1694. Samuel Wesley the elder incorporated M.A. at
       Cambridge

1695. Samuel Wesley the elder appointed rector of
       Epworth and Wroote, Lincolnshire
       Birth of Susanna Wesley the younger
       Samuel Wesley the elder, Elegies (on the deaths
       of Queen Mary and Archbishop Tillotson)

1696. Birth of Mary Wesley

1697. Birth of Mehetabel Wesley

1700. Samuel Wesley the elder, An Epistle to a Friend
       concerning Poetry

1702. Birth of Anne Wesley (died sometime after 1742)

1703. 17 June. Birth of John Benjamin Wesley at
       Epworth

1704. Samuel Wesley the younger enters Westminster
       School
       Samuel Wesley the elder, The History of the Old
       and New Testaments, attempted in Verse

1705. Samuel Wesley the elder, Marlborough, or the Fate
       of Europe (a poem)

1706. Birth of Martha Wesley

1707. 18 December. Birth of Charles Wesley, at Epworth
       Isaac Watts, Hymns and Spiritual Songs

1709. 9 February. John Wesley rescued from the fire
       at Epworth rectory
       Joseph Addison and Richard Steele, The Tatler

1710. Birth of Keziah Wesley
       Stricter measures against Nonconformists urged by
       High Church Tories
       Bishop George Berkeley, Treatise concerning the
       Principles of Human Knowledge

1711. 12 May. John Wesley nominated for admission to
       Charterhouse School by the Duke of Buckingham
       9 June. Samuel Wesley the younger enters Christ

Church, Oxford

1713. Treaty of Utrecht ending the War of the Spanish
       Succession

1714. 28 January. John Wesley admitted to Charterhouse
       Death of Queen Anne
       George I, King of England
       Birth of George Whitefield

1715. Samuel Wesley the younger graduates B.A. from
       Oxford
       Jacobite uprising

1716. Charles Wesley enters Westminster School

1717. Benjamin Hoadley, Bishop of Bangor, The Nature of
       the Kingdom or Church of Christ
       William Penn, Religion Professed by the Quakers

1718. Samuel Wesley the younger graduates M.A. from
       Oxford

1719. Isaac Watts, The Psalms of David Imitated

1720. 24 June. John Wesley enters Christ Church, Oxford
       Bursting of the "South Sea (Company) Bubble"

1721. Robert Walpole, Prime Minister

1722. William Wollaston, Religion of Nature

1724. John Wesley graduates B.A. from Oxford
       Gilbert Burnet, A History of My Own Time

1725. 19 September. John Wesley ordained deacon by Dr.
       John Potter, Bishop of Oxford
       16 October. John Wesley preaches his first sermon
       at South Leigh, Oxfordshire
       League of Hanover (Herrenhausen) by England, France,
       and Prussia against Spain and Austria
       Francis Hutchinson, An Inquiry into the Original
       of Our Ideas of Beauty and Virtue

1726. Charles Wesley enters Christ Church, Oxford
       14 March. John Wesley elected Fellow of Lincoln
       College, Oxford; lectures in Greek, philosophy,

and logic

April-October. John Wesley assists his father at
Epworth and Wroote

12 October. Birth of Sarah Gwynne, wife of Charles
Wesley

Voltaire in England (1726-1729)

Jonathan Swift, Gulliver's Travels

1727. 9 February. John Wesley awarded the M.A. in religion and natural and moral philosophy

August. John Wesley again leaves Oxford to assist his father at Epworth and Wroote

Death of George I at Osnaburg

George II, King of England

1728. John Wesley admitted to priest's orders

Peace of Pardo, with Spain

Alexander Pope, The Dunciad (first version)

William Law, A Serious Call to a Devout and Holy
Life

1729. May. Charles Wesley forms the Oxford "Holy Club";
the group becomes known as "methodists"

November. John Wesley returns to Oxford, presides
over Lincoln College public moderations

December. John Wesley joins the Oxford Holy Club
and assumes its leadership

Treaty of Seville among France, England and Holland

1730. Charles Wesley graduates B.A. from Oxford

1731. Treaty of Vienna with Spain and the Holy Roman
Empire

1732. July. John Wesley meets William Law

Covent Garden Theatre built

Vauxhall pleasure gardens under management of
Jonathan Tyers

1733. 12 March. Charles Wesley graduates M.A. from Oxford

Samuel Wesley the younger becomes master at Tiverton Grammar School, Devonshire

James Oglethorpe establishes the Georgia colony

Robert Walpole withdraws the Excise Act

Alexander Pope, An Essay on Man

1734. Death of Mary Wesley Lamb, daughter of Samuel and
Susanna Wesley

1735. George Whitefield joins the Oxford Holy Club

25 April. Death of Samuel Wesley the elder

21 October. John and Charles Wesley sail for
Georgia aboard the Simmonds

Publication of Samuel Wesley the elder's Disser-
tationes in Librum Jobi

William Hogarth, The Rake's Progress

1736. 5 February. John and Charles Wesley reach Savannah,
Georgia

11 August. Charles Wesley leaves Georgia

2 December. Charles Wesley arrives in England

Samuel Wesley the younger, Poems on Several
Occasions

Bishop Joseph Butler, The Anatomy of Religion,
Natural and Revealed, to the Constitution and
Course of Nature

Bishop William Warburton, The Alliance between
Church and State: or, the Necessity and Equity
of an Established Religion

Witchcraft laws repealed

1737. 2 December. John Wesley leaves Savannah

John Wesley, A Collection of Psalms and Hymns

Theatre Licensing Act

1738. 1 February. John Wesley returns to England

21 May. Charles Wesley's evangelical conversion,
at Bray's, in Little Britain, London

24 May. "The Aldersgate Experience"--John Wesley's
  evangelical conversion, Aldersgate Street,
  London
June. John Wesley visits Count Nicholas von
  Zinzendorf and the Moravians at Herrnhut
John and Charles Wesley, A Collection of Psalms
  and Hymns
War with Spain (The War of Jenkin's Ear)

1739. 6 November. Death of Samuel Wesley the younger
11 November. John Wesley preaches the first ser-
  mon at the Foundery, Upper Moorfields, London
John and Charles Wesley, Hymns and Sacred Poems
The Wesleys establish a Methodist society in
  Bristol
David Hume, A Treatise of Human Nature

1740. John and Charles Wesley, Hymns and Sacred Poems
Admiral George Anson's voyage round the world

1741. Death of Keziah Wesley, daughter of Samuel and
  Susanna Wesley
Charles Wesley, Hymns on God's Everlasting Love
John Wesley, A Collection of Psalms and Hymns

1742. 30 July. Death of Susanna Wesley the elder
Death of Ursula Berry Wesley, wife of Samuel
  Wesley the younger
John and Charles Wesley. Hymns and Sacred Poems
Resignation of Robert Walpole as Prime Minister
War of the Austrian Succession

1743. 29 May. Opening of West Street Chapel, London
English and Hanoverian armies (under personal com-
  mand of George II) defeat French at the
  Battle of Dettingen

1744. 25 June. The first Methodist conference, held at
  the Foundery, London
Death of Alexander Pope
British fleet defeated near Toulon

1745.   John Wesley, Advice to the People Called
            Methodists
        Death of Jonathan Swift
        Jacobite rebellion; Charles Edward, the Young
            Pretender, lands in Scotland
1746.   John Wesley, Sermons on Several Occasions (to
            1760)
        Battle of Culloden; defeat of Charles Edward by
            William, Duke of Cumberland
1747.   9 August. John Wesley's first visit to Ireland
        John Wesley, Primitive Physick
        British victories over the French off Belle-Isle
            and Cape Finnisterre
1748.   John Wesley, English Grammar
        John Wesley, Latin Grammar
        Death of Isaac Watts
        Peace of Aix-la-Chapelle, with France
        David Hume, Philosophical Essays
1749.   8 April. Charles Wesley marries Sarah Gwynne
        Charles Wesley, Hymns and Sacred Poems
        John Wesley, Directions concerning Pronunciation
            and Gesture
        John Wesley (ed.), The Christian Library, 50 vols
            (to 1755)
        Henry St. John, Lord Bolingbroke, On the Idea of
            a Patriot King
1750.   John Wesley, A Compendium of Logick
1751.   18 February. John Wesley marries Mrs. Molly
            Vazielle
        April. John Wesley's first visit to Scotland
        1 June. John Wesley resigns his fellowship at
            Lincoln College, Oxford
        Death of Mehetabel Wesley Wright, daughter of
            Samuel and Susanna Wesley

John Wesley, French Grammar
John Wesley, Hebrew Grammar
Death of Frederick, Prince of Wales
Frederick's son, George, becomes heir to the
 throne of England
1752. The New Style introduced; the year henceforth be-
 gins on 1 January
1753. John Wesley, The Complete English Dictionary
The British Museum established
Death of George Berkeley
1754. David Hume, A History of Great Britain
Thomas Chippendale, The Gentleman's and Cabinet-
 Maker's Director
1755. January. John Wesley, Notes upon the New Testament
1756. "Seven Years" Subsidiary Alliance, with Prussia
Seven Years' War
William Pitt the elder, Prime Minister
Edmund Burke, Philosophical Inquiry into the Ori-
 gin of Our Ideas of the Sublime and Beautiful
1757. 11 December. Birth of Charles Wesley the younger,
 son of Charles and Sarah Wesley (d. 1824)
Robert Clive's victory at Plessey, in India
Soame Jenyns, A Free Enquiry into the Nature and
 Origin of Evil
Sir William Chambers, Designs of Chinese Build-
 ings, Furniture, etc.
Robert Adam, The Ruins of the Palace of
 Diocletian
1758. John Wesley, Reasons against a Separation from
 the Church of England
1759. 1 April. Birth of Sarah Wesley the younger, daugh-
 ter of Charles and Sarah Wesley
British naval victories over Lagos
Admiral Edward Hawke's victory over the French at

Quiberon Bay

British capture Surat, in India

1760. John Wesley, The Disideratum; or, Electricity
Made Plain and Useful

Death of George II

George III, King of England

1761. John Wesley (ed.), Select Hymns: with Tunes
Annext: Designed Cheifly for Use of the People
Called Methodists

John Stuart, third Earl of Bute, Prime Minister

1762. Charles Wesley, Short Hymns on Select Passages
of Holy Scriptures

War with Spain

Conquests of Havan, Trinidad, and Manila

Henry Home, Lord Kames, Elements of Criticism

1763. Charles Wesley, Hymns for Children

Peace of Paris; Canada and India ceded to England

Thomas Reid, An Inquiry into the Human Mind on the
Principles of Common Sense

Lord Bute resigns as Prime Minister

George Grenville, Prime Minister

1764. Death of Susanna Wesley Ellison, daughter of
Samuel and Susanna Wesley

1765. John Wesley, Explanatory Notes upon the Old Testament

John Wesley, Greek Grammar

John Wesley, A Short History of Methodism

Bengal ceded to the East India Company by the
Treaty of Allahabad

Stamp Act passed

Lord Grenville dismissed as Prime Minister

Charles Watson Wentworth, Marquis of Rockingham,
Prime Minister

Sir William Blackstone, Commentaries upon the
Laws of England

1766.   31 January.   John Wesley, A Plain Account of Chris-
        tian Perfection
        24 February.   Birth of Samuel Wesley the third, son
        of Charles and Sarah Wesley (d. 1837)
        Stamp Act repealed
        William Pitt, Earl of Chatham, Prime Minister
        Pitt resigns
        Augustus Henry Fitzroy, 3rd Duke of Grafton,
        Prime Minister
        Henry Cavendish discovers the element hydrogen
1768.   24 August.   Opening of Trevecca College, Wales,
        by the Calvinist Methodists
        Joseph Priestley, First Principles of Government
        Beginning of the John Wilkes agitations
        Royal Academy of Arts founded; Sir Joshua Reynolds
        first president
1769.   Hyder Ali plunders the Carnatic
        Turmoil over John Wilkes' expulsion from Commons
1770.   Death of Emilia Wesley Harper, daughter of Samuel
        and Susanna Wesley
        18 November.   John Wesley preaches George
        Whitefield's funeral sermon (d. 30 September)
        Frederick, Lord North, Prime Minister
        Edmund Burke, Thoughts on the Present Discontent
1771.   23 January.   Molly Vazielle Wesley separates from
        her husband, John Wesley
        Charles Wesley, An Elegy on the Late Reverend
        George Whitefield
        Charles Wesley, An Epistle to the Reverend George
        Whitefield
        The Works of the Rev. John Wesley. Bristol. 32 vols.
        (to 1774)
1772.   Warren Hastings head of the Bengal government
        Boston Port Bill passed

Warren Hastings, governor-general of India

1773.   John Wesley, A Short Roman History

December. John Wesley, Works, vols 12-25

The "Boston Tea-Party"

1774.   John Wesley, Works, vols 26-32

Joseph Priestley isolates oxygen

1775.   John Wesley, A Calm Address to Our American
Colonies

Lord North's conciliatory measures rejected by the
American colonies

The American Revolution

1776.   John Wesley, A Concise History of England, 4 vols

City of London remonstrates against the American
war

The Declaration of Independence

Hessians hired for service in America

Adam Smith, The Wealth of Nations

Sir John Hawkins, General History of Music

Charles Burney, A General History of Music

Edward Gibbon, The Decline and Fall of the Roman
Empire

Jeremy Bentham, A Fragment on Government

1777.   21 April. Foundation stone laid for City Road Chapel, London

John Wesley, A Calm Address to the Inhabitants of
England

Joseph Priestley, A Disquisition on Matter and
and Spirit

General John Burgoyne surrenders at Saratoga

1778.   1 January. First number of John Wesley's Arminian
Magazine

1 November. City Road Chapel opened

Capture of Pondicherry, in India

1779.   John Wesley, Popery Calmly Considered

William Cowper and John Newton, "Olney Hymns"

1780.   John and Charles Wesley, A Collection of Hymns for
        the Use of the People Called Methodists
        Second war with Hyder Ali
        War with Holland
        Lord George Gordon "No Popery" riots in London
1781.   8 October. Death of Molly Vazeille Wesley, wife
        of John Wesley
        John Wesley, A Concise Ecclesiastical History
        Naval victory off the Doggerbank
        British surrender to the Americans at Yorktown
        Sir William Herschel discovers the planet Uranus
1782.   Joseph Priestley, History of the Corruption of
        Christianity
        Lord North resigns
        Lord Rockingham, Prime Minister of England; resig-
        nation
        William Petty, 3rd Earl of Shelburne, Prime Minis-
        ter
        Admiral George Brydges Rodney destroys Comte De
        Grasse's fleet at Dominica
1783.   Robert Blair, Lectures on Rhetoric and Belles
        Lettres
        Peace of Versailles; Britain acknowledges Ameri-
        can independence
        Coalition government of Lord North and Charles
        James Fox
        William Pitt the younger, Prime Minister
1784.   1-2 September. John Wesley ordains preachers for
        America
        Samuel Wesley the third joins the Roman Catholic
        Church
        Death of Samuel Johnson
        Peace with Tippo Sahib
1785.   John Wesley, A Pocket Hymn Book, for the Use of

Christians of All Denominations

1786. Charles, Marquis Cornwallis, succeeds Warren
       Hastings in India
1787. Warren Hastings impeached
       William Wilberforce and Thomas Clarkson found the
       Society for the Suppression of the Slave Trade
1788. 29 March. Death of Charles Wesley
       5 April. Charles Wesley buried at Marylebone,
       London
       John Wesley, Sermons, 2nd series, 4 vols
       George III declared insane
       Death of Charles Edward, the last Pretender
       Trial of Warren Hastings
1789. Jeremy Bentham, Principles of Morals and Legis-
       lation
       The French Revolution
1790. 27 July. John Wesley attends his last Methodist
       conference, at Bristol
       24 October. Last entry in John Wesley's journal
       March. John Wesley, Hymns for Children (selected
       from Charles Wesley's Hymns for Children)
       John Wesley's last major publication, The New Tes-
       tament, with an Analysis of the Several Books
       and Chapters
       Edmund Burke, Reflections on the Revolution in
       France
       Archibald Alison, Essay on the Nature and Princi-
       ples of Taste
1791. 22 February. John Wesley's last sermon, at Leather-
       head
       23 February. The last entry in John Wesley's diary
       24 February. John Wesley's last piece of extended
       writing--a letter of encouragement to William
       Wilberforce

2 March. Death of John Wesley, at 10:00 a.m.

9 March. John Wesley buried at City Road,
    London

Death of Martha Wesley Hall, daughter of Samuel
    and Susanna Wesley

James Boswell, <u>The Life of Samuel Johnson, LL.D.</u>

B. Eighteenth-Century Archbishops of Canterbury

1695-1715. Thomas Tenison (1636-1715). Revived the Arch-
           bishop's Court and assumed a prominent role in
           the founding of the Society for the Propagation
           of the Gospel in Foreign Parts. Fell into dis-
           favor of Queen Anne because of his pronounced
           Whig and Low Church views.

1716-1737. William Wake (1657-1737). Engaged in nego-
           tiations with Gallican (French Catholic) lea-
           ders on a plan for reunion between the Church
           of England and the French Church. Sympathized
           with Protestant Nonconformists and advoca-
           ted changes in the Book of Common Prayer to
           facilitate the easing of tensions between the
           two groups.

1737-1747. John Potter (1674-1747). As Bishop of Oxford,
           he ordained John Wesley into Holy Orders. He
           edited a standard edition of the works of
           Clement of Alexandria.

1747-1757. Thomas Herring (1693-1757). Archbishop of
           York (1743-1757) while he was also Archbishop
           of Canterbury. His York Visitation Returns
           constitute an important document for
           the religious history of the period.

1757-1758. Matthew Hutton (d. 1758). Consecrated Bi-
           shop of Bangor in 1743; Archbishop of York
           in 1747. Editions of his published sermons
           appeared in 1741, 1744, 1745, 1746,and 1747.

1758-1768. Thomas Secker (1693-1768). A former Dissen-
           ter, he nonetheless stood in high favor with

Queen Caroline, who granted him rapid advan-
cement. He stood, generally, for religious
tolerance and common sense. Also, he favored
the posting of Anglican bishops to the
American colonies.

1768-1783. Frederick Cornwallis (d. 1783). Consecrated
Bishop of Lichfield and Coventry in 1749. Published volumes of sermons in 1751, 1752, 1756,
and 1762.

1783-1805. John Moore (1733-1805). Native of Gloucester
and graduate of Pembroke College, Oxford. Dean
of Canterbury (1771), Bishop of Bangor (1776).
Published sermons in 1777, 1781, and 1782.

C. Eighteenth-Century Bishops of London

1675-1713. Henry Compton (1632-1675). Served as tutor
to the Princesses Mary and Anne, but his anti-
Catholic attitude brought him into disfavor
with the girls' father, James II. The Church
restrained him from the exercise of his
spiritual functions because of his failure to
suspend Anglican clerics for their anti-
Catholic sermons. He officiated at the coro-
nation of William III, supported the Compre-
hension Bill of 1689, and took interest in
the missionary work in North America.

1714-1723. John Robinson (1650-1723). Chaplain to the
English ambassador to Sweden (1683); ambassador to Sweden until 1708; Bishop of Bristol
(1710-1714). Generally regarded as a charitable and regular bishop, but did little to
advance the cause of religion or his Church.

1723-1748. Edmund Gibson (1669-1748). A High Church
Whig, he proceeded from Bishop of Lincoln
(1716-1723) to Bishop of London. Under his
jurisdiction, the religious welfare of the
American colonies became a priority. He published his Synodus Anglicana: or, the Constitution and Proceedings of an Anglican Convo-
cation (1702), a manual that became a Church
standard. Further, his Codex Iuris Ecclesi-
astici Anglicani (1713) remains the most complete collection of English Anglican statutes.

1748-1761. Thomas Sherlock (1678-1761). Prebendary of
London (1713), Master of Catherine Hall (1714),

Dean of Chichester (1715), Prebendary of Norwich
(1719), Bishop of Bangor (1727-1728), and
Bishop of Salisbury (1734). In 1747, He declined consideration of an appointment as
Archbishop of Canterbury. When he accepted
the see of London, he had reached his seventieth year; nonetheless, he proved an indus-
trious administrator.

1761-1762.   Thomas Hayter (d. 1762). Bishop of Norwich
(1749)Served as a tutor to the sons of
Frederick, Prince of Wales .

1762-1764.   Richard Osbaldeston (d. 1764). Dean of York
and Bishop of Carlisle (1747). He published
his collected sermons in 1723, 1748, and 1752.

1764-1777.   Richard Terrick (d. 1777). Canon of Windsor
(1742), Prebendary of London (1749), Bishop
of Peterborough (1757). He published seven
single sermons between 1742 and 1764. A
competent preacher and a generally liberal
minded official, he nevertheless opposed the
Roman Catholics, whose chapels he caused to be
closed.

1777-1787.   Robert Lowth (1710-1787). An accomplished
scholar, particularly with Hebrew texts, he
produced an excellent translation of Isaiah
in 1778. Although generally opposed to reform
and to the evangelicals within the Church,
he nonetheless expressed warm admiration for
John Wesley; their correspondence casts important light upon the entire issue of the
evangelical movement in the eighteenth century.

1787-1809.   Beilby Porteous (1731-1808). Himself of American
descent, Bishop Porteous outwardly identified

his thinking with the practical ideals
of the evangelicals. He promoted mission
work among Negro slaves in America and generally lent his support to the abolition of
the slave trade, the Sunday school movement,
and the full observation of the Holy Days.
He gained recognition as an able preacher and
as a liberal donator of Church funds to worthy
causes.

D. Sir Christopher Wren's London Churches

Entries arranged by date of completion of the main structure (excluding the steeple)--followed by the name and
location of the church, the approximate cost (£ . s. d.),
and the date of destruction, serious damage, or gutting.
Sources: Dictionary of National Biography, 21:1004; Gwilt
214; Downes, Wren 129-131.

1672. St. Mary-at-Hill, Lovat Lane.

1673. St. Michael, Wood Street. 1897

1674. St. Bride, Fleet Street. 11,430. 5. 11. 1940.

1674. St. Mary Aldermanbury. 5237. 3. 6. 1940

1675. St. Mary-le-Bow. 8071. 18. 1. 1941

1676. St. Edmund, Lombard Street.

1677. St. Dionis Backchurch, Lime Street and Fenchurch
        Street. 5737. 10. 8. 1878.

1677. St. Mildred, Poultry. 1872

1677. St. Stephen, Coleman Street. 1940

1678. St. Magnus, London Bridge. 9579. 18. 10.

1678. St. Stephen Walbrook. 1941

1679. St. George, Botolph Lane. 1904.

1679. St. Michael Bassishaw, Basinghall Street. 1900

1679. St. Olave, Old Jewry. 5580. 4. 10. 1877

1680. St. Michael, Queenhythe, Upper Thames Street.
        1876.

1681. St. Anne and St. Agnes, Gresham Street. 2488.
        0. 11. 1940

1681. St. Bartholomew, Exchange, Bartholomew Lane.
        5077. 1. 1. 1841.

1681.   St. Benet Fink, Threadneedle Street. 4129. 16.
           10. 1876
1681.   St. Lawrence Jewry, Gresham Street. 11,870. 1. 9.
           1940
1681.   St. Peter, Cornhill. 5647. 8. 2.
1681.   St. Swithin, Cannon Street. 4687. 4. 6. 1941
1682.   All Hallows the Great, Thames Street. 5641. 9. 9.
           1894
1682.   St. Clement Danes, the Strand. 8786. 17. 0. 1941
1682.   St. James Garlickhythe, Garlick Hill. 3357. 10.
           8. 1941
1682.   St. Mary Aldermary, Queen Victoria Street. 1940
1683.   St. Antholin, Budge Row. 5685. 5. 10. 1876
1684.   All Hallows, Watling Street. 5591. 9. 2. 1877
1684.   St. James, Picadilly. 8500. 0. 0. 1940
1685.   St. Benet, Paul's Wharf, Upper Thames Street.
           3328. 18. 10.
1686.   St. Augustine, Watling Street. 3145. 3. 10.
           1941
1686.   St. Martin Ludgate, Ludgate Hill. 5378. 9. 7.
1686.   St. Matthew, Friday Street. 2301. 8. 2. 1885
1687.   Christ Church, Newgate Street. 11,778. 9. 6.
           1940
1687.   St. Alban, Wood Street. 3165. 0. 9. 1940
1687.   St. Benet, Gracechurch Street. 3583. 9. 5½.
           1876
1687.   St. Clement, Eastcheap, Clement's Lane and King
           William Street. 4365. 3. 4. 1940
1687.   St. Margaret Pattens, Rood Lane.
1687.   St. Mary Abchurch, Abchurch Yard. 4922. 2. 4.
           1940
1687.   St. Mary Magdalene, Old Fish Street. 1890
1687.   St. Michael, Crooked Lane. 1831
1687.   St. Mildred, Bread Street. 1941

1688. St. Nicholas, Cole Abbey. 5042. 6. 11. 1941

1692. St. Andrew, Holborn, Holborn Circus. 9000. 0. 0.
       1941

1692. St. Margaret Lothbury. 5340. 8. 1.

1694. All Hallows, Lombard Street. 8058. 15. 6. 1939

1694. St. Andrew-by-the-Wardrobe, St. Andrew's Hill
       (Queen Victoria Street). 7060. 16. 11. 1940

1694. St. Mary Somerset, Upper Thames Street. 6579.
       18. 1. 1871

1694. St. Michael Royal, College Hill. 7555 7. 9. 1944

1700. St. Vedast, Foster Lane. 1940

1702. St. Dunstan in the East, Idol Lane. 1940

1710. St. Paul's Cathedral.

1714. St. Christopher-le-Stocks, Threadneedle Street.
       2098. 12. 7. 1786

LIST OF WORKS CITED AND CONSULTED

The following works have been consulted (and cited in the text) as sources for the preparation of this book. The reader will find entries arranged alphabetically by author, editor, or title:

Abbey, Charles J. The English Church and Its Bishops. 2 vols. London: Longmans, Green, and Company, 1887.

Addison, Joseph, and Sir Richard Steele. The Spectator, ed. Gregory Smith. 4 vols. London: Dent (Everyman's Library), 1907.

Baedeker, Karl. London and Its Environs. London: George Allen and Unwin, Ltd., 1951.

Bell, Colin, and Rose Bell. City Fathers: Town Planning in Britain, from Roman Times to 1900. New York: Frederick A. Praeger, 1969.

Bowen, Marjorie. Wrestling Jacob.A Study in the Life of John Wesley. London: The Religious Book Club, 1938.

Boswell, James. The Life of Samuel Johnson, LL.D., ed. R.W. Chapman, rev. J.D. Fleeman. London: Oxford University Press, 1970.

Bray, William (ed.). The Diary of John Evelyn. 2 vols. London: J.M. Dent and Sons, Ltd., 1966.

Braybrooke, Neville. London Green. The Story of Kensington Gardens, Hyde Park, Green Park, and St. James's Park. London: Victor Gollancz, Ltd., 1959.

Briggs, Asa. A Social History of England. New York: The Viking Press, 1983.

Briggs, Martin S., Wren the Incomparable. London: George Allen and Unwin, Ltd., 1953.

Clifford, James L. Young Sam Johnson. New York: Oxford
    University Press, 1961.

Crook, J. Mordaunt. The British Museum. New York:
    Prager Publishers, 1972

Curnock, Nehemiah (ed.). The Journal of the Rev. John
    Wesley, A.M. 8 vols. London: Charles H. Kelly, 1909-
    1916.

Currie, Robert, Alan Gilbert, and Lee Horsley. Churches
    and Churchgoers. Patterns of Church Growth in the
    British Isles Since 1700. Oxford: The Clarendon Press,
    1977.

Davey, Richard. The Pageant of London. 2 vols. London:
    Methuen and Company, 1906.

Davie, Donald. A Gathered Church. The Literature of the
    English Dissenting Interest, 1700-1930. New York:
    Oxford University Press, 1978

Defoe, Daniel. A Tour through the Whole Island of Great
    Britain, ed. Pat Rogers. Harmondsworth, Middlesex:
    Penguin Books, Ltd., 1971.

Downes, Kerry. Hawksmoor. New York and Washington:
    Prager Publishers, 1969

_____. The Architecture of Wren. New York:
    Universe Books, 1982

Downey, James. The Eighteenth-Century Pulpit. A Study
    of Butler, Berkeley, Secker, Sterne, Whitefield, and
    Wesley. Oxford: The Clarendon Press, 1969.

Escott, Harry. Isaac Watts, Hymnographer. London:
    Independent Press, 1962

George, M. Dorothy (Mrs. Eric). London Life in the
    Eighteenth Century. New York: Alfred A. Knopf, 1926.

Gwilt, Joseph. The Encyclopaedia of Architecture: His-
    torical, Theoretical, and Practical. 1842; rpt. New
    York: Bonanza Books, 1982.

Hare, Augustus J.C. Walks in London. 2 vols. London:

George Allen, 1894.

Harrison, G. Elsie. Son to Susanna. The Private Life of John Wesley. Nashville: Cokesbury Press, 1938.

Hawkins, Sir John. The Life of Samuel Johnson, LL.D., ed. Bertram Davis. New York: The Macmillan Company, 1961.

Hibbert, Christopher. The English: A Social History, 1066-1945. New York and London: W.W. Norton and Company, 1987.

Hill, Douglas. A Hundred Years of Georgian London. London: Macdonald and Company, 1970.

Humphreys, A.R. The Augustan World. Society, Thought, and Letters in Eighteenth-Century England. New York: Harper and Row, 1963.

Hurd, Richard, D.D. (ed.). The Works of the Right Honourable Joseph Addison. A New Edition. 6 vols. London: T. Cadell and W. Davies, 1811

Hymans, Edward. Capability Brown and Humphry Repton. New York: Charles H. Scribner's Sons, 1971.

Kent, William (ed.). An Encylopaedia of London. New York: E.P. Dutton and Company, Inc., 1937.

_____. London for Everyman. London and Toronto: J.M. Dent and Sons, Ltd., 1931.

Latham, Robert, and William Matthews (eds.). The Diary of Samuel Pepys. 11 vols. Berkeley and Los Angeles: University of California Press, 1970-1983.

Lecky, William Edward Hartpole. A History of England in the Eighteenth Century, 3rd ed., rev. 8 vols. London: Longmans, Green, and Company, 1883-1890.

Lewis, Wilmarth Sheldon. Three Tours through London in the Years 1748, 1776, 1797. 1941; rpt. Westport, Connecticut: Greenwood Press, 1971.

Little, David M., and George M. Karhl (eds.). The Letters of David Garrick. 3 vols. London: Oxford University Press, 1963

Livingstone, Elizabeth A. (ed.). The Concise Oxford Dic-
    tionary of the Christian Church. Oxford: Oxford Uni-
    University Press, 1977.

Lunn, Arnold. John Wesley. New York: The Dial Press,
    1929.

Minutes of the Methodist Conferences, from the First,
    Held in London, by the Late Rev. John Wesley, A.M.
    London: Mason, 1862.

Ollard, S.A. Dictionary of English Church History.
    1912; 3rd ed., rev. London: A.R. Mowbray and Co.,
    Ltd., 1948.

Osborn, George (ed.). The Poetical Works of John and
    Charles Wesley. 13 vols. London: Wesleyan Methodist
    Conference Office, 1868-1872.

Pevsner, Nikolaus. Christopher Wren. 1632-1723. New
    York: Universe Books, 1960.

Phillips, Hugh. Mid-Georgian London. London: Collins,
    1964.

A Pictorial and Descriptive Guide to London. London:
    Ward, Lock, and Company, n.d. [c. 1936].

The Pictorial Handbook of London. Comprising Its Anti-
    quities, Architecture, Arts, Manufacture, Trade,
    Social, Literary, and Scientific Institutions,
    Exhibitions, and Galleries of Art. London: Henry G.
    Bohn, 1854.

Plomer, Henry G., et al. A Dictionary of the Printers
    and Booksellers Who Were at Work in England, Scot-
    land, and Ireland from 1688 to 1725. London: The Bib-
    liographical Society, 1968.

_____, G.H. Bushnell, and E.R. McC. Dix. A
    Dictionary of the Printers and Booksellers Who Were
    at Work in England, Scotland, and Ireland from 1726
    to 1775. London: The Bibliographical Society, 1968.

Pottle, Frederick A. (ed.). Boswell's London Journal,

1762-1763. New York: McGraw -Hill Book Company, Inc.,
    1950.

Pratt, Helen Marshall. Westminster Abbey. Its Architec-
    ture, History, and Monuments, 2 vols. New York: Duf-
    field and Company, 1911.

Rasmussen, Steen Eiler. London: The Unique City. 1934;
    rpt. Cambridge, Massachusetts: The M.I.T. Press, 1967.

Riddaway, T.F. The Rebuilding of London after the Great
    Fire. 1940; rpt. London: Edward Arnold and Company,
    1951.

Robertson, C. Grant. England under the Hanoverians.
    8th ed. London: Methuen and Company, Ltd., 1927.

Rogal, Samuel J. John and Charles Wesley. Boston: G.K.
    Hall (Twayne Publishers), 1983.

Routley, Erik. The Musical Wesleys. London: Herbert
    Jenkins, 1968.

Rude, George. Hanoverian London: 1714-1808. Berkeley
    and Los Angeles: University of California Press, 1971.

Ryskamp, Charles, and Frederick A. Pottle (eds.).
    Boswell: The Ominous Years (1774-1776). London: William
    Heinemann Ltd., 1963.

Seckler, Eduard F. Wren and His Place in European Archi-
    tecture. New York: The Macmillan Company, 1956.

Southey, Robert. The Life of John Wesley and the Rise
    and Progress of Methodism. London: George Bell and
    Sons, 1901.

Stephen, Sir Leslie. History of English Thought in the
    Eighteenth Century, 2 vols. 1876; rpt. London:
    Rupert Hart-Davis, 1962
    _____, and Sidney Lee (eds.). Dictionary
    of National Biography, 63 vols. London, 1885-1900.

Summerson, John. Architecture in Britain. 1530 to 1830.
    Harmondsworth, Middlesex: Penguin Books, Limited,
    1953.

_____. Georgian London: An Architectural
Study. New York: Praeger Publishers, 1962.

Telford, John (ed.). The Letters of the Rev. John Wesley,
M.A. 8 vols. London: The Epworth Press, 1931.

_____. The Life of the Rev. Charles Wesley,
M.A. London: Wesleyan Methodist Book Room, 1900.

_____. The Life of John Wesley. London: Hodder
and Stoughton, 1886.

Tyerman, Luke. The Life and Times of the Rev. John Wesley,
M.A., Founder of the Methodists. 3 vols. New
York: Harper and Brothers, 1872.

Watts, Michael R. The Dissenters. From the Reformation
to the French Revolution. Oxford: At the Clarendon
Press, 1978.

Weinreb, Ben, and Christopher Hibbert (eds.). The London
Encyclopaedia. London: Macmillan London, 1983.

Wellsman, John (ed.). Panorama of London, 1749. From
an original engraving made by the Buck Brothers in
1749. London: Sidgwick and Jackson, 1972.

Wesley, John. Sermons, ed. Albert C. Outler. 4 vols.
Nashville, Tennessee: Abingdon Press, 1984-1987.

_____. Sermons on Several Occasions, ed. Thomas
Jackson. 2 vols. New York: Carlton and Phillips,
1854.

_____. The Works of John Wesley, ed. Thomas Jackson.
14 vols. 3rd ed. London: The Wesleyan Methodist
Book Room, 1872.

Wimsatt, William K., Jr., and Frederick A. Pottle.
Boswell for the Defence, 1769-1774. London: William
Heinemann, Ltd., 1959.

INDEX OF BIBLICAL REFERENCES

Genesis
3:19   191, 205
6:3   179, 301
6:5   80, 375
17:1   142
27:38   179
28:20   308
28:22   342
32   220
49:4   125, 190, 315
49:5   82

Exodus
3:14   286
14:3   164
14:15   88
32:10   52, 170
14:16   312
34:6   291

Leviticus
26:11   343
26:34   80

Numbers
13   50
23:10   50, 289, 299,
        308, 344

Deuteronomy
10:12   48, 54, 57-58,
        122-123, 308-309
12:10   28
29:12   197

Joshua
10:12   185

1 Samuel
17   92, 195, 377
21:8   361

2 Samuel
24:17   215-216

1 Kings
2:21   346
5:13   163
8   140
18:21   55, 78, 157, 159
19   67, 166

2 Kings
5:10   143
5:11   300
5:12   79, 158, 159

Nehemiah
1:10   291-292
13:16   86, 193

Job
5:18   366
6:27   214
7:18   121
22:21   64, 301, 361
28:28   292

Psalms
2:12   303
4:6   169
4:7   169
8   303
9:17   192
10:4   65, 180
10:12   343

Psalms (cont'd)

10:14	59
14:1	96
16:4	187
23	302-303, 373
25:13	80
29	168
29:10	164
31:1	254-255
33:4	172
33:6	172
34:8	74, 222, 262, 376
34:10	297
34:11	97
35:27	87, 127
37:1	68, 69, 262
40:16	365
42	303
46:2	168
46:7	168
46:10	50
49:6	79
50:13	125
50:22	56, 292
51:8	86
51:9	86
61:2	284
61:4	284-285
62:1	85, 193, 205, 306
66:18	67
68:1	317
69:30	288

69:33	306
71:4	187
71:14	301-311
74:20	317
75:1	128
75:2	128
76:11	69
77:3	204, 317
78:9	287
81:1	218
84:1	283
84:11	375
90:4	213
90:12	27, 288, 299
91:11	73, 74
93	303
93:1	76, 307
96:1	188
96:2	188
101:1	70, 72
101:2	70, 72, 81, 124
103:2	84, 192
103:3	318
103:13	174
103:19	323
107	228
107:2	195, 318
115	177
116:12	169
188:28	54, 172
119:137	190
120:5	348
122:6	276
122:9	276

Psalms (cont'd)

130:1	288
130:7	306, 376
130:8	306, 376
138:7	156, 172-173
139	53
141:3	89
144	185-186, 308
147	26
147:3	29, 120, 218
147:20	66, 220

Proverbs

2:1	81, 192
2:5	192
2:6	81
3:17	127
4:23	180
12:27	75-76
19:7	64-65
22	217
23:23	76, 182
28:14	53

Ecclesiastes

3:18	127
4:1	185
4:2	185
6:12	60
9:10	172, 314
11:1	65, 122
12:13	345

Isaiah

1	203
1:3	93, 121, 125, 186, 263
1:18	34-35
2	203
2:22	93
3	203
3:10	214
5:6	255
9:6	171
9:11	342
11:9	148, 203
19:11	144
24:4	190
24:6	183, 220-221
24:15	222
24:16	222
24:17	183, 340
26:8	311
26:12	93
26:20	221
26:21	72
30:18	53, 211, 315
30:20	286
35:8	343
38:18	82
40:1	70, 82, 189
40:6	170
40:8	170
40:28	316
42:19	63, 300
44:22	73
45:22	365
49:22	167
51:11	77
51:12	221
51:16	193-194

Isaiah (cont'd)

51:22	77
53:5	77, 316
53:6	77
55:1	153, 212
55:6	345, 351
55:7	27, 49, 218, 286
58:5	123, 204
58:6	123-124
58:10	182
58:12	49, 204
58:13	49
59:1	142
59:2	142
60:18	288
62:11	164, 297, 344
66:8	167

Jeremiah

?:?	183
4:1	220, 221, 222
4:2	220, 221
4:9	221, 222
5:29	61-62, 181
6:13	67
8:20	192
8:22	28
18:5	67
18:22	27
23:6	71, 81, 312
50:4	69
50:5	69

Lamentations

| 3:39 | 124 |

Ezekiel

18:31	158, 158-159
33	349
36:25	227
37:1	123, 220

Daniel

3	96, 210
4:1	183
4:27	190-191
7:9	171
9:7	71
9:24	81

Hosea

11	367
13	339
14:4	34, 156, 185, 224, 263, 340-341, 376

Joel

2:12	84, 164
2:13	87, 126-127
2:14	90
2:16	65

Amos

| 4:12 | 72, 207 |
| 5 | 217 |

Micah

2:10	254
6	136
6:7	26, 35
6:8	142-143, 222, 269, 304
6:8	182, 303, 375

Habakkuk

| 2:5 | 75 |

Haggai
  2:7   73, 144, 188
Zechariah
  4:7   195, 318
  12:10   366
  13   338-339
Malachi
  3:2   59, 175, 296
  3:3   223

Matthew
  1:21   61, 141-142,
          307-308
  1:22   372
  3:2   350
  3:8   61, 73
  3:10   156
  3:12   88-89, 316-317
  4:3   294
  4:7   303
  5:2   224
  5:4   224, 338
  5:20   297, 350
  5:48   194
  6:13   171
  6:20   66
  6:24   74
  7   372
  7:8   317, 339
  7:14   361
  7:16   308
  7:20   92
  7:24   277

  8:2   165, 377
  8:3   165
  8:13   378
  8:19   183
  9:2   252-253
  9:5   277, 304
  9:11   284
  9:13   284, 354
  9:22   70-71
  9:24   77
  10:13   186
  10:16   65
  10:21   78, 187, 264
  10:32   263, 377
  10:34   168
  11   289
  11:12   263, 299
  11:25   50, 77
  11:28   27, 81, 87, 154, 202
  12   270
  12:22   190, 343
  12:26   226
  12:42   181
  12:43   61, 297-298
  13:3   211
  13:9   221
  13:16   158
  13:27   73, 74, 304
  14:31   210
  15:20   177
  15:28   90, 377
  16:23   64, 210, 220, 375
  16:26   27, 234
  17   294

Matthew (cont'd)   Mark
  17:20 209, 314   1:1   221
  18:3   77, 86   1:5   187
  18:15 59, 124-125, 175,   1:15   26, 226
         375   2:11   71
  18:35 175   2:17   80, 284
  19:21 211   2:18   181, 303
  19:22 190   2:26   202
  19:29 61, 298   3:8   338
  20   289   4:1   62, 298
  20:12 188, 312   4:26   122, 223, 312
  20:15 84, 87, 95, 315   4:27   177
  20:16 194, 222, 254,   4:36   163
         351   6:12   186, 308
  20:17 304   8:38   221
  21:21 88, 379   9:23   127, 179, 195, 196
  22:4   124, 263-264   9:24   65
  22:12 192, 213   9:44   158
  22:20 343   10   54
  22:21 55, 134   11:24 83-84
  22:27 197   12:32 370, 380
  22:37 92, 146   12:34 120, 122, 360
  22:39 147, 209   13   191
  23   294   13:27 305
  23:23 72   15:17 181
  23:37 72-73, 89   16:6   209
  24:4   26   Luke
  24:17 210   1:6   191
  24:37 314   1:26   54
  25:1   61, 289, 297   1:58   289
  25:34 177   1:68   176
  26:12 80   1:72   211, 299
  26:46 190   2   307
  27   303   2:14   95

Luke (cont'd)

2:21	48
2:42	219
3:8	167
5:13	194, 317
5:31	284
5:32	221
6	301
6:1	303
6:22	304
7	227
7:16	183-184
7:36	26, 289
7:41	184
7:42	177, 263, 321
8:10	83, 205
8:14	213
8:18	62, 211
8:25	289
8:48	312
9:23	149, 182
9:55	141, 166, 175, 296
10:11	189
10:23	169, 309
10:28	191
10:42	93, 127, 180, 254, 305, 348, 349, 365
12:7	70, 340
12:13	317
12:19	50
12:20	63-64, 71, 91
12:42	121
13:1	301
13:2	90
13:4	221
13:12	224
13:23	56
13:24	66
13:27	218
14:20	314
15:7	42, 110, 121, 174
15:11	26
15:22	91-92
16	253
16:2	227
16:3	187, 342
16:9	52, 76, 170
16:12	167
16:26	25
16:31	63, 174, 211, 223-224
17:6	186
17:20	128, 305
18:10	95
18:12	157
18:14	187
18:18	227
18:41	188-189
18:42	68, 172
19	302
19:1	295
19:17	71
19:41	68
20:1	303
20:34	206
21	189

Luke (cont'd)

21:34 69-70, 72, 219,
       340, 381
21:36 72
22:24 164
22:31 165
22:37 70
23:39 305
23:43 222
24   339
24:8   121, 310
24:25 309
24:48 318
24:49 155

John

1   165
1:47   67
2   165
3   165
3:7   55, 66, 174, 226,
       314, 343, 349
3:8   123, 295
3:14   55
3:16   197
4   165
4:13   26, 165
4:14   296, 307
4:24   28, 81, 218, 220,
       222, 234, 320,
       377
4:34   189
5:5   321
5:6   321
5:12   56

5:25   136, 187-188, 311-
       312
5:39   191-192
6:27   255
6:28   166
6:29   306
6:37   265
6:38   166
6:40   339
6:45   26
6:69   184
7:7   166
7:17   166, 186
7:37   121, 137, 155,157,
       309, 318
8:12   206, 210
8:29   67
8:31   347
8:32   66
8:36   70
9   165, 227-228, 292,
       302
10:12 168
11:25 296
11:26 186
11:36 373
11:47 263
11:48 121, 212, 218, 287,
       295
11:49 122
13:27 75, 306
13:28 183, 219
14   135-136
14:1   286, 374

John (cont'd)

14:2	310
14:6	195
14:16	54, 174
14:21	54-55, 174
14:22	156-157, 373
14:27	186
15	67, 339
15:1	287
15:2	71
15:7	210
15:16	74-75
15:17	67
15:21	171-172
15:22	63
16	293
16:8	56
16:9	338
16:22	55, 63, 292
16:27	291
17:3	28, 52, 120, 136, 170, 173, 218, 262, 290
18:11	291, 375
18:13	173
18:28	340
18:36	55, 173
19:5	174
19:10	311
20	306
20:18	263
20:25	184
20:27	76
20:29	292

21:15	310
21:19	88, 318
21:22	60

Acts

1:4	68
1:8	71, 71-72
1:25	87, 266
2	302, 322, 353
2:8	321-322
2:14	88
2:28	293
2:42	76
3:12	43, 46
3:26	68
4	322
4:2	313
4:10	182
5	322
5:18	293
5:30	34
5:31	155
5:32	310
6	322
6:1	306
6:8	307
7	322
7:55	320
8	323
8:5	293
8:13	69
9:31	84-85, 193
10:35	125
11	163-164
11:21	81

Acts (cont'd)

11:26	27, 218, 224, 226, 262-263
11:32	160
13	367, 372
14	323
14:22	193, 316
15:8	69
15:18	302
15:27	318
16:22	290
16:31	153, 212, 229, 323, 365
17	323
17:8	205
17:10	191
17:20	371
17:23	60, 288
17:27	205
17:30	211
18	323
18:17	311
18:19	125
19	323-324
19:2	311
20	324
20:27	369
20:28	38
21	324
21:14	316
22	324
22:16	93, 170, 220, 293-294, 345
23	324

24:14	60
24:16	84
24:25	132
24:26	297
24:27	300, 314
26	324
26:8	50, 169, 266
26:18	65, 183, 355
26:23	73
26:24	60-61, 324
26:25	294
26:27	136
28	324-325
28:22	34, 57, 153-154, 297, 313, 365

Romans

?:?	316
1	43
1:3	69
1:16	320, 335
2	43
2:23	54, 285
2:28	57
3	43-44
3:1	219
3:10	196
3:19	180, 265, 337
3:21	372
3:22	29, 90, 120, 262, 294
3:23	244
3:28	193
4:5	44, 349

Romans (cont'd)

4:7	65, 291
4:13	76-77
5	44
5:14	44
6	44
6:1	37
6:3	374
6:4	167-168, 374
6:23	64, 91, 158, 179, 308
7	44-45, 284
7:4	196
7:24	92
8	46
8:1	45
8:2	45
8:4	45
8:7	45
8:13	179, 304
8:15	45-46, 367
8:16	46
8:18	66-67
8:21	179
8:22	51
8:29	45
8:30	45
8:32	149
8:33	120, 360
9	294
9:32	244
10	78-79
10:4	195, 196, 264, 315, 318, 373
10:7	335
10:13	291
11:6	367
11:33	173, 325
12:1	144, 344
12:2	57, 125-126, 185
12:5	91, 193
12:11	82
12:21	80, 122, 188
13	265
13:1	164
13:8	145
13:10	289, 317, 352
13:11	51, 60, 118
13:12	78, 145
13:14	167
14:7	91, 126, 254, 266
14:17	34, 61, 154
14:23	85-86, 126
15:2	184
15:4	64, 95
15:5	52, 56, 95, 167
15:6	52-53
15:9	171
16:16	314

1 Corinthians

1:14	276
1:17	61
1:24	121, 182, 315, 339
1:27	68
1:30	291, 381
2:5	55, 173
2:12	92, 343
2:14	49, 223, 288, 308

1 Corinthians (cont'd)   206, 295, 315, 341

   3:8   311   14:20 61

   3:11   35, 277   15   324

   3:12   194, 344   15:19 83, 181, 298, 339

   4:7   301   15:20 78

   4:12   86   15:33 289

   5:8   178-179   15:55 254

   5:11   86   15:56 170

   5:18   181   2 Corinthians

   6:2   186   1:22   298, 305

   6:3   186   2:2   50-51

   6:9   58, 220, 266,   3   308
          294
                             3:8   83
   6:19   82-83, 262, 289-
          290, 342   3:17   366

   7:29   61, 86, 126   3:18   25

   7:35   126, 194   4:1   372

   7:37   126   4:5   276

   9:22   194-195, 196   4:6   25, 26

   9:24   79-80   4:18   245

   9:27   178, 300, 344   5:7   35

   10:12 145, 308   5:8   63, 375

   10:21 83   5:15   121

   10:22 66   5:17   73, 96, 243, 315,
                                    373
   12:7   179, 300
                             5:18   122, 156, 345
   13   350
                             5:19   89, 264, 351, 355
   13:1   50, 137, 228,
          241, 367, 271,   6   289, 352
          342
                             6:1   96, 213, 227, 299,
   13:2   50   300

   13:3   50, 212, 218   6:2   182, 206

   13:10 77, 186   7:1   286, 307, 308

   13:13 28, 51, 112-113,   8:9   27
          124, 186, 205-
                             9:10   63

                             10:5   89, 341

11:2	80		5:25	123
11:3	86-87, 315		6	366
11:14	87		6:3	92
13:5	55-56		6:12	127
13:8	49		6:14	29, 66, 73, 74,
13:14	301			157, 202, 255, 289,
Galatians				298, 369
1:3	345		6:15	146, 299, 300
1:4	307		6:16	155
2:17	68, 70, 285		**Ephesians**	
2:20	87, 305		1:10	171
3:3	88		1:12	305
3:12	89		1:13	55, 205, 346
3:20	127		2:1	307
3:22	29, 120, 127-		2:2	25-26, 285
	128, 150, 229		2:8	30, 95, 142, 268,
4:3	53-54			336, 344, 358-359,
4:4	57, 128			379
4:5	60		2:9	194
4:10	344		2:11	166
4:18	83, 90		2:12	166, 197
4:19	172		2:13	166, 184
4:30	91		2:17	166
5	194		2:19	66, 88
5:1	222, 301		3:1	189
5:5	90, 146, 195		3:3	90
5:6	91, 202, 317,		3:13	320
	344, 359		3:14	77
5:16	303		4	226, 227
5:18	51, 122, 157,		4:1	64, 177
	205		4:3	74, 95
5:22	55, 87, 91, 157,		4:22	76
	174, 192		4:28	64
5:23	304		4:29	74

Ephesians (cont'd)   3:1   89
  4:30   90, 92, 96, 195   3:3   57, 203, 285, 293,
  5:1   97   307
  5:2   97   3:8   56-57, 91
  5:8   78   3:9   58
  5:12   317   3:10   51, 58, 63, 169-
  5:14   380   170, 290
  5:15   206, 212, 221   3:11   58
  5:16   67, 84, 170   3:13   195-196, 373
  5:24   316   3:14   58
  5:29   192   3:17   179
  6   163   3:19   311
  6:10   144, 184, 293   3:20   58, 78, 166, 213
  6:11   184, 213, 301   4:4   84
  6:12   192   4:7   58, 79, 212-213,
  6:13   62   294, 374, 376
  6:14   62, 77   Colossians
Philippians   1   175
  1:4   203   1:9   299
  1:9   64, 189, 206,   1:10   96
           212, 291   1:12   294-295
  1:12   189   1:14   75, 222
  1:13   58   2   175
  1:21   64, 114, 127   2:6   182, 301
  1:23   52   2:9   59
  1:27   56, 292, 374   2:10   295
  1:29   203-204   3:4   59, 175, 255
  1:30   56   3:5   317
  2:1   292   3:9   123
  2:2   292   3:10   147, 298
  2:5   187   3:11   59, 295, 296
  2:16   28   3:16   59-60, 296
  2:17   28   3:18   60
  3   135, 174   3:22   124

Colossians (cont'd)

  3:23   346

  4:5   123

1 Thessalonians

  ?:?   176

  1:4   154

  3:3   375

  3:11   309

  3:12   309

  4:1   146, 189

  4:3   210, 212

  4:7   54, 90, 173

  4:8   81

  4:13   78

  5:12   62

  5:16   181, 219

  5:19   62, 178, 292,
           295, 302

2 Thessalonians

  1   296

  2   177, 286

  2:1   295

  2:7   76, 184

  3   177

  3:5   311

1 Timothy

  1   177

  1:5   96, 196-197, 320

  1:7   226

  1:8   180, 265, 342

  2   177

  2:4   34

  3   177-178

  3:16   156, 264, 309,

         318

  4:1   182

  4:5   68, 92

  4:6   68

  4:7   304

  4:8   70, 182, 319-320

  6:6   219

  6:17   58, 175, 295-296

2 Timothy

  ?:?   183

  1:6   304

  1:7   291, 292-293

  2:4   219, 221, 340

  2:6   81, 124, 312

  2:11   340

  2:19   285

  2:20   75

  3:4   68, 209

  3:5   216, 262, 340

  3:12   306

  3:16   298, 305

  4:5   74, 310

Titus

  ?:?   187

  2:11   68

  2:12   145

  2:14   181, 264-265, 293,
         302

  2:15   122

  3:5   53, 171

  3:8   154, 366

Hebrews

  1:1   88

  1:4   88-89

1:14	296, 313	9:11	78
2:1	87, 127, 245	9:12	312
2:3	296	9:13	54, 59, 91, 126,
2:4	72, 250		173, 285-286
2:13	285	9:14	343
2:15	48	9:27	150, 158, 183, 219,
3	350		262, 340, 361, 376
3:7	68, 343, 375	10:19	142, 164, 337
3:9	310	10:22	337-338
3:12	176	10:35	52, 380
3:13	178, 300	10:36	78, 244, 245, 286-
3:14	79, 264, 376		287, 306, 374
3:15	70	10:38	51
4:9	48	11:1	82, 342, 343
4:11	372	12	351
4:12	165, 219	12:1	62, 290, 318
4:13	310	12:2	52, 287-288, 290,
4:14	219		374
5:12	62, 143, 316,	12:3	290
	373-374	12:5	52, 92, 290
5:13	301	12:6	52, 190
5:14	69	12:14	245
6:1	93, 172, 341	12:22	290
6:4	293, 302	12:24	341
6:5	293	12:28	67, 120, 145, 255,
6:10	49		262, 287, 343
6:11	49, 143	13	269
7:15	157	13:1	53, 180, 302
7:19	91, 125, 314	13:8	79
7:25	157	13:9	53, 184
8:10	287, 313	13:14	171
8:11	121, 156, 202,	13:20	79, 144, 264, 302
	381	13:21	144
9	169		

James

1:27	81-82, 205, 313
2:4	175
2:12	85, 172
2:14	287, 313
2:22	57, 123, 313
2:26	231
2:27	231
3:2	86, 126, 194, 197, 266
3:17	145, 181, 196, 369
4:4	184-185
4:14	306-307, 376
4:16	341
4:17	175
5:20	88

1 Peter

1:1	312
1:2	188, 312
1:3	312
1:4	300
1:6	63, 69, 178
1:9	79, 92, 127, 195, 223, 264, 318, 321, 366
1:13	176
1:14	188
1:18	210
1:24	122, 254
2:1	120, 292, 342
2:2	52, 170, 290
2:7	376
2:12	290, 302

2:13	80
2:14	342
2:24	63
3	189
3:3	170
3:8	124, 189
3:17	265
3:18	205, 265-266
3:22	276
4	338
4:2	187
4:3	313
4:7	26, 114, 190, 287
4:8	190
4:10	195
4:11	82
4:12	175
4:17	84
4:18	254, 294
4:19	83
5	189, 190
5:5	83
5:8	188, 312, 344
5:12	314

2 Peter

?:?	192
1:16	176-177, 307
2:14	173
2:15	173
3:5	180
3:7	66, 180
3:8	85, 125, 193, 315
3:10	85, 176, 193, 265
3:11	93

2 Peter (cont'd)

3:17	125
3:18	85, 125

1 John

1	325, 330
1:1	180, 302
1:3	65, 155, 276, 293
1:7	76, 79, 185, 223
1:9	104, 319
2:1	93, 196, 318
2:3	288
2:12	313-314
2:13	290
2:20	93
3:1	49, 124, 288, 297, 350, 377
3:7	66
3:8	60, 80, 160, 176, 265, 369
3:9	76, 253
3:22	127
4:3	223
4:7	178
4:13	311
4:19	55, 229
5:3	28, 268
5:5	291
5:7	27, 156, 178
5:11	28, 227, 238, 335, 367
5:12	28, 57, 238, 265
5:19	53, 92, 302, 317
5:20	294

2 John

8	346

Jude

3	176, 286
22	92, 317

Revelation

1:5	197
1:8	188
3:1	145
3:6	90, 171
7:8	92
7:9	51, 75
7:10	75
7:13	86
14	43, 46
14:1	73, 320, 345-346
14:4	53
14:5	53
17:15	51
19:8	70
19:9	75
20	27
20:1	196
20:8	120, 196
20:11	176
20:12	254, 334-335
21:4	179-180
21:6	214
22	155
22:1	177
22:17	26, 118, 223

INDEX OF NAMES, PLACES AND EVENTS

Abney, Sir Thomas 22–23

Act of Settlement 151

Acton, J. Adams 248

Adam, James 239–240

Adam, John 239–240

Adam, Robert 239–240, 362, 392

Addison, Joseph 101, 129, 232, 246, 250, 386

Adelphi, The 239–240

Admiralty Court 149

Africa 330

Agutter, Jonathan 101

Aix-la-Chapelle, Treaty of 237, 391

Albert Embankment 281

Albert Square 353

Aldersgate Street 128–131, 281, 390

Alfred, King 117

Algiers 333

Alison, Archibald 397

All Hallows, Lombard Street 267–269, 407

All-Hallows-on-the-Wall 147–148

All Hallows the Great, Upper Thames Street 332, 406

All Hallows, Watling Street 406

All Saints, Oxford 129

Allen, Edmund 115

Allen, Rev. Fifield 131

Allestree, Richard 155

Almonry 250

American Revolution 395

Amsterdam 137

Ancaster, Duke of 358

Anglican Church. See under Church of England

Anglo-Austrian Alliance 261

Anne, Queen 6, 105, 200, 231, 333, 387

Anson, Admiral George 390

Archenholz, Johann W. von 7

Archer, Thomas 243

Arlington House 238

Armstrong, Colonel 161

Armstrong, John 241

Arne, Thomas Augustine 237

Arthur Street 269

Austin, John 233

Austrian Succession, War of 237, 390

Avison, Charles 237

Ayerst, Dr. William 275–276

Bacharach, Lower Palatinate 129

Bacon, Sir Francis 332

Bailey, Arthur 352

Baptist's Head, Saint
    John's Lane 100- 101

Barbault, Rev. Thomas L.
    134

Barbon, Nicholas 47

Barclay and Perkin's Brew-
    ery 321

"Barn," Deptford 372

Barnard Castle, Yorkshire
    207

Barningham, Yorkshire 207

Basilica of Maxentius,
    Rome 273

Bateman, Richard Thomas
    113

Bath 242, 270, 328

Bath, Lady 359

Battersea 363-364

Battersea Bridge 4

Bear Yard, Sheffield Street
    97-98

Bedford, Rev. Arthur 134-
    135

Bedford, Francis, Fifth
    Earl of 240

Bedlam. See Mary of Be-
    thlehem, Hospital of

Beech Lane, Whitecross
    Street 118-119

Belgravia 6

Bell, George 207, 345

Bellamy, George Anne 369-
    370

Belle-Isle 391

Bennet, Earl of Arlington 238

Bentham, Jeremy 395, 397

Berkeley, George 11, 386,392

Berkeley, John 331

Bermondsey Mission 282

Berridge, Rev. John 206

Bethnal Green 5, 215-224

Bexley 374

Binknell, June 319

Bishopsgate 150,152,198

Bishopsgate Street 272

Blackfriars 256

Blackfriars Bridge 4

Blackfriars Road 283

Blackstone, Sir William
    101, 393

Blackwell 6, 354

Blair, Hugh 257

Blair, Robert 396

Blake, Reverend John
    137

Blenheim Palace 239

Bloomsbury 6, 39ff

Bloomsbury Square 6

Bohler, Peter 106, 358

Bolt Court, Fleet Street
    115-117, 146

Bolton 22

Bond Street 233

Bonner, Edmund 217

Bonner's House, Bethnal
    Green 217-224, 245

Book of Common Prayer
    108

Borough High Street,
    Southwark 282

Bosanquet, Mary 24

Boston 216

Boston Port Bill 394

Boston Tea Party 395

Boswell, James 14-15,
    109, 112, 115-116,
    199, 232, 240, 242,
    249, 251, 257-258, 273,
    336-337, 398

Boulogne Harbor 119

Bow 6, 228, 229

Bower Street 353

Boyce, William 237

Boyle, Richard, Lord Bur-
    lington 6, 249, 275

Bray, John 129, 131, 389

Bray, Thomas 273

Bread Street 270

Brentford 97

Bretagne, John, Duke of
    129

Brewer Street, Goswell
    Road 104

Bridewell Prison 103,
    256

Bristol 6, 24, 235, 390

British Museum 39-40, 241,
    392

Brixton 5, 367

Broad Street 353

Bromley 385

Brompton 232

Brompton Park Nursery 232

Brompton Road 234

Brown, Tom 30

Brown, William 378

Brune, Roas 200

Brune, Walter 200

Buckingham 247

Buckingham House 238

Buckingham Palace 239

Buckingham, Rev. William
    208-209

Bull and Mouth Inn 119

Bullock, Rev. Richard 241

Bunker Hill 216

Bunyan, John 261

Burch, Dr. Thomas 331-332

Burgoyne, Gen. John 395

Burke, Edmund 392, 394,
    397

Burlington House 6

Burnet, Gilbert 387

Burney, Dr. Charles 240,
    395

Burney, Mrs. Charles 199

Burney, Frances 242

Burton, Mrs. 336

Butcher Hall Lane 119

Butcher Row 353

Butcher, Samuel 283
Butler, Bishop Joseph
    11, 348, 389
Butler, Joseph the youn-
    ger 348
Butler, Samuel 241
Butterfield, William 349

Caesar, Sir Julius 149
Calvinist Methodists
    191, 209, 238, 371,
    372, 394
Camberwell 5, 367-368,
    380
Cambridge University 386
Cannon Street 275
Cannon Street Station
    269
Canterbury 310
Canterbury Tales 259
Carnaby Market 238
Caroline of Anspach 231
Catherine of Braganza
    333
Catholic Relief Act 141
Cavendish, Henry 394
Caxton, William 250
Cennick, John 372
Centlivre, Susannah 241
Central Criminal Court
    108
Central Markets 111
Chambers, Sir William 392

Chandler, Mr. 278
Chandos House 266
Chapel Royal, the Strand
    251-252
Chapman, George 328
Chapman, Mr. 328
Chapman, Rev. William 328
Charing Cross 7, 43, 229
Charing Cross Road 47
Charles I 98
Charles II 5, 14, 119, 155,
    252, 333, 362
Charles Edward, Prince 48,
    164, 391, 397
Charles Square, Hoxton 135-
    137
Charles Street, Hoxton 135
Charlotte, Queen 239
Charterhouse School 101-
    102, 239, 386, 387
Chatterton, Thomas 112
Chaucer, Geoffrey 259
Cheapside 270
Chelsea 6, 232, 357-363,
    364
Chelsea College 362
Chelsea Hospital 362
Chelsea Physic Garden 363
Chester Street 236
Chesterfield Street, Mary-
    lebone 37-38, 144
Cheyne, Lord 358
Children's Home, Bonner
    Road 217

Chippendale, Thomas   392
Christ Church, Newgate
    Street   406
Christ Church, Oxford
    101, 113, 386-387
Christ Church, Spital-
    fields   214
Christ Hospital   332
Church, Brother   372
Church, Sister   372
Church of England   10,
    11, 12, 13, 14, 16,
    128, 130, 150, 159,
    206, 250, 268, 309,
    379-380
Church Street, Wapping
    347
Churchill, John, Duke of
    Marlborough   161
Churchill, Charles   249
Cibber, Colley   20
City Road   100, 398
City Road Chapel   111,
    138-147, 163, 282,
    283, 395
Clapham   5, 380-381
Clapham Sect   381
Clare Market   97-98
Clare, Mr.   30
Clark, Adylena   29-30
Clark, George   30
Clarke, Virginia   20
Clarkson, Thomas   397
Clavel, Sister   372

Claxton, Marshall, 22, 213-
    214
Clerkenwell Green   103
Clink Street, Southwark
    283
Clippingdale, Mrs.   354
Clive, Robert   392
Clugni, Abbots of   130
Clulow, William   19
Coade's Factory   252
Cochrane, William   257
Cock Lane, Shoreditch   138
Cock Lane, Smithfield   138
Cock Lane, York Street   138
Colebrook, James   20
Colebrook, Row, Islington
    100
Colet, John   228
College Graveyard, South-
    wark   283
Colley, Rev. Benjamin   206
Collins, William   20
Commercial Road, East   353
Commons Journals   138
Compton, Bishop Henry   112,
    401
Concord   216
Constantine, Emperor   149
Cornhill   272, 277
Cornwall   158
Cornwallis, Charles   397
Cornwallis, Frederick   400
Couse, Kenton   381
Covent Garden   240, 370

Covent Garden Theatre 388
Coverlet Fields   225
Cowper, William   99,
   395
Cox, James   241
Cox's Museum, Spring
   Gardens   241-243
Crabbe, George   11
Crichton, Michael   236-
   237
Cripplegate   16, 152
Crooked Lane   269
Crosby Sir John   149
Crosby, Lady   149
Croutch, Mr.   270
Crowe, Rev. Dr. William
   151
Croxall, Dr. Samuel   274
Crucifix Lane, Bermond-
   sey   283
Culloden, Battle of   364,
   391
Cut-throat Lane, Stoke
   Newington   22

Dance, George the elder
   5, 10, 137, 150, 216
Dance, George the younger
   10, 148
Daniel, Mary, 257
Davies, Rev. Howell   113
Davies, Tom   241

Day, Thomas   283
Deal   1
Debonair, Susanna   141
Declaration of Independence
   272, 395
Defoe, Daniel   1, 22, 29,
   30,33, 357, 367-368,
   370-371, 380
Defoe Road, Stoke Newing-
   ton   22
Deleznot, Dr.   346
Deptford   6, 370-380
Derby   164, 232
De Salis, Jerome   271
Dettingen, Battle of   390
Dickens, Charles   266
Doggerbank   396
Doulton's Pottery   252
Dowbiggin, Launcelot   20,
   349
Dowgate Hill   270
Dresden   328
Drury Lane   106
Drury Lane Theatre   228,
   237
Dryden, John   108
Dunciad   335-336, 388
Durbin, Alice   21
Durbin, Henry   21
Durham Yard   239

East India Company   241,
   393

East Smithfield 352
Easterlings 117
Edgware Road 233
Edinburgh 333
Edmund, Earl of Lancas-
  ter 325
Edward I 19
Edward VI 217
Edwards, Mr. 253, 255
Edwards, Mrs. 255
Edwin, Charles 360
Edwin, Lady Charlotte
  360
Eleanor of Provence 251
Elizabeth I 217, 248
Emhurst, Sussex 208-209
Epworth 386, 388
Erasmus 228
Essay on Man 364, 389
Established Church. See
  under Church of Eng-
  land
Ethelbert, King 150
Eton College 155
Evelina 242
Evelyn, John 362, 370
Everton, Bedfordshire
  206
Exeter 129
Exeter College, Oxford
  385
Exeter Exchange 251
Excise Act 389
Eye Brook 232

Faerie Queene 332
Fetter Lane 16, 42, 106-
  108, 163, 328
Fetter Lane Chapel 106-108
Fielding, Henry 257
Fifty New Churches Act 10,
  334
Finch, Robert 272
Finnisterre, Cape 391
Finsbury 138-139
Finsbury Circus 152
Finsbury Dispensary, Rosomon
  Street 104. 105
Finsbury Square 152
Fish Street 269
Fisher, Elizabeth 141
Fitzroy, Augustus Henry 394
Fleet Prison 256
Fletcher, John 280
Fletcher, Rev. John William
  23-25, 309-310
Flitcroft, Henry 260
Ford, Sister 368
Fordyce, Dr. James 257
Forster, Sir Thomas 100
Fort Duquesne 261
Fox, Charles James 396
Fox, George 119
Fox, Sir Stephen 362
Frederick II 333
Frederick, Princeof Wales
  392
French Protestant Chapel,
  Grey Eagle Street 201-

202, 202-203, 204,207
French Revolution 397
Friday Street, Cheapside
    270
Friend, George 104
Fulham 4
Furnival, William de 98
Furnival's Inn, Holborn
    98

Gambold, Mrs. John 358
Garden, Rev. Mr. 284
Garden, Rev. Nathaniel
    131
Garrick, David 35, 100,
    225, 240, 249
Garrick, Eva Marie 240
Gascoigne, Sir Crisp 5
Gay, John 19
Gayer, Sir John 330
Gentleman's Magazine 20,
    103, 234, 242
George I 40, 249, 252,
    387, 388
George II 6-7, 10, 151,
    231, 239, 261, 388,
    390, 393
George III 7, 10, 239,
    252, 333, 347, 392,
    393, 397
George, Prince of Wales
    34
Georgia 1, 8, 16, 131,

148, 279, 281, 363, 389
Germany 5. 328
Giardini, Felice de 237
Gibbon, Edward 395
Gibbs, James 10, 36, 105-
    106
Gibson, Dr. Edmund 113, 401
Gifford, Henry 225
Gilbank, William 150
Giles, Brother 373
Giltspur Street 138
Ginn, Madame 282
Girdler's Hall, Basinghall
    Street 29
Glasgow 240
Godalming, Surrey 101
Godwin, George 329
Golden Square 7
Goldsmith, Oliver 100, 357,
    368
Goodman's Fields Theatre 225
Goodman's Fields, Whitechapel
    225
Gordon, Lord George 108, 141,
    396
Goring House 238
Goswell Road 100, 104
Gould, James 150
Gower, John 280
Gracechurch Street 3
Gravel Lane 148-149
Gray's Inn Walks, Holborn
    98-99
Great Fire 89, 110, 112,

115, 131, 132, 133,148,
149, 150, 224, 256,
267, 269, 270, 271,
272, 273, 273-274,
275, 329, 331, 332
Great Gardens, Whitechapel
    Road 225-226
Great Hall, Southwark
    283
Great Marlborough Street
    238
Great Plague 133
Great Queen Street 97
Great St. Helen, Bishops-
    gate Street 149-150
Great Wild Street 130
Green Park 237
Greenwich 7
Greenwood, Charles 23
Grenville, George 393
Gresham Street 131-132
Gresham, Sir Thomas 149
Grey Eagle Street 201
Greyhound Lane, White-
    chapel 226-228
Grossley, A.M. 47
Grosvenor Place 236
Guilford, John 118-119
Gutter Lane 117
Guy, John 277
Guy, Thomas 277, 278
Guy's Hospital 277-278
Gwyn, Nell 362

Haberdashers' Hospital 134
Hackney 5, 6, 30-31
Hall House, Nettleton Court
    130-131
Hampton 274
Hanover, League of 387
Harley, Robert, Earl of
    Oxford 36
Harris, Howell 128, 372
Harris, Renatus the elder
    110, 228
Harrys, Thomas 99
Hartopp, Sir John 22
Harvard, John 280
Hastings, Warren 394, 395,
    397
Havering Street 353
Hawk, Admiral Edward 392-
    393
Hawkins, Sir John 116, 395
Hawksmoor, Nicholas 10, 40,
    117, 352
Hay, Rev. Dr. John 133
Hayter, Thomas 402
Heidelberg 129
Helena 149
Hell in Epitome 278-279
Henesey, Dr. 233
Henry I 41
Henry III 19, 251, 333
Henry VII 251, 370
Henry VIII 101, 105, 119,
    248

Henry, Prince of Wales
   332
Hereford 274
Herne Hill 367
Herrick, Robert 250
Herring, Thomas 399
Herrnhut 326
Herschel, Sir William
   396
Heylyn, Dr. John 267,
   365
Hicks, Sir Baptist 100
Highbury Place, Isling-
   ton 21-22
Highgate Road, Kentish
   Town 19
Hill, Rowland 104
Hill, Thomas 24
Hilliard, Col. 359
Hinton 274
Hoadley, Bishop Benjamin
   387
Hog Lane 47
Hogarth, William 8, 41,
   106, 389
Holborn 108, 233
Holborn Viaduct 111
Holland 396
Holland, William 107
Holy Trinity, Clapham
   381
Home, Henry, Lord Kames
   393
Hopkey, Sophia Christi-
   ana 131

Horne, James 329
Horneck, Dr. Anthony 128-129
Horsemonger Lane 279
Horton, John 21
Horton, Mary Durbin 21
Hotel des Invalides 362
Hotham, Sir Charles 360
Hotham, Lady Gertrude 360
Houghton-le-Spring 201
House of Commons 243
House of Lords 248
Howard, John 108
Hoxton 5, 134-137
Hudson, Henry 150
Huggitt, Mr. 235
Hughes, John 112
Huguenot Chapel, Wapping
   346-347
Huguenots 200, 203, 215, 238,
   252
Hume, David 390, 391, 392
Humphreys, John 371
Hunter, Dr. John 236
Hutchinson, Francis 387
Hutton, James 106-107, 108,
   131, 358
Hutton, Matthew 399
Hyde Park 234
Hyder Ali 394, 396

Independents 134
Innys, William 106
Ireland 261, 297, 391
Isle of Man 347

Islington   5, 20-22
Italy   275

Jackson, John   22
Jackson, Sister   353
Jacobites   364, 387, 391
James I   332, 363
James II   239
James, John   117, 334
Jenyns, Soame   392
Jewin Street, Barbican
    132
John Street   36
John the Baptist   19
Johnson, Joel   347
Johnson, Michael   129
Johnson, Samuel   3, 15,
    100, 115-117, 129,
    138, 146, 199, 240,
    242, 251, 336, 396
Johnson's Court   115
Jones, Inigo   98, 240-
    241, 256, 330
Jones, Mr.   225
Joyner Street   284
Judith   237

Karnaby House   238
Keats, John   150, 278
Kennington Common   16,
    364-367
Kennington Road   252

Kensington   243
Kensington Common   5
Kensington Gardens   231-232
Kensington Gardens   232
Kensington Palace   231
Kentish Town   19
Ketch, John   233
Ketterage, Mr.   106
King William Street   269-270
King's Bench Prison   5
King's Foundery, Windmill
    Street   37, 107, 118-119,
    138, 139, 161-198, 204,
    244, 345, 390
King's Street, St. Giles   43
Kingswood   199, 202
Knightsbridge   6, 233-235

Labelye, Charles   4
Lagos   392
Lambeth   5, 252-256
Lambeth Marsh   253
Lambeth Road   199
Lambeth Walk   252
Lambeth Wells   252
Lane and Trotman   234
Lanesborough House   235
Larwood, Samuel   261
La Tremblade   47
Law, William   388
Leatherhead   397
Leeman Street East   225
Leicester Fields   7, 141

Leipzig, University of
    328
Lewis, Louisa 115
Lewisham 23
Lexington 216
Licensing Act 225
Life Guards 207
Lime Street 328
Lincoln College, Oxford
    12, 281, 387-388, 391
Lincoln, Sister 278
Lincoln's Inn 98
Lincoln's Inn Fields 6
Lincolnshire 258
Lindsay House 358
Little Lombard Street 277
Little Wild Street 106
Liverpool 6
Lock Hospital Chapel
    236-238
London Association 331
London Bridge 3, 4, 54,
    272
London Chest Hospital
    217
London Corporation 4
London, George 232
London Spa 103
London Wall 152
London Workhouse, Bish-
    opsgate Street 151-
    152
Long Lane, Bermondsey
    283, 321-325

Long Lane Chapel 282, 321
Louis XIV 362
Lovelace, Richard 101, 115
Lowth, Bishop Robert 402
Ludgate 256
Ludgate Church 257
Luther, Martin 130

Macklin, Charles 241
Madeley, Shropshire 24, 144
Magdalene Hall, Oxford 148
Maiden Lane 117
Manchester 6
Manhead, Devonshire 246
Manley, Mary de la Riviere
    256-257
Mansion House 5, 275
Marble Arch 233
Markham, Dr. William 249
Marriott, Thomas 135
Marriott, William 135
Marshall, Mr. 328
Marshalsea Prison 217, 278-
    280
Mary I 217
Mary II 386
Marylebone 6, 33-34, 37-38,
    360, 397
Marylebone Fields 33-35
Massinger, Philip 280
Matilda, Queen 41, 330
Maxfield, Thomas 206, 207
Maze 282

Maze Pond Chapel   282
Merchant Taylors   101
Meriton, Rev. John   347
Methodist Conference
    390, 397
Methodist Record   253
Michel, Simon   105
Middlesex   3, 9
Middlesex House, Bar-
    tholomew Close   105
Milner's Academy, Peck-
    ham   368
Milton, John   115, 332
Minden, Battle of   85
Minories, Aldgate   325-
    328
Mohocks   111
Monks Orchard, Becken-
    ham   199
Monkwell Street   257
Montague House   See un-
    der British Museum
Moore, John   400
Moorfields   16, 138-139,
    152-200
Moravian Brethren   2,
    107-108, 128, 131,
    321, 328, 358, 371
More, Hannah   240
Morning Chapel, City Road
    146-147
Morocco, Emperor of   333
Morton, Charles   385
Morton Magna   274

Muncy, Jane   42

Nantes, Edict of   200
Nash, John   348
Navy Office   329
New England Coffee House
    272
New Prison, Clerkenwell
    102-103
New Queen Street   270
New Street   23
New Style   392
New Wells, Lower Roscommon
    Street   103
Newburyport, Massachusetts
    378
Newcastle House   103
Newcastle-upon-Tyne   354
Newgate   7, 233
Newgate Prison   16, 42, 103,
    108-110, 200, 216, 232,
    233, 256
Newington   5
Newington Green   29-30, 385
Newington Green Academy   29
Newport, Earl of   47
Newton, Sir Isaac   108
Newton, Rev. John   395
Nicholls, William   117
Nichols, John   20
Nicholson, John   129
Nightingale, Lady Elizabeth
    246, 247

Nightingale, Joseph Gas-
    coigne 246
Nine Elms 252
Nonjurors 130
Norfolk, Duke of 101
North, Sir Edward 101
North, Frederick, Lord
    394, 395, 396
North Side, Clapham 381
Northburgh, Michael de
    102
Northiam, Kent 334
Norwich 6
Nottingham House 231

Oglethorp, James 1, 279,
    389
Old Ford 228, 229
Old Jewry, Meeting-house
    Court 131-132
Old Street 200
Old Street Road 139
Old Swan Street 270
Oldys, William 257
Order de la Trappe 23
Ordnance Department 325
Osbaldeston, Richard 402
Otway, Thomas 108
Oxford Holy Club 281,
    388, 389
Oxford Market 36-37
Oxford Street 7, 36-37,
    108, 233, 243

Oxford University 155
Oxted Cottage, Surrey 107

P----, Mr. 361
Paddington 33
Packington, Lady Dorothy
    154
Palmer, Elizabeth 47
Pardo, Peace of 388
Pardon Church, Charterhouse
    102
Parents' Director, The 208
Paris 7
Paris, Peace of 393
Parker, Peter, Sr. 330
Patrick, Betty 278
Paved Alley 326
Peckham 5, 367, 368-370,
    380
Pembroke 328
Penn, William 387
Pepys, Samuel 14, 98, 115,
    329, 353, 381
Peter of Savoy 251
Peter the Great 370
Peto, Henry 98
Petty, William, Lord Shel-
    burne 396
Picadilly 6, 233
Piddock, Thomas 237
Pierce, Edward 250
Pitt, William, the elder
    392, 394

Pitt, William the younger
    396
Plautus 249
Plymouth 341
Pondicherry 395
Pope, Alexander 335-336,
    364, 388, 389, 390
Poplar 6, 354-355
Port Isaac, Cornwall 209
Porteous, Bishop Beilby
    402-403
Portland Market 36
Potter, Bishop John 387,
    399
Poultry 272
Presbyterians 131-132,
    134, 257-258, 261
Price, John 266
Priestley, Joseph 394,
    395, 396
Primrose Hill 232
Prince, John 37
Providence Row, Moor-
    fields 162
Pulteney, William, Earl
    of Bath 360
Purcell, Henry the youn-
    ger 250
Putney Bridge 4

Quaker Meetinghouse,
    Bull-and-Mouth Street
    119-128

Quebec 85
Queen's College, Oxford
    129
Queen's House, St. James
    Park 238-239
Queen's Square, Westmins-
    ter 6

Rag Fair 335-336
Raleigh, Sir Walter 332
Randal, Mrs. 327
Ranelagh, Earl of 362
Ranelagh Gardens 358, 361
Ratcliff 348
Ratcliff Cross 353
Ratcliff Highway 352-353
Ratcliff Square, Stepney
    353-354
Read, Nathaniel 247
Redcross Street 118
Redriff. See under Rother-
    hithe
Regent's Park 34, 331, 333
Reid, Thomas 393
Reynolds, Sir Joshua 240,
    352, 394
Richard III 273
Richard III 225
Richardson, John 208-209
Richardson, Samuel 115
Richmond 231
Richmond College 140
Richmond, Earl of. See un-

der Bretagne

Robinson, John   401

Rodney, Admiral George
   396

Rogers, Hester Ann   213-
   214

Rosemary Lane, Whitecha-
   pel   335

Rotherhithe   349-352, 371

Rotherhithe Tunnel   353

Roubillac, Louis Fran-
   cois   246, 247

Rowe, Henry   30

Rosomon Street   104

Rowe, Thomas   29

Rowlands, Daniel   372

Royal Academy of Arts
   394

Royal Academy School   22

Royal Artillery   161

Royal Exchange   149, 272

Royal Gardens   232

Royal Hospital, Chelsea
   362-363

Royal Mint Street   335

Royal Navy Victualling
   Yard   370

Royal Society of London
   198, 358, 363

Ruth   237

Rysback, John Michael   363

S., Mr.   199

Sacheverell, Henry   105,
   112

Sadler's Wells   103

Sancte Katerinae Trinitatis
   329

Sandemanians   119

Savage, Richard   100

Savannah, Georgia   3, 113

Savoy Chapel   128, 129

Sayes Court, Deptford   370

Schalch, Andrew   161-162

Scotland   351, 391

Secker, Bishop Thomas   10,
   11, 399-400

Sedley, Catherine   239

Senegal   333

Seven Years' Alliance   392

Seven Years' War   392

Seville, Treaty of   388

Shacklewell   30-31

Shadwell High Street   348

Shaftesbury Avenue   41

Shakespeare, Edmund   280

Shakespeare, William   332

Sheffield, Sir Charles   239

Sheffield, John, Duke of
   Buckingham   238-239, 386

Sheridan, Richard Brinsley
   242

Sherlock, Dr. Thomas   113,
   401-402

Shirley, Selina, Countess
   of Huntingdon   24, 35,

48, 104, 104, 191,
209, 238, 246, 271,
358, 359-360
Shoe Lane   241
Shoreditch   134, 137-
138
Shoreditch Workhouse
137-138
Short's Gardens, Drury
Lane   42, 43-47
Shropshire   274
Simmonds   389
Simpson, William   352
Sims, Peter   326
Sims, Mrs. Peter   326
Sir George Wheeler's
Chapel   201, 214
Sisson, Marshall   330
Sloane, Sir Hans   39-40,
357-358, 363
Sm---, Miss   253
Smirke, Robert   39
Smirke, Sydney   39
Smith, Adam   395
Smith, Rev. Samuel   148
Smithfield   105, 112
Snow Hill, Holborn   111-
112
Snowsfields   244, 282-320
Snowsfields Chapel   310
Snowsfields Meetinghouse
283
Soane, Sir John   362
Society for Promoting

Christian Knowledge   273
Society for the Propagation
of the Gospel   273
Society of Apothecaries   363
Society of Friends   119
Soho Square   6
Somerset House   239
Sorores Minores   325
South Leigh, Oxfordshire
387
South Sea Company   387
Southwark   4, 259-267, 319
Southwark CAthedral   260,
280, 282
Spain   393
Spanish Succession, War of
161, 387
Spectator   129, 232, 246,
250
Spitalfields   200-215, 224,
244
Spitalfields Chapel   208
St. Alban, Wood Street   406
St. Albans, Duke of   239
St. Andrew, Holborn   112-
113, 385, 407
St. Andrew-by-the-Wardrobe
407
St. Anne, Gresham Street
131, 243, 405
St. Anne's Lane, Westmins-
ter   250
St. Antholin, Watling Street
271, 406

St. Augustine, Watling
  Street 406
St. Bartholomew, Exchange
  405
St. Bartholomew the Great,
  Smithfield 105, 113-
  114
St. Bartholomew's Hos-
  pital, Smithfield
  105-106
St. Benet, Gracechurch
  Street 406
St. Benet, Paul's Wharf
  256-257, 347, 406
St. Benet Fink, Thread-
  needle Street 272,
  406
St. Botolph, Bishopsgate
  150-151
St. Bride, Fleet Street
  114-115, 273, 405
St. Christopher-le-Stocks
  407
St. Clement Danes, the
  Strand 47, 243, 250-
  251, 406
St. Clement Eastcheap
  406
St. Dionis Backchurch
  405
St. Dunstan, Fleet Street
  99-100
St. Dunstan, Stepney 228
St.-Dunstan-in-the-East

  407
St. Edmund, Lombard Street
  405
St. Ethelburga, Bishops-
  gate 150
St. Ethelburga Society 269
St. Francis, Order of 325
St. Gabriel, Fenchurch Street
  331
St. George, Botolph Lane
  405
St. George, Hanover Square
  236, 243, 334
St. George, Hart Street 40-
  41
St. George, Southwark 321
St. George, Spitalfields
  214-215
St. George the Martyr,
  Southwark 266-267
St. George's Hospital, Hyde
  Park 235-236
St. George's-in-the-East,
  Ratcliff 352, 353
St. Giles, Cripplegate 16,
  117, 233
St. Giles-in-the-Fields,
  High Street 41-42
St. James, Clerkenwell 105,
  243
St. James Garlickhythe 406
St. James, Picadilly 406
St. James's Park 153
St. John, Carnaby Street 238

St. John, Clerkenwell
102, 104-105

St. John, Henry, Vis-
count Bolingbroke
112, 364, 391

St. John Horsleydown,
Tower Bridge Road
334-335

St. John of Jerusalem,
Order of 105

St. John Street 102

St. John the Evangelist,
Friday Street 270

St. John, Wapping 257,
347-348

St. John, Westminster
243

St. John the Evangelist,
Milbank 243

St. Katharine Cree, Lea-
denhall Street 329-
330

St. Katharine Docks 331

St. Katharine near the
Tower 330-331

St. Katharine's Royal
Chapel 331

St. Katharine's Royal
Hospital 330

St. Katherine Coleman,
Fenchurch Street 329

St. Katherine de Christ-
church, Aldgate 329

St. Lawrence Jewry,

Guildhall Yard 132, 133,
406

St. Leonard, Shoreditch
137, 138

St. Luke, Old Street 104,
117-118

St. Luke's Hospital, Moorfields 199, 200, 207

St. Magnus, London Bridge
405

St. Margaret Lothbury 407

St. Margaret, Southwark 280

St. Margaret, Westminster
243

St. Margaret Moses, Friday
Street 270

St. Margaret PAttens, Eastcheap 331-332, 406

St. Mark, Lambeth 364

St. Martin-in-the-Fields
240, 243

St. Martin-le-Grand 119

St. Martin Ludgate 406

St. Mary Abchurch 406

St. Mary Aldermanbury, 405

St. Mary Aldermary 406

St. Mary-at-Hill, Lovat Lane
405

St. Mary, Bow 228, 229

St. Mary-le-Bow, Cheapside
272-273, 405

St. Mary le Strand 243,
267, 365

St. Mary Magdalene, Bermond-

sey   280, 321
St. Mary Magdalene, Old
    Fish Street   406
St. Mary Matfelon   224
St. Mary Mountshaw   274
St. Mary of Bethlehem,
    Hospital of, Moor-
    fields 198-200
St. Mary Overy's Priory
    281
St. Mary, Priory and
    Hospital of   200
St. Mary, Rotherhithe
    349
St. Mary Somerset, Hox-
    ton   274
St. Mary Somerset, Upper
    Thames Street   273-
    274, 407
St. Mary, Spital Square
    201
St. Matthew, Bethnal
    Green   215, 216-217
St. Matthew, Friday
    Street   270, 406
St. Michael, Basingshall
    Street   132-133, 405
St. Michael, Crooked Lane
    269-270, 406
St. Michael, Queenhythe
    405
St. Michael Royal   407
St. Michael, Wood Street
    405

St. Mildred, Bread Street
    406
St. Mildred, Poultry   405
St. Nicholas, Cole Abbey
    407
St. Olave, Hart Street   282,
    329
St. Olave, Old Jewry   405
St. Olive, Tooley Street
    260
St. Pancras   19, 38-39
St. Paul's Cathedral   16,
    159, 228, 257-259, 274,
    407
St. Paul's, Covent Garden
    240-241, 243
St. Paul's, Deptford   370
St. Paul's School   228
St. Paul's, Shadwell   348-
    349
St. Peter, Cornhill   332-
    333, 406
St. Saviour, Southwark   260,
    280, 321
St. Sepulchre's, Snow Hill
    110-111, 233
St. Stephen, Colman Street
    133, 405
St. Stephen Walbrook 274-
    275, 405
St. Swithin, London Stone
    275-277, 406
St. Swithin's Lane   275
St. Thomas, Southwark   282

St. Thomas's Hospital 277, 278, 281, 282

St. Vedast, Foster Lane 133-134, 407

Stamp Act 393, 394

Stationers' Company 277

Steele, Sir Richard 101, 129, 357, 386

Stephen, King 330

Stepney 4, 6, 348, 354

Stepney Causeway 353

Stocks Market 5

Stoke Newington 22-30

Stonehouse, George 20-21

Strahan, William 23

Strand, The 239, 240

Stratford, Bishop Ralph 102

Stuart, John, Lord Bute 393

Sundon 84

Surat 393

Surrey 3, 5

Surrey Chapel, London 104

Sutton Hospital 239

Sutton, Thomas 101

Swalwell 354

Swift, Jonathan 112, 388, 391

Tabernacle Street 161

Tamworth, Warwick 277

Tartar 341

Tatler 386

Tattersall, Richard 234, 235

Taylor, Richard 238

Temple Bar 7, 106, 243, 364

Tenison, Thomas 399

Terence 249

Terrick, Richard 402

Thames Marshes 275

Thames River 3, 5, 6, 232, 239, 240, 243, 259, 270, 353, 362

Thanet, Lady 360

Theatre Licensing Act 389

Thomas, Count of Savoy 251

Thomas, John 332

Thornton, Mr. 280

Threadneedle Street 272

Tickell, Thomas 232

Tillotson, Archbishop John 386

Tippo Sahib 396

Tiverton Grammar School 389

Tollerton, Yorkshire 206

Tooley Street, 284

Tothill Fields 6

Tottenham 6

Tottenham Court Road Chapel 35-36, 360

Toulon 390

Tower Bridge 352

Tower Hill 331

Tower of London   141, 326,
    330, 333-334, 335, 336,
    353
Townsend, Lady   360
Townsend, Lord   359
Trevecca   24, 394
Trinity Hall, Little Bri-
    tain   129-130
Truman, Bixton, and Han-
    bury Brewery   201-202
Turner, William   278
Tunis   333
Tyburn   16, 41, 42, 110,
    232-233
Tyburn Road   233
Tyers, Jonathan   388
Tyrell, Admiral Richard
    247
Tyssen, Francis   30-31

Unitarian Chapel, Snows-
    field   282, 283
Upper Bryanston Street
    233
Upper Hospital Row   361
Upper Moorfields   16
Utrecht, Treaty of   387

Vauxhall Gardens   388
Vauxhall Plate Glass Works
    252
Venn, Henry   271

Venn, Dr. Richard   271
Versailles, Peace of   396
Victoria Park Chest Hospi-
    tal   217
Vienna, Treaty of   388
Voltaire   388

Wake, William   4, 399
Walbrook   270
Wales   273, 372
Walpole, Horace   359
Walpole, Sir Robert   4,
    357, 387, 389, 390
Walsh, John   234-235
Walsh, Thomas   47
Walworth   5, 367
Wapping   148-149, 336-348
Warburton, Bishop William
    389
Water Lane   99
Watermen, Company of   3-4
Watling Street   108, 233,
    270
Watts, Isaac   22, 29, 326,
    386, 387, 391
Weales, Thomas   111
Weldron, Sister   353
Welling   377
Wells   129, 371
Wentworth, Charles Watson
    393, 396
Wesley, Anne   386
Wesley, Charles   12, 34,

35-36, 37-38, 42, 106,
112, 118, 129, 131,
139, 144, 168-169,
198, 199, 208, 215,
233, 248, 253, 282,
327, 328, 332, 347
360, 365, 386-397
Wesley, Charles. Works:
Elegy on the Late Rev.
    George Whitefield
    394
Epistle to the Reve-
    rend George White-
    field 394
Hymns for Children
    393, 397
Hymns Occasioned by
    the Earthquake,
    March 8, 1750 169
Hymns on God's Ever-
    lasting Love 390
Short Hymns on Select
    Passages of Holy
    Scriptures 393
Wesley, Charles the youn-
    ger 37-38, 392
Wesley, Eliza 332
Wesley, Emilia 385, 394
Wesley, John. Works:
Advice to the People
    Called Methodists
    391
Arminian Magazine 13,
    31, 368, 369, 395

Calm Address to Our Ame-
    rican Colonies 395
Calm Address to the In-
    habitants of England
    395
Complete English Dictio-
    nary 392
Concise Ecclesiastical
    Dictionary 396
Concise History of Eng-
    land 395
Christian Library 391
Collection of Psalms and
    Hymns 389, 390
Compendium of Logic 391
Deed of Declaration 19
Directions concerning
    Pronunciation and Ges-
    ture 391
Disideratum; or, Electri-
    city Made Plain and
    Useful 393
English Grammar 391
Explanatory Notes upon
    the Old Testament 393
French Grammar 392
Further Appeal to Men of
    Reason and Religion
    23
Greek Grammar 393
Latin Grammar 391
Lessons for Children 272
Letter to a Friend con-
    cerning Tea 23

Wesley, John. Works
    (cont'd)
New Testament 397
Notes upon the New
    Testament 392
On the Power of Music
    237
Plain Account of Chris-
    tian Perfection
    394
Pocket Hymn Book 396-
    397
Popery Calmly Consi-
    dered 395
Primitive Physick 391
Reasons against a Se-
    paration from the
    Church of England
    392
Select Hymns: with
    Tunes 393
Sermon Preached at St.
    Matthew's, Bethnal-
    Green 215-216
Sermons on Several
    Occasions 23, 391,
    397
Short Account of the
    Rev John Fletcher
    23, 24-25
Short Hebrew Grammar
    272, 392
Short History of Me-
    thodism 393

Works of the Rev. John
    Wesley 394, 395
Wesley, John and Charles.
    Works:
Collection of Hymns for
    the Use of the People
    Called Methodists 396
Collection of Psalms and
    Hymns 390
Hymns and Sacred Poems
    390, 391
Wesley, Keziah 386, 390
Wesley, Martha 386, 398
Wesley, Mary 386, 389
Wesley, Dr. Matthew 99-100
Wesley, Mehetabel 386, 391
Wesley, Molly Vazielle 367,
    391, 394, 396
Wesley, Hetty 246
Wesley, Samuel the elder
    112, 238, 246, 385, 386,
    389
Wesley, Samuel the fourth
    37-38
Wesley, Samuel the third
    246, 332, 394, 396
Wesley, Samuel the younger
    112, 246, 247, 248, 385,
    386, 387, 389
Wesley, Samuel Sebastian
    332
Wesley, Sarah Gwynne 38,
    198, 388, 391
Wesley, Sarah the younger
    392

Wesley, Susanna the elder   246, 365, 385, 390

Wesley, Susanna the younger   246, 386, 393

Wesley, Ursula Berry   246, 248, 390

Wesley, Ursula the younger   246

Wesleyan Methodist Central Hall   244

West Bourne   234

West End   7, 16

West Street   24

West Street Chapel, Seven Dials   47-97, 111, 143, 204, 244, 253, 382, 310, 360, 390

Westminster   3, 129, 168, 243, 243-250, 252, 334

Westminster Abbey   102, 244, 245-248, 257, 365

Westminster Bridge   4, 5-6

Westminster Hospital   235

Westminster Plays   249

Westminster School   106, 248-249, 386, 387

Whalley, Peter   332

Wheeler, Sir George   201

White, John   341

White Lion   279

Whitechapel   16, 224-228

Whitechapel Road   225

Whitecross Street   118

Whitefield, George   11, 13, 24, 35-36, 48, 104, 107, 128, 135, 153, 191, 201, 256, 271, 329, 352, 359-360, 371, 378, 387, 389, 394

Whitefield's Tabernacle   140

Whitehall   24, 310

Whittington, Sir Richard   108

Whole Duty of Man   154-155

Wilberforce, William   397

Wilkes, John   394

Wilkes, Robert   241

William III   231, 251, 252, 362

William, Duke of Cumberland   391

Williams, Anna   116

Williams, John   353

Willis, Rev. Dr. Francis   347

Wilson, Rev. Mr.   103

Winchester, Marquis of   325

Winchester Palace   283

Winchester Yard, Southwark, 320-321

Windham, William   336

Windmill Street   161

Wine-Office Court   23

Wise, Henry 232

Witchcraft Law 389

Wolfe, Gen. James 85

Wollaston, William 387

Woodbridge Street, Cler-
    kenwell 104

Woolchurch Market 5

Woolwich 162

Wren, Sir Christopher 10,
    110, 112, 115, 131,
    132, 133, 250, 256,
    267, 269, 271, 272,
    273, 274, 275, 331,
    332, 362, 363, 405-
    408

Wroote 386, 388

Wyatt, J.D. 332

Wyatt, James 19

Wycherley, William 241

Yorktown 396

Zinzendorf, Nicholas von
    2, 98-99, 100, 107,
    131, 258, 390

Zoar Chapel, Southwark
    158, 261-266, 283

Zulendahl, Baron 360

TEXTS AND STUDIES IN RELIGION

1. Elizabeth A. Clark, **Clement's Use of Aristotle: The Aristotelian Contribution to Clement of Alexandria's Refutation of Gnosticism**

2. Richard DeMaria, **Communal Love at Oneida: A Perfectionist Vision of Authority, Property and Sexual Order**

3. David F. Kelly, **The Emergence of Roman Catholic Medical Ethics in North America: An Historical-Methodological-Bibliographical Study**

4. David Rausch, **Zionism Within Early American Fundamentalism,1878-1918: A Convergence of Two Traditions**

5. Janine Marie Idziak, **Divine Command Morality: Historical and Contemporary Readings**

6. Marcus Braybrooke, **Inter-Faith Organizations, 1893-1979: An Historical Directory**

7. L. William Countryman, **The Rich Christian in the Church of the Early Empire: Contradictions and Accommodations**

8. Irving Hexham, **The Irony of Apartheid: The Struggle for National Independence of Afrikaner Calvinism Against British Imperialism**

9. Michael Ryan, editor, **Human Responses to the Holocaust: Perpetrators and Victims, Bystanders and Resisters**

10. G. Stanley Kane, **Anselm's Doctrine of Freedom and the Will**

11. Bruce Bubacz, **St. Augustine's Theory of Knowledge: A Contemporary Analysis**

12. Anne Barstow, **Married Priests and the Reforming Papacy: The Eleventh-Century Debates**

13. Denis Janz, editor,**Three Reformation Catechisms: Catholic, Anabaptist, Lutheran**

14. David Rausch, **Messianic Judaism: Its History, Theology, and Polity**

15. Ernest E. Best, **Religion and Society in Transition: The Church and Social Change in England, 1560-1850**

16. Donald V. Stump *et al.*, editors, *Hamartia:***The Concept of Error in the Western Tradition**

17. Louis Meyer, **Eminent Hebrew Christians of the Nineteenth Century: Brief Biographical Sketches**, edited by David Rausch

18. J. William Frost, editor, **The Records and Recollections of James Jenkins**

19. Joseph R. Washington, Jr., **Anti-Blackness in English Religion 1500-1800**

20. Joyce E. Salisbury, **Iberian Popular Religion, 600 B.C. to 700 A.D., Celts, Romans and Visigoths**

21. Longinus, **On the Sublime,** translated by James A. Arieti and John M. Crossett

22. James Gollnick, *Flesh* **as Transformation Symbol in the Theology of Anselm of Canterbury,**

23. William Lane Craig, **The Historical Argument for the Resurrection of Jesus During the Deist Controversy**

24. Steven H. Simpler, **Roland H. Bainton: An Examination of His Reformation Historiography**

25. Charles W. Brockwell, **Bishop Reginald Pecock and the Lancastrian Church: Securing the Foundations of Cultural Authority**

26. Sebastian Franck, **280 Paradoxes or Wondrous Sayings,** Translated & Introduced by E. J. Furcha

27. James Heft, **John XXII and Papal Teaching Authority**

28. Shelley Baranowski, **The Confessing Church, Conservative Elites, and the Nazi State**

29. Jan Lindhardt, **Martin Luther: Knowledge and Mediation in the Renaissance**

30. Kenneth L. Campbell, **The Intellectual Struggle of the English Papists in the Seventeenth Century: The Catholic Dilemma**

31. William R. Everdell, **Christian Apologetics in France, 1730-1790: The Roots of Romantic Religion**

32. Paul J. Morman, **Noel Aubert De Verse: A Study in the Concept of Toleration**

33. Nigel M. de S. Cameron, **Biblical Higher Criticism and the Defense of Infallibilism in 19th Century Britian**

34. Samuel J. Rogal, **John Wesley's London: A Guidebook**

35. Andre Seguenny, **The Christology of Caspar Schwenckfeld: Spirit and Flesh in the Process of Life Transformation,** translated by Peter C. Erb and Simone S. Nieuwolt

36. Donald E. Demaray, **The Innovation of John Newton (1725-1807), Synergism of Word and Music in Eighteenth Century Evangelism**